Electronic Document Preparation and Management for CSEC® Examinations

Kyle Skeete

Electronic Document Preparation and Management for CSEC® Examinations is an independent publication and has not been authorised, sponsored, or otherwise approved by CXC

CAMBRIDGE
UNIVERSITY PRESS

CAMBRIDGE
UNIVERSITY PRESS

University Printing House, Cambridge CB2 8BS, United Kingdom

One Liberty Plaza, 20th Floor, New York, NY 10006, USA

477 Williamstown Road, Port Melbourne, VIC 3207, Australia

314–321, 3rd Floor, Plot 3, Splendor Forum, Jasola District Centre, New Delhi – 110025, India

103 Penang Road, #05-06/07, Visioncrest Commercial, Singapore 238467

Cambridge University Press is part of the University of Cambridge.

It furthers the University's mission by disseminating knowledge in the pursuit of education, learning and research at the highest international levels of excellence.

www.cambridge.org
Information on this title: www.cambridge.org/9780521184670

© Cambridge University Press 2011

First published 2011

20 19 18 17 16 15 14 13 12 11 10 9 8 7 6 5

Printed in Great Britain by CPI Group (UK) Ltd, Croydon CR0 4YY

A catalogue record for this publication is available from the British Library

ISBN 978-0-521-18467-0 Paperback with CD-ROM for Windows and Mac

Contents

Part 4 – Document preparation 251

Part 5 – Document management and ethics 337

Part 6 – Practice papers and SBA guidelines 354

Introduction

Welcome to *Electronic Document Preparation and Management* for CSEC® Examinations. This book covers the new CSEC Electronic Document Preparation and Management (EDPM) syllabus, which will be taught from September 2011.

It will take you on an in-depth journey of all aspects of document preparation. By the end of this journey, you will have all the skills that you need to do well in your EDPM exam – skills that are also vital in the 21st century workplace.

This book requires no prior knowledge of computers. Do you type with two fingers? Do you feel like pulling out your hair whenever you try to format a document in Microsoft® Word? Don't know what type of paper to use? Not sure how to type a business letter? Don't worry. By the end of this book, you will know all this and much more. Once you have finished Parts 1 and 2, you will have a strong foundation in computer theory, know how to type and how to use Microsoft Windows. And, after Part 3, you will have all the Microsoft Word, Excel, PowerPoint and Access skills needed for this course.

Part 4 is all about Document Preparation. You will learn how to combine the techniques you've already mastered in order to produce professional-looking documents such as business correspondence, wills, invoices and newsletters. You will be provided with a sample of each type of document complete with tips on what stationery, margins and orientation to use. In many cases, you will be asked to reproduce these documents, paying special attention to any manuscript correction symbols. Not only will this give you lots of practice, but the documents you produce can be used as part of your SBA portfolio.

In Part 5 you will look at the Document Management part of EDPM. You will also learn about ethics at work and at school, intellectual property, how to write bibliographies and how to make sure you are not guilty of plagiarism.

Between the book itself and the accompanying CD-ROM, you will have a wealth of resources at your disposal, which cater to a variety of learning styles. At the beginning of each chapter is an overview of the topics to be covered. Exercises and summaries at the end of each chapter reinforce the main points of each topic covered. There are also several interactive questions on the CD-ROM. If you are a more visual person there are even a few videos showing you how to perform some of the more challenging tasks in Microsoft Office. Teachers and students alike can take advantage of the PowerPoint presentations (revision slideshows). And of course, there is also a comprehensive glossary.

In keeping with this theme of flexibility, multiple versions of Microsoft Office and Microsoft Windows are covered. Not only that, but the similarities and differences between the different versions are highlighted. This is especially important since the newer versions of Office and Windows have radically different interfaces from the older versions still being used in many schools and businesses. Whether you are using Office 2003, 2007 or 2010, Windows XP, Vista or 7, we have got you covered.

When it is time to do your SBA or study for the exams, you will want to take a look at Part 6, which tells you what to expect and how to prepare. There are also practice papers with exam-style questions. When you are finished doing the questions, you can see how well you did by comparing the answers to those provided on the CD-ROM.

As you can see, a lot of effort went into this book. I hope you enjoy reading it, and want to take this opportunity to wish you the best of luck in your EDPM exam.

Kyle Skeete

Acknowledgements

The author and publisher acknowledge the following sources of copyright material and are grateful for the permissions granted. While every effort has been made, it has not always been possible to identify the sources of all the material used, or to trace all copyright holders. If any omissions are brought to our notice, we will be happy to include the appropriate acknowledgements on reprinting.

Microsoft product screenshots throughout used with permission from Microsoft Corporation.

Cover seed/Shutterstock; p. 1 ep-stock/Shutterstock; pp. 2-a, 2-c Oleksiy Mark/Shutterstock; p. 2-b cobalt88/ Shutterstock; p. 2-d Andrew Buckin/Shutterstock; p. 2-e blackred/iStock; p. 4 janrysavy/iStock; p. 6l Mau Horng/Shutterstock; p. 6r Iakov Filimonov/ Shutterstock; p. 7tl Art Directors & TRIP/Alamy; p. 7tr edgamon/iStock; p. 7bl bluudaisy/Alamy; p. 7br Edin/iStock; p. 8tl vladacanon/iStock; p. 8tr John Kwan/Shutterstock; p. 8bl wacpac/Shutterstock; p. 8br Voznikevich Konstantin/Shutterstock; p. 8br-insert Pastushenko Taras/Shutterstock; p. 9l KonstantinPetkov/iStock; p. 9r Tischenko Irina/ Shutterstock; p. 10tl gmnicholoas/iStock; p. 10tr David J. Green/Alamy; p. 10bl kosmozoo/iStock; p. 11 Goygel-Sokol Dmitry/Shutterstock; p. 11 (inset) Mikhail Khusid/Shutterstock; p. 12 bedo/iStock; p. 13l bigworld/ iStock; p. 13r George Dolgikh/Shutterstock; p. 14 Andrew Barker/Alamy; p. 15l scubabartek/iStock; p. 15r rafalstachura/Shutterstock; p. 37t screenshot from Roxio Easy CD and DVD Burner; p. 37b Mozilla Firefox screenshots used with permission; p. 41 gvictoria/ iStock; p. 42 Google screenshots © 2011 Google; p. 49 GgWink/iStock; p. 50 ericlefrancais/Shutterstock; p. 238 actionplus sports images/TopFoto; p. 252tl tradigi/iStock; p. 252tc Ferenc Cegledi/Shutterstock;

p. 252tr Alexandra Kalina/Shutterstock; p. 252bl blinow61/Shutterstock; pp. 252bc, 256br iStockphoto/ Thinkstock; p. 252br Stockbyte/Thinkstock; p. 255t Hemera/thinkstock; p. 255b emily2K/iStock; p. 256l BrianAJackson/iStock; p. 256tr Gunnar Pippel/ Shutterstock; p. 343 Norton Anti-Virus by Symantec Corporation; p. 345 Karam Miri/Shutterstock; p. 346 Brad Wynnyk/Shutterstock; p. 358 300dpi/iStock

System requirements to successfully install the CD-ROM:

Windows
Intel Pentium III 1GHz or faster processor, 512MB of RAM
Recommended: Pentium 4 2GHz or faster, 1GB RAM
Windows Vista SP1, Windows XP SP2 and SP3

MAC OS X
Intel Core Duo 1.83GHz or faster processor; PowerPC G4 1GHz or faster processor
Mac OS X 10.4.11 or Mac OS X 10.5.4 and 10.5.5
512MB of RAM

Recommended screen resolution: recommended minimum is 1024x768. Ideally bigger should be used.

The recommended browser for the interactive questions is Firefox 3 or above and we also support Microsoft Internet Explorer 7 or above (IE for Mac not supported). Browsers should have Adobe Flash Player 10 or above and must be Java and JavaScript enabled.

Author's acknowledgements

First of all I'd like to thank my father Kelvin for helping me get into writing in the first place. I also wish to express heartfelt gratitude to my mother Margaret and my brother Jamario for their encouragement throughout the entire process.

Thanks to everyone who helped or supported me while I was working on this book. Kimmy, Alison, Terricia, I couldn't have done it without you guys! I also want to give a special shout out to my aunt Valerie, who helped check the technical content, and my cousin Lenda, who helped me with some of the legal documents.

I want to thank Cambridge University Press for all the assistance they have provided, for their suggestions and for their patience.

And last, but by no means least, I'd like to thank Almighty God, through whom all things are possible.

Computer basics

Part 1

1 Introduction to computers

In this chapter, you will learn:

- the definition of a computer
- the different types of computers
- advantages and disadvantages of computers
- health risks associated with computers

What is a computer?

Since this chapter is all about computer systems, it would be remiss of me not to start by giving a definition of what a computer is. A **computer** is an electronic device that can accept data and instructions, process them, then store the result or produce output.

In the context of computing, **processing** is when you manipulate data in some way e.g. sorting it or performing calculations on it.

Types of computers

Computers may be categorised according to their size and form factor. From largest to smallest, the main categories are: mainframe, minicomputer and microcomputer.

Mainframe

Mainframes are very large (about the size of a small room) and powerful computers which support hundreds of simultaneous users via connected terminals (Figure 1.1). To support so many users, a mainframe must have vast amounts of memory and secondary storage.

Mainframes are typically only found in large organisations (no doubt because they are so expensive) such as universities, banks and utility companies.

Minicomputer

A **minicomputer** is a multiuser computer that is smaller and less powerful than a mainframe. The

'mini' in minicomputer is only in relation to their larger mainframe counterparts, however; they are still much larger than your average PC.

Figure 1.1 A mainframe computer.

As the computing power in microcomputers jumped by leaps and bounds, minicomputers became obsolete but in their heyday they could be found in many a company department.

Microcomputer

Technically, the term **microcomputer** refers to a particular class of computer which contains a microprocessor. However, you would know it by its more common name – the PC (personal computer). This is the smallest (and by far the most popular) type of computer (see Figure 1.2). It comes in a variety of form factors:

1 Desktop – A desktop computer is the largest type of PC, typically consisting of a separate monitor, tower, keyboard and mouse.
2 Laptop (or notebook) – These are smaller, portable PCs which come with the monitor, keyboard and CPU in a single unit.
3 Tablet – This type of PC is also smaller than a laptop computer but unlike a netbook it does not usually come with a keyboard. Instead, you interface with it using a touchscreen. The popular iPad is a tablet PC.
4 Netbook – These are smaller, lighter, less powerful notebooks that are best suited for web browsing.

5 Palmtop – These are handheld PCs which have touchscreens. Some require a pen-like stylus but the more modern ones are controlled by making gestures on the screen with your fingers. Smartphones fall into this category.

Of these form factors, only numbers 1, 2 and 5 are on the CXC syllabus. But it is good to know the others as well.

Embedded systems

Rather than functioning as standalone devices, some computers are part of other devices like MP3 players, household appliances and digital cameras. These computers are known as **embedded systems**.

Advantages of computers

Computers have had a profound impact on our society, making our lives significantly easier and much more productive. Let us look at the main advantages that computers provide.

Speed and accuracy

Computers are widely known for their speed and accuracy. How long would it take you to multiply 1734590 by 8986? Computers can perform millions of calculations like this each second, and get every single one correct!

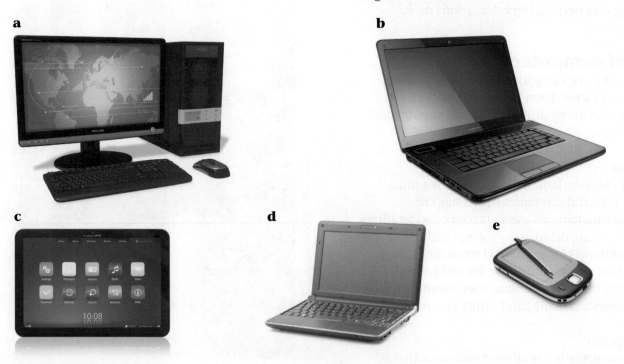

Figure 1.2 Different PC form factors: a. desktop; b. laptop; c. tablet; d. netbook and e. palmtop.

But it is not just mathematical calculations that computers are good at. Computers can quickly and accurately retrieve information, even if it was stored years ago. Contrast that to the average human who would be hard pressed to remember what he had for breakfast yesterday.

Storage capacity

Computers have an unbelievable ability to store lots of data in a tiny space. They can store a library's worth of information on a drive the size of a human thumb. And as was mentioned before, not only can they store all that information; they can retrieve it in a split second.

They do not get bored or tired

If you give a computer a sequence of instructions to perform, no matter how complex they are, it will carry out each step correctly and reliably. Unlike humans, computers do not get bored or tired and as such are not prone to fatigue-induced mistakes.

Disadvantages of computers

Hard as it is to believe, there are some disadvantages associated with computers. We will look at three of the main ones below.

Downtime from power outages and hardware failures

As people and businesses rely more and more on computers, they become increasingly susceptible to power outages and hardware failures. How often have we heard this sheepish response 'Our system is currently down. Could you call back again later?'

Health risks

Improper or extended usage of computers can result in a number of health risks including:

1 Carpal Tunnel Syndrome – This painful condition which affects the wrists and arms is common among people who do a lot of typing. In the Keyboarding section, we will look at how to properly position your hands on the keyboard to mitigate this risk.
2 Eyestrain – If you spend too long looking at the screen, particularly if there is poor lighting, you run the risk of eyestrain. To reduce the chance of this happening, use antiglare screens and take regular breaks from looking at the screen.

3 Neck and Shoulder Pain – Incorrect posture, inappropriate furniture and poor positioning of the monitor can all lead to neck and shoulder pain.

Job losses

The computerisation of certain aspects of business has the unfortunate side effect of costing some people their jobs. Using a computer is often cheaper than paying people to do the same thing. And since in some cases the computer can do the job better than a human can, it makes the person's job redundant.

Summary

- A computer is an electronic device that can accept data and instructions, process them, then store the result or produce output.
- Mainframes, minicomputers and microcomputers are the main types of computers.
- Desktop, laptop and palmtop PCs are all examples of microcomputers.
- Advantages of computers include increased speed and accuracy, increased storage capacity and the ability to work without getting bored or tired.
- Disadvantages of computers include job losses, downtime due to power/hardware failures and health risks like carpal tunnel syndrome, eyestrain, neck and shoulder pain.

Review exercises

Exercise 1

1 In your own words, explain what a computer is.
2 Explain the difference between:
   a A mainframe and a minicomputer.
   b A mainframe and a microcomputer.
3 Put the following PC form factors in <u>descending</u> order of size and power: notebook, desktop, palmtop.
4 Give three advantages of computers. Can you think of any others?
5 Shanika, who works at a data-entry company, has been complaining of pain in her wrists. What is the name of the condition she is most likely experiencing? List two other ailments that affect frequent computer users.

② Computer systems

In this chapter, you will learn:

- the components of a computer system
- the difference between hardware and software
- about the 'brains' of the computer
- the two main types of software
- the difference between data and information

Components of a computer system

In the last chapter we established what a computer is. Now we will turn our attention to the elements that comprise a computer system. A computer system is made up of the following components: hardware, software, people, procedures and data.

Let us look at each component in turn.

Hardware

These are the parts of the computer that you can touch such as the monitor, keyboard, mouse and speakers. They may be divided into five categories:

1 Input devices.
2 Output devices.
3 Storage devices.
4 Communication devices.
5 The CPU.

We will look at the other types of hardware in future chapters, but right now, let us look at the 'brains' of the computer – the CPU.

The CPU

CPU stands for 'Central Processing Unit'. Remember the processing that we talked about in Chapter 1? This is where it is done. So it is no exaggeration to say that this tiny chip is the brains of the computer. The CPU is responsible for:

- decoding instructions
- executing instructions
- performing calculations (e.g. adding, subtracting etc.)
- performing comparisons and other logic operations.

The CPU is found on the **motherboard** (the main system board) as shown in Figure 2.1.

Figure 2.1   The CPU Chip on a Motherboard.

Peripheral devices

The term 'peripheral devices' refers to a particular set of computer hardware devices. The formal definition is that a **peripheral device** is any device (apart from the CPU, primary memory and motherboard), that is part of the computer system. According to this definition, all of the following are peripheral devices:

- all input devices
- all output devices
- all communication devices
- some storage devices (secondary storage devices only).

Software

The term **software** refers to the programs that run on the computer, for example Microsoft Windows and Internet Explorer. There are two main categories of software:

1   Operating Systems like Microsoft Windows which control the computer hardware as well as the other programs.
2   Applications Software which runs on the operating system e.g. Internet Explorer, Microsoft Word or Adobe Photoshop.

We will cover these in more depth in later chapters.

People

It is easy to overlook the human element of computer systems, but that does not make it any less important. After all, people (also known as end users) are the ones who use the computer hardware, the ones who enter the data and tell the computers what to do. Other persons ('surprisingly' called programmers) write the software that the end users work with.

Procedures

Every computer system has several procedures that the users must follow. For example, there are procedures for starting up the computer, shutting it down, backing up data and copying files.

Data

The last, but by no means least part of a computer system is the actual data. This data may be entered by the end user, stored on disk, retrieved later or processed to generate information.

> Data is raw facts and figures. Information is data that has been processed, for example by sorting or summarising.

Summary

- The five components of a computer system are hardware, software, people, procedures and data.
- Hardware refers to the physical components of the computer whereas software refers to the programs that run on the computer.

- People are part of the computer system either in the role of end users or programmers.
- Data is raw facts and figures whereas information is data that has been processed.

Review exercises

Exercise 2

1   What are the components of a computer system? Give descriptions of each.
2   What is the difference between hardware and software?
3   Give four categories of hardware.
4   What do the letters CPU stand for?
5   Give four things the CPU has to do.
6   What are the two main categories of software? Give examples of each.
7   Give two types of people associated with computer systems.
8   What are some of the procedures you have to follow in your school's computer lab?
9   Explain why a set of ages is considered raw data, but if you sort them or find the maximum, minimum and average, it becomes information.

3 Input and output devices

Input devices

Input devices are peripheral devices that allow users to enter information into the computer. Keyboards, mice, microphones, digital cameras, webcams, scanners and light pens are all examples of input devices.

Keyboard

The most common type of input device is the **keyboard**, which, of course, gets its name from the several keys it contains (see Figure 3.1). There are keys for each letter of the alphabet, the numbers 0–9 and for common symbols like the full stop and question mark. You will learn more about the keys on the keyboard in Part 2 of this book.

Although the keyboard can be used for a variety of purposes, it is most suited for data entry and typing documents.

Figure 3.1   A wireless mouse and keyboard.

Mouse

As you can see in Figure 3.1, a computer mouse does bear some resemblance to its namesake. The typical mouse has two buttons on top as well as a scroll wheel. If you turn the mouse over, you'll see a red light, which is actually a low-powered laser beam that is used to track the movement of the mouse. If you have an older mouse, there may be a small ball instead.

As the mouse moves, the pointer on the screen moves as well. When the pointer is over the item that the user wishes to select, he or she clicks one of the mouse buttons. You can use a mouse:

- to select a menu command or 'press' a button on the screen
- for highlighting icons and text
- to draw in graphics programs (although light pens and graphics tablets are more suited to this task).

Even though the mouse is a very versatile input device, it can only be used for items on the screen. In addition, mice that use a laser may move erratically if placed on reflective surfaces. Mice that use a ball can cause erratic movement on screen when they need cleaning.

Laptops do not usually come with a mouse; instead they have a touchpad that serves a similar function.

Light pens and graphics tablets

The best way to create drawings on the computer is by using either a **light pen** (Figure 3.2) or a **graphics tablet** (Figure 3.3). While both allow you to actually draw images, the light pen allows you to draw directly on the screen. Of course this requires a special screen.

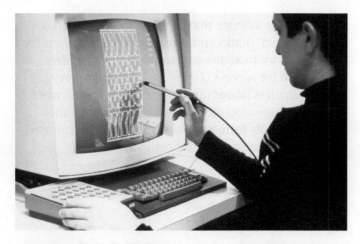

Figure 3.2 A light pen.

Figure 3.3 A graphics tablet and stylus (pen).

Scanner

A **scanner** is a device that scans existing photographs or printed documents and converts them to digital images. Most scanners are <u>flatbed</u> like the one in Figure 3.4, where you put a page of the document face-down on the flat surface and close the lid. However, all-in-one printers often come with <u>sheet-fed</u> scanners, where you put all the sheets of paper in the tray and the scanner pulls them through one by one like a fax machine does.

Scanners are useful when you do not have the original document or image on your computer. They save you from having to retype the document. However, because documents are scanned as images, you need to use optical character recognition software if you want to edit the scanned text in a word processor.

Figure 3.4 A flatbed scanner.

Digital camera

A **digital camera** (see Figure 3.5) is a camera that uses an electronic sensor instead of film. The images are stored digitally on removable flash memory cards.

Cameras nowadays have resolutions of about 14 megapixels (approximately 14 million pixels). A **pixel** is simply a dot in the image: the more dots, the higher the resolution and the more detail that can be recorded.

Figure 3.5 The back of a digital camera showing the LCD screen.

Digital cameras are more convenient than their film counterparts. They have LCD screens that allow you to compose shots and view images right after you take them, to make sure they come out properly. The memory cards are reusable and store hundreds of images at a time, compared to the 36 on a typical roll of film. You do not have to send them to get developed either, so you save a lot of money. And because the images are stored digitally, they can easily be edited on the computer, imported into documents or uploaded to the Internet.

Webcam

A **webcam** is a small camera that you use to send live video over the Internet (see Figure 3.6). The video quality is not usually very good but this does not matter since you do not use webcams to do professional videos. Instead, webcams are normally used so you can see the people you are videoconferencing or chatting with.

Figure 3.6 A webcam.

Microphone

Computer microphones (see Figure 3.7) work the same way as normal ones – the only difference is that they are smaller. Common uses are voice chatting online, recording audio and giving voice commands to the computer. However, all of these applications require special software.

Figure 3.7 A computer microphone (and headset).

Optical Mark Reader (OMR)

Have you ever done a multiple-choice exam where you had to shade the correct answers? After the exam, the batch of answer forms would most likely be placed into a device called an **Optical Mark Reader (OMR)**.

An OMR is a device that can detect the position of pen and pencil marks and determine which options they correspond to. In addition to multiple-choice quizzes, it is also used for surveys (Figure 3.8). OMRs are very fast and require less labour (and the associated costs) when inputting large amounts of data. Unfortunately they require specially formatted forms and can get confused if the answers are not shaded correctly.

Figure 3.8 A survey sheet that can be read by an OMR.

Optical Character Reader (OCR)

An **Optical Character Reader (OCR)** is a device that detects characters in printed documents. It allows you to quickly enter printed text into the computer, without having to retype it. This technology is used to capture data from airline tickets, envelopes and utility bills. However, OCRs have trouble reading handwriting and low quality text.

Barcode scanner

You probably are already familiar with barcode scanners used in supermarkets (Figure 3.9). These

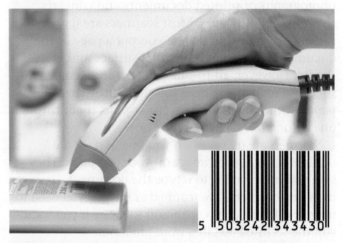

Figure 3.9 A barcode scanner being used to read the barcode on a bottle of shampoo. Inset: a barcode.

devices scan patterns of parallel black lines (called barcodes) which are used to identify items. The particular store or supermarket maintains a database which associates each barcode with the item's current price. This system is much faster and more accurate than manually keying in the prices into a cash register.

Output devices

Output devices are also peripheral devices but they are like the opposite of input devices – they allow you to get information <u>out</u> of the computer so that humans can read or understand it. The most obvious examples are computer monitors and printers, but speakers are output devices as well.

Monitor

A **monitor** is what people commonly refer to as the computer screen. In the past, all monitors were **CRT** monitors (see Figure 3.10) – big, bulky devices that looked, and worked, similar to an old television set. Nowadays, computers come with thin **LCD** monitors like the one in Figure 3.11 instead.

Printer

A **printer** is a device that produces hard-copy output on paper. Let us look at the four main types of printers:

- inkjet printers
- laser printers
- dot-matrix printers
- thermal printers.

What is the difference between hard copy and soft copy? A **soft copy** is the digital form of a document whereas a **hard copy** is the printed, human-readable copy of that document.

Inkjet printers

These are the small printers found in most homes and offices like the one in Figure 3.12, see page 10. They work by squirting tiny droplets of ink on the paper. Their initial cost is cheap but the ink is expensive. Despite printing fairly quickly, they produce high quality images and text.

Figure 3.10   A CRT monitor.

Figure 3.11   An LCD monitor.

Figure 3.12 An inkjet printer.

Laser printers

Laser printers (see Figure 3.13) are the biggest, fastest, most expensive printers so they are usually only found in offices that do a lot of printing. Instead of ink, they use lasers to fuse toner onto the paper, which results in excellent text quality.

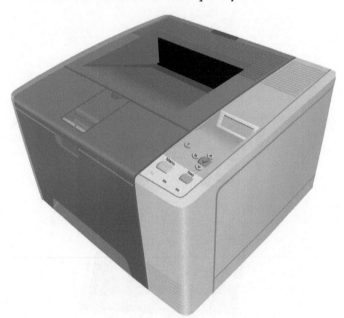

Figure 3.13 A laser printer.

Dot-matrix printers

A dot-matrix printer (Figure 3.14) works almost like a typewriter. Tiny pins in the print-head strike the paper through an inked ribbon and the resulting dots form text and images. This makes dot-matrix printers slow and noisy but also makes them uniquely able to print in duplicate using carbon paper.

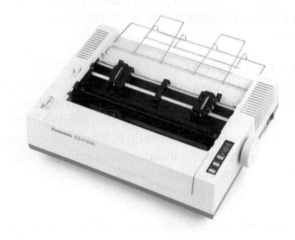

Figure 3.14 A dot-matrix printer.

Thermal printers

As the name suggests, this class of printer works by using heat. A thermal printer does not require ink, toner or a ribbon, only heat-sensitive paper. So its running cost can be as cheap as, or even cheaper than, a dot-matrix printer. Thermal printers are used when low quality text is acceptable, for example when printing cash register receipts or movie tickets. They are also used in some fax machines.

Impact printers versus non-impact printers

Like the names suggest, impact printers print by striking the paper whereas non-impact printers print by other means. So a dot-matrix printer is an example of an impact printer whereas inkjet, laser and thermal printers are non-impact printers.

Page printers versus line printers

The terms 'page printer' and 'line printer' refer to how fast a printer appears to be printing. Inkjet and laser printers, which print so quickly that they appear to print an entire page at a time, are called **page printers**. A **line printer**, on the other hand, is a printer that appears to print an entire line at a time.

Multimedia projector

A multimedia projector is an output device that connects to a display port on your PC and uses a lens to project whatever is showing on your screen onto a flat surface such as a wall or a board. You usually plug one into your laptop when you are doing PowerPoint presentations so the audience can see your slides.

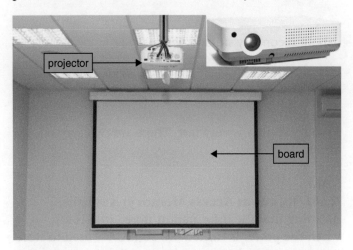

Figure 3.15 A typical set up of a projector and a board on which the content of the screen is projected. Inset: A close up of a typical projector.

Speakers

Computer speakers are output devices as well, even though users hear the data as opposed to seeing it. They work and look like normal speakers, only smaller.

Summary

- Input devices allow you to put information <u>into</u> the computer whereas output devices are used to get information <u>out</u>.
- Keyboards, mice, light pens, graphics tablets, scanners, digital cameras, webcams, OMRs, OCRs and microphones are all input devices.
- The most common output devices are monitors, printers, multimedia projectors and speakers. Printers produce hard copy.
- There are four types of printers: inkjet, laser, dot-matrix and thermal.
- Page printers appear to print a page at a time; line printers appear to print a line at a time.
- Impact printers print by striking the paper.

Review exercises

Exercise 3A

1 a What is an input device?
   b What is an output device?

   c List three input devices and three output devices.
2 Give a similarity and a difference between a light pen and a graphics tablet.
3 Give two uses of a keyboard.
4 What are three things you can use a mouse to do?
5 Timothy goes to use a PC in his school's computer lab but finds that the mouse is, in his words, 'jumping all over the place'. Give two possible causes.
6 Describe the two types of scanners.
7 Cynthia has lost an important document from her computer but has managed to find an old printed copy. Explain how she can get the information into Microsoft Word so she can make changes to it.
8 What is a pixel? Using the word 'pixel', explain how the resolution of a digital camera relates to its image quality.
9 How are digital cameras more convenient than normal film cameras?
10 What are webcams normally used for?
11 What input device would you use to enter voice commands into your computer?
12 What is the biggest difference between the two types of monitors?
13 Give a brief description of how the four types of printers work.
14 What does the term 'soft copy' refer to?
15 Give the advantages and disadvantages of:
    a a laser printer over an inkjet printer
    b an inkjet printer over a dot-matrix printer
    c a thermal printer over a laser printer.
16 What is the input device best suited for:
    a Reading telephone bills?
    b Recording the results of a survey?
    c Determining the prices of items in a retail store?
    d Grading quizzes?
17 Give two disadvantages of optical mark readers.
18 Explain what a page printer is and give two examples.
19 Why is an inkjet printer not considered an impact printer?

④ Storage devices

In this chapter, you will learn:

- the difference between a kilobyte, megabyte and gigabyte
- about main memory
- about secondary storage devices
- the similarities and differences between different storage devices

Two types of computer storage

In the first chapter, we mentioned that computers need some way of storing information. Computers have two types of storage – primary storage and secondary storage – and each has a role to play. But before looking at each type, you will have to learn the units of storage in order to understand just how much data the storage devices can hold.

Units of storage

A single letter, digit or symbol is called a **character** and takes one **byte** of space to store. But computers store so much data that we rarely talk about 'bytes' – instead we use terms like **kilobyte**, **megabyte** and **gigabyte**. In Table 4.1, each unit of storage is roughly 1000 times bigger than the one above it.

Table 4.1 Units of storage.

Unit of storage	Number of bytes	Symbol
Kilobyte	Roughly one thousand	KB
Megabyte	Approximately one million	MB
Gigabyte	About one billion	GB
Terabyte	Approximately one trillion	TB

As a point of reference:

- the average document is between 30 KB and 100 KB
- a compressed song is a few megabytes
- a DVD video takes up a few gigabytes
- programs may be as small as a few kilobytes or as large as hundreds of megabytes.

Primary storage

Primary storage, also known as **main memory**, is memory that is directly accessible to the CPU.

Primary storage is very fast. There are two types: RAM and ROM.

RAM

RAM (**Random Access Memory**) is volatile, meaning that the information stored in it is lost when the power is turned off. So RAM is used to store temporary calculation results as well as instructions of currently running programs. You can see what RAM looks like in Figure 4.1.

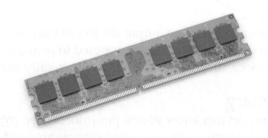

Figure 4.1 A RAM module.

ROM

The acronym **ROM** stands for **Read-Only Memory**. The name should tell you that ROM (usually) can only be read i.e. it cannot be changed. Data stored in ROM is permanent, making it perfect for storing the instructions used to boot up (start up) the computer.

There are some types of ROM that can be reprogrammed but this is beyond the scope of this course.

Secondary storage

Unlike primary storage, the CPU cannot directly access secondary storage. So data in secondary storage must first be loaded into RAM before the CPU can use it. As you can imagine, secondary storage is not nearly as fast as primary storage (and the technology used by secondary storage devices makes them even slower).

So why would you use secondary storage? First, it is much cheaper. Secondly, secondary storage can in most cases hold a lot more information than primary storage. And lastly, data in secondary storage (unlike RAM) is not lost when the computer is turned off.

Let us compare and contrast some of the secondary storage devices.

Floppy disks

Figure 4.2 shows a typical 3½ inch **floppy disk**. You cannot tell from the image, but inside a floppy disk is a round magnetically coated piece of plastic where up to 1.44 MB of data can be stored. This is not very much storage space, so floppy disks are mainly limited to storing documents and small programs.

Floppy disks are portable but slow and unreliable. And although individual floppy disks are pretty cheap, they hold so little information that they are not cost effective. So it is no surprise that they have been made virtually obsolete by USB drives, which have none of these disadvantages.

write-protect <u>off</u> (tab closed)

Figure 4.2 A floppy disk.

Overwrite protection
A floppy disk has a tiny square in the corner that you can slide up and down, called the **write-protect tab** (see Figure 4.2). It is normally closed by default. If you slide the tab open (so that there are now two square holes on the disk), overwrite protection will be turned on.

When overwrite protection is turned on, you can not delete or save over the files on the disk. This is a simple but effective way to protect important data.

In order for the computer to access the data stored on a floppy disk, the disk must be inserted into the floppy disk drive. When you are inserting a disk, you hold it by the label.

Hard disks

A **hard disk** is a rigid, large-capacity disk. Like floppy disks, hard disks are magnetic. But that is where the similarities end. A hard disk is built into its drive and cannot usually be removed. This is why the terms 'hard disk' and 'hard drive' are used interchangeably. The hard drive is stored inside the main 'box' of the computer so you cannot see it unless you open the computer up. Inside the drive there is a **read/write head** that moves across the surface of the disk retrieving (reading) and storing (writing) data (Figure 4.3).

A hard disk is larger than a floppy, both physically and in terms of the amount of information it can hold. Even the cheapest hard drives can store several GB of information, and terabyte drives are becoming more common. This is more than enough space to store the operating system, application programs, your documents, photos, videos and music!

hard disk

read/write head

Figure 4.3 The inside of a hard drive, showing the hard disk and read/write head.

External hard drives

Although hard drives are normally built into the computer, <u>external hard drives</u> are increasing in popularity. These drives are put in special enclosures to help protect them and can be connected to the computer via USB ports.

Magnetic tape

Magnetic tape, similar to that found in cassette tapes, is a very cheap medium on which to store data. Magnetic tape also has a similar capacity to a hard drive. This makes it ideal for backing up and archiving data. It comes in two forms – as a cassette or as a reel. Unsurprisingly, the device used to read from and write to magnetic tape is called a <u>magnetic tape drive</u>.

CDs and DVDs

Not all storage media utilises magnetic technology. CDs and DVDs (Figure 4.4) are examples of **optical storage media**. To the naked eye a CD and a DVD look the same since they both use similar technology (they are read by lasers). However, a DVD can hold much more information than a CD (4.7 GB as opposed to 700 MB).

The terms disk and disc are somewhat interchangeable but as a general rule, disk (with a 'k') is used for magnetic storage devices and a disc (with a 'c') is used for optical storage media. So you would say 'floppy disk' but 'DVD disc'.

Figure 4.4 A CD (or DVD) in an open CD/DVD-ROM drive.

CD-ROMs and DVD-ROMs

Although computers can play audio CDs and the DVD videos, these are not the types of optical discs you associate with a computer. Computer programs are typically distributed using CD-ROMs and DVD-ROMs. As you might guess, the ROM part means that no information can be written to these media (i.e. they are read only). Instead they are mass produced using a process not unlike that used to produce books; a master copy is created, from which the other copies are produced.

Because DVD technology is newer, DVD drives can read CDs but CD drives cannot read DVDs.

Recordable and Rewritable CDs and DVDs

If you want to save information on CD or DVD, the first thing you need is a drive capable of doing so (called a <u>burner</u>). Then you need a recordable or rewritable CD or DVD.

Recordable optical media have an 'R' at the end e.g. CD-R. DVD-R and DVD+R. This R' at the end stands for <u>recordable</u>, meaning that data can be written to the media in question but not erased. The 'RW' at the end of CD-RW, DVD-RW and DVD+RW stands for <u>rewritable</u>. You can erase a rewritable disc and burn new information on it multiple times.

Writing information to a CD or DVD is called 'burning', no doubt because of the lasers that are used in the process.

Unlike a CD-ROM or DVD-ROM, the underside of a recordable disc is not silver. Instead it is purple, green, blue or even gold – a result of the coloured dye used on the reflective surface of this type of disc. When this dye is heated using the laser, its composition changes, allowing information to be stored. Unfortunately, this same property makes recordable (and rewritable) optical media susceptible to sunlight.

What is the difference between a DVD-R and a DVD+R? These are two competing technologies that allow recording on DVDs. In some cases, a drive may only be able to use one of these types. Fortunately, this is very rare.

Flash memory

Flash memory (Figure 4.5) is a form of secondary storage that utilises solid-state electronics. Although it can hold a lot of information (up to a few GB), it is very small, making it ideal for use in portable devices such as digital cameras and MP3 players.

When used in such devices, it is in the form of a tiny card. To copy data from the card, you remove it from the slot and put it in a card reader which you then connect to your computer. Many laptops have a card reader built into them.

Figure 4.5 Compact flash memory.

USB drives

A **USB drive** is a tiny portable drive (about the size of a person's thumb) that can plug directly into your computer's USB port. Because they use flash memory, USB drives are also referred to as **flash drives**. The flash memory is built into the USB drive so it cannot be removed.

Figure 4.6 USB drive inserted into a laptop.

Flash drives are smaller than floppy disks, more reliable, much faster and can store a lot more information (a few gigabytes as opposed to 1.44 MB). It is also easier to copy information to a flash drive than a CD or DVD. For these reasons, flash drives are the preferred way of transferring files from one computer to another.

Comparison of secondary storage devices

Table 4.2 compares and contrasts the different types of secondary storage.

Table 4.2 Comparing different types of secondary storage.

Storage device	Capacity	Technology	Portable	Used for
Floppy disk	1.44 MB	Magnetic	Yes	Storing small documents
CD	700 MB	Optical	Yes	Storing music, installation programs and backing up data
DVD	4.7 GB	Optical	Yes	Storing movies, installation programs and backing up data
USB drive	A few GB	Flash	Yes	Transferring files between computers
Hard drive	Hundreds of GB	Magnetic	External hard drives	Stores the OS, application programs, documents, music and videos
Magnetic tape	Hundreds of GB	Magnetic	Yes	Backing up data

Summary

- Each character such as a letter, digit or symbol takes one byte of space to store.
- You can write information to RAM but not to ROM. However, the contents of RAM are lost when the computer is turned off.
- Secondary storage is slower than primary storage but is also much cheaper.
- Floppy disks, CDs and DVDs and magnetic tape must be placed within drives on the computer in order for the computer to access their information; hard disks are built into their drives within the computer.
- You can only burn a CD or DVD if it is recordable (or rewritable) and you have a burner.
- USB drives have made floppy disks obsolete because they are smaller, faster, hold more information and are more reliable.

11 What is the difference between a CD-R and a CD-RW?
12 Why can DVD-ROM drives read CDs but CD-ROM drives cannot read DVDs?
13 What is the relationship between flash memory and USB drives?

Review exercises

Exercise 4

1 How many kilobytes are there in a gigabyte?
2 Sort the following storage sizes in descending order: 1200 KB, 500 KB, 3000 MB, 1 MB, 2 GB.
3 Explain the difference between the two types of primary memory.
4 a What is ROM used for?
    b What type of information is stored in RAM?
5 What is the difference between primary storage and secondary storage?
6 Give five examples of secondary storage devices as well as the type of information typically stored on each.
7 Explain what a burner is.
8 Give three reasons why flash drives are replacing floppy disks.
9 Explain how you can tell the difference between a recordable DVD and an ordinary DVD-ROM by looking at them.
10 If you put a DVD in a DVD drive but are unable to burn it, what are two possible reasons?

5 Introduction to Microsoft® Windows

In this chapter, you will learn:

- the most common versions of Microsoft Windows
- about the Microsoft Windows interface
- common window controls
- how to use the mouse
- how to start programs
- how to minimise, maximise and close windows
- how to switch between running programs

Different versions of Windows

The most commonly used version of Microsoft Windows is Windows XP which was released in 2001. Then came Windows Vista which overhauled the user interface. At the time of writing, the current version is Windows 7. Its interface is very similar to Vista's, but with a few important enhancements.

We will be covering all three versions in this book.

The Microsoft Windows interface

The desktop

When you first log into Windows, you will notice a rectangular area with a few tiny images on it (see Figure 5.1, page 18). This area is known as the **desktop** and the tiny pictures are known as **icons**. Each of these icons may represent a program, a folder or a document that you may open by double-clicking. (I will explain what 'double-clicking' is shortly.)

Some of the icons commonly found on the desktop are:

- *My Documents* – this is a folder where you can find most of your documents.
- *My Computer* – this allows you to view and manage the files on your computer.
- *Recycle Bin* – this allows you to retrieve files that were deleted.
- *Internet Explorer* – this allows you to browse the Internet.

You can change your desktop 'wallpaper' (background) so yours may look different from the one in Figure 5.1

The taskbar

At the bottom of the desktop is a rectangular bar that stretches across the width of the screen. This is called the **taskbar** and it is used to switch between currently running programs.

The *Start* button

To the far left of the taskbar is the **Start button** which you click to open the **Start menu**. This is where you usually go when you want to start a program. Surprisingly, the option to shut down the computer is also found in the Start menu.

In Windows Vista and Windows 7 the Start button is a circle with a Windows logo in it.

The notification area

To the right of the taskbar is an area with tiny icons called the **notification area**. Besides containing the clock, it allows you to adjust the volume, stop any USB devices so you can unplug them, and receive notifications from programs that are running.

Mouse basics

Windows is a **GUI** (graphical user interface) and it contains several elements with which you can interact using a mouse. Any movements you make

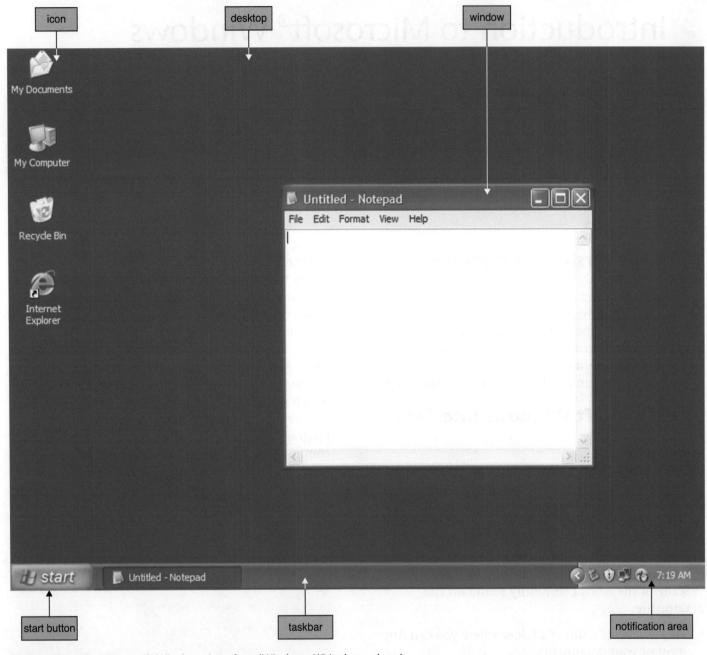

icon   desktop   window

My Documents

My Computer

Recycle Bin

Internet
Explorer

Untitled - Notepad

File   Edit   Format   View   Help

start   Untitled - Notepad   7:19 AM

start button   taskbar   notification area

Figure 5.1   The Microsoft Windows interface (Windows XP is shown here).

with the mouse are mirrored by an arrow on the screen (known as the <u>mouse pointer</u>).

The appearance of the mouse pointer may vary, as shown in Table 5.1.

Here are some mouse terms with which you need to be familiar:

- **Click –** To quickly press and release the <u>left</u> mouse button, while the mouse pointer is over the intended target. This is used for 'pressing' buttons,

choosing items from menus, repositioning the cursor in text areas and much more.

- **Right-click –** The same as clicking but with the <u>right</u> mouse button. This brings up a context menu for the object you right-clicked on. A **context menu** is a menu that only displays menu items relevant to the particular item. So, for instance, if you right-click on the *Recycle Bin*, you'll see the menu in Figure 5.2. However, if you right-click on the desktop itself, you'll see something similar to Figure 5.3.

- **Double-click** – When you click on an item twice in quick succession, without moving the mouse. This is used for opening items on the desktop.
- **Drag and drop** – To 'drag' an object, hold down the <u>left</u> mouse button while the pointer is over it, then move it to another location. When you release the left mouse button, the object is 'dropped' at the new location. This is used to move selected text as well as other objects on the screen.

Table 5.1 Mouse pointers and their meanings.

▷	This is what the mouse pointer normally looks like.
⧖	The hourglass lets you know when a program is busy working on something. When you see it, you usually will not be able to use that program as normal.
✛	Usually when you see this four-headed arrow, it means that you can move an object (such as a window) from one location to the next.
I	The pointer changes to an I-beam whenever you move over a text area. You can click on any such area and start typing.
↔	When you move over the borders of some objects (e.g. windows), the mouse changes to a double-headed arrow indicating that you can resize the object. Just hold down the left mouse button and drag the mouse in one of the directions indicated.
⇞	When you are surfing the Internet, this lets you know which phrases or images are links that you can click to visit other web pages.

Figure 5.2 The context menu for the *Recycle Bin* appears when you right-click on the *Recycle Bin* icon.

Figure 5.3 The context menu for the desktop appears when you right-click on the desktop.

Starting programs

You can start a program by either double-clicking on its icon on the desktop or by clicking the *Start* button and selecting it from the *Start* menu.

Using the *Start* menu

When you click the *Start* button, you will see the *Start* menu which only shows the most recently used programs (see Figure 5.4). In order to see all the programs installed on your computer, click the *All Programs* option.

Figure 5.4 The *Start* menu. You can open this menu by clicking on the *Start* button.

The *All Programs* section is divided into groups (which each have icons of folders on their left). In Windows XP, the groups have black triangular arrows next to them as well. You can see the contents of the 'group' by clicking on the black arrow.

In Windows XP, when you move the mouse over a group, a menu pops up to reveal the programs it contains as shown in Figure 5.5.

In Windows Vista and Windows 7, you have to click on the group in order to see its contents. The group is then expanded inside the *Start* menu itself (see Figure 5.6). If there are too many programs being shown in the *Start* menu, you may have to drag the scroll box to get to the one you want.

When you start a program, it opens up in a new window.

tip

You can quickly find items in the Windows Vista and Windows 7 *Start* menus by typing the first few letters of the program you are looking for.

Common controls

The good thing about Windows is that it uses standardised controls, meaning that they work the same way in most programs. Below are brief descriptions of the most common parts of a window and how they function. Although Windows XP is shown here, the later versions of Windows work the same way; they are just prettier.

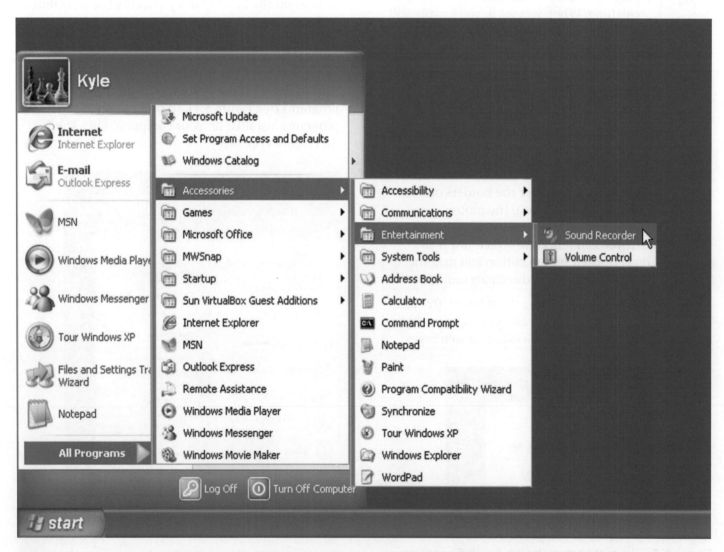

Figure 5.5 Program groups in Windows XP. Here the mouse was moved over *All Programs, Accessories, Entertainment* and *Sound Recorder* (in that order). The programs and sub-menus in each highlighted menu item are shown on its right.

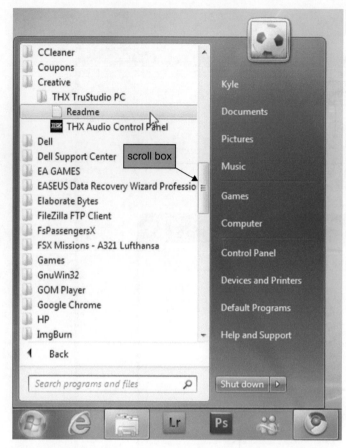

CCleaner
Coupons
Creative
   THX TruStudio PC
      Readme
      THX Audio Control Panel
Dell
Dell Support Center   scroll box
EA GAMES
EASEUS Data Recovery Wizard Professio
Elaborate Bytes
FileZilla FTP Client
FsPassengersX
FSX Missions - A321 Lufthansa
Games
GnuWin32
GOM Player
Google Chrome
HP
ImgBurn
◄   Back

Search programs and files

Kyle

Documents

Pictures

Music

Games

Computer

Control Panel

Devices and Printers

Default Programs

Help and Support

Shut down ▶

Figure 5.6 The *Start* menu in Windows 7 and Vista. Each folder represents a program group. When you click one (e.g. THX TruStudio PC), its contents are shown as an indented list of further folders or items.

The window

In Figure 5.7, see page 22, there are actually two windows being displayed. Although you can open as many windows as you like, only one may be active at a time. The <u>active window</u> is the one currently 'on top'; any keystrokes you press will go to this window. The title bar in an inactive window normally has a more faded look, though in Windows Vista and Windows 7 it is hard to tell the difference. In the example shown in Figure 5.7, the *Options* window is currently active.

Not every window is a separate program. In Figure 5.7, the *Options* window was displayed as a result of the user clicking on *Options …* inside WordPad's View menu.

Title bar

At the top of every window is the title bar which displays the name of the program that is currently being run (and usually the name of the document currently open). In this case, the program is *WordPad*.

Menu bar

Underneath a window's title bar, you can usually find the menu bar. Clicking on a menu item will 'pull down' that menu's list of items and submenus. (If an item has a submenu, it will have a black triangle next to it.) In Figure 5.8, see page 22, the *Picture* submenu of an *Insert* menu is being displayed.

Toolbars

Not all windows have toolbars, but those that do may have more than one. Toolbars have buttons for the most common program tasks, and these buttons usually have icons on them.

Status bar

Located at the bottom of many windows, the status bar displays information related to the current program.

Tabs

When a window has too many options to be displayed at once, they may be grouped into tabs (much like the tabs of a folder). You can only view one tab at a time; in Figure 5.7, the *Text* tab is the one currently active in the *Options* window.

Command buttons

Command buttons, which we will simply refer to as 'buttons' from now on, allow you to make the program take some action. You click on the appropriate button to activate it.

Radio buttons

Radio buttons allow you to switch between a list of options. To select an option, click it, and a bullet will be displayed next to it indicating that it is now selected. In Figure 5.7, the *No Wrap* option is currently selected.

Combo boxes

Combo boxes also allow you to choose from a list of options. However, only one option is displayed

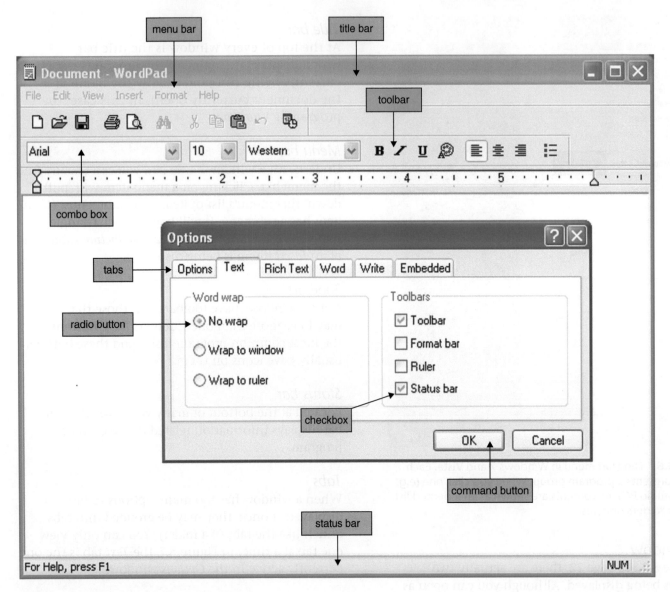

Figure 5.7 Typical window components.

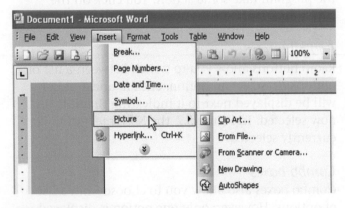

Figure 5.8 A menu and a submenu.

at a time. To choose another option, click the down 'arrow' to the right of the combo box which will cause the list of items to drop down. When you click an item from the list, the list closes and the new item replaces the old one.

Checkboxes

A checkbox works like a switch. You click it once in order to turn an option on and click it again to turn it off. Options that are currently turned on have check marks (ticks) next to them.

As you can see in Figure 5.7, more than one checkbox can be turned on at a time. In this example, the toolbar and status bar options are turned on.

Minimising, maximising or closing a window

To the right of a window's title bar, there are normally three buttons, as seen in Figure 5.9. These buttons are (from left to right): the *Minimise*, *Maximise* and *Close* buttons.

a   b

Figure 5.9 The *Minimise*, *Maximise* and *Close* buttons in **a** Windows XP and **b** Windows 7/Vista.

Minimising a window

If you click the *Minimise* button, you will hide the window without closing it. In order to make it visible again, you have to select it from the taskbar by clicking on the appropriate button. In some cases, all the windows for a particular program may be grouped together as shown in Figure 5.10. In such a case, you click on the group and then click the correct window.

In Windows 7, the windows are always grouped. When you move the mouse over a program's icon in the taskbar, you get a preview of the windows for that program (see Figure 5.11).

Maximising a window

If you click the *Maximise* button, the window will get expanded so that it takes up the entire desktop. The button will change to the *Restore* button, which consists of overlapping rectangles like this: 🗗 .

When you click this button, the window will return to its original size.

Closing a window

When you click the *Close* button in a window's title bar, it will close the window. In some cases you will be asked if you want to save the changes.

Moving and resizing windows

You can use the mouse to move and resize a window as long as it is not maximised. To move a window, drag it by its title bar from one part of the screen to the next.

To resize a window, position the mouse over one of its edges. The mouse pointer should change to a double-headed arrow. Then drag the edge until the window is the size you desire.

Switching between windows

The taskbar is not only used to restore minimised windows; it also allows you to switch between open windows. Simply click the window's button in the taskbar to make it the active window.

If you can see a window in the background that you want to make active, you can click on a part of that window.

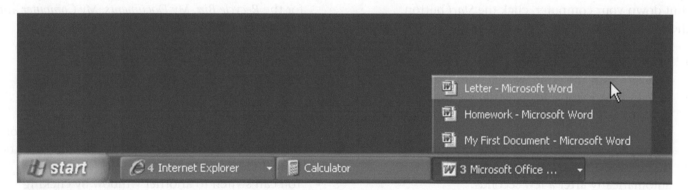

Figure 5.10 Program groups in the taskbar (Windows XP). You can see there are 4 Internet Explorer windows available and 3 Microsoft office Word windows.

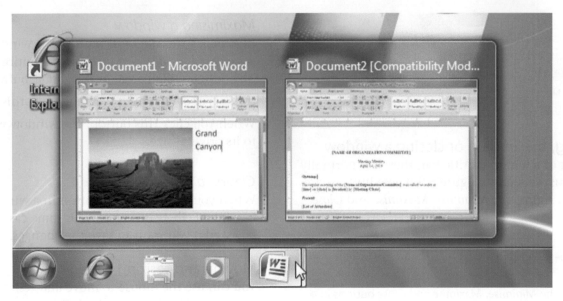

Figure 5.11 Program groups in Windows 7.

Shutting down the computer

When you have finished using your computer, you should not physically turn it off before shutting it down properly. Doing so can leave remnants of temporary files on your drive and cause files that were open at the time to become corrupted. To correctly shut down your computer, click the *Start* button, then:

- In Windows XP, click *Turn Off Computer* and click *Turn Off* from the window that pops up.
- In Windows Vista, click the triangle near the bottom of the *Start* menu, then select *Shut Down* (see Figure 5.12).
- In Windows 7, click the *Shut Down* button.
- If you have a modern computer, it will turn off automatically after a few seconds.

Figure 5.12 Shutting down Windows Vista.

Summary

- Some icons commonly found on the desktop are for the *Recycle Bin*, *My Documents*, *My Computer* and *Internet Explorer*.
- You can open programs via the *Start* menu or by double-clicking their icons on the desktop.
- The taskbar at the bottom of the screen is used to switch between open windows and to restore windows that have been minimised.
- The three buttons in the top right-hand corner of a window allow you to minimise it, maximise it and close it respectively.
- You can switch to another window by clicking inside the window itself, clicking on its button in the taskbar, or pressing *Alt + Tab*.
- You should not turn off the computer without shutting it down.

Review exercises

Exercise 5A

1 What is an icon? List two icons commonly found on the desktop.
2 Explain the following terms:
   a drag and drop
   b double-click
   c right-click.
3 If the mouse pointer is currently an hourglass, what does that mean?
4 Sarah accidentally clicked on a button in a window causing it to disappear. Give two explanations of what could have happened.
5 List six components found in the typical window and describe the purpose of each.
6 Explain where the notification area is and the kind of information displayed in it.
7 Explain how to shut down the version of Windows installed on your computer.

Exercise 5B

After logging into Windows, perform the following tasks:
1 Write down the names of the icons on your desktop.
2 Rearrange the icons on your desktop by dragging them to other locations.
3 Right-click on the following items:
   a The desktop
   b The *Start* button
   c The taskbar
   d Any of the icons in the notification area.
   Are there any differences among the resulting context menus?
4 Double-click an icon on your desktop (for example, *My Documents*). Then do the following to its window:
   a If it is currently maximised, restore it to its normal size.
   b Resize it by dragging each of its edges.
   c Drag it to the centre of the screen.
   d Minimise the window.
   e Maximise the window then restore it.
5 Open the *Notepad* and the *Calculator* via the *Start* menu. (Both programs are found in the *Accessories* group.) Reposition and resize them as you see fit.
6 Switch between the open windows using the various methods that you have learnt.
7 Close all the windows.
8 Shut down the computer via the *Start* menu.

6 File management

In this chapter, you will learn:

- about the *My Computer* window
- common file types and their extensions
- how to create folders
- how to copy, move, rename and delete files and folders
- about the *Recycle Bin*
- how to create shortcuts

Folders and files

In Chapter 4, we looked at different types of disks and the drives that read them. Think of a disk as an electronic filing cabinet. The data within that 'filing cabinet' is usually organised into several **folders** (also called directories). Although a folder can be empty, it usually contains one or more **files**.

Most of the files you will work with will be documents (e.g. letters, pictures). Other files will be programs you can run (e.g. Microsoft Word) or data files needed for those programs to work.

Managing your files

Windows provides comprehensive file management tools. Among the things you can do are:

- organise your files into folders
- copy, move, delete and rename files and folders
- see what files are on a particular disk
- find out information about the files, e.g. how much disk space they take up or when they were last modified
- open programs or documents.

You can do all of this via the *My Computer* window or *Windows Explorer* (which are two views of the same program). On many computers there is an icon for *My Computer* on the desktop. If you cannot see the icon on your computer desktop, you can still open the *My Computer* window by:

- clicking the *Start* button
- then clicking *My Computer*.

The *My Computer* window looks similar to that in Figure 6.1.

In Windows 7/Vista it is simply called *Computer*.

The My Computer window

The *My Computer* window is divided into two panels as you can see in Figure 6.1.

In the right-hand panel, you will see a list of the files in the current location, whether it is a folder, the desktop, a drive or the entire computer.

In the left-hand panel there is normally a high-level view of important folders on your computer as well as the different drives (the *Folders* view). However, if you are using Windows XP, sometimes it displays a list of file-related tasks. If this is the case with your *My Computer* window, you can show the *Folder* view by clicking the *Folders* button (Figure 6.2).

Drive letters

When the *My Computer* window first opens, it will display a list of the drives on your computer, with icons for each type of drive.

Each drive is assigned a letter which is displayed in brackets after its name. The typical drive letters on a Windows computer are shown in Table 6.1.

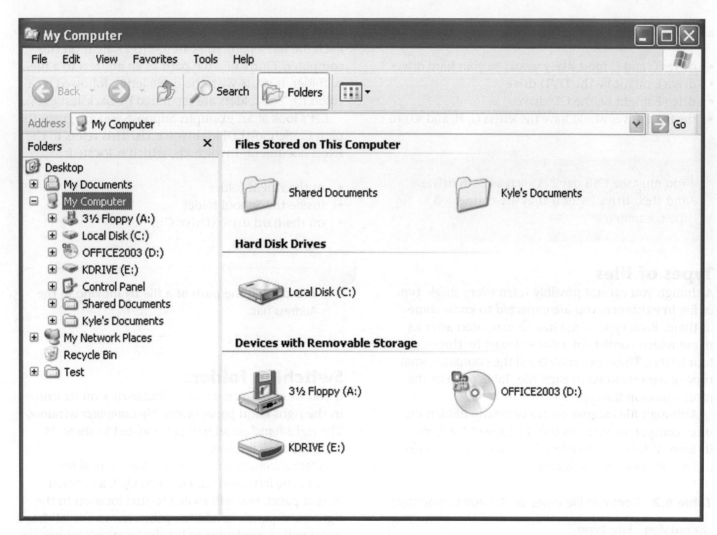

Figure 6.1 The *My Computer* window (in Windows XP).

Figure 6.2 Enabling the *Folder* view.

Table 6.1 Typical drive letters on a Windows computer.

Letter	Drive
A:	Floppy disk drive
C:	Hard drive (the drive that is built into your computer)
D:	CD-ROM or DVD-ROM drive
E, F, G, etc.	USB drives (also called flash drives or thumb drives)

Your computer may have different drive letters. For example, if your computer has two hard drives, a DVD drive and a CD burner:

- drives C and D most likely would be your hard drives
- drive E might be the DVD drive
- drive F might be the CD drive
- the flash drives would have the letters G, H, and so on.

> You only see USB devices such as flash drives and their drive letter if they are connected to the computer.

Types of files

Although you cannot possibly learn every single type of file in existence, you are expected to know some of them. Each type of file has an extension after its name which consists of a dot followed by three or four letters. These extensions tell the computer what type of data is stored in each file. Table 6.2 lists the most common file types.

Although file extensions are normally hidden on most computers, you can tell the type of file from its icon. When you double-click a file, it gets opened using the associated program.

Table 6.2 Common file types on Windows computers.

Extension	File type
.accdb	Access file 2007/10
.bmp	Bitmap Image file
.doc	Microsoft Word document
.docx	Microsoft Word 2007/2010 document
.exe	Executable program
.gif	GIF image file
.jpg	JPEG image file
.mdb	Access file 2003
.mp3	MP3 music file
.pdf	Adobe Acrobat file
.ppt	Microsoft PowerPoint document
.pptx	Microsoft PowerPoint 2007/2010 document
.txt	Plain text file
.xls	Microsoft Excel document
.xlsx	Microsoft Excel 2007/2010 document
.zip	Compressed file

File paths

Each file has a path you can use to locate it on the computer. Think of a file path as an address to a file or folder. It starts with the drive letter, followed by a colon (:). The folders are separated by backslashes (\).

Let's look at an example. Suppose you are given the path C:\School\EDPM\Invoice.xls. This refers to the Excel document, Invoice.xls, which is located:

- in the EDPM folder
- inside the School folder
- on the hard drive (Drive C:).

> You can tell the path of a file by looking in the *Address* bar.

Switching folders

If you want to open a folder, *double-click* on its icon in the right-hand panel of the *My Computer* window. The right-hand panel will get updated to show the contents of that folder.

Alternatively, you can use the hierarchical folder view in the left-hand panel. If you click a location in that panel, you will switch to that location in the right-hand panel. In addition, the view in the left-hand panel will be expanded to list the location's folders.

If you want to expand the list of folders in a particular location without actually opening that location, click the plus sign or arrow (depending on your version of Windows) to the left of the location in the *Folders* view. Figure 6.3 shows the user to expand the EDPM folder.

You will notice that in Figure 6.3 the folders that have been expanded have minus signs getting ready or diagonal triangles (a) (b) next to them. If you click one of these, such as the one next to the *School* folder, you will collapse the view for that location.

Using the *Address* bar in Windows XP

The *Address* bar in Windows XP works like a regular combo box. If you click the *down arrow* to the right of the *Address* bar, it will display a list of locations you can choose from (see Figure 6.4), including:

- the Desktop
- your *My Documents* folder

- the parent folder of the one you are currently in
- and the drives on your computer.

If you click on a location from the list, you will be taken to that location. You can also type the path directly into the *Address* bar and press the *Enter* key.

Using the *address* bar in Windows 7 and Vista

The *address* bar in more recent versions of Windows is more advanced. After each folder in the path, there is an arrow that you can click in order to see a list of that folder's subfolders. If you click on one of the subfolders in the list, you will be taken to that location.

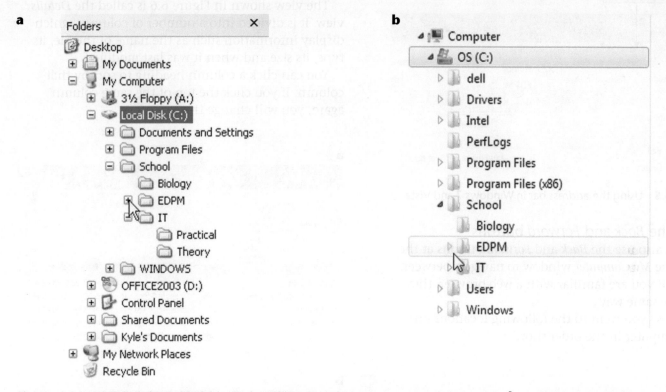

Figure 6.3 Expanding the EDPM folder in the *Folders* view of *My Computer*: **a** in Windows XP; **b** in Windows 7 and Vista.

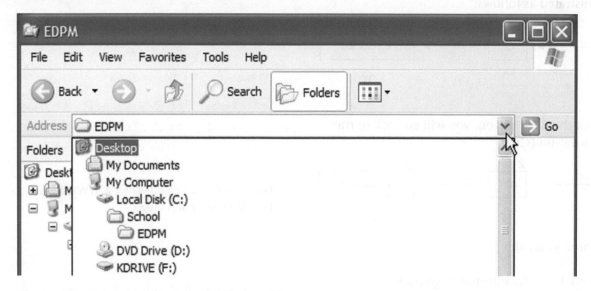

Figure 6.4 Using the address bar in Windows XP.

For example, in Figure 6.5, the user has clicked the arrow to the right of the *School* folder in the *Address* bar, causing a list of its subfolders to be displayed. When the user clicks the *IT* folder from the list, he will be taken to the path C:\School\IT.

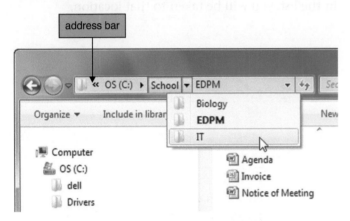

Figure 6.5 Using the *address* bar in Windows 7 and Vista.

Using the *Back* and *Forward* buttons

You can also use the *Back* and *Forward* buttons at the top of the *My Computer* window to navigate between folders. If you are familiar with a web browser, they work the same way.

Suppose you went to the following locations on your computer in the order shown:

1 E:\
2 C:\
3 E:\Games

This is illustrated as follows:

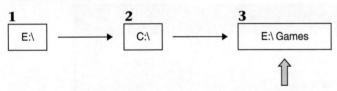

If you click the *Back* button, you will go back to the previous location (C:\).

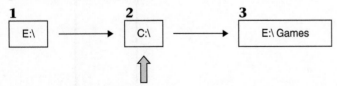

At this point, you can:

- either click the *Back* button to go back to E:\
- or click the *Forward* button to go to E:\Games.

Switching views

The right-panel of the *My Computer* window has a number of views you can choose from. To switch the view you can click a button near to the top of the window, which unfortunately is not labelled (see Figure 6.6). When you click the button, you will be shown a list of the different views to choose from.

The view shown in Figure 6.6 is called the *Details* view. It is divided into a number of columns which display information such as the name of the file, its type, its size and when it was last modified.

You can click a column heading to sort by that column. If you click the top of the same column again, you will change the sort order.

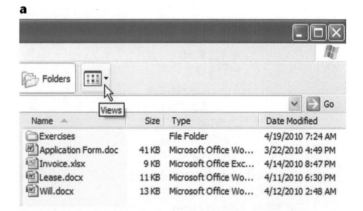

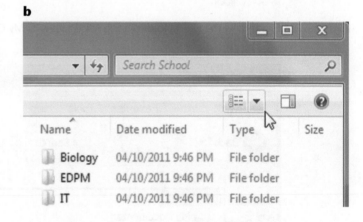

Figure 6.6 Switching views: **a** in Windows XP; **b** in Windows 7 and Vista.

An easy way to find the last file you worked on in a folder is to switch to the *Details* view, then click on the *Date Modified* column heading to sort the modification dates in descending order. (You may have to click the column heading twice.)

Other possible views include:

- Icon views to show just the name of the file and its icon
- the Thumbnail view shows small previews of the images in the folder (in Windows Vista and Windows 7 the equivalent view is the *Extra Large Icon* view)
- the Filmstrip view, which is only found in Windows XP, is great for viewing the images in a folder (see Figure 6.7).

Working with folders and files

Creating a folder

To create a folder:

1 Go to the drive or folder where the new folder is to be placed.

2 Right-click on an empty area.

3 Click *New, Folder*.

4 Type the name of the new folder.

5 Press the *Enter* key when done.

Blue hills.jpg   Sunset.jpg   Water lilies.jpg   Winter.jpg

Figure 6.7   The Filmstrip view in Windows XP.

Renaming a file or folder

If at any time you want to rename a file or folder:

1 Right-click on the folder.

2 Type the new name.

3 Press *Enter* when done.

Copying files

To copy a file from one folder to another:

1 Right-click on the file's icon.

2 Click *Copy* from the context menu that appears.

3 Go to the folder where you want the copy to be placed.

4 Right-click inside the view of that folder.

5 Click *Paste* from the context menu that appears.

You can also use this process to copy folders.

If the files are very big, a window will appear in order to keep you updated on the progress.

To copy multiple files at the same time, select the first file, then while holding down the *Ctrl* key, click on the other files to select them. The selected files will be highlighted in blue. Then right-click on any of the files you selected, click *Copy* and proceed as before.

Moving files

To move a file from one location to another:

1 Right-click on the file's icon.

2 Click *Cut* from the context menu that appears.

3 Go to the folder to which you want the file to be moved.

4 Right-click inside the view of that folder.

5 Click *Paste* from the context menu that appears.

You can also move files by dragging them from the right-hand panel of the *My Computer* window and dropping them on the desired location in the folder list on the left-hand panel.

Deleting files or folders
If you want to delete files or folders, you first select them then press the *Delete* key. In order to reduce the chance of you accidentally deleting the wrong thing, the computer will require you to confirm the deletion.

The Recycle Bin
When you delete files from your hard drive, they are not deleted right away (unless you specifically tell the computer to do so). Instead, they go to a special folder called the *Recycle Bin*.

This only works for files deleted from hard drives. Files deleted from removable disks like floppy disks or flash drives bypass the *Recycle Bin* and are deleted immediately.

You can access the *Recycle Bin* by double-clicking its icon on the desktop. If it contains any files, the waste paper basket in its icon will contain a crumpled piece of paper. To 'unerase' a file that has been sent to the *Recycle Bin*, right-click on the file then click *Restore*.

Finding files

In Windows XP, if you want to find a file in a particular location (and its subfolders), you can go to that location in the *My Computer* window and click the *Search* button. The *Search Companion* (see Figure 6.8) will then be displayed in the left-hand panel of the *My Computer* window. From there it is simply a matter of choosing the appropriate option and following the instructions.

In Windows Vista and Windows 7 finding files is even easier. You simply type the name of the file you are looking for in the *Start* menu's search box (see Figure 6.9).

Figure 6.8 Searching for files in Windows XP.

Creating shortcuts

You may want to create a shortcut on your desktop to a file or program you find yourself using all the time. To do so, right-click on the desktop and then click *New*, *Shortcut* in the context menu. A window similar to the one in Figure 6.10 will be displayed.

If you know the location (path) to the file you can type it directly into the box. In most cases you will need to click the *Browse...* button and locate the file in the window that pops up.

Figure 6.9 Search results for files in Windows 7 or Vista.

Figure 6.10 The *Create Shortcut* window.

After clicking *Next*, you'll have to choose a name for the shortcut and click the *Finish* button.

Summary

- The *My Computer* window allows you to manage your files and view information about them.
- You can change the current location in the *My Computer* window by clicking a location in the left-hand panel, double-clicking a folder in the right-hand panel, using the address bar or the *back* and *forward* buttons.
- If you want to copy, move or rename a file/folder, the first step is usually to right-click on it.
- If you delete a file from the hard drive, it goes to the *Recycle Bin* so it can be restored later. If you delete a file from a flash drive or floppy disk it is deleted permanently.
- You can use the *Ctrl* key to select multiple files or folders at a time.

Review exercises

Exercise 6A

1 Give three file extensions that are used for image files.
2 What extension does the average program have?
3 Explain how you can use the *My Computer* window to see the largest file in a folder.
4 Explain how to place a shortcut to a file (which is located on your hard drive) on the desktop.
5 Explain how you would copy a file from the *My Documents* folder, to a folder called Business. How would the steps change if you were moving the file instead?
6 Tim accidentally deleted a file from his A:\ drive. Will he be able to get it back?
7 Give the path to a Microsoft Word 2007 document called 'Newsletter' located in the Correspondence folder of the Sunday School folder on the main hard drive.

Exercise 6B

1 Open the *My Computer* window.
2 Using the Folder view on the left-hand side, go to your class folder.
3 Create a new folder with your name.
4 Inside that folder, create a new folder for each day of the week.
5 Rename these folders to Mon, Tue, Wed, and so on.
6 Delete the weekend folders.
7 Move the Tue folder inside the Mon folder.
8 Move the Wed folder inside the Tue folder
9 Move the Thu and Fri folders inside the Wed folder.
10 Go to the folder for Exercise 6B (by default it will be C:\EDPM for CSEC\Computer Basics\ Exercise 6B).
11 Copy the files one by one to the Thu folder. (It will be a lot faster if you use the *Back* and *Forward* buttons.)
12 Select all the files in the Thu folder.
13 Right-click on the selected files and click Copy.
14 Use the Address bar to go to the Fri folder. (You will need to go to the Wed folder first if you are using Windows XP.)
15 Right-click inside the folder contents and click Paste.
16 Switch between the various views.
17 Switch to the Details view and sort the files in reverse alphabetical order. Then sort them in descending order by modification date.
18 Delete the files in the folder then restore them from the *Recycle Bin*.
19 Create shortcuts to any two of the files in the Fri folder and place them on the desktop.

7 Systems and application software

In this chapter, you will learn:

- the difference between systems software and application software

- the different categories of application software

As was previously mentioned, computer software can be divided into two broad categories: Operating Systems (also called Systems Software) and the application software which runs on it.

Operating systems

You should have already encountered an operating system, the one we have been looking at in chapters 1 to 6: Microsoft Windows.

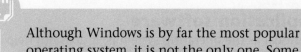

Although Windows is by far the most popular operating system, it is not the only one. Some alternatives are Mac OS X (shown in Figure 7.1), MS-DOS, Linux and Unix.

The **operating system** (OS) is a special program that manages the other programs on the computer

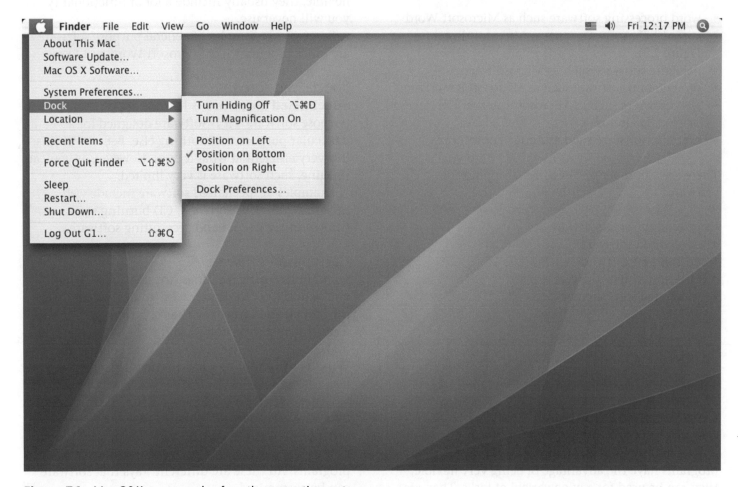

Figure 7.1 Mac OS X, an example of another operating system.

as well as the computer hardware. Among its many responsibilities are:

- acting as an interface between the computer hardware and software
- managing the hardware resources
- allowing you to run, switch between and close other programs
- allowing you to manage your files.

Application software

As critical as the operating system is, it does not help you get your work done; that is the job of application software. **Application software** is software used to solve problems that are not related to the computer itself. Such 'problems' include enabling the user to write a letter or play a computer game. This type of software runs <u>on top of</u> the operating system. Examples of application software include:

- word processing software such as Microsoft Word
- spreadsheet software such as Microsoft Excel (see Figure 7.2)
- database software such as Microsoft Access
- presentation software such as Microsoft PowerPoint
- web browsers such as Microsoft Internet Explorer or Mozilla Firefox
- graphics software such as Adobe Photoshop.

There are a number of categories of application software:

- general purpose software
- specialised software
- customised software
- custom-written software
- integrated software package.

A program can be in more than one category.

General purpose software

The programs you will working with in this course will be mainly **general-purpose software**. Such programs have the advantage of being very flexible; they can be used for a wide variety of tasks. They are

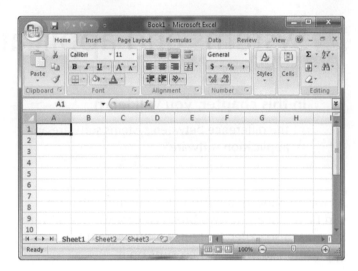

Figure 7.2 Microsoft Excel, an example of general purpose software.

also usually mass produced, making them relatively cheap. Unfortunately, because the programs are *so* flexible, they usually include a lot of functionality you will never use.

Some good examples of general purpose software are office programs like Microsoft Word and Excel.

Specialised software

Specialised software is like the opposite of general purpose software – it is software designed for a particular purpose and nothing else. Because of this, it is very efficient at what it does. However, as you can imagine, such software is very limited.

Examples of specialised software include web browsers, antivirus software, CD burning software (shown in Figure 7.3) and accounting software.

Customised software

Sometimes a program does not do exactly what you would like. In some cases, you can customise it in much the same way that you would customise a car. For instance, companies like Dell may make changes to the programs that come with Windows in order to add functionality specific to their brand.

Other software like Mozilla Firefox and Photoshop allow the user to install plug-ins to extend their functionality. And many Microsoft programs have support for macros which are like programs <u>inside</u> the programs. All these are different ways that software can be customised.

Figure 7.3 CD burning software such as that shown are an example of specialised software.

a

b

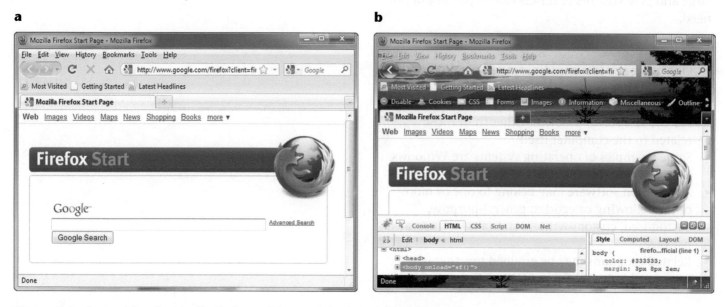

Figure 7.4 Customising the Mozilla Firefox web browser: **a** original; **b** customised.

Figure 7.4 shows the dramatic change that customising a program can have. Here both the appearance and functionality of Firefox have been changed.

Custom-written software

Despite the level of customisation available in many programs, sometimes companies want software written from scratch. Such software is called **custom-written software**. The beauty of custom-written software is that you can get *exactly* what you want. Unfortunately, this comes at a price. Not only do you have to wait for the software to be written; you also have to pay quite a bit of money.

Integrated software packages

Large software companies like Microsoft and Adobe give you the option of buying their programs in **integrated software packages** which are cheaper than buying all the programs separately. Integrated software packages are groups of programs designed to work together and share data.

For example, although programs like Microsoft Word and Excel are general purpose software, together they form a package called Microsoft Office. Similarly, the Adobe Creative Suite package contains a variety of programs including Photoshop and Dreamweaver.

As you can imagine, integrated packages are very large and give you lots of functionality you might not need.

Summary

- Operating systems coordinate the operation of the computer hardware and software.
- Application software runs on top of the operating system and solves problems other than those related to the computer itself.
- Some examples of operating systems are Windows, Linux, Unix, Mac OS X and MS DOS
- Application software may belong to one or more of the following categories: general-purpose, customised, custom-written, specialised, integrated package.
- Related programs may be grouped together in Integrated Software Packages like Microsoft Office.

Review exercise

Exercise 7

1 Give four functions of systems software.
2 What is the difference between application software and systems software?
3 Can application software run without an OS? Can an OS run without application software?
4 Explain the differences between the following types of software:
   a Customised and custom-written
   b General purpose and specialised
   c General purpose software and integrated software packages.
5 Why would a business opt to pay for custom-written software instead of using general purpose software?
6 Give an advantage and a disadvantage of specialised software over general purpose software.

8 Computer care

In this chapter, you will learn:

- how to take care of your computer
- how to take care of your working environment

A computer is an expensive piece of equipment so it is important to take care of your computer, whether it is at school or at home. Below are some guidelines to help you do so.

General care

1. Cover the computer when you are not using it in order to reduce the accumulation of dust.
2. Shutdown the computer when you are finished using it. If you turn off the computer without shutting it down, you run the risk of corrupting any files that were open at the time.
3. Do not plug the computer components directly into the wall socket; use a surge protector instead. Every now and again, particularly after an electricity outage, there are power surges which can damage electrical equipment (such as computers) that are not plugged into a surge protector.
4. Do not eat or drink around the computer. Food can get between the keys on the keyboard and if liquids get into contact with the circuits inside your computer they will destroy the computer.

Taking care of disks/drives

1. Do not write on floppy disks, CDs or DVDs unless you are using a felt tip pen or marker. Ball point pens can scratch these disks.
2. Keep magnetic storage media like floppy disks, hard disks or magnetic tape away from magnets. Magnets, even those in devices such as speakers, can scramble the information on magnetic media causing corruption or loss of data.
3. Keep disks out of direct sunlight. Disks are mostly plastic so if the sun is hot enough they can melt. Also, the UV rays can affect recordable CDs and DVDs rendering them unreadable.

4. Do not bend floppy disks, CDs or DVDs.
5. Do not move the computer tower when it is turned on. If you do so while the hard drive is in operation, you run the risk of damaging it.
6. Eject USB devices via Windows before you remove them from the computer. To do so, click the *Safely Remove Hardware* icon 🔌 in the notification area of the Taskbar. If the icon is not visible you may need to click the arrow. If you fail to do so, data in any files on the flash drive that were open at the time may be corrupted.

Caring for your working environment

It is not only your computer you need to care for – you also need to care for your working environment. The table surface should be kept clean at all times. Avoid keeping clutter on your desk since it makes your workspace look unprofessional.

Summary

- If you turn off a computer without shutting it down or remove a USB device without ejecting it in Windows, you run the risk of data corruption.
- Keep computer equipment away from food, dust and moisture.
- Keep storage devices away from magnets and direct sunlight.
- Do not plug computer equipment directly into the wall sockets. Plug them into surge protectors instead.
- Keep your workspace clean and tidy.

Review exercises

Exercise 8

1 List five ways you can protect your computer hardware.
2 For each of the following types of storage media, explain how improper handling can result in data corruption or data loss:
   a CD-R
   b Hard drive
   c Floppy disk.

9 The Internet

Networks

Simply put, a network is a group of computer devices that are connected in some way. The best known and largest network is the Internet, but networks may be found in offices, universities and companies of all sorts. If the network is in a limited geographical area like a university it is called a **LAN** (Local Area Network); otherwise it is called a **WAN** (Wide Area Network).

Connecting the computers makes it easier to share files as well as resources such as printers and Internet connections. Unfortunately, this makes them susceptible to hackers and computer viruses.

In LAN networks, devices may be connected wirelessly or using cables plugged into network cards. For WAN networks, telephone lines, fibre optical cables or even satellites may be used.

Bandwidth

The communication channel determines the available **bandwidth** (how fast data can be transmitted). For example, cables are normally faster than wireless and fibre-optic cables have a much higher bandwidth than regular telephone lines.

The Internet

The Internet is a worldwide network of networks. In order to access the Internet, you, or your company must first sign up with an Internet Service Provider (ISP) such as LIME. Your computer, or your office network, will also need to be connected to a modem, which is normally provided by the ISP.

You plug the telephone or cable line into the modem which is in turn connected to your computer. The modem then converts the digital data into a form that can be transmitted over the line. A modem on the other end does the reverse.

Figure 9.1   A DSL modem.

The World Wide Web

The World Wide Web is not the only part of the Internet, but it is certainly the most visible. It consists of billions of documents called **web pages** that are linked together. A group of related web pages forms what is known as a **website**. Each web page and website has an address called a **URL**, normally in the form http://www.whatever.com (though the http://www. part may be omitted).

Web browsers

Web pages are written in a special language called **HTML**. In order to view a web page, you need to use a program called a **web browser** that interprets the HTML and displays it accordingly. The most popular web browsers are Internet Explorer and Mozilla Firefox, although Google Chrome is steadily gaining momentum.

Although there are a number of web browsers, they all work in the same way. Here are some of the things they have in common.

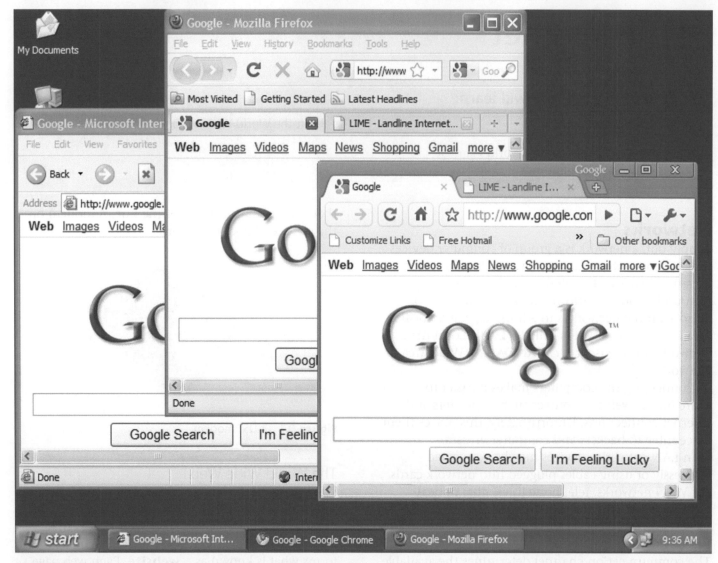

Figure 9.2 The Google home page displayed in 3 different browsers.

Address bar

Near the top of every web browser is an address bar, where you type websites' URLs (if you know them). The address bars also keep track of the most recently visited addresses.

Going from one web page to the next

The typical web page contains several <u>hyperlinks</u> (called links for short) which you can click to go to other web pages. Links may be in the form of words or images. When the mouse pointer passes over a link, it changes to a hand, like in Figure 9.3. Links are often, but not always, distinguished from normal text by putting them in blue or underlining them.

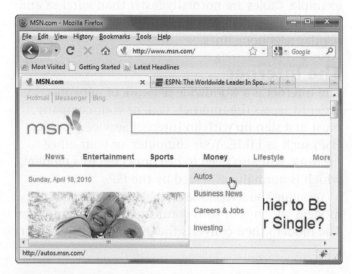

Figure 9.3 Clicking a link.

When you point at a link, the URL of the page it points to is displayed in the status bar at the bottom of the browser. For instance, in Figure 9.3 when the user clicks on the Autos link he/she will get taken to the URL http://autos.msn.com.

You can also go from one web page to the next by using the *Back* and *Forward* buttons at the top of the web browser. These work in much the same way as those in the *My Computer* window.

Downloading

The process of transferring data from a remote computer to your own is called downloading. When you click on a download link, such as those used for email attachments, the web browser will begin downloading the file. You will have the option of running the file automatically or saving it so you can access it later (see Figure 9.4).

Figure 9.4 Downloading a file in Internet Explorer.

If you choose the Save option, the file will be saved in the *Downloads* folder, on the *Desktop* or in another folder of your choosing.

Search engines

If you do not know the URL of a particular website or web page, which is most of the time, you can search for it using a special type of website called a **search engine**. You will probably be familiar with at least one search engine, Google.com but there are others like Bing.com.

When you type in what you are looking for and click *Search*, the search engine returns a list of web pages that contain the search terms. For each result,

the title of the page, its URL and a sample of the matching text is displayed (see Figure 9.5).

Figure 9.5 Results from a search engine.

Summary

- A network is a group of interconnected computer devices.
- The Internet is a worldwide network of networks; the World Wide Web is its most visible aspect.
- In order to gain access to the Internet, you must sign up with an Internet Service Provider.
- A program used to view websites and web pages is known as a web browser.
- Websites such as Google that allow you to find information on the Internet are called search engines.

Review exercises

Exercise 9

1. Explain what a network is. Give some advantages and disadvantages of using a network.
2. What does the word 'bandwidth' mean?
3. What communication device do you need in order to access the Internet?
4. What is the relationship between websites and web pages?
5. Explain the difference between a web browser and a search engine.
6. How can you tell if a phrase in a webpage is a link to another page?
7. Describe three ways you can get from one web page to another.

10 Electronic mail

How email works

Email is a vital part of the Internet (so much so that it merits its own chapter in this book). Let us take a look at how it works.

In order to send or receive an email, you must have an email address. Email addresses are usually in the form: my_account_name@myprovider.com. Your email provider might be your ISP, but in many cases people choose from a range of free alternative such as Windows Live Hotmail (Hotmail.com), Gmail (gmail.com) or Yahoo Mail (mail.yahoo.com).

> Email addresses do not have spaces in them. Instead, words are usually separated by underscores or dots e.g. john_doe@hotmail.com or john.doe@yahoo.com.

Suppose Alice (alice@hotmail.com) wants to send an email to Bob (bob@gmail.com). The process would normally go something like this:

1 Alice logs into her email account.
2 She composes an email message, including Bob's email address and clicks *Send*.
3 Hotmail's servers send the message to Gmail's servers (this process normally takes a few seconds at most).
4 The Gmail server forwards the message to Bob's mailbox.
5 When Bob logs into his Gmail account, he will see a new message from Alice in his Inbox.

Advantages of email

The main advantage of email is of course its speed. Messages can be delivered across the globe in seconds, instead of days.

Another major advantage is that a single email can be sent to multiple recipients simultaneously at the push of a button. And since you do not have to pay for stamps, emails are also cheaper to send.

Disadvantages of email

However, like most things in life, email has some disadvantages as well. It can only be used by people who have valid email accounts and access to the Internet (a surprising number of people do not). In addition, of course, it cannot be used to send packages.

But, there are even more serious problems than those, which can arise from using email. Viruses can easily spread via email attachments. Also, specially crafted emails can trick you into visiting websites that *seem* legitimate but are designed to steal your personal information.

Getting a free email account

As was mentioned earlier, there are a number of sites you can visit to obtain a free email account. Since there are so many alternatives, each of which is constantly evolving, I will not teach you a particular email service. Instead, I will explain how to use email in general.

When you visit the website of the email provider, you will be given two options. If you already have an email account <u>with that provider</u> you can type in your username and password in the boxes provided and click *Sign In*. If you do not, you will need to sign up for a new account.

When you sign up you will be asked to choose a username (which is not already taken) and password, in addition you will be asked to provide certain information like:

- Your real name.
- Your date of birth.
- What country you are from.

You will also be asked to choose a secret question and provide an answer. This information will be used to verify your identity in the event that you forget your password and need to reset it.

You may also be asked to type a word that is displayed in an image (called a CAPTCHA). This is done to make sure it is a human signing up for the email account as opposed to an automated junk mail program (Figure 10.1). (Programs are not nearly as good at recognising text in images as humans).

Figure 10.1 System designed to thwart automated signups.

When you finish the sign up process, your account will be created in a matter of seconds, complete with a welcome email explaining some of the features that are provided.

The inbox

When you first login to your email account, you will be taken to the Inbox which displays a list of the emails you have received. Figure 10.2 shows what a typical Inbox looks like.

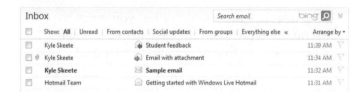

Figure 10.2 The Inbox.

There are a few things to note. An Inbox normally has at least three columns, listing, for each email:

- who it is From
- the Subject
- the Date the email was sent.

Some email providers may also list additional information such as the size of the email. You can arrange any of these columns in ascending or descending order, but by default the messages are arranged by the date, with the most recent messages being shown at the top.

Next to the email subject you will see envelopes which indicate the status of the email – a closed envelope means that the email is unread whereas open envelopes show which messages you have already read. Email providers automatically mark an email as Read after you open it for a few seconds.

In Hotmail, Read emails may also have arrows (in addition to the icon of an opened envelope) that indicate whether you have forwarded an email. A purple left arrow means that you have replied to the email in question; a blue right arrow indicates that you have forwarded the email.

Other folders

The Inbox is just one of the folders found in a typical email account. Some of the other common ones are:

- Junk Mail/Spam – This is where emails that you or your email provider flag as junk mail get sent.
- Sent – Maintains a list of the emails you have sent.
- Trash/Deleted Items – Temporarily stores emails that you have deleted.

tip

If someone says they've sent you an email but you haven't received it after a few minutes, check your junk mail folder. Your provider might have incorrectly flagged it as spam.

Common email operations

Sending an email

The process of sending an email generally goes like this:

1. Click *New* (or Create mail or something similar).
2. Type the address of the person(s) you want to send the email to, or select it/them from the contact list.
3. Type the subject of the email.
4. Type the message.
5. Attach any additional files that need to be sent with the email.
6. Click *Send*.

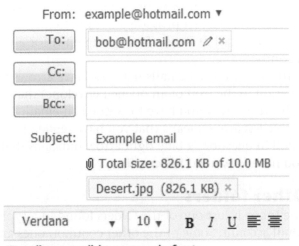

Figure 10.3 Composing an email.

The Cc and Bcc fields

If you want to send an email to multiple recipients, you can type them in the <u>To</u> field, separated by commas. But if you look closely in the Figure above (Figure 10.3), you will see fields labelled <u>Cc</u> and <u>Bcc</u>. What are those for?

When you click Send, a copy is sent to any email addresses in the Cc and Bcc (carbon copy and blind carbon copy) fields. People receiving these copies will know that the email is not addressed to them directly (if it were, their email addresses would be in the To field instead).

But what is the difference between the two? Well, if you put an email address in the Bcc field, none of the other recipients will see it (hence the reason it is called a *blind* carbon copy).

tip

The Cc and Bcc may be hidden by default unless you explicitly enable them.

Sending attachments

If you need to send a file in an email, you have to send it as an attachment. When you click on the *Attach File* option, a window will pop up allowing you to select a file that has already been saved on your computer. The file may take a while to be uploaded depending on how large it is.

Emails that have attachments are normally displayed with a paperclip icon next to them in the Inbox. When you open such an email, images that were attached are normally displayed automatically. However, you will have to download the other types of attachments on to your computer.

Only open attachments that you were expecting to receive and from people you know. Email viruses (called worms) can be transmitted via attachments. If you open one of these malicious attachments, it will send infected emails to all the contacts in your list (who will think they came from you).

Replying to an email

When you want to reply to an email that you are reading, you click the *Reply* button. This will create a new email with Re: in front the original subject and a copy of the original message. However, you can change this information if you wish.

Do not click *Reply to All* unless you mean to send the reply to all the people in the email. This can lead to embarrassing situations!

Forwarding email

If you come across an interesting email you want to send to your friends or workmates, click the *Forward* button. The subject of the created email will have Fw: in front the original subject.

Emails that say that Hotmail is closing down or promise money if you forward them to all your friends are hoaxes. If you forward them, all you will do is make your friends think you are really gullible.

Deleting email

In the inbox there will usually be checkboxes next to each email that is listed. You place ticks in the box next to the emails you want to delete, and then click *Delete* (or something similar). The emails will go to a special folder called *Trash*, where they will stay a few days before they are deleted permanently.

If you want to delete old email, you can sort your Inbox in ascending order by date and then select the emails you want to delete.

Signing out

When you have finished reading or sending your emails, remember to click *Sign Out* so that people who use the computer after you cannot read your email.

Contact lists

Email providers also provide a way for you to manage your list of contacts (even those that do not have email addresses). When you create a contact, you can store the bare minimum (the contact's name) or you can include additional information such as the contact's email address(es), telephone number(s), birth-date, company and home address.

The cool thing about saving contact information is that when you want to send an email to a contact, you can start typing his/her name in the To field and the email address will popup (see Figure 10.4).

Figure 10.4 Sending an Email to a Contact.

Summary

- Email is faster and cheaper than regular mail and allows you to send email to multiple recipients simultaneously, but malicious emails may spread viruses and try to scam you.
- You can get a free email address by signing up with Hotmail, Yahoo or Gmail.
- In addition to the Inbox, which contains the email messages you have received, there are also folders for Junk Mail, Sent Items and Deleted Items.
- Use the Cc and Bcc fields to send carbon copies and blind carbon copies respectively.
- If you want to send files via email you have to send them as attachments.

Review exercises

Exercise 10

1 Suppose you, as group leader, receive an email from your History teacher with the subject 'Project Submission Guidelines', that you want to forward to the rest of your group members (whose email addresses are listed below).

- Sue – sue.ellen@hotmail.com
- Christopher – cmoney@gmail.com
- Joshua – josh_man@yahoo.com

The email is going to be addressed to Joshua but copied to Christopher and Sue. Now suppose that you want to send a copy to your friends from another group, Janelle (j_smith@hotmail.com) and Tyler (t_perry@bet.com) without *your* group members knowing.

Complete the table below using the supplied information.

To:	
Cc:	
Bcc:	
Subject:	

2   What are the disadvantages associated with email?

3   List 3 free email providers.

4   What is the name of the location in which the emails that you receive are stored?

5   What sort of information do you need to provide when signing up for an email account?

6   Explain how to send a Word document via email.

7   How can you tell whether an email is a reply or a forward by looking at its subject?

8   Alice accidentally deleted an important email yesterday. Explain why she will most likely be able to get back the email.

9   Why is it important to sign out after you have finished reading your email?

10 Explain the purpose of the Spam and Sent Items folders.

11 Types of electronic communication

Ways to communicate electronically

Technology has made it easy to communicate electronically with people all over the world. Let us look at a few of the ways you can do so.

Email

As you learnt in the last chapter, you can use email to type messages to people all over the world. Also, if you want to send a file, you can send it by using an attachment.

Telecommuting

Telecommuting is the process by which an employee works remotely from his office by utilising telecommunication channels such as a telephone line. It normally requires a modem and special networking software to be installed, both inside the office and the remote computer.

As you would expect, this is a very appealing way of working since an employee can work from the comfort of his home if he chooses. He would not have to travel to and from work every day, saving time, money and sanity (from not having to deal with rush hour traffic).

So what happens if he has to go to a meeting? Actually, he can do this from home as well through a process called **videoconferencing**. Videoconferencing is the use of computer, video, audio and communications technology to allow people in different locations to see and talk to one another. It also saves the company the cost of having to fly employees to meetings.

The office could have a conference room with a video camera and a large screen so all the people in the meeting can see and hear the remote employee(s). The person at home, (the remote employee), would need a webcam, microphone and speakers so that the people in the meeting could see and hear him, and *he* can also *see*, *hear* and *speak to* the people at the meeting.

You can also have meetings via teleconferencing. In this case you would not be able to see the participants, but it has the benefit of not requiring cameras.

Figure 11.1 A room set up for videoconferencing.

Unfortunately telecommuting has a few disadvantages, the main one being the lack of proper supervision. There is also a lack of social interaction.

Fax machines

Fax machines are another way to communicate electronically. A fax machine is a device that allows you to electronically transmit printed or written documents over the telephone line. In order for this technology to work it requires a fax machine (or fax-capable device) on both ends. I say 'fax-capable' because a computer can send a fax as well, once it is connected to a phone line.

Instead of a dedicated fax machine, many businesses (particularly small ones) tend to use multifunction printers like the one on page 50 which have built-in fax capability.

Figure 11.2 A multifunction printer with built-in fax.

Scan-to-mail/scan-to-file

Fax machines are not the only way to electronically transmit documents that were originally on paper. You can also use a scanner to scan the document and then send the resulting file as an email attachment. This process is known as scan-to-mail or scan-to-file.

Choosing a means of electronic communication

Now that you have seen the different ways you can communicate electronically, let us look at factors affecting which one you choose.

Degree of urgency

Because all of the methods outlined are electronic, they are all pretty quick. However, if the matter is urgent it is best to communicate via telecommuting (in the form of teleconferencing or videoconferencing). This is because using the other approaches can involve a lot of back and forth (I send you a message, you send me one back etc.). Also with those approaches you have to wait for the intended recipient to see your message.

You can flag an email as urgent so it would stand out from the other emails in the recipient's inbox. But this still does not guarantee that the recipient will check her email in a timely fashion.

Location/time zone

If you are communicating with people in countries on the other side of the globe, chances are they are in another time zone. This can make conferencing very challenging since when it is day in one country, people might be sleeping in the other country.

In a case like this, if the message is not urgent, it is better to use one of the other methods such as faxing or emailing. That way the recipient can check it when he/she comes into work the next day.

Level of confidentiality

If the message is confidential you certainly do not want to send it by fax where anyone in the office can see it. It is much better to send an email or use telecommuting.

Since telecommunications channels are not entirely secure, you can use encryption technology for additional security.

Cost

Of the methods mentioned, fax machines and telecommuting are the most expensive, due to the cost of the equipment involved. And in the case of faxes, long distance charges may apply.

Genre

In this case 'genre' refers to whether the communication will be oral, written or visual. If written or typewritten documents are being transmitted, then you have to use fax machines or scan-to-email. If the written document is already on the computer, then you can send it as an ordinary email attachment. And if the communication is oral or visual, you can use teleconferencing or videoconferencing respectively.

Summary

- Electronic communication can be done via email, telecommuting, fax or scan to email.
- Telecommuting allows an employee to connect to his office remotely and do work from home.
- Teleconferencing and videoconferencing are cost effective ways of having meetings with people in different locations.

- The choice of electronic communication media depends on urgency, location, confidentiality, cost and the genre of communication.

Review exercises

Exercise 11

1 Explain what telecommuting is and why an employee would want to do it.
2 What is the difference between teleconferencing and videoconferencing?
3 What hardware and software are required for videoconferencing?
4 Explain two ways that a company can send printed documents electronically even if it does not have a dedicated fax machine.
5 List four factors that affect the selection of communications media.
6 Which communications method would you use in the following scenarios? In each case, justify your answer:
   a You are in the Caribbean and want to send a completed application form to someone in England.
   b You want to be able to see the person's reaction when you are talking to them.
   c You have an urgent message that you want to send to someone in Japan (and you are in Jamaica).
   d A company wants to send a mockup of a top secret new product to one of its overseas employees.

Part 2   Keyboarding

① Keyboarding basics

In this chapter, you will learn:

- about the correct posture for typing
- how to erase text
- how to type capital letters
- about the *Num Lock* key
- about special keys on the keyboard

Correct posture

When you are typing – indeed whenever you are sitting at your desk – it is important to maintain the correct posture (Figure 1.1). This is not just to look professional; improper posture can cause health problems such as carpal tunnel syndrome, eyestrain and other aches and pains. Carpal tunnel syndrome is pain or numbness in your hands and fingers caused by placing too much pressure on the wrists (e.g. by holding your hands incorrectly while typing).

Here are some guidelines for maintaining the correct posture.

- Adjust the height of your chair so that your thighs are horizontal (i.e. your knees and hips are at the same level).
- Rest your feet comfortably on the floor or on a foot rest.
- Sit upright in the chair (don't slouch!).
- Position the monitor about an arm's length away with the top of the monitor at eye level.
- Position your keyboard at a height that has your forearms almost parallel to the floor.
- Keep your arms near to your body.

Figure 1.1   The correct typing posture.

- Avoid bending your wrists. Keep them as straight as possible.
- Keep your fingers relaxed.

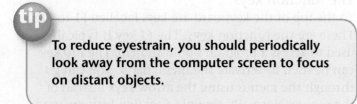

tip

To reduce eyestrain, you should periodically look away from the computer screen to focus on distant objects.

Opening WordPad

Throughout the keyboarding chapters, we will be using the WordPad program to practise typing. There are two reasons we will be using WordPad instead of another program like Microsoft Word.

1 It is installed on every computer that has Microsoft Windows.
2 It does not try to automatically correct things while you're typing (the way that Word does).

In order to open the WordPad program, click the *Start* button, then *Programs*, *Accessories*, and then click the *WordPad* icon.

The cursor

When you open WordPad, one of the first things you will notice is a thin vertical line that is flashing on

and off. That is the **cursor**. It tells you where the next letter that you type will go.

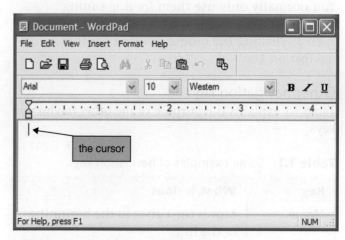

Figure 1.2 The cursor in Wordpad.

The typical keyboard layout

The typical keyboard has over 100 keys, so they are grouped in order to make them easier to find. The main grouping contains the letters of the alphabet (in no obvious order) with a row of numbers at the top. To the right of the letters are some symbols, and to their right you can find the *Enter* key and *Backspace* key. To the bottom of this same grouping is the space bar which is flanked on both sides by the *Shift*, *Ctrl* and *Alt* keys.

The most important key groupings are highlighted on Figure 1.3.

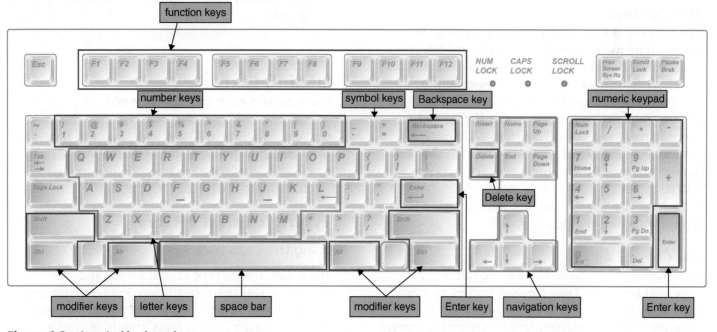

Figure 1.3 A typical keyboard.

The arrow keys

The arrow keys can be used to move the cursor. You normally only use them for fine tuning since there are quicker ways to move the cursor, such as clicking the mouse or using another navigation key.

Other navigation keys

Table 1.1 explains the purpose of the other navigation keys.

Table 1.1 Some examples of navigation keys.

Key	What it does
Home	Moves the cursor to the beginning of the line
End	Moves the cursor to the end of the line
Page Up (Pg Up)	Sends the cursor up to the previous page
Page Down (Pg Dn)	Sends the cursor down to the next page

The Space bar

The easiest key to find on the keyboard – because of its size and location – is the Space bar. Like the name suggests, you use it to insert spaces between words.

The Shift keys

The *Shift* key is known as a <u>modifier key</u>. You do not use it by itself. Instead, it is used to modify the usual behaviour of a key. You will notice that some keys have two characters on them. Normally, when you press one of those keys, you will get the bottom character. But if you hold down the *Shift* key while pressing that key, you will get the top character instead. For example, if you held down the *Shift* key and press the 4 in the number row, a dollar sign ($) will be typed.

You can also use the *Shift* key to type capital letters, but we will cover that later on.

The Ctrl and Alt keys

Like the *Shift* key, you do not use the *Ctrl* or *Alt* keys by themselves. They are used in combination with other keys to form keyboard shortcuts. For example, *Ctrl* + S is the shortcut for saving the current

document and *Ctrl* + *Shift* + *End* takes you to the bottom of a document.

The function keys

To the top of the keyboard are keys labelled F1 to F12. These are the <u>function keys</u>. The *F1* key is typically used to access a program's built-in help. The *F10* key can be used to activate the menu bar so you can go through the menus using the arrow keys instead of the mouse. Normally though, function keys are used in combination with the *Alt* or *Ctrl* keys (as opposed to by themselves).

One common shortcut involving a function key is *Alt* + *F4*. This closes the active program.

The *Enter* key

Also called the *Return* key, the *Enter* key forces the cursor down to a new line, moving down any text below it in the process.

There are actually two *Enter* keys on the keyboard: one in the middle of the keyboard and another to the right of the numeric keypad.

Erasing text

There are two ways you can erase text.

- Press the *Delete* (Del) key if you want to erase the character to the <u>right</u> of the cursor.
- Press the *Backspace* key in order to erase the character to the <u>left</u> of the cursor.

Typing capital letters

Using the Caps Lock key

The easiest way to type capital letters, and indeed the way many beginners do so, is to use the *Caps Lock* key. This key works like a switch – press it once to turn it on and press it again to turn it back off. There may be a light on the keyboard to tell you when *Caps Lock* is turned on. Once it is on, any letters that you type will appear in ALL CAPS.

Using the *Shift* key

If you only want part of the word to be in capital letters (e.g. at the start of a sentence) it is quicker to use the *Shift* key. If *Caps Lock* is <u>off</u>, holding down the *Shift* key while you type will give you <u>uppercase</u> letters. If *Caps Lock* is <u>on</u>, holding down *Shift* will give <u>lowercase</u> letters.

tip

> It may help to think of the *Shift* key as overriding the effect of the *Caps Lock* key.

Using the numeric keypad

To the right of the keyboard, you will see the numeric keypad. This is especially helpful in cases where you have to type a lot of numbers, such as processing invoices or doing spreadsheet calculations. But in order to use the numbers on the keypad, *Num Lock* must be turned <u>on</u>.

Like the *Caps Lock* key, the *Num Lock* key works like a switch. When it is off, the keys on the numeric keypad perform the actions underneath the numbers. For example, the 7 key will work like the *Home* key and pressing the number 2 will cause the cursor to move down.

Summary

- Having the correct posture helps reduce the chance of health problems like carpal tunnel syndrome.
- The *Enter* key forces the cursor down on to a new line.
- To type the character at the top of a key's label, hold down the *Shift* key.
- The preferred way of typing individual capital letters is to use the *Shift* key. But for typing a sequence of uppercase letters using *Caps Lock* may be easier.
- The *Ctrl*, *Alt* and *Shift* keys are used with other keys.
- To use the numbers on the numeric keypad, *Num Lock* must be turned on.

Review exercises

Exercise 1

1. Explain two ways to type capital letters.
2. Suppose the cursor is located after the 'a' in the word 'chair'. Which key would you press if you want to:
   a erase the 'a'?
   b erase the 'i'?
3. What do the *Page Up* and *Page Down* keys do?
4. List five guidelines you should follow if you want to maintain the correct posture while typing.
5. Give two functions of the *Shift* key.
6. What are the *Ctrl* and *Alt* keys used for?
7. Jason is trying to type numbers using the numeric keypad but they do not seem to be working. For example, when he presses the number 2, the cursor goes down to the next line. What is the reason for this?

2 The home row

In this chapter, you will learn:

- how to find the home row
- the a s d f keys (left hand)
- the j k l ; keys (right hand)
- which fingers to use when pressing the Space bar

Figure 2.1 The home position.

The home row

In the middle of the keyboard is what is known as the home row (Figure 2.1). Whenever you are going to type, you start with your fingers placed on certain keys in this row. This is referred to as the **home position**. Even though you will have to move your fingers as you type, you will keep coming back to the home position to help you re-establish your bearings.

tip

If at any time you want to see which finger to use when pressing a particular key, consult the finger positions chart at the end of the Keyboarding section. There is also a printable version of this chart on the accompanying CD-ROM.

Left hand

Table 2.1 shows how the fingers on your left hand should be positioned.

Table 2.1 Finger positions for the left hand.

Finger	Key
Left pinkie (smallest finger)	A
Left ring finger (next to the pinkie)	S
Left middle finger	D
Left index finger	F
Left thumb	Space bar

Right hand

The fingers on your right hand should be on the keys indicated in Table 2.2.

Table 2.2 Finger positions for the right hand.

Finger	Key
Right index finger	J
Right middle finger	K
Right ring finger	L
Right pinkie	;
Right thumb	Space bar

tip

Two of the keys in the home row have little bumps to show you where to place your index fingers. Use these bumps to find the F and J keys without having to look down on the keyboard. Then the rest of your fingers will fall into place.

Typing practice

Exercise 2A

In this exercise you will be using the <u>left</u> hand only.
```
asdf fdsa a s d f f d s a aa ss dd ff ff
dd ss aa a d d s s a f f a f s d sa fs sd
as af sf ad da fd ds fa df asd fas fds sfa
adf saf sad fsa dfs afs das ads sfd dsf
sdf daf fad afd sda dfa asf fda fsd dsa
asdf safd fdsa sadf fdas sdaf fsad adsf
dfsa sfda sfad dsaf dasf dafs afsd sdfa
fads dsfa dfas adfs afds fasd asfd fsda
```

Exercise 2B

For this exercise, use the <u>right</u> hand only.
```
jkl; ;lkj j k l ; ; l k j jj kk ll ;; ;;
ll kk jj ; ; j j j k l k l ; k l ;k k; lj
kj lk kl j; jl jk ;l ;j l; ljk lkj k;j l;k
jlk k;l ;kj kjl ;kl kl; l;j ;jk j;k jkl klj
;lj kj; jk; ;lk ;jl lj; j;l lk; jl; jk;l k;lj
k;jl lkj; jlk; l;kj lk;j lj;k ;ljk ;jkl jl;k
j;kl ljk; kl;j klj; kjl; j;lk kj;l jkl; ;kjl
;klj ;jlk ;lkj l;jk
```

Exercise 2C

For this exercise and all those that follow, use <u>both</u> hands.
```
asdf jkl; ;lkj fdsa ajskdlf; jaksld;f
a;sldkfj a s d f j k l ; ; l k j f d s a
aa ss dd ff jj kk ll ;; ;; ll kk jj ff dd
ss aa ;s fa l; ls fs la a; jf ;f aj sf kl
df f; fd ;k kf ak ;a ld ks da d; fj jd sdk
lk; fsj j;d alk akf ;sa daf dks jas akj
;la kld kjf ;lk l;f fak slf ;fa fsk flk k;a
jds ;fj ;kd
```

Exercise 2D

```
f;lj ajdk f;as fjkd fdj; f;jd fk;d sj;d ;ajd
alsd jafl lksa kda; ;jsd klaf kjsa jkd;
askf ljdk lfd; flk; ;jal fasl akfj ajlf f;aj
sla; ;alj fsdj s;kd lkf; ;ksl ;fks fslk
fkl; jld; skjd asfd da;f jkl; kdlf skdj
s;fd fklj alsj ;dfk dlsf slaj kad; sa;j
;sfl fj;d akjf fsla ksfa jsdl ;ksd dfjk j;ld
sjal lad fall salad a all ask as alfalfa
flask la flak dal dad ala fad ass add ad sad
lass
```

③ The g and h keys

In this chapter, you will learn two more keys in the home row: the letters g and h

Figure 3.1 How to type the letter g.

Finger positions

You'll notice that the letter g is to the right of the f. So when you want to press it, you slide your <u>left index finger</u> to the right (as shown in Figure 3.1).

Similarly, because the letter H is to the left of J (which you would normally press with your right index finger), you slide your <u>right index finger</u> across to the left when you want to type H.

Typing practice

Exercise 3A

gh hg g h h g gg hh hh gg g h h h g g g ghg
hgg hhg hgg ggh hgh ghg ghh ghgh hggg
hhgg ghhg hhgh hggh hghh ghgh hghg gggh
hhgh gghg ghhg gghh hhgg ghhg hhghh ggghg
gghhh ghggh gghgg hhggg gghhg ghggg hhhgg
hghgg ghghh ghhgg ghhgh hgghh hghgh hhhgh
hghgg gggh hghhg hgggh hhghg ghhgh hgghh
hhggh gghgh

Exercise 3B

asdfg lkjh; hasdf gjkl; jgd hlk lhd ag;
ajg kgd jh; sh; kah hda dh; gsk kgk haf
hfd kga lg; fkh dgd haf sgd shk ahf lgs
gsa ashg h;ja ggjs ghld ggld dgaf jlg; ghg;
ggs; jhjf kgg; sfhl shgk hgjd hhjl sag;
ggak gkhf hkgf hkf; ahdg gjf; ggjs kgh;
kfsg ajlh lkh; hlkf gjfa lfg; lgfs fhh;
dgsg ldhf aggk

Exercise 3C

gash saga ha shad flag; shah hall glass
lash gaff; jag gad has; shall sash lakh
flash half alga; ash lag slag gala gal; gag
hash; ah dash gall glad sag slash gas had
algal gash gal has gad ash hall; had flag
lakh shah sash; shall shag saga alga

4 The e and i keys

In this chapter, you will learn how to type some letters above the home row: the letters e and i

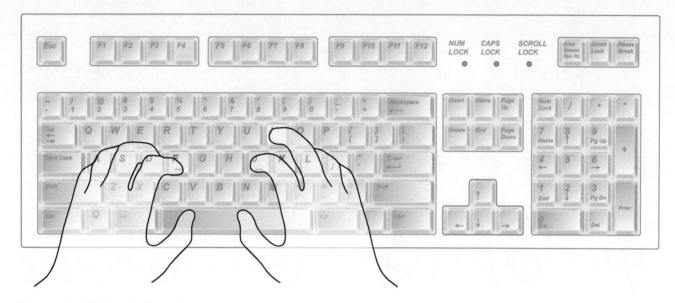

Figure 4.1 Typing the letter i.

Finger positions

The letters e and i are pressed with your middle fingers. Since the letter e is above the letter d (which you would normally press with your left middle finger), you press it using your <u>left middle finger</u> as well. You just move this finger up a row in order to press the e.

Naturally, you do something similar when typing the letter i. The only difference is that you use your <u>right middle finger</u> instead (as shown in Figure 4.1).

Typing practice

Exercise 4A

ei ie e i i e ee ii ii ee e i i e i e iie
eie eei iei eii iee iei eei eeii eiie ieei
eeie ieie iiei eiie ids ehd dil ail aki kke
ded efj dik lke ji; eas ekl asi sih ijj eak
aje dle ed; dea ik; ial shi edh ekhk gli;
jisj jkei gfed dkeg i;l; dhae eea; eif; iej;
hilj sife ehkj eeks hlei jse; aki; glhi ilj;
ekjs gjeg ejd; fiih dese gdeg; efif; hdish
kdiae dieag hdhij gfsej adlis edigg esfsh
sdei; kiidd fkeka higji iefls fifdg jijl; lkdki
dlgde hikld akjee hkile aejkk efikk ;kje;

Exercise 4B

feed ell hill held dish ledge egg gee
hill disk; geld jail flea sleigh seed ill;
fee dais shelf halide alike aegis kid
khaki alkali degas fail lead lifelike
fiddle alia isle fig fake dial leash sleek
shellfish agile flee glee hale fledge gage
illegal shill geese allele added lakeside
assail hassle jade eagle haggis gila added
giggle age;

Exercise 4C

egg seek fed sail keel dill flesh safe deaf
geese easel hellish file flee sage; dais
skill skiff isle field gage adage gases
slid giggle id hedge ahead siege ease
shake skied deal; hiss eggshell ill sake
allied legal allege hale fell fish fig shade
life filled gaffe seaside deed shied hi;
failsafe lake fledge sleek led laid glee
seashell his ledge algae jail sea gild
silk dish hike jig; khaki sedge idea lid
sleigh flail held self shell said feed dell
aside fiddle kiddie aid like

⑤ The r and u keys

In this chapter, you will learn how to type some letters above the home row: the letters r and u

Figure 5.1 Pressing the u key.

Finger positions

You type the letters r and u using the left and right index fingers, respectively. Figure 5.1 illustrates how you would do so for the letter u.

Typing practice

Exercise 5A

ru ur r u u r rr uu uu rr r u u u r r uru
rru uur rur rur ruu urr uru urur rurr
urru uurr rrru urru ruur uuru uuuu rrur
uruu ruuu rruu uuur rurr ruru ruuur ruurr
ururu rruuu rruru urrur ruurr rurrr uuuru
ruuru uruuu ruruu uuruu uurrr uruur rruur
urruu rurur ururr urrru rurru uurru urrrr
uurur rrrur

Exercise 5B

fsr jra rsa ug; ars lhu uff uas lr; hir
rhi luk ahu gfu kgr jr; liu dju udk ira rj;
ull jre suf lkr aukj rhsr ejiu erd; aurl
jrrd uak; efrl isua lrdr urfs uri; uua;

uddf udfr fuju uugj usuh skul rfar rsgr
rrea gkkr gdru freu ireag ijrgd lusuk hujsl
aker; kdfhu gfuhk ulhku riafg jurh; rsul;
euldd eujd; urgij erssd fegrs uhjud edud;
suhfu kgaau ggkue rujg; uair; rude; srkia

Exercise 5C

slug affair fuss suds guard figural sir;
salaried seagull surge flu; fluff deer use
fare flare hearse grease laurel dagger
rueful rehearse shirk freakish safeguard
hue slur huddle degrade friar; seller
dare; skull regal fur defuse; gradual
grief gleeful headdress heard reef fire
elder herself agar girlie serif refugee
deride feud reddish heir guise dud girl
rural rear herd gush gurgle dread gauge
sue referral fuse frail regress aerial
guile druid sire lieu afresh gargle duffel
issue sidereal freer deluge lull shuffle
herald fear harass grad rare era; alder
radish ague failure flair;

6 The t and y keys

In this chapter, you will learn how to type some letters above the home row: the letters t and y

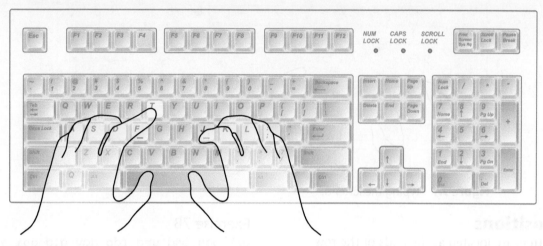

Figure 6.1 Typing the letter t.

Finger positions

As with the letters r and u, the letters t and y are located in the row above the home row, but you have to reach a little further to get to them. They too are typed using the index fingers.

- The letter t is typed with the <u>left index finger</u> (see Figure 6.1).
- You use the <u>right index finger</u> to type the letter y.

Typing practice

Exercise 6A

ty yt t y y t tt yy yy tt y t t y t y yty
tyt tyy yyt ytt tty ytyt tyty yyty tytt
yytt tef tik ugt yue hrt kta ray tls tak
yfu yru hyh jyh hfy yf; trk dat rtf ly;
kry jy; jry gte kyg utd gyj fhy dyr ;y;
hyl yhl; kyi; jtk; tkfs ufay fktr dsys
fyhy fayl dytd yete guyt dta; iskt rety
uyfe y;af dtuu haay kyyf tsgd ldte fhjt
deyt tyhk ysii rttk yltf ukte jhty

Exercise 6B

the ester faithful trailhead treatise
restaurateur stature rite left ted; tartar

august truss straddle athlete flutter fleet
sightseer data the right tart thirsty
artery shaky get the girth frigate
surfeit deterred desert; artistry tailgate
ladylike eyelash sally dirty jest terry
stifle leathery fight rift flute ethereal
hardhearted salute alliterate hilly just
hiatus guest saturate stadia light gift
altar hairy startle allay height ye teak
stay sat hearty feisty

Exercise 6C

diet eta dressy firelight safety sheathe
fetus gradate aft shrift shaft tattle
talus gusset thesis farthest trill
frustrate tie; fusty stare latter fiat
starlet irrigate hath tether fraught
suggest ugly heyday heresy ruthless flat
heat sturdy faith lateral hast hysteria
eight hereditary faulty fest jittery
futile stake great lethargy shut regretful
tasteful sherry terrify either future
distillery allergy stutter estate defy
fruit segregate daylight garter tassel

7 The q, w, o and p keys

In this chapter, you will learn four new keys above the home row: the letters q, w, o and p

Figure 7.1 Typing the letter o.

Finger positions

These four letters are located at the ends of the row above the home row; q and w on the left and o and p on the right. The fingers you use to press them are:

- for the letter q, the left pinkie
- for w, the left ring finger
- the right ring ringer for the letter o (see Figure 7.1)
- the right pinkie to type the letter p.

tip

If you keep forgetting the first six letters on a standard keyboard, just remember the word 'qwerty'.

Typing practice

Exercise 7A

qwop powq q w o p p o w q qq ww oo pp pp
oo ww qq q w w p w o q q o o p p wqo qpo
wpo wpq opq owq woq wop pow pwq qop wqp
pqw oqp qwp qpw opw owp poq qwo oqw pwo
pqo qow powq pwoq qowp poqw woqp wpqo
wpoq qopw oqpw qwop pqow wqpo qpwo owqp
wopq opqw pqwo qwpo owpq opwq oqwp pwqo
wqop qpow owqoo pqqwo poppw pqoqw oppqo
wqwoq woqwo owqpp oopqo ooqqo wwppw wqwqq
oqwwo qwwoo qpqwo opqow wqpqo qwwpp
opowp woopw wqwwq qppqw qpqqw qppqo wooww

Exercise 7B

prk oau pjd upd fdp doy glq qgi awl oeg oed
wjg oht plr yiq apl gpi gqe pgf lw; lwh wfy
sps yuq ygw fkqp ohpj awqa pyqf oss; rfok
iowu ulwf uwpi owif ltro ootf ghwi yqsy
gqla dqlu ;uwq aupp oeip shqq rhwp poga
raop puoi oakq eqega oplde khdkq jfpws
iwkll hyqfr wato; ipalw qph;u jllpf lopfr
fgqtu g;kw; orjq; qlukp aojdi hrutq hfhfo
euqfd ithos tgieo lhhjw fqlrr kokfi upuha

Exercise 7C

headquarters silo hilltop fossil spell
too spree groggy hyper atop workhorse
dispersal quadrupedal quiet quid falloff
writeup prophet iota sprawl hypothesis
root; trio portray tower sweater upward
throat uphold swag shot wasteful floor
splashy afoul sulphur hideout golf roast
our two today pastoral prodigious slough
westerly log; weld kudos troll putty
house shepherd joyous leapt gross upsurge
offset flood offstage wisp; profile solo;
fog shutoff puppet equipped applied orate
holdup toward ghostlike lookup; assiduous
surrogate parasol praise; equity lodge
uproar proof plate paprika shout throttle
lipid wisp peal squatter riot stratosphere
sloth peek lottery tulip toggle dapper
thoughtful sporty awful;

8 The v, b, m and n keys

Figure 8.1 The correct way to type the letter b.

Finger positions

Having finished with the middle and top rows, we turn our attention to the bottom row. The letters v, b, m and n are all typed using the index fingers:

- v and b with the <u>left</u> index finger
- m and n with the <u>right</u> one.

Figure 8.1 shows how you type the letter b, which some people find tricky because you have to reach pretty far.

Typing practice

Exercise 8A

```
vbmn nmbv v b m n n m b v vv bb mm nn nn
mm bb vv b n v n v m v m b n m b mbv vmb
mnv nbm nvb bvm mvn bvn bmn nmv vbm nmb
mnb nbv vnb bmv mbn vbn nvm vmn vnm mvb
bnm bnv vnbm nbmv vmbn mnbv mnvb bvnm
```

```
nmvb vmnb vbnm vbmn nmbv bnvm mvnb nvmb
mbnv bmvn nvbm mbvn mvbn vnmb bvmn bmnv
bnmv nbvm mmbmn mvnnm bvmnb vnvmb mbmmm
bnmnb bmnmn nbvnb mvmmn nmbnv mvmbb
bbmbb vnmnm nvmvb vmmvn bbbnv vmbnv
vbbmv nmbmm vmbmn vbmmb nbvmm bnmbb
mmnnm mnvmb
```

Exercise 8B

```
bad rvu qvl bhj mpl umr ran oqv lim gqv
ifv vlk ttv ffb hvj ggb nuh qna vlf gv;
sv; wba sgv unw hma voyn nwmq aldv vghr
wyvt wnen nkwb fnjq nowe dvhp thv; gvu;
nwe; mnyt iwns iyne joev lsun mrrl onbl
wmv; bbd; mym; plmy plnp tkbbq iagrm
wpvbt bvspe ikymg snjvs fiqbr luvf; nyhdm
vyvai ktyuv aaubw negwh morvt eveti flakn
negf; ybeid bnwhp vymas ;jqvf vivqp mvfod
arygm btmrw
```

Exercise 8C

pervasive honorarium mustang urbane
resignation neurophysiology pushpin
prohibit snippet pretentious merriment
amphibious retardant blustery
differential fable binge insubordinate
headmaster transferral worn jamming
mania soundproof termite; shedding
sheepskin admit vibrate month tonight
tomato distributive instep swampland
pilgrimage sunrise plane job northwest
tinker immodest trainee evaluable feign
reverse mount tidings rendition orient
plump farmland wineskin ruinous blind

threadbare substitute stump pang tense
monster lumpy waken fumble tango abut
utmost lunge derisive mew; indefatigable
limp mournful immigrant opportune evil
realisable maternal sterling tabular
oblique kingdom distributor skimming
aboveground revelation repairmen paternal
lukewarm mainframe deem bridesmaid
determinate bluefish seminar different
tension turnabout twain; fatten indelible
nutritious automobile hunt derision
typesetting atmosphere king seventh
mystique keyboard

9 The z, x and c keys

In this chapter, you will learn to type some letters below the home row: the letters z, x and c

Figure 9.1 Typing the letter c.

Finger positions

The remaining three letters in the bottom letter row are z, x and c. Here is how you type them.

- To type z you use the <u>left pinkie</u>.
- To type x, use the <u>left ring finger</u>.
- To type c, use the <u>left middle finger</u> (see Figure 9.1).

Typing practice

Exercise 9A

zxc cxz z x c c x z zz xx cc cc xx zz x z
c z c x c x z czx xcz zcx zxc cxz xzc cxzx
xzcz czxc xccx cczx czxz zczz xzxc xcxz
xccx xzxz zcxz cxxz cxxc czxx zxcc zczx
xzxc zcxz cxcx zzxc xxcc cxcz zzxx xccz
xzxcz xczxc xzxzz xczzx cxxzx xczxx czxxz
zzxcc czxxc zcccx zxcxx zxczz zcccz xzzxz
cczzc zzczc zcxxc zxczc xzxcz zxzcx zcxzc
xzcxc xxcxz zxzcc cxczc

Exercise 9B

daz lzv bc; wyc bzt oxm lpc ddx bce yic
ix; zij kxa bzo kdc vzs exg wcd pcb uhc uck
zgh bpz tgc wex zzby azrz tzke cfxg scpn
cfxt zszy tix; ymxd gpzp jjvc tchx ckmz

rxc; cllk zjzg yzu; aych zxtn xnpu gzpx
rxlr braz xlse cntq lczqy nlccs wgkvc bkqax
dvxxe vorxu zykdz rxlco mfxzd cijzj jeczb
pxizy mwctc cdlzo ggpzp gdqjz mxmxg lzcew
vqsxz oxbcu lcqmc cxnt; weack cktyh lncma

Exercise 9C

zebra tweeze galaxy space cohort crucifix
sleazy fuzzy gizmo apex fixate taxicab zoo
exist constitute reckon; nuisance forceful
procession ache cancel flaxseed pica
incomprehension recipient connect tactile
bronze slack waistcoat recurred nomadic
euphoric contestant ocean cognac blackout
objectify instinct productivity contact
match grace czar cashmere toothache
cough; compliant axes accurate document
starch exceptional boxcar maxim gizmo
matrix duplex projectile zinc; gigahertz
colonel terrace honeysuckle logarithmic
screwdriver vehicle perceive consent
since fireplace meticulous practise debacle
career article grocer recess fraction
zigzag zoom; xenophobia xerox zeal extra;
expedite exhort; hydroxyl hotbox scarce
armchair correspond induce object custom
classify locomotive extremes slacken
secede castor chore scribble

⑩ Some punctuation marks

In this chapter, you will learn the correct way to type full stops, commas and apostrophes

Figure 10.1 How to type a full stop.

Typing full stops

As you know, the full stop (.) is most commonly used to indicate the end of a sentence. But it is also used:

- in abbreviations like Jr. and St.
- in acronyms like U.S.A. and e.g.
- after initials, for example John T. Flynn or George W. Barker.

Traditionally, when typing, you would leave two spaces after a full stop that comes at the end of a sentence.

As Figure 10.1 shows, you press the full stop using the <u>ring</u> finger of your <u>right</u> hand.

Typing commas

The comma is located to the right of the M key (and to the left of the full stop). You press the comma with the <u>middle</u> finger of your <u>right</u> hand.

Commas are most often used to separate lists of items or adjectives. For example, 'This morning, I saw three trucks, twenty cars, two motorcycles and one donkey cart' or 'She is a very kind, patient, compassionate and understanding person'. Notice that you normally do not put a comma before the last item in the list.

It is considered standard practice to leave <u>one</u> space after a comma.

Typing apostrophes

On the keyboard, the apostrophe is easy to confuse with the comma since they look very similar on the keys. The apostrophe is found on the key to the right of the semicolon. You press it with your <u>right pinkie</u>.

The apostrophe denotes ownership, e.g. Kelly's computer or Curtis' football. It is also used in contractions such as *doesn't* (as opposed to *does not*).

> **tip**
>
> The key containing the apostrophe is also used to type single quotes

Typing practice

Exercise 10A

,' ',, . ' ' ., ,, .. " " .. ,, ' , , ' , ' . in the ark were cats, dogs, sheep, goats, pigs, ducks, geese, lions, tigers, hippos, rhinos, snakes, cows and bears. she's funny, smart, kind, gentle, humble, pretty, loving and exciting. he's stubborn, arrogant, careless, foolish, unkind and boring.

Exercise 10B

rep. abbrev. lect. comp. trig. compl. coll. sp. p.m. sing. chem. illustr. subst. assoc. struct. compar. desc. brit. bef. corresp. attrib. corr. obj. subj. comb. def. prec. transl. reg. arch. transf. eng. concr. man. cf. conc. var. mr. bot. fig. psych. opp. freq. pop. gen. tr. eccl. lang. adv. orig. dict. pl. app. st. cal. esp. bull. refl. e.g. ult. math. col. chron. fem. exc. comm. etc. ser. mrs. conj. quot. syll. rev. crit. pict. prop. dat. adj. org. prob. yrs. a.m. pref. conf. lit. i.e. pol.

Exercise 10C

we'd you'll who's what's who're who's she's you've haven't mightn't hadn't there's she'd don't aren't that's they'd wouldn't who'll didn't what'll who've she'll they'll we're he's what're couldn't isn't where's they're shouldn't shan't they've hasn't let's won't you're he'll mustn't he'd you'd weren't can't doesn't we've what've

11 Typing capital letters

In this chapter, you will learn how to type capital letters using the *Shift* key

Figure 11.1   How to type a capital F.

Using the Shift keys

We mentioned before that you can use the *Shift* key to type capital letters. The correct way to do so is to press the letter with one hand, while holding down the *Shift* key using the other hand. Figure 11.1 illustrates how this is done.

If you want to type an f you use your <u>left</u> index finger. So to type a capital F, you hold down the <u>right</u> *Shift* key while doing so. Similarly, to type a capital J, you hold down the <u>left</u> *Shift* key and press the j key.

Using this principle:

- you hold down the <u>left</u> *Shift* key when typing capital A, S, D, F, G, Q, W, E, R, T, Y, Z, X, C, V and B
- you hold down the <u>right</u> *Shift* key to type capital H, J, K, L, Y, U, I, O, P, N and M.

Typing practice

Exercise 11A

A B C D E F G H I J K L M N O P Q R S T U
V W X Y Z Y   X W V U T S R Q P O N M L K
J I H G F E D C B A

Exercise 11B

Cuba Peru I'd Dominica Venezuela, Aruba
Chile Bahamas Ecuador, Grenada D.A.

Barbuda I'm USA D.C. Belize Argentina
Honduras Trinidad Tobago, Colombia
Bolivia Barbados, Guatemala, Paraguay A.D.
Suriname, Uruguay Bermuda Scotland I'll
Jamaica Cayman Antigua England Montserrat
Mexico Caribbean Nicaragua Canada Brazil
Haiti B.C. Guyana Panama I've E.S.T.
Michelle Henry Veronica Claude Alvin,
Mathew Jacqueline Herbert Karla Eve Sheila
Myra, David A.S.T. Adele Martina Tanisha
Margaret Corey Don Sonja Reginald Sheena
Isaac Caroline Julie Pedro Shauna Angelina
Keisha Charmaine

Exercise 11C

The five vowels are A, E, I, O and U. E
is the most common one in the English
language, but A is popular as well. All
the other letters are consonants. Letters
like B, L, P and R. Words without vowels
are rare; a few notable ones are hymn,
rhythm and shy. Notice that in these
words, the letter Y is used like a vowel.
I can't imagine life without vowels. Q
shouldn't have to be without U. So let's
be grateful for these underappreciated
letters.

⑫ Symbols I: ? " :

In this chapter, you will learn which fingers to use when you are typing the colon (:), the question mark (?) and the double quotation mark (")

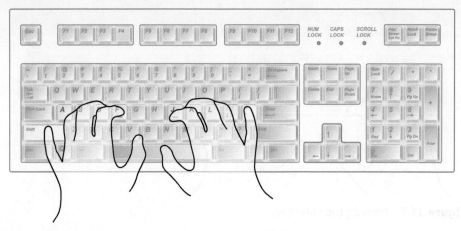

Figure 12.1 How to type a double quotation mark.

Finger positions

For all of these symbols, you hold down the <u>left</u> *Shift* key with your <u>left</u> pinkie and press the key that contains the symbol with your <u>right</u> pinkie (as shown in Figure 12.1).

> Some word processors like Microsoft Word use what are known as 'smart quotes'. So the quotation marks look different depending on whether they are in front of a word or after it. This applies to both single (') and double (") quotation marks.

Typing practice

Exercise 12A

:"? ?": ":? "?: :"? :?" ?": ?:" ::": "::"
"??" "?"" :""? ?"": ":?" "":? ::"" :":" ":??
::?? "?": :?:: ?::" "":? :??: "?"? :?:" ?:??
??:: ""?" ?"?? :"?" ::"? ""?? ":"? ?"?" ??"?
":"" :"?? ??:" "?:" ?:": "":: ?"?: ::?: :"::
":": :?:? :?"? ?:?" :::? "::? ":?: :"?: ?:"?
:?": :":? ??:? ?::? ?:?: ??": ?:"" "??: ??""
:""" ""::" :??" ?":? ?""? ?":: "?:? "?:: :?""
::?" ?":" ":?" ?"": ?":?

Exercise 12B

Many of life's deepest questions centre around two things: happiness and purpose. Have you ever wondered what your life's purpose is? Or about what true happiness is? How, sometimes, poor people seem happier than wealthy ones? I think, at some point in time, all of us have. Here's what some greater minds than mine had to say on these topics. Helen Keller: "Many people have a wrong idea of what constitutes true happiness. It is not attained through self-gratification, but through fidelity to a worthy purpose". James Thurber: "All men should strive to learn before they die, what they are running from, and to, and why". Marie Curie: "I never see what has been done; I only see what remains to be done". Mark Twain: "Good friends, good books and a sleepy conscience: this is the ideal life". Abraham Lincoln: "Most people are about as happy as they make up their minds to be". All these are great quotes, but I've saved the best for last. "Being happy doesn't mean that everything is perfect. It means that you've decided to look beyond the imperfections." Do you agree?

13 The *Enter* key

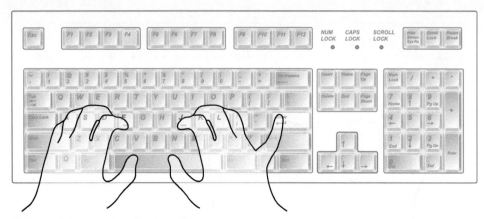

Figure 13.1 Pressing the *Enter* key.

Finger position

As was mentioned before, there are two *Enter* keys on the typical keyboard. We will be looking at the one to the right of the letters. You press it with your <u>right pinkie finger</u> as shown in Figure 13.1.

Typing practice

Exercise 13A

In this exercise press the *Enter* key <u>once</u> after each sentence to move down to the next line.

Typing is so much fun.
Anyone can learn how to type.
The most important thing is that you don't look down while you are typing.
That way, your fingers get accustomed to the position of the keys.
You start in the middle row, known as the Home Row.
Your index fingers go on the two keys with "bumps", F and J.
You press the Space bar with either thumb.
Sometimes you'll have to move your fingers, but you keep coming back to the starting position on the Home Row.
At first it'll feel weird, but it soon gets better.
You'll be typing quickly in no time.Some typists can reach over one hundred W.P.M.

But forty W.P.M. is a good goal for a beginner.

Exercise 13B

Press the *Enter* key <u>twice</u> after each paragraph.

Do you know what the term "peripheral device" means? A peripheral device is a device that is connected to computer but not found on the motherboard. Let's look at three categories of peripheral devices: input devices, output devices and storage devices.

Input devices are devices that allow you to put information into the computer. Examples include: keyboards, mice and digital cameras.

In contrast, output devices allow you to get information from the computer. Monitors, speakers and printers are all output devices.

Storage devices store data so that it can be retrieved later. They can be divided into two categories: primary and secondary. Examples of primary storage are RAM and ROM. Secondary storage is slower but cheaper and can hold more information. Hard disks, floppy disks and CDs are all storage devices.

14 The numbers 1, 2 and 3

In this chapter, you will learn which fingers to use to type the numbers 1, 2 and 3

Figure 14.1 Typing the number 3.

Using the number row

You will recall that there are two sets of number keys on your keyboard: the numeric keypad and the number row above the letters. In this chapter, as well as the next two, we will be using the numbers in the number row. Normally you would use this row for typing the occasional number; for large sets of numbers, the numeric keypad is more convenient.

Finger positions

To type the numbers 1, 2 and 3 you use the <u>left</u> hand as follows:

- Press the number 1 with the *left* pinkie.
- Press the number 2 with the *left* ring finger.
- Press the number 3 with the *left* middle finger (see Figure 14.1).

Typing practice

Exercise 14A

123 321 1 2 3 3 2 1 211 333 3 331 231 12 13
331 121 121 1 2 3 11 23 1 1 13 32 12 312
322 21 3 2 21 13 21 323 1 1 2 11 213 132 11
1 213 311 3 2 1 32 121 31 212 1 2 233 322
211 333 3 331 231 12 13 331 121 121 1 2 3
11 23 1 1 13 32 12 312 322 21 3 2 21 13 21
323 1 1 2 11 213 132 11 1 213 311 3 2 1 32
121 31 212 1 2 233 322

Exercise 14B

12.23 212.2 211.12 2.3 33 131.31 2.21 1 212.3
3,312.3 2.1 3,231.22 2,211 3.2 12.21 232
2,313.3 11 2,331 3,332.13 2,111.22 2 1,321.3
1.3 232.3 311 1.3 3,233 22 312 3,132 213.12
2,221 131 133.22 2,112.12 3 321 33 1,112 3.23
1 3,122.32 2 222.1 333 3,311.3 3.1 2 131 32.3
322.1 231.33 11.3 2,123.3 2.1 22.33 211.1 2
312.1 22.1 2,231.11 2,331.32 3.3 231 1,231
1.2 211.22 2,323.3 131.13 1,131 23.31 3,122.21
112.3 123.3 23.1 212.32 23.21 31 313 1 21.1
3 322.13 23.3 122.21 32.2 21 121 222.31 1.23
1,233.22 32 131.1 12.22 12 322 1 2.1 2,211.12

Exercise 14C

Corey has 3 siblings: 2 sisters and 1 brother. Even though he'll tell you otherwise, his family isn't really that big. "Yeah right", you're thinking? Not so long ago, it wasn't that surprising to hear of families with 12 and 13 children. Now THOSE were large families; a bit more than the typical 2 children, don't you think? Nowadays, people tend to want 1 boy and 1 girl. Now even 3 children are seen as a lot.

Can you imagine having 2 sets of twins or 3 sets of triplets? Even though I don't know of any examples of the latter, the former has happened so often that there are at least 2 websites devoted to it. What's more, twins seem to run in families, so if you or your parents are a part of a twin, you have a better chance of getting twins yourself. Just something to think about.

Exercise 14D

1st 2nd 3rd

A hat trick is 3 of something in a match, e.g. 3 goals or 3 consecutive wickets.

3, 2, 1, GO.

If a double is 2 and a triple is 3, what do you call 1 of something?

In golf, a "birdie" is when you score 1 under par for a given hole; an "eagle" is when you get 2 under par. A bogey is 1 over par whereas double bogey and triple bogey mean 2 over par and 3 over par respectively.

Tiger Woods won the Masters by 2 shots. In the final round, he had 3 birdies and 1 eagle.

Barcelona beat Real Madrid, 3 goals to 2.

In the 1st innings, Timothy scored 123 runs. Unfortunately, he only scored 31 in the 2nd innings.

Canada earned a dramatic 3 to 2 win over Team U.S.A. in the 2010 Men's Hockey Finals.

15 The numbers 4, 5 and 6

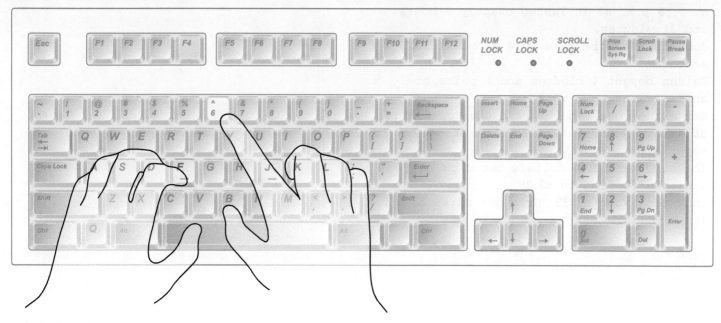

Figure 15.1 Pressing the number 6.

Finger positions

Now let us look at three more keys: the numbers 4, 5 and 6. You press the numbers 4 and 5 with the left index finger, but you press the 6 with the right index finger. You may find typing the number 6 a bit awkward at first (I know I did) since it is so far away from the home row. Figure 15.1 illustrates how you would press this key.

Typing practice

Exercise 15A

456 654 4 5 6 6 5 4 64 456 4 465 55 645 46
5 564 656 46 4 45 44 545 4 564 56 646 656
5 654 546 45 4 5 56 65 6 4 656 566 4 64 56
646 5 46 4 5 4 6 5 454 64 55 4 4 645 5 656
454 64 5 6 466 554 5 466 45 664 466 465 45
556 54 56 46 465 44 656 66 455 5 6 445 4

556 6 54 44 544 5 6 45 56 65 5 45 665 466
645 556 64 5 45 6 445 565 45

Exercise 15B

42.1 6.61 434.3 6.45 1.31 42.64 512.34
5.6 216.6 62.2 5,635.44 13.62 62.5 4,114
465 512.16 6,333.26 5,142.1 52 12 12.64
42 6,255.65 651 55 1,515.3 5.1 5.56 6,556
1,565.51 163 1.6 6,516.3 6.46 6,144.14 6.2
443.41 662.26 44.6 413.4 166.4 5 2,412.6 52
66.15 53.42 1,153.16 642 4,346.62 3,635.16
3,515.2 334 53.4 1,261 3,163 5,235.11 265
4,623.56 6,332.3 344.5 6,243 3,525.54 26.42
4,651 3.15 1,634 63 126.1 352 5.1 2.2 2.51 43
226.41 46 21 456 15.6 2 5,662 23.3 3,622.1
13.66 5.32 4,523 53.4 615.62 1.22 163.2 22.4
35.65 3,362.63 232.6 42 52.4 53 164.14 23.6
5.6 444.5

Exercise 15C

4th 5th 6th 13th 16th 51st

Jamaica is divided into 14 parishes.

Barbados has an area of 166 square miles;
it is also 21 miles long.

There are 5 oceans: the Arctic, Atlantic,
Indian, Pacific and Southern oceans.

The meeting started at 4:24 p.m. and ended
at 6:55 p.m. so it lasted exactly 2 hours
and 31 minutes.

John finished the race in 4 minutes, 32.5
seconds.

Keisha bought 4 blouses and 6 pairs of
shoes at the mall yesterday.

Her mother got 5 packs of biscuits, 4 tins
of sardines and 6 cans of tuna at the
supermarket.

The bill was 56.44 dollars but with VAT
included it came to 63.25.

In 4 tests out of 35, Greg got marks of 26,
14, 32 and 35.

16 The numbers 7, 8, 9 and 0

In this chapter, you will learn which fingers to use to type the numbers 7, 8, 9 and 0

Figure 16.1 Typing the number 9.

Finger positions

Now we will finish off the numbers in the number row by looking at the last four numbers. You press these keys using the same fingers you would use to type j, k, l and ;.

- Press the number 7 using the <u>right index finger</u>.
- Press the number 8 using the <u>right middle finger</u>.
- To press the number 9 you use the <u>right ring finger</u> (see Figure 16.1).
- To press the 0 you use the <u>right pinkie</u>.

Typing practice

Exercise 16A

7890 0987 7 8 9 0 0 9 8 7 77 88 99 00 00 99
88 77 7 9 9 8 8 7 0 0 7 0 8 9 970 890 807
978 980 708 097 798 987 907 790 709 870 789
809 089 879 079 780 908 098 897 078 087 8970
7089 9087 9708 8709 0897 8790 9807 0879 0798
0987 7908 8079 9870 7809 8907 7890 9780 0789
7980 8097 7098 0978 9078 80 97 70 789 99 79
0 89 9 988 70 9 7 8 8 788 8 9 807 7 78 0 88
897 977 0 80 0 79 889 987 88 778 988 9 7 8
908 0 989 0 7 988 987 89 09 800 877 9 90 9

0 9 79 99 700 87 700 97 9 88 0 78 8 0 7 70
899

Exercise 16B

52.0 3.88 3,684.05 5,113.17 5,095.44 4.26
5,132.0 6,913.4 503.4 521 648.09 2,013.65
2,040.92 8,207 329.96 534.0 326.5 0.8 3,807.34
9 6.39 293 7 73.8 1 80.81 8,788.6 99.44 2,161
21.5 0.25 4,632.1 4.8 4,925.11 5,558.82 13
86.40 41.0 1.24 3,628.7 936 96.88 531.93 48.9
271.7 8,302.3 218.7 336 2.7 5 895 786.3 1.8
5.70 1.4 5 1,367.1 1,420 29.20 978.54 8 5,784
88.9 0.4 8 1,314.17 7 5.3 45 629.20 4.25
100.5 236.88 156.45 318.21 6,173 735 99.30 11
71 127.6 4,246 6 7.25 6 9.08 439 9 5,840 26
6,146.25 7,672 94.9 4,918 8 951.8 298 464.93
7.68 4.6 6,218 827 503.05 3 2,214.85 90 3.68
7.0 1,752 75 379 4,536.4 6,888 70.17 21.6
2,620.4 94 2,832 424 521 921 17 5.5 6,333.26
1,248.28 130 7,774.07 31.9 4 5,161.43 55.1
821 942 635.7 2,670.0 255.35 3 906.0 62.65
75.10 8.3 8,895 4.9 21 9,433 9.1 2 3.78 388.28
3,749.4 4.13 3.0 21.61 2,884 7.5 4,851.15 86.70
6,658 27.01 52 66.0 597 311.4 397.2 7.01 300
385 1.6 7 91.7

Exercise 16C

"On the 12th day of Christmas, my true
love gave to me:
12 drummers drumming,
11 pipers piping,
10 lords a-leaping,
9 ladies dancing,
8 maids a-milking,
7 swans a-swimming,
6 geese a-laying,
5 golden rings,
4 calling birds,
3 French hens,
2 turtle doves,
And 1 partridge in a pear tree"

But soon afterwards I was singing a
different tune. First of all, the song
is a bit repetitive, don't you think?
And secondly, what does one do with 23
birds? My "true love" seems to think
that I want a zoo. At least the 6 geese
were contributing; the other 17 were just
taking up space.

There was also the question of where those
50 people were going to fit in my 2 bedroom
apartment. Especially the 8 maids; they
brought cows with them as well. And do
you know how high maintenance 10 leaping
lords are? Speaking of lords, my landlord
wasn't too thrilled about the racket the
23 "musicians" were keeping.

So ultimately, I sent everything back,
except the 5 rings of course. And not a
moment too soon. I found the 9 ladies
dancing extremely distracting. The 10
lords didn't seem to mind though.

17 Symbols II: ! @ # $ %

In this chapter, you will learn:

- how to type some symbols found on the number keys: !, @, #, $ and %
- how they are used in contemporary English

Figure 17.1 Pressing the @ key.

Finger positions

Now that you are familiar with the numbers in the number row, you can now learn some of the symbols that are found on the same keys. The symbols we are covering in this chapter are found on the same keys as the numbers 1 to 5. So to type them, you need to hold down the right *Shift* key as shown in Table 17.1.

Table 17.1 Typing the symbols ! @ # $ and %.

Symbol	Number key	Press with this finger while holding down the right *Shift* key
!	1	left pinkie
@	2	left ring finger
#	3	left middle finger
$	4	left index finger
%	5	left index finger

Usage

The $ and % signs need no introduction, but let us look at the others in turn.

The exclamation mark (!)

The exclamation mark is used at the end of sentences to indicate when a person is excited about something or shouting. Here are some examples:

- 'Help!'
- "That movie was great!"

The at symbol (@)

The @ symbol is used as shorthand for the word 'at'. You see this all the time in email addresses such as johndoe@hotmail.com. But it is also used when talking about rates. For example, on some invoices you might see things like:

- 20 hours @ $30 per hr
- 10 bags @ 50 kg

The number sign (#)

Like, the @ symbol, the number sign is very specialised in its use. The only time you use it is in addresses or as shorthand for the word 'number'.

> The number sign is also referred to as the hash symbol or 'pound'. The latter term is used primarily when dealing with telephone calls.

Typing practice

Exercise 17A

!@#$% %$#@! ! @ # $ % % $ # @ ! 1! 2@ 3#
4$ 5% %5 $4 #3 @2 !1 !1! 11! !!1 1!! !11 1!1
@@2 @22 22@ 2@@ 2@2 @2@ 3## #3# ##3 #33
33# 3#3 ##4 #4# 44# 4## 4#4 #44 %55 5%5 %%5
55% 5%% %5% 5% #3 %5 $4 $4 %5 !1 @2 4$ 2@
5% 5% 1! #3 #3 4$ 4$ %5 !1 2@ 1! $4 4$ @2
!1 %5 $4 #3 1! %5 @2 @2 #3 3# 3# !1 3# @2
4$ $4 2@ 5% 2@ 1! 2@ 1! 3# 3# !1 5%

Exercise 17B

!@#$% %$#@! ! @ # $ % % $ # @ !
$#@ @$# $%# $!@ %$@ $@# #$@ !$@ @!% $@!
%$# $#! #!@ !$# !@% @#% $!# !%# ##@ $@% #%$
$!% @%# @!$!@# @#$ #@! %@# #!$!$% #$% !#@
#$! %$! !%$!@$ @%! %!@ @#! %!# @$! #%! $%@
!%@ #@$ %!$ %#$!#$ %#@ %#! #!% $%! #@% %@!
%@$!#% @!# @$% @%$ $#%
%@#! !@%# !$#@ @$%! @!#% @!#$ #!@% %$#!
#$@! %$@# #!$@ !@#$ %#!$ @%$# $!%@ #$@%
$#!% $#%! !@$% %#$! $@#% %$@! #$!@ !$@#
%!#$ @#%! $#!@ @$%# %#@! @#%$ %#$@ !@#%
$@#! !$@% %@$! $!#@ @$#! $#@! $!%# @$!#
%!$@ %#@$ %@!# !$#% #@%! !@%$ $!@# @!$#
@#!% %$!# %!@# %@!$!$%@ $#@% #!%$ #!@$

Exercise 17C

"Amazing!", "That was awesome!", "Incredible!", the fans exclaimed after seeing James Cameron's 3D epic, Avatar. It made a mindboggling 2.7 BILLION US$ worldwide! That's over 180,000,000 people @ $15! In contrast Titanic, #2 money earner, made $1.8 billon, a number once considered unsurpassable. As was the $600 million it made in the United States. But Avatar blew past that as well, making $740 million to become the #1 grossing movie of all time!

An email address such as janedoe@yahoo.com consists of 2 parts: the username and the domain name. The username is the part before the @. The domain name is the part after the @. Neither part can be blank. So the following addresses are valid abc@test.com, frank.hardy@myseries.net, whereas bob@ isn't.

Exercise 17D

Jennifer lives at #123 Main Street. Her telephone # is 555-1111 and her email address is jennifer@example.com. Her sister Janice lives 2 houses away at #124 Main Street. Her cell # is 222-1234 and her home # is 555-3333. Her work email is janice@acme.com.

He bought 5 pens @ $1, 20 pencils @ $0.25, 2 rulers @ $0.50 and 1 sharpener @ $0.25. So his total bill was $11.25. He paid with a $20 bill so he got back $8.75 in change.

The highest mark in the exam was 88% but several students got below 50% with the lowest being a mere 2%. As expected, the average was low. It was only 45%. Since the school's pass mark was 60%, the teacher added 15% to everyone's mark. But rather than giving the top student 103%, the teacher "only" gave him 100%.

18 Symbols III: ^ & * ( )

In this chapter, you will learn:

- how to type some more symbols: ^, &, *, (and)
- how they are most commonly used

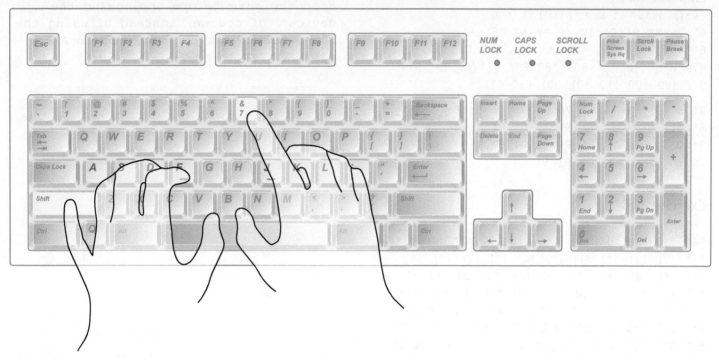

Figure 18.1 Pressing the & key.

Finger positions

These symbols are above the numbers 6 to 0 on the number row. To type them, you need to hold down the left *Shift* key as shown in the table.

Table 18.1 Typing the symbols ^ & * (and).

Symbol	Number key	Press with this finger while holding down the left *Shift* key
^	6	right index finger
&	7	right index finger
*	8	right middle finger
(	9	right ring finger
)	0	right pinkie

Usage

Listed below are some of the symbols (the brackets need no introduction) and the way they are typically used.

The caret (^)

The caret is normally handwritten to indicate a missing word. It is hardly, if ever, used in normal typing.

The ampersand (&)

The ampersand is known as the 'and' sign because it is used to replace that word. So rather than typing 'black and white', you might type 'black & white' or even 'B&W'.

The asterisk (*)

The asterisk (what people call 'star') has a variety of uses. It may be used to emphasise words when typing, to indicate footnotes or even in place of bullets. But you will most commonly use it when you are doing spreadsheet calculations. That is because the asterisk is used as the multiplication sign. So instead of typing 4 × 6, you would type 4 * 6.

Typing practice

Exercise 18A

```
^&*() )(*&^ ^ & * ( ) ) ( * & ^
6^ 7& 8* 9( 0) )0 (9 *8 &7 ^6
6^^ 66^ ^66 6^6 ^^6 ^6^ 77& &&7 7&7 &77 7&&
&7& 8*8 **8 *8* 88* *88 8** 9( ((9 99( 9(9
9(( (99 )00 ))0 )0) 00) 0)0 0))
```

```
9( 6^ 0) 9( 7& 6^ 7& 7& 7& 0) 9( 8* 6^ 8*
8* 0) 8* 7& 6^ 8* 9( 6^ 0) 9( 0) 0) 8* 7&
8* 0) 6^ 6^ 9( 8* 8* 7& 0) 6^ 8* 9( 6^ 7&
7& 6^ 7& 0) 9( 0) 9( 9(
```

Exercise 18B

```
^&*() )(*&^ ^ & * ( ) ) ( * & ^
^&^ ^*^ ^(^ ^)^ &^& &*& &(& &)& *^* *&* *(*
*)* (^( (&( (*( ()( )^) )&) )*) )() (^) (&)
(*) (!) (@) (#) ($) (%) (1) (2) (3) (4) (5)
(6) (7) (8) (9) (0) *1* *2* *3* *4* *5* *6*
*7* *8* *9* *0* 1*1 2*2 3*3 4*4 5*5 6*6 7*7
8*8 9*9 0*0 1^1 2^2 3^3 4^4 5^5 6^6 7^7 8^8
9^9 0^0 &1& &2& &3& &4& &5& &6& &7& &8& &9&
&0& 1&1 2&2 3&3 4&4 5&5 6&6 7&7 8&8 9&9 0&0
```

```
(1*1) (2*2) (3*3) (4*4) (5*5) (6*6) (7*7)
(8*8) (9*9) (0*0) (1*2) (2*3) (4*5) (5*6)
(6*7) (7*8) (8*9) (9*0) (1&1) (2&2) (3&3)
(4&4) (5&5) (6&6) (7&7) (8&8) (9&9) (0&0)
(1&2) (2&3) (3&4) (5&6) (6&7) (7&8) (8&9)
(9&0) (1^1) (2^2) (3^3) (4^4) (5^5) (6^6)
(7^7) (8^8) (9^9) (0^0) (1^2) (2^3) (4^5)
(5^6) (6^7) (7^8) (8^9) (9^0)
```

Exercise 18C

```
Trinidad & Tobago, St. Kitts & Nevis,
Antigua & Barbuda, Turks & Caicos, St.
Vincent & The Grenadines, B&W, A&E, R&D,
AT&T.
From left to right, Mrs. Cynthia Sue
(Marketing Manager), Mr. Harold Francis
(General Manager), Cameron Greenidge
(Chief Executive Officer), Keisha Jones
```

(I.T. Manager) and Tanya Yearwood (Human Resources Manager).

When using a typewriter, the asterisk (*) can be used to emphasize words (as an alternative to bold or italics). So if a word or phrase is *really* important, you could surround it with * * to make it stand out. For example, "Do *not* open the case before unplugging the device". Of course, instead of using the * you could just put the word in ALL CAPS.

19 Symbols IV: - _ = +

In this chapter, you will learn:

- how to type the last four symbols in the number row: - _ = +

- the difference between a dash and an underscore

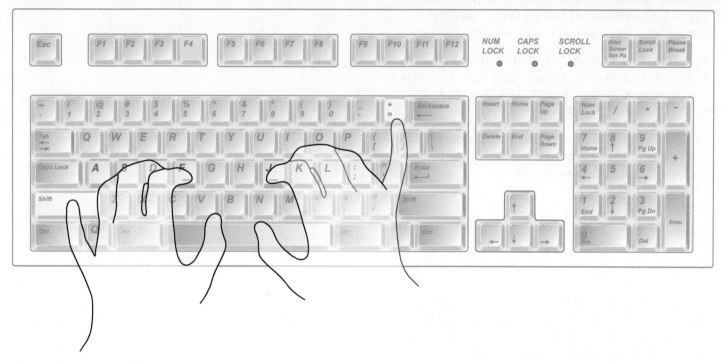

Figure 19.1 Typing the + sign.

The dash and the underscore

If you look to the right of the 0 in the number row, you will see a key that looks as if it has a longer dash on top of a shorter one. But only the bottom one is a dash (or minus sign, or hyphen, depending on how it is used). The top one is actually the underscore (_), which is sometimes used to indicate blanks or to join words in email addresses: e.g. john_bates@microsoft.com or al_jones@dodge.com.

To type the dash/minus sign/hyphen you use your right pinkie. So naturally, if you want to type an underscore, you have to hold down the left shift key as well (with your left pinkie).

The equals sign and the plus sign

To the right of the dash is a key with the equals sign (=) underneath and a plus sign (+) on top. You press this key using the right pinkie as well. Normally that would produce an = sign, but if you want the + sign you just hold down the *Shift* key with your left pinkie as well (see Figure 19.1).

Typing practice

Exercise 19A

```
-_ _- =+ += -= =- _+ +_ -+ +- -=+_ _+=-

1-1 2-2 3-3 4-4 5-5 6-6 7-7 8-8 9-9 0-0 2-1
3-2 4-3 5-4 6-5 7-6 8-7 9-8 1-0 1-10 9-5

son-in-law, daughter-in-law, mother-in-
law, father-in-law, brother-in-law, sister-
in-law, governor-general, side-by-side,
signal-to-noise, silky-haired, yellow-
breasted, yellow-bellied, x-ray

a_b b_c c_d d_e e_f f_g g_h h_i i_j j_k
k_l l_m m_n n_o o_p p_q q_r r_s s_t t_u
u_v v_w w_x x_y y_z 1_1 2_2 3_3 4_4 5_5
6_6 7_7 8_8 9_9 0_0

jim_jones@hotmail.com joe_hardy@mysteries.
com nancy_drew@mysteries.com i_cant_
choose_a_name@example.com
```

Exercise 19B

```
-_ _- =+ += -= =- _+ +_ -+ +- -=+_ _+=-
-+_ _-+ _=+ -=_ -_+ +=_ =_+ +-= _+= -=+
_=- +-_ -+= =+_ _+- =-+ +_= -_= =_- +_-
_-= +=- =-_ =+-

1+2 2+3 3+4 4+5 5+6 6+7 7+8 8+9 9+0 1+1=2
2+2=4 3+3=6 4+4=8 5+5=10 6+6=12 7+7=14
8+8=16 9+9=18 10+10=20 9-2=7 33-22=11 91-
10=81 60-20=40 87-78=9 5-6=-1 10-12=-2 70-
65=5
```

20 Symbols V: the slash (/)

In this chapter, you will learn about the last symbol we will be covering (the slash) and how to type it

Figure 20.1 Pressing the slash.

Using the slash (/)

The slash (/), not to be confused with the backslash (\), is located next to the right *Shift* key. Sometimes it is called the forward slash in order to further emphasise the distinction between the two. It is used:

- as a substitute for the word 'or', e.g. Yes/No
- when typing fractions, e.g. 1/2 or 3/4
- as a division sign when working with spreadsheets
- when typing Internet addresses.

You press the slash using the <u>right pinkie</u> as shown in Figure 20.1.

Typing practice

Exercise 20A

```
/? ?/

1/1 2/2 3/3 4/4 5/5 6/6 7/7 8/8 9/9 0/0 1/2
2/2 1/3 2/3 3/3 1/4 2/4 3/4 4/4 1/5 2/5 3/5
4/5 5/5 1/6 2/6 3/6 4/6 5/6 6/6 1/7 2/7 3/7
4/7 5/7 6/7 7/7 1/8 2/8 3/8 4/8 5/8 6/8 7/8
8/8 1/9 2/9 3/9 4/9 5/9 6/9 7/9 8/9 9/9

128/2=64 64/2=32 32/2=16 16/2=8 8/2=4 4/2=2
2/2=1

Yes/No True/False Black/White On/Off Male/
Female
```

Exercise 20B

Use underscores when typing the blank spaces where information is to be inserted. Hold down the key to quickly type multiple underscores.

```
I, Mr/Mrs/Miss _____
_____ , give/do not give
permission for my son/daughter/ward
_____ to go on the trip to
Cuba from April 1st - 14th, 2012.

In case of emergency, I can be reached
at the following home/work/mobile
number _____. If for
some reason you don't get me, you can
contact his/her father/mother/brother/
sister _____ at

_____

I am/am not able to pay the airfare on/
before February 20th 2012.

Medical Information:
Is your child diabetic? (Yes/No)
Does he/she suffer from asthma? (Yes/No)
Is he/she allergic to Penicillin? (Yes/No)
Does he/she suffer from allergies? (Yes/No)
If yes, please list:

_____
_____
_____
```

21 The numeric keypad

In this chapter, you will learn which fingers to use to type the keys on the numeric keypad

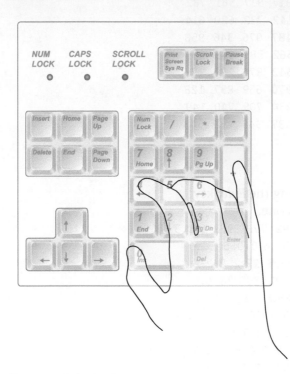

Figure 21.1 The starting position for the numeric keypad.

Using the numeric keypad

Although you have learnt how to type numbers using the number row, this is best suited when you have one or two numbers to type in a sentence. For heavy-duty number typing, especially when you are working with spreadsheets, the numeric keypad is the way to go.

Finger positions

Typing with the numeric keypad is easy. For the most part, each finger is assigned to a column:

- right index finger: 1, 4, 7 and Num Lock
- right middle finger: 2, 5, 8 and /
- right ring finger: full stop, 3, 6, 9, *
- right pinkie: Enter, +, -
- right thumb: 0

Remember to make sure that the Num Lock key is turned on before trying to type numbers using the numeric keypad.

Starting position

Just like the letters F and J, the number 5 has a 'bump' on it. But in this case, it indicates where your right middle finger should go. Then the rest of the fingers fall in place. As Figure 21.1 shows, the other fingers are positioned as follows:

- right index finger: number 4
- right ring finger: number 6
- right pinkie: + sign
- right thumb: 0.

Typing practice

Exercise 21A

Type the following numbers, but instead of putting spaces between them, press the *Enter* key (on the numeric keypad) after each one.

456 789 123 321 654 987 348 073 603 082 064
541 628 963 208 742 297 783 817 917 561 782
861 394 093 239 396 624 467 142 732 620 614
250 695 964 306 978 019 567 487 076 346 958
029 274 519 068 504 376 720 562 589 049 280
028 473 078 748 943 892 670 642 875 287 183
651 653 912 413 813 109 719 970 659 837 128
067 137 824 936 568 206 318 234 709 740 149
984 854 697 281 718 608 436 387 948 819 543
374

Exercise 21B

Type the following numbers, pressing the *Enter* key (on the numeric keypad) after each one.

0 4.4 3 37.6 12 6.3 641.32 43.92 77.9 9.3 959.3
300.96 27.7 161.4 1 61.8 3.44 68 6.0 985 52.0
7.2 85.15 52 0 55 5.0 6 43.1 69.5 12.2 3.21
690.61 37 39.2 68.2 8 302 40.6 91 305.84 6.5
12.21 34.95 1.20 37.70 92 4.6 85.8 11.4 72.5
3.19 890 0.0 65.98 870 858.62 9.9 60.58 9 98.01
310 643 7 13.75 4.04 746.76 1.24 91.9 8 7 3.36
20.4 95 36.19 42.8 4 25.96 176 720.4 518 561
18.10 722.07 231 3.89 9.32 75 373 1 555.95
433.1 450.75 206.8 4.4 9.20 84.69 5.61 0.17 450

Exercise 21C

Type the following, pressing the *Enter* key (on the numeric keypad) after each one.

46/73 4-44 5+28 20*6 891*1 5/545 67+94 64-625
317+4 33/8 108+333 20*6 747-164 45+21 54/7
60+43 9*4 269/72 28*86 67+49 56+0 76-175
13*40 80+4 897*75 831/6 577-541 396*72 721*4
70/76 18*46 945/29 99+0 76/6 21/37 64-48
650/7 580+41 3+757 20/74 7/1 5/5 0-0 1/874
38-596 3*6 722+783 382+0 691*2 534*200 8*30
2+92 52/19 71+949 646/107 9+2 623/7 0+795
23*33 738-951 570+5 6+957 9+54 39/572 612+5
98+3 994*85 0/833 7-86 56-4 886-70 881/8
583/626 821*4 78-8 156+5 75+1 65*94 409*5
28-8 94*77 16+2 292/26 13/78 303-702 0-2
705/18 89-6 8/4 0*944 454+377 8-127 549+9
631*3 5*83 9*900 2*194 7+234 781+9 68+10

Finger position chart

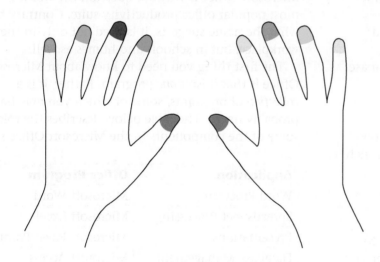

Part 3 Productivity tools

① Choosing the right tool for the job

In this chapter, you will learn:

- about productivity tools
- a little about Microsoft Office
- the programs that make up Microsoft Office
- where to find Microsoft Office on your computer
- how to choose the right Office program for your task

Productivity tools

In this course, you will learn how to use a number of office productivity tools. These programs allow you to perform most of the tasks required in a modern office including: Word Processing, Spreadsheet Processing, Presentations and Database Management.

Word processing

A **word processor** is a type of program that allows you to create and manipulate textual documents such as letters, reports, flyers and manuscripts.

Spreadsheet processing

Spreadsheet programs allow you to work with large amounts of numerical data, making it easy to manipulate the figures and to perform calculations on them.

Presentations

Presentation software allows you to create slideshows that can be used during teaching, reports or even speeches. It also makes it easy to insert animations and sound effects to help keep your audience's attention.

Database management

A Database Management program is a piece of software that allows you to efficiently store, retrieve and manipulate data stored in database tables.

About Microsoft Office

Microsoft Office is without question the world's most popular office productivity suite. Contrary to what the name suggests, it is used not only in the workplace, but in schools and homes as well.

The first thing you need to know about Microsoft Office is that it isn't *one* program. Rather, it is a *collection* of programs, some of which you may have probably heard. The table below describes the roles of some of the components in the Microsoft Office suite.

Application	Office Program
Word Processing	Microsoft Word
Spreadsheet Processing	Microsoft Excel
Presentations	Microsoft PowerPoint
Database Management	Microsoft Access

This is by no means an exhaustive list. There are other Microsoft Office programs such as Microsoft Outlook, OneNote, Publisher and Visio.

Microsoft Office comes in various versions so the edition you have may not include all of the programs mentioned.

These programs form what is known as an **integrated software package**. Individually, each serves a very specific purpose; combined they complement each other, allowing users to perform all sorts of tasks.

Because these programs are designed to work together, it is very easy to copy data from one Office program and paste it into another. Another benefit is that the programs have similar interfaces, so if you know your way around one program, you will be right at home in the others.

Where to find Office on your computer

The individual Office programs are usually listed under the Microsoft Office group in the Start Menu. (I know, this is not exactly earth shattering news). So to open Microsoft Word, for example, you would click on *Start*, go to the Microsoft Office program group, then click *Microsoft Word*.

Figure 1.1 Searching for Microsoft Word in Windows 7.

If you are using Windows Vista or Windows 7, you can use the search function that is built into the Start Menu. So to search for Microsoft Word, click on the *Start* button, then start typing W-O-R (see Figure 1.1).

If you do not see the Office programs in the Start Menu, try searching for them on the desktop. Sometimes people move the icons there for quicker access.

In order to cut costs, many computers come with Microsoft Works installed instead of Microsoft Office. Unfortunately, Microsoft Works is very limited compared to Microsoft Office.

Determining which Microsoft Office program to use

If you want to do a presentation or slideshow, your choice is simple – you have to use Microsoft PowerPoint. Similarly, if you are writing a textual document or doing a poster, you are going to want to use Word.

If you are working with lots of data, either Microsoft Excel or Microsoft Access can be used. Determining which to use can be challenging, since there is some overlap in the functionality. However, if your data consists of mainly figures and a lot of calculations are involved, it is better to use Excel. Excel is also better for plotting graphs.

If you are going to frequently perform queries or need more control over your data, then Access is the better bet.

Sometimes multiple programs are used together. For example, you may plot a graph in Excel and copy it into PowerPoint to use in a presentation.

Old versus new

Up until Office 2003, the Office interface was pretty consistent. Sure, there were some menu items added and the introduction of the Task Pane, but for the most part the interface remained unchanged.

All this changed in Office 2007 when Microsoft completely overhauled the interface. Office 2010 uses the same interface, with a few minor wrinkles. Where the two interfaces diverge, this book will highlight the differences (starting with the next two chapters).

Summary

- Microsoft Office is an integrated office productivity package.
- This course will be covering Word Processing, Spreadsheet Processing, Presentations and Database Management using Microsoft Word, Excel, PowerPoint and Access respectively.
- Office 2007 and 2010 have a very different interface from previous versions.

Review exercises

Exercise 1

1 What is an integrated software package?
2 What are the advantages of an integrated software package?
3 Name four programs that are part of the Microsoft Office suite.
4 Suppose you go to start Microsoft Excel but you do not see it in the Start Menu. What are two possible explanations?
5 Match the following application types to the corresponding Office program.

Spreadsheet Processing	Microsoft Word
Presentations	Microsoft Access
Word Processing	Microsoft Excel
Database Management	Microsoft PowerPoint

6 For each of the following, state whether you would use Word Processing, Spreadsheet Processing, Presentation or Database Management software. In each case, justify your answer:
  a If you want to plot the number of new cars sold each year for the past 5 years.
  b In order to produce a slideshow on Healthy Living.
  c To do a flyer promoting your annual school fair.
  d To determine the percentage each student in a class got on his report.
  e If you need to store the names and addresses of all your friends.

② The Office 2003 interface

In this chapter, you will learn:

- the main components of the Microsoft Office 2003 interface

- about the common menus and toolbars

- how to show, hide and reposition toolbars

- about the task pane

The Office 2003 interface

The programs in Office 2003 and earlier look just like typical Windows programs. Most of their functionality can be found in toolbars and menus.

But Office 2003 has a few additional tricks up its sleeve, the most notable of which is the task pane. Using Microsoft Word 2003 as an example, let us take a look at the Office 2003 interface (see Figure 2.1).

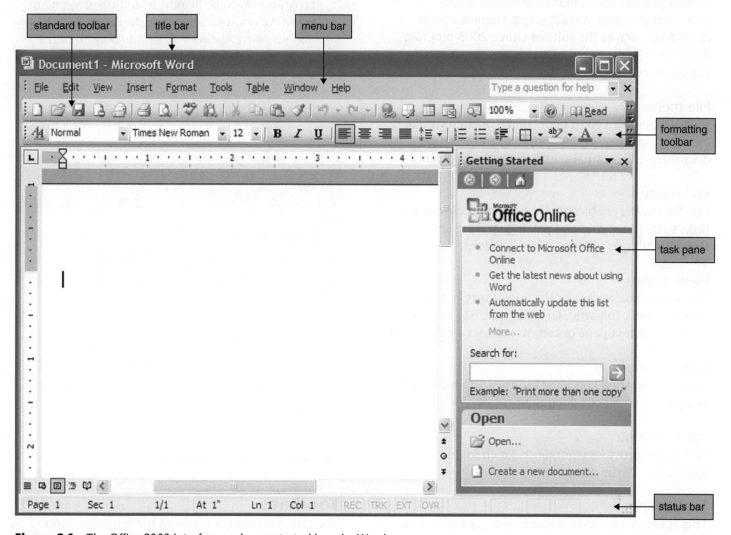

Figure 2.1 The Office 2003 interface as demonstrated here by Word.

Title bar

The title bar of a Microsoft Office program displays the name of the program as well as the document currently open in it. In Figure 2.1, the current document is *Document1* and it is being displayed in *Microsoft Word*.

Menus

Although some menu items are unique to the particular program you are using, there is a lot of consistency across the suite of Office 2003 programs. Below are the common menus as well as an explanation of what each one is for.

File menu

This is where you go to perform file operations like creating, opening, saving, printing and closing documents. You can also exit the entire program.

Edit menu

The Edit menu enables you to perform basic editing tasks such as copying and pasting, finding and replacing text, as well as undoing actions.

View menu

This allows you to change the appearance of the program itself. In particular, you go here to control whether the task pane or certain toolbars are displayed.

Insert menu

You go here when you want to insert an object such as a picture into your document.

Format menu

This menu provides commands for changing the appearance of the document.

Tools menu

This is where you go to perform more complex tasks. At the bottom of the *Tools* menu is the *Options* command which allows you to change the settings of the particular program.

Window menu

If you have multiple documents open within the same Office program, you can use this menu to manage them and switch between them.

Help menu

You can go here for Microsoft Office help. At the bottom of the menu is the *About* command that tells you what version of the program you are running.

If you do not see items in a menu that you know should be there, they may be hidden. Office programs try to be helpful by hiding menu items you have not used in a while. In Figure 2.2, the double down 'arrows' (⌄) at the bottom of the *Insert* menu show that there are hidden items. If you click the arrows or wait for a few seconds, the full menu will be displayed.

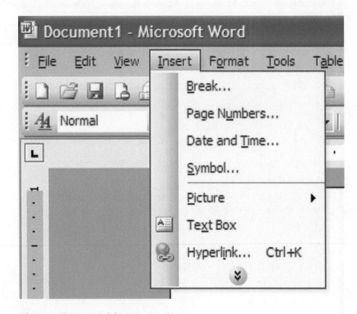

Figure 2.2 Hidden menu items.

Toolbars

The toolbars provide access to the most common commands. Of course, there are many functions that cannot be found on the toolbars – for these you have to search through the menus.

There are two main toolbars which most Microsoft Office programs display by default.

- The <u>Standard toolbar</u> has buttons for basic tasks such as creating, opening, saving and printing documents, copying and pasting as well as undoing and redoing actions.
- The <u>Formatting toolbar</u> allows you to format the appearance of the document.

tip

If you cannot remember what a particular button does, just position the mouse over it for a few seconds. A yellow tooltip will tell you what the button is for. In Figure 2.3, the tooltip is telling you that the button with the floppy disk icon in the Standard toolbar is the *Save* button.

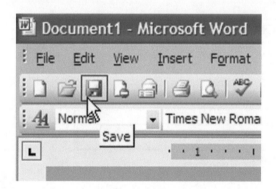

Figure 2.3 Tooltip for the *Save* button. Tooltips are displayed when you move the mouse pointer over a button.

Repositioning toolbars

When you first open a Microsoft Office program, the Standard and Formatting toolbars may be positioned on the same line in order to save space. Unfortunately this prevents you from seeing all the toolbar items on either toolbar. If your toolbars are displayed this way, you should reposition the Formatting toolbar (the one with the B, I and U buttons) underneath the Standard toolbar.

To reposition a toolbar:

1 Position the mouse over the vertical dots at the start of the toolbar. The mouse pointer should change to the *Move* icon which is a four-headed arrow (see Figure 2.4 below).

2 Hold down the <u>left</u> mouse button and drag the toolbar to new position.

3 Release the mouse button.

If you drag the toolbar too far down, it will 'float' above the main program window in its own window. If this happens, just drag it back into position using its window's title bar (see Figure 2.5, see page 94). (The *Move* icon will not be displayed until you hold down the left mouse button.)

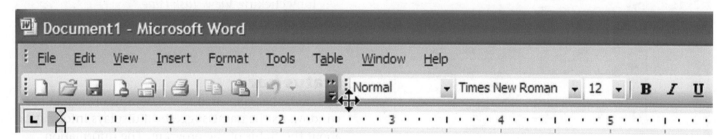

Figure 2.4 Moving the Formatting toolbar.

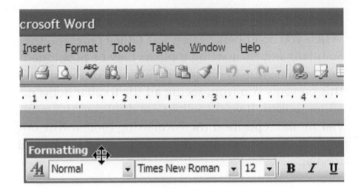

Figure 2.5 A floating toolbar.

Showing or hiding toolbars

In order to maximise screen space, most of the toolbars are hidden.

To show or hide a toolbar:

1 Click *View, Toolbars*.

2 Click the menu item for the desired toolbar.

If the selected toolbar was not currently being shown, it will now be displayed and a check mark will be placed next to its menu item. To hide the toolbar, click on its ticked menu item. It will now not be ticked and will be hidden. So in the example shown in Figure 2.6, the Formatting toolbar is currently visible as shown by the tick next to the 'Formatting' menu item. But when the Formatting option is clicked, the Formatting toolbar will be hidden.

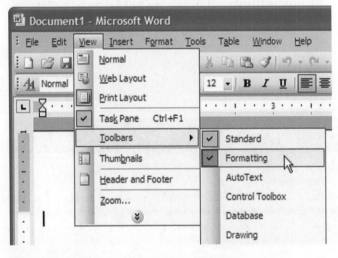

Figure 2.6 Hiding the Formatting toolbar.

Task pane

By default, Office 2003 programs display the task pane to the right of their windows. The task pane is a feature that made its debut in the 2002 version of Microsoft Office (Office XP). For certain tasks (such as inserting a picture), the task pane automatically appears, guiding you through the steps.

There are several different task panes, each corresponding to a particular task.

To switch to another task pane:

1 Display the *Task Pane* menu by clicking the *down arrow* in the top right-hand corner of the task pane.

2 Click the name of the task pane you want.

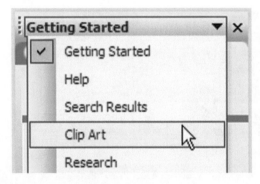

Figure 2.7 Changing the task pane.

 If you do not see the task pane, you can display it by clicking *View, Task Pane*.

Status bar

The status bar is located at the bottom of each Office window. As the name suggests, it displays information about the status of the program. The information displayed varies depending on the program.

Summary

- Office 2003 programs look like typical Windows programs, except for the inclusion of the task pane.
- By default, only the Standard and Formatting toolbars are shown, but additional ones may be enabled via the *View* menu.
- Toolbars can be dragged to other positions.

Review exercises

Exercise 2A

1 What two toolbars are displayed by default in each Office 2003 program?
2 What is the difference between the View menu and the Formatting menu?
3 Under which menu would you find each of the following?
  a The command that allows you to change the program options.
  b The Find and Replace commands.
  c The Cut, Copy and Paste commands.
  d The Print command.
  e The command that allows you to exit the program.
  f Commands to display toolbars or the task pane.
4 Explain how to reposition a toolbar.
5 Look at Figure 2.8 (see page 96) and state:
  a whether or not the task pane is being displayed
  b which Office program is being shown
  c the name of the document currently open
  d which toolbars are currently being displayed
  e which toolbars are currently 'floating'
  f what the current status is
  g whether all the items in the View menu are currently being displayed.

Exercise 2B

This exercise only applies to people using Office 2003.
1 Open Microsoft Word.
2 Make sure that the Formatting toolbar is currently displayed and that the task pane is hidden.
3 Move the Formatting toolbar so that it floats in its own window. Then drag it underneath the Standard toolbar.
4 Hide the Standard toolbar.
5 Display the Standard toolbar and the task pane.
6 Switch to the Mail Merge task pane.
7 Close Microsoft Word.

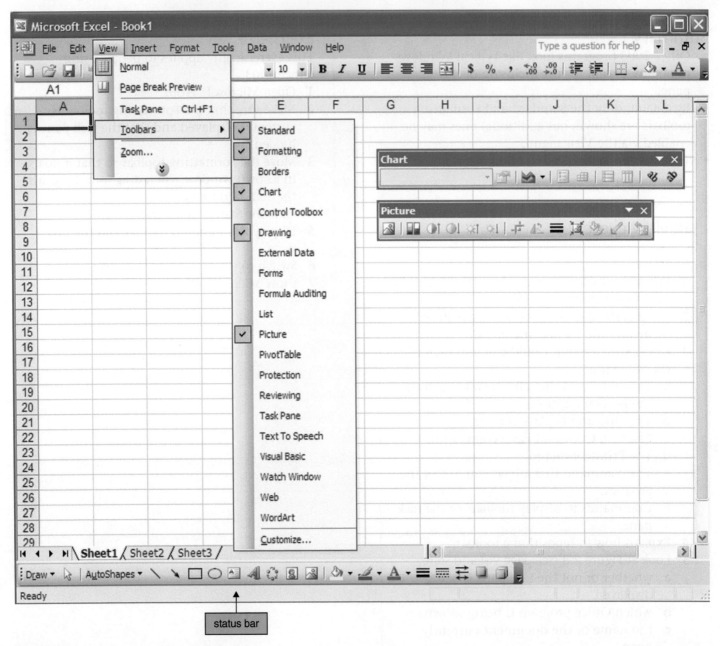

Figure 2.8 For Exercise 2A, question 5.

3 The Office 2007 and 2010 interfaces

In this chapter, you will learn:

- the components of the interface used by Microsoft Office 2007 and 2010

- how to use the Ribbon

- about the Microsoft Office button and the new Backstage view

The Ribbon

As you can see from Figure 3.1, the Office 2007 interface does not look like that of a standard Windows program. It does not have any menus or toolbars *per se*. Instead, it combines the two into a unique feature called the <u>Ribbon</u>.

The Office 2010 interface, shown in Figure 3.2, see page 98, is almost identical with one notable exception – in place of the Microsoft Office button there is a File tab (highlighted in blue).

The Ribbon (shown in Figure 3.3, see page 98) was introduced in Office 2007 (and continued in Office

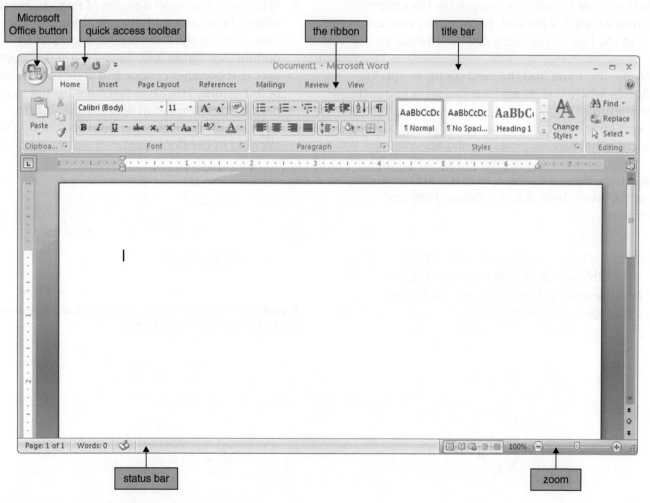

Figure 3.1 The Office 2007 interface (Word shown here).

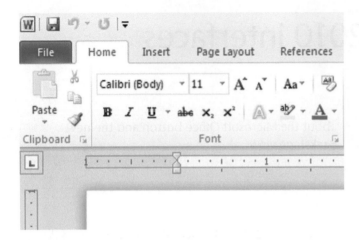

Figure 3.2 The Office 2010 interface with *File* tab highlighted.

2010) because the menus in the Office programs had become so complex that users could not find where commands were located.

At the top of the Ribbon you can see the various tabs into which it is divided. For example, here are some of the tabs in the Word 2007/2010 Ribbon:

- *Home* – here you find the most common options
- *Insert* – where you go anytime you want to insert something
- *Page Layout* – this allows you to change page settings such as the margins, paper size and orientation.

In addition, there are some tabs that will only display when you need them, e.g. the *Picture*, *Table* and *Chart* tabs.

Your Ribbon may not look exactly like this because items get resized according to how much space your screen has.

Switching between tabs

Only one tab can be selected at a time. When a tab is selected, all of the buttons belonging to that tab are displayed underneath it. In Figure 3.3, the Home tab is selected.

To switch to another tab on the Ribbon:

1 Click on its name at the top of the Ribbon.

You do not have to click on tabs nearly as much as you would expect though. There are three reasons for this:

- The Ribbon intelligently guesses which tab you currently need. So, for example, when you first insert an image, the Picture tab is automatically selected.
- When you first select a region of text, the mini toolbar (a small semi-transparent toolbar) appears. This contains the most common formatting options (see Figure 3.4). As you move the mouse over it, it becomes opaque and you can click on any of its buttons. This saves you from having to switch back to the *Home* tab in order to format text.
- You can always access the mini toolbar by right-clicking in the document.

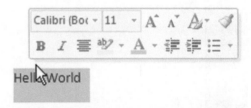

Figure 3.4 The mini toolbar. It automatically appears when the text 'Hello World' is selected.

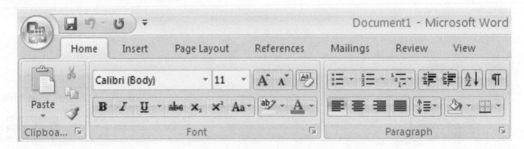

Figure 3.3 An example of the Word 2007/2010 Ribbon.

Button groups

The buttons on the tabs are grouped into logical sections. In Figure 3.3 you can see three of the sections on the Home tab: *Clipboard*, *Font* and *Paragraph*.

At the bottom right of some sections, you will see this button: 🗗. Clicking it will give you more options to choose from. For example, if you click the one in the *Font* section, it will open the *Font Options* window.

tip

If you cannot remember what a particular button does, leave the mouse pointer over it for a few seconds and a tooltip will eventually appear (see Figure 3.5).

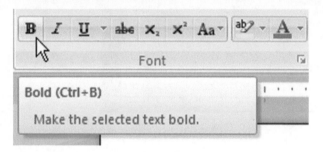

Figure 3.5 A tooltip appears when you hover the mouse over a button.

The Microsoft Office button (Office 2007 only)

Office 2007 programs have a round button to the top left of the Ribbon. This is the Microsoft Office button (see Figure 3.1, see page 97). Clicking here will display the Microsoft Office menu (see Figure 3.6). This menu has the items you would find in a typical *File* menu, such as *New*, *Open*, *Save*, *Print*, *Close* and *Exit*.

The File tab (Office 2010 only)

Users new to Office 2007 often did not realise that they could access the typical *File* menu items by clicking the Office button. So Office 2010 has a highlighted *File* tab to the left of the Ribbon in place of the button in the 2007 version.

But this tab acts differently from a normal *File* menu. When you click it, the Office program switches to the oddly named *Backstage* view (see Figure 3.7, on page 100). Here, not only can you do things like work with files, but you can also manage various options to do with your document.

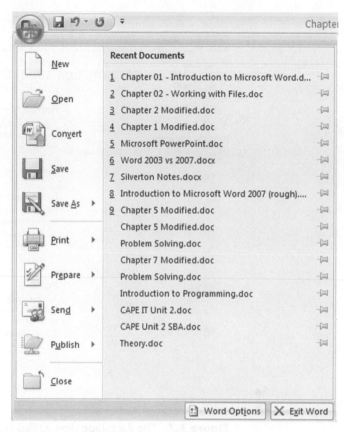

Figure 3.6 The Microsoft Office menu (Office 2007).

The Quick Access toolbar

In both Office 2007 and 2010, to the left of the title bar is the Quick Access toolbar. It contains buttons that allow you to quickly:

- save the document
- undo the last thing you did
- redo the last thing you undid.

Task pane

Although they are not used nearly as much as in Office 2003, task panes are found in Office 2007 and 2010 (not pictured in Figures 3.1 and 3.2). When you are performing certain tasks, particularly in PowerPoint, the corresponding task pane appears to the right of the window to guide you through the process.

The status bar

Each Office program has a status bar at the bottom to provide you with information about its current status. By default, Office 2007/2010 status bars display a lot less information than the ones in previous versions.

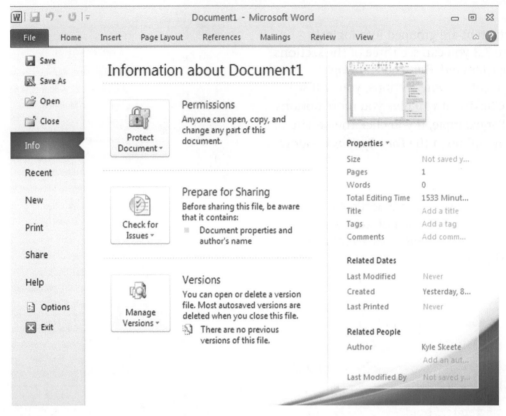

Figure 3.7 The *Backstage* view (Office 2010).

To the far right of the status bars are the zoom buttons which show you the current magnification of the document and allow you to zoom in (+) or out (−) (see Figure 3.1, page 97).

Summary

- Instead of toolbars and menus, Office 2007 and 2010 use the Ribbon.
- Some tabs in the Ribbon are only displayed when you need them.
- The normal *File* menu items can be accessed by clicking the Office button (Office 2007) or the *File* tab (Office 2010).

Review exercises

Exercise 3A

1 In your own words, explain how the Ribbon works.

2 Which tab of the Ribbon would you go to if you wanted to:
  a change the orientation of the page?
  b put a picture in the document?
  c change the size of the margins?
3 Where would you find commands such as Save, Open and Exit, in:
  a Office 2007?
  b Office 2010?

Exercise 3B

This exercise only applies to students who are using Office 2007 or 2010.

1 Open Microsoft Excel.
2 Switch to the *Insert* tab.
3 Switch to the *Page Layout tab*.
4 Click the *More Options* button at the bottom of the *Page Setup* group.
5 Close the window that appears.
6 Exit Microsoft Excel by using either the *Office* button or the *File* tab.

4 Working with files

In this chapter, you will learn:

- about file extensions
- how to open, save and close files
- how to use templates and how to create your own

File extensions

Having looked at the Microsoft Office interfaces, we turn our attention to the documents that you might work on within those same interfaces. Each document is stored as a file on your computer, the format of which depends on the document type. So a Microsoft Word document is stored in a different format to an Excel one.

Since there are a variety of file formats, the computer needs to make sure that it opens each document using a program that knows how to 'understand' it. If it does not, the data will look like gibberish. Figure 4.1 shows what happens when you try to open an Excel spreadsheet in Microsoft Word.

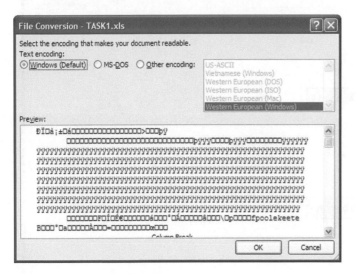

Figure 4.1 A document opened in the wrong program.

So how does the computer know what program to open a document with? As you saw in Part 1 Chapter 5, each file has an <u>extension</u> (a dot followed by three to five letters) that tells you its type. Table 4.1 shows some of the Microsoft Office file extensions.

Table 4.1 Microsoft Office file extensions.

Document type	Office 2003 extension	Office 2007/ 2010 extension
Word document	.doc	.docx
Excel spreadsheet	.xls	.xlsx
PowerPoint presentation	.ppt	.pptx
Access database	.mdb	.accdb

Some computers are configured to hide the file extensions. The extensions are still there – they are just hidden from the user.

Incompatibilities between new and old Office versions

You may have noticed that the table above has two sets of extensions – one for Office 2003 and another for Office 2007/2010. This is because Office 2007 did not just introduce a new interface; it also brought new file types as well.

Unfortunately, the two sets of file types are incompatible. Office 2007 and 2010, since they are more recent, can open the older file types in addition to the newer ones. But Office 2003 can only open the newer formats if a special convertor is installed. For that reason, it is best to save your files in the Office 2003 format even if you are using office 2007/2010.

tip

The Office 2007/2010 file extensions are often the same as the 2003 ones, but with x's at the end.

Opening files

To open a file using any Office program:

1 Click *File* or the Microsoft Office button.

2 Click *Open*.

3 Choose the file from the *Open* window.

As you can see in Figures 4.2a and 4.2b, the appearance of the *Open* window depends on the version of Windows you have installed. What both versions have in common, however, is that the heart of the window lists the folders and documents in the current location. If you double-click on a folder, the contents of *that* folder will be shown instead.

Once you have found the file you want to open, you can double-click it to open it, or select it and click the *Open* button.

The *Open* button will be disabled until you select an item.

How do you know the current location? It is displayed in the box at the top of the *Open* window. In Windows XP this box is called the *Look In* box (in Windows 7 and Vista it does not have a name). You can click in the box to change the location or type the location directly.

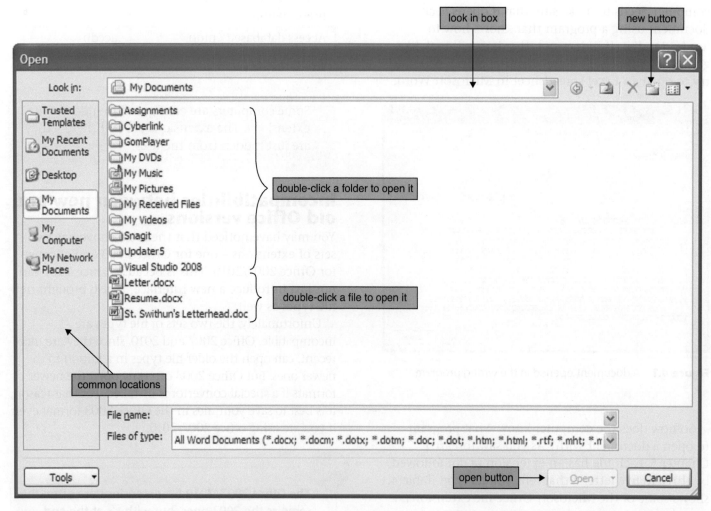

Figure 4.2a Word's *Open* window (in Windows XP).

Figure 4.2b The Word's *Open* dialog window in Windows 7 and Vista.

tip

You can also click on one of the common
locations located to the left of the Window
e.g. *My Documents*.

Saving a document

To save a document:

1 Click *File* or the Microsoft Office button.

2 Click *Save*.

3 If this is your first time saving the document,
the *Save As* window will appear. You will then
have to type the name of the file and choose
the location where it is to be saved.

4 (Optional). If you are using Office 2007 or
later, you should change the file type to an
Office 97–2003 format as shown in Figure 4.3,
see page 104 to ensure other people can open
it if they are using an older version.

5 Click the *Save* button.

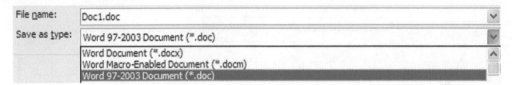

Figure 4.3 Changing the file type.

Saving documents in Office 2007/2010

As was mentioned earlier, Microsoft Office 2007 and later use new file formats that previous versions of Office cannot normally read. Fortunately, the programs in these versions of Office give you the option of saving in the previous Office 97–2003 format (Figure 4.3).

Saving under a new file name

To save a file under a new name:

1 Click *File* (or the Microsoft Office button).

2 Click *Save As*.

3 Go to the folder where you want to store the file.

4 Type the new name of the file.

5 Click *Save* when you are done.

Closing files

To close a file, click *File* (or the Microsoft Office button), then click *Close*. You will be prompted about any unsaved changes.

Exiting a Microsoft Office program

To exit a Microsoft Office program click *File* (or the Microsoft Office button), then click *Exit*. You will be prompted to save changes if necessary.

Alternatively, you can click the *X* in the right-hand corner of the window.

Templates

The Microsoft Office programs come with several templates you can use while typing documents. For example, there are templates for application letters, memos, invoices and much more. When you create a document using one of these templates, a lot of the work is done for you already – you just have to fill in the placeholders with your relevant information (see Figure 4.4).

[Street Address]
[City, ST Zip Code]
[phone]
[fax]
[Web address]

Fax

To:

Fax:

Phone:

Re:

Figure 4.4 Part of a Fax Template.

Creating a document using a template (Office 2003)

If you are using Office 2003, in order to create a document using a template, you:

- Click *File, New...*
- Under the Templates section of the *Task Pane*, click *On My Computer...*
- Choose the document category e.g. *General, Letters and Faxes* or *Memos*.
- Then double-click on the icon for the template.

Creating a document using a template (Office 2007/2010)

To create a new document using a template in Office 2007 or 2010:

- Click *File* (if you are using Office 2010) or the *Microsoft Office* button.
- Then click *New*.
- Choose the appropriate category.
- Then double-click on the particular template.

> **tip**
>
> **Although there may be templates for a particular type of document you are working with, you should still make sure you know how to produce the document on your own.**

Saving your own templates

If you find yourself using a common format when typing a particular type of document, you may want to create your own template. In order to do so:

- Create a new document and insert the information to be reused e.g. the company's letterhead.
- Click *File* (Or the *Microsoft Office Button*).
- Click *Save*.
- Change the document type to an Office 2003 template (for compatibility reasons).
- Change the location to an easily accessible location such as the *Desktop*. (Alternatively you can save it in the template folder so it will be listed among the other templates.)
- Type the name of the template.
- Then click the *Save* button.

If you double-click a template file that is saved on your desktop, a brand new document based on that template will automatically be created. If you want to edit the template file, right-click on it and click *Open*.

Summary

- The file extension of a file is given by three to five letters after a dot; the extension tells the computer the format of the file and helps it figure out what program to open it with.
- The file extensions of the new Office file formats normally end with an x.
- By default, Office 2007 and 2010 use new file formats that are incompatible with Office 2003.
- When saving files in Office 2007 and 2010, you should change the file format to the Office 97–2003 format.
- Office comes with a variety of templates you can use; you can also create your own.

Review exercises

Exercise 4A

1 Explain how you would save a file.
2 Explain how you would open a file you previously saved.
3 Why should you save files using the Office 2003 format?
4 Explain why someone would want to create a template.

Exercise 4B

1 Open Microsoft Word and type a sentence or two in the blank document.
2 Save the file as TEST in a new folder inside your class folder. To create the new folder:
   a First go to your class folder.
   b Click on the *New* button at the top of the Save window.
   c Type the name of the new folder and press *Enter*. You will be taken inside the new folder.

3 Close the TEST file.

4 Open the LARA file from the exercise folder.

5 Save a copy of the file as LARA1 in your class folder, then exit Microsoft Word.

6 Open the Microsoft Excel file called CLIMATE.

7 Save a copy of the file as CLIMATE1 in your class folder, then exit Microsoft Excel.

8 Open PowerPoint file called ISLAND.

9 Save a copy of the file as MY ISLAND in your class folder, then exit Microsoft PowerPoint.

Exercise 4c

1 Open Microsoft Word.

2 Create a new document based on a memo template.

3 Type some random characters in the document.

4 Save the document as a template on the Desktop called MY MEMO.

5 Exit Microsoft Word.

6 Double-click the *MY MEMO* template on your desktop.

7 Note the name of document that appears in the Title bar.

8 Exit Word again without saving any changes.

9 Right-click on the *MY MEMO* template and click *Open* in order to edit it.

10 What name do you see in the title bar now?

11 Exit Microsoft Word without saving any changes.

5 Formatting text

In this chapter, you will learn:

- how to select text using either the mouse or the keyboard
- how to format text
- about fonts

Introduction

One thing you'll find yourself doing a lot of is formatting text. By 'formatting text', I mean changing the appearance of text – its size, its colour or some other characteristic. The good thing about formatting text in Office is that the process is similar in all the programs.

The way you normally format text is:

1 Select the text you want to format.

2 Choose the appropriate *Formatting* option from the formatting toolbar (2003) or the *Home* tab (2007/2010).

Selecting the text

If you want to change the appearance of text, you have to have some way of telling the computer which text you want to format. That is why when you are formatting text the first step is normally selecting it. There are two ways to select text:

- by using the mouse
- using the keyboard.

Using the mouse

To select text using the mouse:

1 Position the mouse pointer at the <u>beginning</u> of the text you want to select (the mouse pointer should be an I-beam) as shown in Figure 5.1a.

2 Hold down the <u>left</u> mouse button.

3 Drag the mouse to the <u>end</u> of the text you want to select. As you move the mouse, the text will be highlighted, indicating the selected region (see Figure 5.1b).

4 Release the mouse button.

a

I The programs in Office 2003 and earlier look just like the typical Windows program. The majority of their functionality can be found in toolbars and menus. But Office 2003 has a few additional tricks up its sleeve, the most notable of which is the Task Pane. Using Microsoft Word 2003 as an example, let us take a look at the Office 2003 interface.

b

The programs in Office 2003 and earlier look just like the typical Windows program. The majority of their functionality can be found in toolbars and menus. But Office 2003 has a few additional tricks up its sleeve, the most notable of which is the Task Pane. Using Microsoft Word 2003 as an example, let us take a look at the Office 2003 interface.

Figure 5.1 Selecting text: **a** before; **b** after.

Using the keyboard

To use the keyboard to select text:

1 Position the cursor at the beginning of the text you want to select. (Recall that the cursor is the flashing black line that indicates your current position in the document.)

2 Hold down the *Shift* key.

3 Use the arrow keys to increase or decrease the selected region. Use the right (or down) arrow to expand the selection. Use the left (or up) arrow to reduce the selection.

4 Release the *Shift* key.

Choosing the appropriate formatting option

Once you have selected the text, you have to tell the computer how you want to format it. You can format text via the Formatting toolbar in Office 2003 (Figure 5.2) or the *Home* tab of the Ribbon in Office 2007/2010 (Figure 5.3).

Let us look at some of the most common formatting options.

Bold, italics and underline

You can use the three buttons in Figure 5.4 to:

- make the text **bold**
- put it in *italics*
- <u>underline it</u>.

This is a great way of making text words or phrases stand out. Each one of these buttons works like a switch – click it once to turn it on, click it again to turn it off. When a button is on, it is highlighted in orange.

Figure 5.2 The Word 2003 Formatting toolbar.

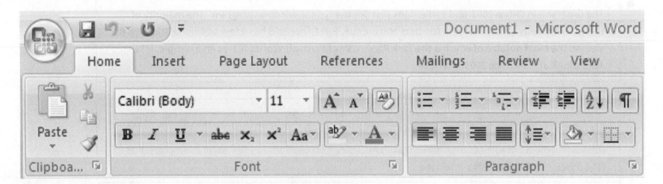

Figure 5.3 The Home tab of the Ribbon (Word 2007 and 2010).

Figure 5.4 The *Bold, Italics* and *Underline* buttons.

Aligning text

The alignment buttons (shown in Figure 5.5) control the alignment of the text, whether it is to the left of the page, centred, or to the right. By default, text is aligned to the left.

The rightmost button fully justifies the text so that the paragraphs have no jagged edges on either side.

Unlike the Bold, Italics and Underline buttons, only one of these may be on at a time.

Figure 5.5 The Alignment buttons.

The lines in these buttons represent lines of text. So you can tell what a button does by just looking at it. For example, since the lines in the first button are lined up to the left, you can tell it is the *Align* Left button.

Changing the font and font size

You probably have heard the word 'font' many times. A **font** is a style of type. Here are a few of the fonts that come installed with Microsoft Office:

- Times New Roman is the default font in Office 2003.
- Calibri is the default font in Office 2007 and 2010.
- **Arial Black is great for headings.**
- Comic Sans MS is a nice casual font.
- *Monotype Corsiva is an elegant cursive font.*

The Office programs provide combo boxes like those in Figure 5.6, that allow you to change the font and the font size. A **combo box** looks like a text box with a down arrow on the right. You can type in the text-box portion or click the arrow in order to get a list to choose from.

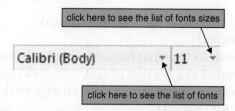

Figure 5.6 The *Font* and *Font Size* combo boxes.

To change the font:

1 Click the down arrow at the right of the *Font* combo box.

2 Choose the font you want from the list.

To change the font size:

1 either choose the size you want from the *Font Size* combo box

2 or type the size directly into the text-box portion.

The bigger the number, the bigger the text will be.

Changing the colour

Another great way of making text stand out is to change its colour. This is easy to do via the *Font Colour* button (which looks like a capital A). Underneath the A there is a colour (usually red or the last colour you used). If you click on the <u>left</u> side of the button (the bit with A on), that is the colour the selected text will become.

If you click on the arrow on the <u>right</u> of the button, you will get a drop-down list of colours to choose from (see Figure 5.7, see page 110). As you move the mouse over a colour, a tooltip tells you the colour.

How to tell what formatting options are selected

If you want to tell what formatting options have been applied to a portion of text, just click inside the text. The formatting buttons will change to show the settings for that text.

This does not work for the font colour.

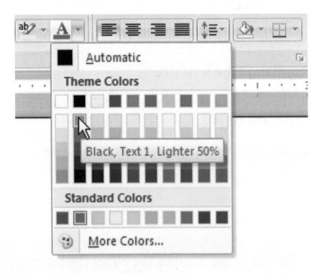

Figure 5.7 Changing the colour.

Additional formatting options

Thus far, we have covered the most common formatting options. Now let us look at some of the less common options, including some that do not have dedicated formatting buttons.

Subscripts and superscripts

If you want to do a subscript like the 2 in H_2O or a superscript like the 3 in x^3, the easiest way to do so is via their dedicated formatting buttons x^2 x_2. Unfortunately you usually will not find these buttons in Office 2003. Instead, you can go through the Font window.

Font window

The *Font* window (see Figure 5.8) gives you a number of formatting options including super^script,

Figure 5.8 The *Font* window.

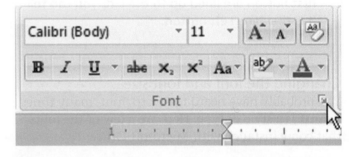

Figure 5.9 Opening the *Font* window in Office 2007 and 2010.

~~strikethrough~~ <u>double underline</u> and character spacing.

To access this window in Office 2003, click *Format, Font* (or *Format, Cells* if you are using Excel).

In Office 2007 and 2010, you can access it by clicking the *More Options* button in the *Font* group of the Ribbon's *Home* tab (see Figure 5.9).

In Microsoft Excel the *Font* 'window' is actually a tab in the *Format Cells* window.

Summary

- When you format text you change its appearance.
- To select text using the mouse, drag from the beginning of the region you want selected to the end.
- To select text using the keyboard you need to hold down the *Shift* key.
- You can format text using the buttons on the Formatting toolbar or the Home tab of the Ribbon.

Review exercises

Exercise 5A

1 What is the first thing you need to do when you are formatting existing text?
2 What is a font?
3 Why would you not use a font like Comic Sans MS in business documents?
4 Explain how to change the colour of text.

Exercise 5B

Open the BARGAINS file from the exercise folder and make the following changes.

Use the mouse when selecting the text for questions 1 to 4.

1 The first main title, 'BargainShopper™', should be centred and in Arial Black font, size 28. It should also be blue.
2 The second main title, 'Reducing the Cost of Living', should be bold, centred and in italics. Use a font size of 18.
3 The section headings, 'How does it work?', 'What are the benefits?' etc., should no longer be underlined. Instead they should be changed to Comic Sans MS font, made bold and placed in italics.
4 After each occurrence of the word BargainShopper, place the letters 'TM' as a superscript.
5 Save the file in your class folder as BARGAINS1.

Use the keyboard when selecting the text for questions 6 to 10.

6 The first two sentences, 'For years Caribbean…solution', should be bold and have a font size of 16.
7 Fully justify the text in the first paragraph.
8 Right-align the second paragraph.
9 Make the words 'Figure 1' (above the chart) green and underline them. Do the same for the word 'Key' underneath the chart.
10 Save the file in your class folder as BARGAINS2.

6 Editing text

In this chapter, you will learn:

- how to move text or copy it
- an easy way to delete regions of text
- how to find and replace text
- how to undo mistakes

Introduction

Unlike formatting text, editing text changes its structure. For example, you can copy text from one location to another, delete it or replace it with something else. Knowing how to effectively edit text can save you a lot of time and reduce frustration.

Copying text

The first thing to look at is copying text to another location – either in the same document or another one altogether. This can significantly reduce the amount of typing you have to do.

To copy text:

1 Select the text to be copied.

2 Right-click on it and click *Copy* from the popup menu that appears (see Figure 6.1).

3 Right-click at the point where the copy is to be placed.

4 Click the *Paste* option.

In Office 2010 the word '*Paste*' is not displayed in popup menu. In its place is a *Paste* icon, which looks like a clipboard.

This process is called 'copying and pasting'. But what is really happening behind the scenes? Well, first of all, by selecting the text you tell the computer which text you want to copy. When you right-click on it, the computer displays a menu of things you can do with that particular text, one of which is to copy it.

When you click on *Copy*, the selected information is copied to the *Clipboard*, which is a temporary storage area to which all running programs have access. Right-clicking on the desired destination and clicking *Paste* causes the information in the *Clipboard* to be copied there. The process is illustrated in Figure 6.2.

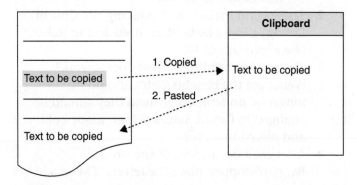

Figure 6.2 Copying and pasting.

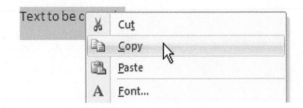

Figure 6.1 Copying text.

When you click *Paste*, the information is not removed from the *Clipboard*. It stays there until it is replaced by something else being copied to the *Clipboard*. This means you can paste the same bit of text over and over without first having to copy it again.

tip

These techniques are not limited to text or to Microsoft Office. You can copy images, tables and other types of information between Windows programs. For instance you can copy an image from Internet Explorer.

Moving text

Moving text from one location to another is very similar.

To move text:

1 Select the text to be moved.

2 Right-click on the selected text and click *Cut*.

3 Right-click on the point to which you want the text to be moved.

4 Click the *Paste* option.

The main difference is that when you click *Cut* (as opposed to *Copy*), the text is <u>moved</u> to the Clipboard as shown in Figure 6.3. As before, when you click *Paste*, the information is copied from the *Clipboard* to the new location, but remains on the *Clipboard* as well.

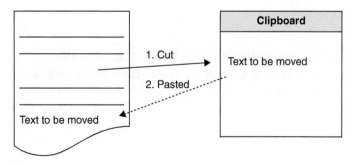

Figure 6.3 Cutting and pasting.

Other ways to copy or move text

Although I showed you one way to copy or move text, there are a number of alternatives. We will look at some of them.

Using the *Cut, Copy* and *Paste* buttons

For starters, you can use the *Cut, Copy* and *Paste* buttons which are found in Office 2003 on the *Standard* toolbar, and in Office 2007/2010 on the *Home* tab of the Ribbon. Figure 6.4 shows what the buttons look like in the newer version of Office. In Office 2003 they do not have the words next to them and all the buttons the same size but the image used on each icon is the same.

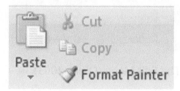

Figure 6.4 The *Cut, Copy* and *Paste* buttons in Office 2007/2010.

To use the *Cut, Copy* and *Paste* buttons:

1 Select the text you want to move or copy.

2 Click the *Cut* or *Copy* button.

3 Position the cursor where you want the text to be inserted.

4 Click the *Paste* button.

Using the Edit menu (Office 2003 and earlier)

If you are using Office 2003 or earlier, you can use the *Edit* menu instead (although there are very few cases in which you would want to do so).

Using the keyboard shortcuts

If you look at Figure 6.5, see page 114, you will see that on the right of certain items like *Cut, Copy* and *Paste* there are the keyboard shortcuts for those commands – for example, *Ctrl+C* for *Copy*. These are standard keyboard shortcuts and work in all versions of Microsoft Office.

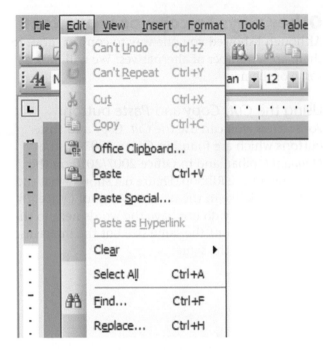

Figure 6.5 The Edit Menu (Office 2003).

Dragging and dropping

You can also use the drag-and-drop approach. If you want to move text from one location to another, select it then drag it to the destination. The mouse pointer will change so that there is a tiny rectangle at the bottom of it, signalling that the data is being moved. A dotted vertical line indicates where the data will be inserted when you release the mouse button.

In Figure 6.6 the word 'lazy' is going to be moved and put before the word 'dog'.

The lazy quick brown fox jumps over the dog.

Figure 6.6 Dragging and dropping.

If you want to copy the text instead of moving it, hold down the *Ctrl* key while dragging the mouse.

> **tip**
>
> If you inadvertently find yourself dragging data to another location and want to stop it, press the *Esc* key <u>before</u> you release the left mouse button.

Deleting regions of text

If you want to delete a large chunk of text at a time, holding down the *Delete* (or *Backspace*) key can be time consuming. A much quicker way is to select the region of text, then press the *Delete* key once.

> **tip**
>
> If you want to type something in place of a region of text, you do not even have to press the *Delete* key. Instead you can start typing immediately after selecting the text. As soon as you type the first letter, the selected text will be erased and the letter you typed will be put there instead. You then continue typing as normal.

Finding and replacing text

The *Find* and *Replace* feature in Microsoft Office is a real time saver. Instead of having to manually search through lengthy documents – which is also error prone – you can have the computer do the work for you.

Finding text

To find a word or phrase:

1 Click *Edit* (or the *Home* tab), then *Find*.

2 Type the word or phrase in the window that appears.

3 Click the *Find Next* button (this can be repeated to find other occurrences of the word or phrase).

The computer will start searching from the position of the cursor. If you have text selected, the computer will search the selected region only.

Finding text in word 2010

In Word 2010, when you click the *Find* button on the *Home* tab, instead of the *Find* and *Replace* window, the *Navigation Pane* is displayed (see Figure 6.7).

The handy window makes finding text very easy since it displays a list of the occurrences of the search phrase and shows them in context. You can click the up and down arrows to quickly move between occurrences.

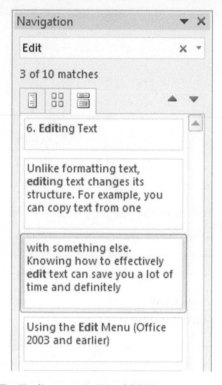

Figure 6.7   Finding text in Word 2010.

Replacing text

To use the replace function:

1 Click *Edit* (or the *Home* tab), then *Replace*.

2 In the window which appears (see Figure 6.8):

- Type the text you want to search for in the 'Find what' box.

- Type the text you want to replace it with in the 'Replace with' box.

3 Use the *Find* and *Replace* buttons as described below.

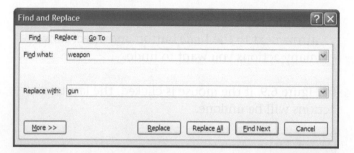

Figure 6.8   Replacing text.

tip

The *Find* and *Replace* functions are on two tabs in the same window. So you can quickly switch between the two functions by clicking on the appropriate tab.

Replacing all occurrences of the search text

If you want to replace all occurrences of the search text, click the *Replace All* button. Be careful, though: blindly using the *Replace All* button can have unintended side effects. For instance, if you replace 'the' with 'a' you may change the world 'these' to 'ase'.

Replacing occurrences one by one

For the reason mentioned above, along with others, people sometimes prefer to replace occurrences one by one.

To replace each occurrence one by one:

1 Click *Find Next* to go to the first occurrence of the word.

2 If you want to replace it, click *Replace*, which will also cause the computer to find the next occurrence of the word. Otherwise click *Find Next* to skip that occurrence and move on to the next one.

3 Repeat Step 2 as often as is required.

Undoing mistakes

Any time you make a mistake, you can undo it by clicking the *Undo* button. The *Undo* button is on the Office 2003 Standard toolbar or on the Quick Access toolbar in Office 2007/2010.

- To undo the last thing you did click on the *Undo* button itself.

- To undo several things at once, click on the down arrow next to the *Undo* button and select how many actions you want to undo.

In Figure 6.9, if the mouse is clicked, the last two actions will be undone.

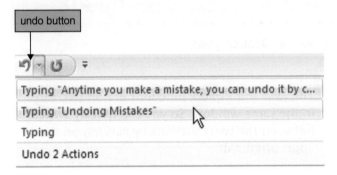

Figure 6.9 Undoing actions.

Common keyboard shortcuts

Table 6.1 lists common keyboard shortcuts that may be used in any Office program (and in many Windows programs). It looks like a lot but they are easy to remember. Usually the shortcut is *Ctrl* + (this means press *Ctrl* and the appropriate key at the same time) the first letter of what you want to do, except for some cases (underlined in the table) where that letter was already taken.

Table 6.1   Common keyword shortcuts for any Office program.

Category	Shortcut	What it does
Copying and moving text	Ctrl + C	Copy
	Ctrl + <u>X</u>	Cut
	Ctrl + <u>V</u>	Paste
Finding and replacing	Ctrl + F	Opens the Find window
	Ctrl + <u>H</u>	Opens the Replace window
Emphasising text	Ctrl + B	Bold
	Ctrl + I	Italics
	Ctrl + U	Underline
Alignment	Ctrl + L	Left align
	Ctrl + <u>E</u>	Centre
	Ctrl + R	Right align
File commands	Ctrl + N	Creates a new document
	Ctrl + O	Opens an existing document
	Ctrl + S	Saves the current document
	Ctrl + P	Opens the Print window
Moving around documents	Home	Moves cursor to the beginning of the line
	End	Moves cursor to the end of the line
	Page Up	Moves cursor up a page
	Page Down	Moves cursor down a page
	Ctrl + Home	Moves to the top of the document
	Ctrl + End	Moves to the bottom of the document
Selecting text	Shift + Arrow key	Increases or decreases the selection region
	Shift + Move shortcut	Selects from the current location to the new location where the cursor is moved
	Ctrl + A	Selects all the data in the document
Miscellaneous	Ctrl + <u>Z</u>	Undoes the last thing you did

Summary

- You copy text from one location to another by copying and pasting.
- You move text to another location by cutting and pasting or dragging it from one location to another.
- You can use the *Find* and *Replace* window to quickly find or replace text.
- Office programs have a button that allows you to undo mistakes.
- For most commands the keyboard shortcut is *Ctrl* + the first letter in that command.

Review exercises

Exercise 6A

1 What is the difference between editing text and formatting it?
2 Explain how you would quickly delete an entire paragraph.
3 Explain how cutting and pasting works.
4 Give three ways to move text from one location to another.
5 What are the keyboard shortcuts for:
   a copying text?
   b centring text?
   c saving a document?
6 If the cursor is on one page and you want to go to the next one, what key would you press?
7 Explain how you would quickly get to the bottom of a long document by only using the keyboard.
8 Explain how the replace all occurrences of the word 'difficult' with 'impossible'.
9 You want to copy the entire document to another program so you press *Ctrl* + A to select all the text. But when you try to copy it, your entire document disappears. Explain what could have happened and two easy ways to solve this problem.

Exercise 6B

1 Open Microsoft Word and type the following sentence:
   The quick brown fox jumped over the lazy dog and then it ran away.
2 Place nine copies of the sentence underneath the original, using as many methods as possible.
3 Starting from the first sentence, make every other sentence bold using keyboard shortcuts.
4 Move all the bold sentences to the top of the document, using as many methods as possible.
5 Replace all occurrences of the word 'quick' with 'speedy'.
6 Replace all occurrences of the word 'dog' with 'cat'.
7 Replace the <u>third</u> occurrence of the word 'fox' with 'wolf'.
8 Replace all occurrences of the word 'the' with 'a' and observe what happens.
9 Save the document in your class folder as FOXES AND DOGS.

Exercise 6C

Open the CAMERAS file from the exercise folder and do the following:

1 Change the main heading to the Verdana font and make it bold.
2 Right-align the second heading 'Choosing the Right One for You'.
3 Use the keyboard to go to the bottom of the document.
4 Swap the Introduction and Summary sections.
5 Find the word 'wildlife' and change its colour to red.
6 Place the word 'particularly' in italics.
7 Change all occurrences of the word 'camera' to 'photo-taking device'.
8 Undo the last thing you did (using either the keyboard or the mouse).
9 Press *Ctrl* + S.
10 Save the document in your class folder as CAMERAS1.
11 Press *Ctrl* + A to select the entire document.
12 Press *Ctrl* + C to copy the information to the Clipboard.

13 Press *Ctrl* + O and open the CAMCOPY file from the exercise folder.
14 Use the keyboard to select the line of text in the CAMCOPY file.
15 Press *Ctrl* + V.
16 Save the document as CAMCOPY1 in your class folder.

⑦ Microsoft® Word basics

In this chapter, you will learn:

- about the Microsoft Word interface
- how to manually create a new document
- how to switch between the different views in Microsoft Word

The Microsoft Word interface

Microsoft Word is a general-purpose application known as a **word processor**. Word Processors allow you to create and manipulate textual documents such as letters, reports and manuscripts. They also have several useful features such as find and replace, automatic spelling and grammar checking, page numbering and mail merge.

Figure 7.1 shows the interface for Word 2007 but the components described are found in Word 2003 and 2010 as well.

The cursor

The cursor is a flashing vertical black line that indicates the current position in the document. When you type, paste or insert something, it gets put where the cursor is positioned.

The ruler

The ruler shows you the margins for your document, allows you to change indentation and set tabs stops. This will be covered in later chapters. Microsoft Word has both vertical and horizontal rulers but for the

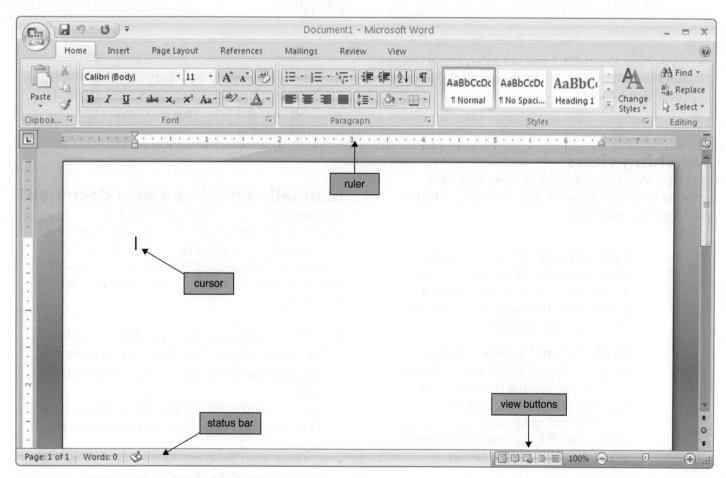

Figure 7.1 The Microsoft Word interface (Word 2007 shown here).

rest of this book I will use the term 'ruler' to refer to the horizontal ruler located above the document. If your ruler is not visible, you can display it by clicking *View, Ruler*.

The status bar

At the bottom of the Microsoft Word window – in all versions – there is a status bar that provides you with information about your document. Here is some of the information you can find on the status bar:

- the number of pages in your document
- what page you are currently on
- whether or not there are any spelling errors; if there are any errors, the indicator will show an X
- the line and column position (Word 2003 only)
- an indicator (OVR) that tells you if Overtype mode is on (Word 2003 only)
- the word count (Word 2007 and 2010 only).

tip

If you have Word 2003 you can always view the number of words in the document by clicking *Tools, Word Count*.

Switching views

Microsoft Word has a variety of views that have different purposes. Below is an explanation of when you might use each view:

 Print Layout – This is the default view. The good thing about it is that while you are typing you can get a good idea of how your document will look when it is printed.

 Draft/Normal Layout – This is a simplified layout which allows you to focus on composing the document. Elements like headers, footers, page numbers and some images are hidden. This is also the best view for removing manual page or section breaks.

 Reading Layout (Full Screen Reading) – This is the best view to use if you are reading a lengthy document.

 Web Layout – Whenever you are working on the contents of a web page, Word will switch to this layout. It shows you what your document would look like in a web browser.

 Outline – This view is useful when you do not know what to write but want to create an outline to help organise your thoughts. It makes it easy to structure your document using different types of headings.

You can switch between views by using either the *View* buttons at the bottom of the window, the *View* menu (in 2003) or the *View* tab of the Ribbon (in 2007/2010).

In Word 2003 the *View* buttons are on the bottom left of the window whereas in Word 2007 and 2010 the *View* buttons are on the bottom right.

Manually creating a new document

Whenever you start Microsoft Word, it automatically creates a new blank document for you to work with. The first document is called '*Document1*', the second '*Document2*' etc. If you want to manually create a new document, do the following:

- In Word 2003, click *File, New*, then click *Blank Document* from the *Task Pane*. Alternatively you can click the *New* icon in the Standard toolbar.
- In Word 2007, click the Microsoft Office button, click *New*, then click *Create* in the window that appears.
- In Word 2010, click *File, New*, then click the *Create* button to the right of the *Backstage* view.

Summary

- Word Processors allow you to manipulate text documents.
- The cursor indicates where the next thing you type or insert will go in the document.
- You can use the *View* menu (in Word 2003) or View tab (in Word 2007/2010) to switch views and to show or hide the ruler.
- You can also use the *View* buttons at the bottom of the Word window to switch views.
- The default view is the *Print Layout* view.
- To manually create a new blank document, click *File* (or the Office button) then click *New*.

Review exercises

Exercise 7A

1 In your own words explain what a Word Processor is.
2 List three features Word Processors provide.
3 Say which is the best view to use in each of these situations:
   a When you are perusing a long document.
   b When you want to focus on typing your document without any visual distraction.
   c When you want to remove manual page and section breaks.

Exercise 7B

1 Open the VIEWS document from the exercise folder.
2 How many words are in the document?
3 Ensure that the ruler is visible.
4 Switch between the views, first by using the View buttons, then by using the View menu/tab.
5 Close the document without saving it.

8 Helpful word processing features

In this chapter, you will learn:

- how to perform spelling and grammar checks
- how to use Word's thesaurus capabilities
- easy ways to make text to uppercase or lowercase
- how to use the bullets and numbering features
- how to insert footnotes and endnotes
- how to insert symbols that are not on your keyboard

Spelling and grammar checks

Have you ever found something so useful that you wondered how you ever managed without it? Microsoft Word has a number of features like that, and we will cover some of them in this chapter.

Perhaps the most useful are the spelling and grammar features. First of all, Word checks your spelling and grammar as you type, highlighting errors with wavy lines. Spelling errors are underlined in red, whereas grammar errors are underlined in green.

In Word 2007 and 2010 there is a similar feature called 'contextual spell checking' which checks for words that are correctly spelt but used in the wrong context. For example, 'The boy is over their.'. The word 'their' is used in the wrong context so it is underlined with a blue wavy line.

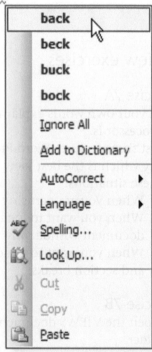

Figure 8.1 Correcting a spelling error.

To correct an individual error that has been highlighted:

1 Right-click on the wavy line.

2 Choose the appropriate correction option from the list that is displayed (Figure 8.1).

The spelling and grammar checks are not perfect. For example, if you type a name that Word does not 'know' it will get underlined as a spelling error even if it is spelt correctly.

At the top of the correction options there are suggested replacements that can be made. These are displayed in order of what Word thinks is most relevant. When you click on one of the suggested replacements, Word replaces the underlined text accordingly.

If you accidentally type a word twice, Microsoft Word underlines the second word in red.
In such a case, when you right-click on the offending word choose the first option, *'Delete repeated word'*.

In addition to the suggested replacements, you are given the following correction options:

- *Ignore* – ignores the error
- *Add to dictionary* – adds that particular spelling to MS Word's internal dictionary so that if you type it again (even in another document), Word will not highlight it as a spelling error; use this for names that Word does not recognise.

Word automatically corrects common typos. To see it in action, try typing 'teh'.

Finding and correcting errors

If your document contains errors, the proofing errors indicator in the status bar will show an X. To find and correct those errors, press the *F7* key. Word will start searching for errors from the point where the cursor is positioned, displaying the *Spelling and Grammar* window (Figure 8.2) when it finds one.

You can also display this window by clicking on *Spelling & Grammar* in the *Tools* menu (Word 2003) or in the *Review tab* of the Ribbon (Word 2007/2010).

The window looks slightly different if the error is a grammatical error.

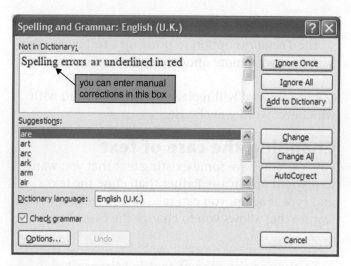

Figure 8.2 The *Spelling and Grammar* window.

A message at the top indicates what the error is; examples are 'Not in dictionary' for a spelling error or 'Subject–verb agreement' for a grammatical error. In Figure 8.2, the text is displayed with the error highlighted. You can:

- apply a suggestion by choosing it from the list and clicking the *Change* button
- manually make a correction by replacing the text in the box under the error message and clicking the *Change* button
- add a word to the dictionary
- ignore the error and move to the next one.

When Word has finished searching for errors, it will say that its check is complete.

You can use the *Explain* button to get an explanation of what Microsoft Word <u>thinks</u> is the cause of a grammar error.

Using the thesaurus

Word makes it very easy to find alternatives to words since it has built-in thesaurus capabilities. If you want to find a synonym for a word:

- Right-click on the word
- Choose *Synonyms* from the context menu which pops up

- Select one of the synonyms from the list or click the *Thesaurus* option to bring up a full blown thesaurus with more options to choose from.

Microsoft Word will replace the original word with whichever word you choose.

Changing the case of text

Suppose you have some existing text that you want to place in uppercase. Rather than erase the text and type it again, you can take advantage of a Word feature that allows you to change the case of text.

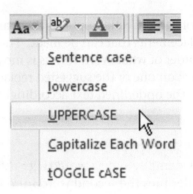

Figure 8.3 Changing case in Word 2007/2010.

To change the case of text in Microsoft Word 2003 or earlier:

1 Select the text.

2 Click *Format, Change Case...*

3 Select the case you want from the window that appears, then click *OK*.

In Word 2007/2010, the steps are a little different:

1 Select the text.

2 Click the *Change Case* button.

3 Select the case you want (see Figure 8.3).

Understanding the different cases

You may have noticed that there are several options to choose from. Table 8.1 explains what each one is for.

Bullets and numbering

Microsoft Word makes it easy to create numbered lists like this:

1 First item.
2 Second item.
3 Third item.

or bulleted items like this:

- Bananas.
- Apples.
- Oranges.

In fact, it has buttons dedicated to these tasks (Figure 8.4).

Table 8.1 Options for changing case in Word.

Option	What it does
Sentence case	Puts the first letter in uppercase and the rest in lowercase.
lowercase	makes the selected text lowercase.
UPPERCASE	MAKES THE SELECTED TEXT UPPERCASE.
tOGGLE cASE	cHANGES aLL tHE lOWERCASE lETTERS tO uPPERCASE aND vICE vERSA
Title Case (2003) Capitalize Each Word (2007)	Capitalises The First Letter In Each Word

Figure 8.4 *Bullets and Numbering buttons.*

In addition, if you start manually typing a numbered list, sometimes Word will recognise what you are doing and convert it to a numbered list automatically.

To reproduce the numbered list given in the first example:

1 Click the *Numbering* button to turn it on. The number '1.' should appear.

2 Type 'First item' and press the *Enter* key to go to the next item, which should be numbered automatically as '2.'.

3 After typing the third item, press the *Enter* key twice to automatically turn off the numbering.

You do not have to type the numbers. Microsoft Word does that for you!

Using another style of bullets or numbers

Suppose that, instead of numbering your items 1, 2, 3, …, you want to number them a, b, c. Or maybe you want to have square bullets instead of the normal round ones. You can do this by choosing what style of bullets or numbers you want.

To choose a different style of bullets or numbers in Word 2003:

1 Click *Format, Bullets and Numbering.*

2 Click the appropriate tab in the window that appears (see Figure 8.5).

3 Choose the style you want.

4 Click the *OK* button.

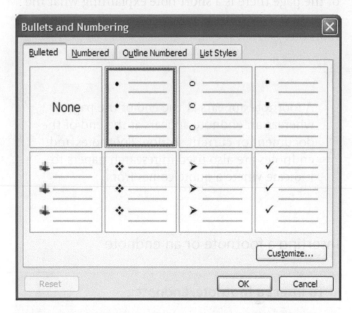

Figure 8.5 *Bullets and Numbering window (Word 2003).*

To do this in Word 2007/2010, just click the *arrow* next to the button and choose from the list that appears. This is shown in Figure 8.6.

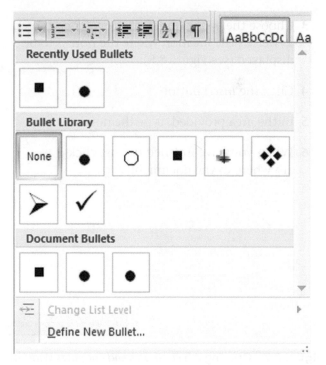

Figure 8.6 Choosing another type of bullet in Word 2007/2010.

Footnotes and endnotes

When you are reading certain types of books, e.g. the Bible or Shakespearean plays, you may see a little number or letter next to a word. Then, at the bottom of the page there is a short note explaining what the particular word/phrase means. This is known as a footnote.

A footnote appears at the end of the page whereas an endnote appears at the end of the document or current section. Footnotes and endnotes are also used in research papers to indicate where a quote comes from.

Inserting a footnote or an endnote

To insert a footnote/endnote:

1 Position the cursor to the right of the text being explained.

2 Open the *Footnote and Endnote* window (see Figure 8.7).

3 Choose the type of note (footnote or endnote), as well as the location where the note is to be displayed (see Figure 8.8).

4 Click the *Insert* button.

5 In the area provided, type the note.

6 When you have finished typing, click anywhere in the document.

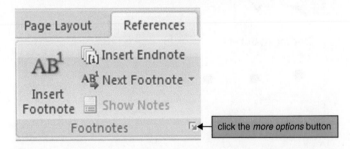

Figure 8.7 Opening the *Footnotes and Endnotes Window* via the Ribbon.

Figure 8.8 The Footnote and Endnote window.

Opening the *Footnote and Endnote* window

To open the *Footnote and Endnote* window in Word 2003:

1 Click *Insert, Reference, Footnote...*

To open it in Word 2007/2010:

1 Switch to the *References* tab of the Ribbon.

2 Click the more options button at the bottom of the *Footnotes* section (see Figure 8.8).

Deleting a footnote or an endnote

To delete a footnote or endnote, you must delete the footnote/endnote number from within the document.

Inserting symbols

Sometimes you will want to insert a symbol that is not found on the keyboard, e.g. the pound symbol. You can do so via the *Symbol* window (Figure 8.9), which can be accessed as follows:

- in Word 2003, click *Insert, Symbol*
- in Word 2007/2010, click the *Insert* tab of the Ribbon, then, *Symbol, More Symbols…*

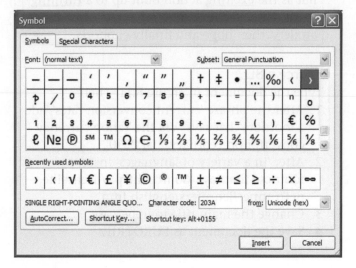

Figure 8.9 The *Symbol* window.

Summary

- Microsoft Word highlights errors in documents with coloured wavey lines: red for spelling, green for grammar and blue for contextual errors.
- To run a spelling and grammar check, press the *F7* key or select from the appropriate menu.
- You can change the case of text without retyping it.
- Footnotes appear at the bottom of the page. Endnotes are at the end of document.
- To insert symbols like '£' that are not found on your keyboard, you have to use the *Symbol* window.

Review exercises

Exercise 8A

1 Give two ways that you can tell if a document contains errors.
2 Rewrite the following sentence using **a** title case and **b** toggle case:
   PETER PIPER picked a Peck of Pickled Peppers.
3 What is the difference between an endnote and a footnote?
4 Explain how to create a bulleted list with square bullets.

Exercise 8B

Open the file WONDERS from the exercise folder and type the text in Figure 8.10 under the first paragraph.

Here are the wonders we will look at:

- The Seven Wonders of the Ancient World
- The Seven Wonders of the Medeival World
- The Seven Natural Wonders
- The Seven Wonders o the Underwater World

Seven wonders of the ancient world

1) Great Pyramid of Giza
2) Hanging Gardens of Babylon
3) Statue of Zeus at Olympia
4) Temple of Artemis at Ephesus
5) Mausoleum of Maussollos at Halicarnassus
6) Colossus of Rhodes
7) Lighthouse of Alexandria

Seven wonders of the medieval world

1. Stonehenge
2. Colosseum in Rome
3. Catacombs of Kom el Shoqafa
4. Great Wall of China
5. Porcelain Tower of Nanjing
6. Hagia Sophia
7. Leaning Tower of Pisa

Figure 8.10 For Exercise 8B.

Exercise 8B continued...

Make the following changes.

1 Correct any spelling errors. (Note that the names of some of the wonders will be incorrectly highlighted as errors.)
2 Change the bullets to square bullets.
3 Change the numbering of the medieval wonders to Roman numerals.
4 Change headings to title case and the main title to uppercase.
5 Put a footnote after the heading 'Seven Wonders of the Medieval World' stating 'Some lists also include the Taj Mahal in India'.
6 Put a footnote after the heading 'Seven Natural Wonders of the World' stating 'This list was compiled by CNN'.
7 Insert an endnote at the end of the main title which says 'These lists were obtained from Wikipedia.com'.
8 Change the font of the headings to Verdana, size 14, and make them purple.
9 Locate the word Galapagos and change it to Galápagos.
10 Save the document in your class folder as WONDERS2.

Exercise 8C

Type the following, then use Word's thesaurus feature to replace the underlined words with synonyms.

> We emerged from the cinema breathless. The movie had everything! At times, especially in the beginning, it was scary, sad and depressing. But as the exciting action built up to a thrilling finale, those feelings were replaced with ones of anxiety, then hope and finally euphoria.

Exercise 8D

Type the document in Figure 8.11. Then:

1 After the phrase 'current conversion rates', add a footnote that says 'Via the Yahoo currency convertor on February 21st 2010'.
2 After 'in a variety of languages' insert a footnote that says 'Source: http://users.elite.net/runner/jennifers/english.htm'.
3 Change the main title to uppercase.
4 Save the document as EUROTRIP.

Your Own Eurotrip

Inspired by movie and TV adventures, many people are planning to journey around Europe in so-called "Eurotrips". But before you think of planning your own, here are a few things ayou should know.

Currency

Most of the countries in Europe use the Euro, with Great Britain being the most notable exception. At the time of writing, the current conversion rates are:

- €1 = $2.7286 BDS
- €1 = $8.6418 TT
- €1 = $279.9401 GUY
- €1 = $3.5588 EC
- €1 = $121.2983 JAM
- £1 = €1.1371

Learning the Language

Once you've been able to pay for your tickets, you'll need to start brushing up on your Français... and Español and more. But in case you aren't a natural linguist, here's how to say "Do you speak English?" in a variety of languages:

- French: Parlez=vous anglais?
- Italian: Parla inglese?
- Spanish: ¿Habla usted inglés?
- German: Sprechen Sie Englisch?

That's all for now! Stay tuned next week when we tell you about the local cuisine and attractions. Ciao.

Figure 8.11 For Exercise 8D.

⑨ Margins and indentation

In this chapter, you will learn:

- how to change the paper size and its orientation
- how to adjust the margins
- how to indent paragraphs

The *Page Setup* window

When you want to change the size, orientation or the margins for a page, you can do so via the *Page Setup* window (shown in Figure 9.1).

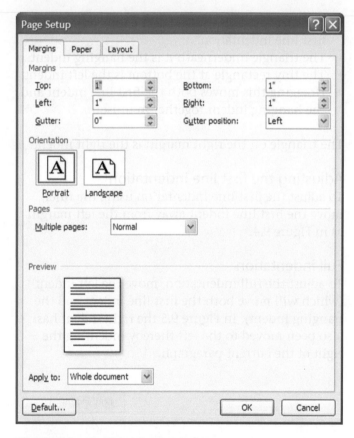

Figure 9.1 The *Page Setup* window.

Opening the *Page Setup* window

To open the *Page Setup* window, click:

- *File, Page Setup* in Word 2003
- *Page Layout, Margins, Custom Margins...* in Word 2007/2010.

Changing the orientation

By default the page is in *Portrait* mode, meaning that it is longer than it is wide. But if you have a wide document, just select the *Landscape* option.

Changing the margins

By default the margins in Microsoft Word are as follows:

- Word 2003: The top and bottom are 1" whereas the left and right margins are 1.25".
- Word 2007/2010: Top, bottom, left and right margins are all 1".

If you wish to change them, open the *Page Setup* window and go to the *Margins* tab. You can type the margin sizes manually or click the *up* and *down* arrows.

Changing the paper size

To change the paper size, switch to the *Paper* tab of the *Page Setup* window and choose a size from the list e.g. A4, A5, Letter or Legal. If the size you want is not in the list, you can type in the dimensions manually.

Indenting paragraphs

The three main types of indentation are first line, full and hanging indentation. The difference between the three is shown below:

With first line indentation, the first line of the paragraph is indented but the rest is not. You would mostly see this in letters or maybe some essays.

With full indentation, the entire paragraph is indented, not just the first line. This style is not very common. You might do it if you want to quote large blocks of text. Whatever the reason, it definitely makes the paragraph stand out from the rest of the text.

With hanging indentation, all the lines in the paragraph except the first one are indented. We will see how to do this later on in the chapter. It is particularly useful while typing plays.

First line indentation
In order to indent the first line of a paragraph, position the cursor at the beginning of the paragraph then press the *Tab* key.

You can remove the first line indentation by positioning the cursor at the beginning of the paragraph and pressing the *Backspace* key.

Full indentation
The *Indentation* buttons (shown in Figure 9.2) allow you to control the indentation of an entire paragraph. The left button <u>decreases</u> the indentation whereas the right one <u>increases</u> it. Just put the cursor inside the paragraph and then click the appropriate button.

Figure 9.2   The *Indentation* buttons.

Using the ruler to adjust margins and indentation
You can use the ruler at the top of the document to precisely adjust the margins and indentation (Figure 9.3).

If the ruler is not visible you can display it by clicking *View* then putting a tick next to the *Ruler* option.

The white region of the ruler indicates the width of the page along which you can type. Remember that even though a letter-sized page is 8.5" wide, the left and right margins are about 1" each. So by default, the lines of text are roughly 6" wide. The ends of this white region are the left and right margins.

On the left margin there are three different items:

- The upside-down triangle at the top controls the first line indentation.
- The triangle underneath it is the hanging indent.
- The tiny rectangle at the bottom is the left indent. Dragging this moves both the first line indent and the hanging indent together in unison.

The triangle on the right margin is the right indent.

Adjusting the first line indentation
To adjust the first line indentation using the ruler, move the first line indent away from the left margin as in Figure 9.4.

Full indentation
To adjust the full indentation, move the left indent (which will move both the first line indent and the hanging indent). In Figure 9.5 the right indent has also been moved to the left thereby indenting the right of the current paragraph.

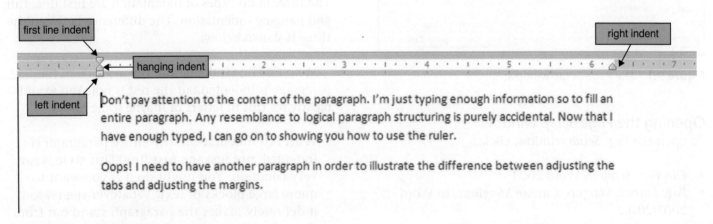

Figure 9.3   The different items on the ruler.

Don't pay attention to the content of the paragraph. I'm just typing enough information so to fill an entire paragraph. Any resemblance to logical paragraph structuring is purely accidental. Now that I have enough typed, I can go on to showing you how to use the ruler.

Oops! I need to have another paragraph in order to illustrate the difference between adjusting the tabs and adjusting the margins.

Figure 9.4   First line indentation via the ruler. The first line indent has been moved to the right.

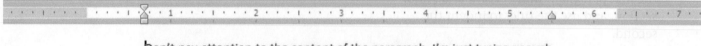

Don't pay attention to the content of the paragraph. I'm just typing enough information so to fill an entire paragraph. Any resemblance to logical paragraph structuring is purely accidental. Now that I have enough typed, I can go on to showing you how to use the ruler.

Oops! I need to have another paragraph in order to illustrate the difference between adjusting the tabs and adjusting the margins.

Figure 9.5   Full indentation via the ruler. The left indent has been moved to the right, taking the first line indent and the hanging indent with it.

Don't pay attention to the content of the paragraph. I'm just typing enough information so to fill an entire paragraph. Any resemblance to logical paragraph structuring is purely accidental. Now that I have enough typed, I can go on to showing you how to use the ruler.

Oops! I need to have another paragraph in order to illustrate the difference between adjusting the tabs and adjusting the margins.

Figure 9.6   Hanging indentation via the ruler. The hanging indent has been moved to the right.

Hanging indentation

Figure 9.6 shows an example of hanging indentation which was done by moving the hanging indent to the right.

Whereas moving the indents only affects the current paragraph, moving the margins affects the entire document. When you position the mouse over one of the margins in the ruler, the pointer changes to a double-headed arrow. In Figure 9.6 the right margin has been moved to the left.

Summary

- The *Page Setup* window allows you to adjust the paper size, orientation and margins.
- You can use the ruler to adjust the indentation of paragraphs as well as their margins.
- The easiest way to indent the first line of a paragraph is to press the *Tab* key.
- To indent an entire paragraph, use the *Indentation* buttons or the indents on the ruler.

Review exercise

Exercise 9

Open the CAMERAS1 file from the exercise folder
then do the questions below.

1 Change the paper size to A4, the orientation
to landscape and the left and right margins to
2 inches.

2 Indent the first line only of the first two
paragraphs, using two different methods.

3 Use the indent buttons to indent the first of
the first paragraph in the 'Point and Shoot'
section, and use the ruler to indent the
second.

4 Use the ruler to make the first paragraph
in the 'Ultra-Zoom' section have a hanging
indent of ½ inch.

5 Use the ruler to indent the left and right of
the second paragraph in the 'Ultra-Zoom'
section by an additional inch.

6 Save the document in your class folder as
CAMERAS2.

10 Enhancing a document's appearance

In this chapter, you will learn:

- how to adjust the line spacing
- to insert pictures, clip art, WordArt and watermarks
- how to use textboxes
- how to draw an organisational chart
- about page borders

Adjusting line spacing

Having the correct line spacing can go a long way towards enhancing a document's readability.

To adjust the line spacing:

1 Select the text.

2 Click the *line spacing* button (see Figure 10.1).

3 Select the line spacing you want.

The default line spacing in Word 2003 is 1, whereas the default in Word 2007/2010 is 1.15.

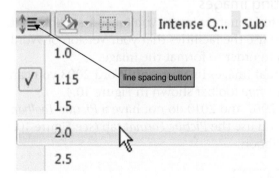

Figure 10.1 Adjusting the line spacing.

Working with pictures

Adding images can quickly enhance the appearance of your document. You can either insert a picture from a file, or from the library of images and other media (called **clip art**) that comes with Microsoft Word. You do not have to know where the clip art files are actually located on your disk – Word takes care of this for you.

Inserting a picture from a file

If you have an image (e.g., a .jpg, .bmp, .gif or .tiff) file, to insert it into a Microsoft Word document:

1 Position the cursor where the picture is to be inserted.

2 Click *Insert, Picture, From File* (Word 2003) or *Insert, Picture* (Word 2007/2010).

3 Go to the folder where the picture is located.

4 Select the correct file.

5 Click the *Insert* button.

This causes a <u>copy</u> of the image to be inserted into the document. So if you change, delete or move the original file, the image you see in the document is not affected. Similarly, if you change the copy in your file, the original will not be affected.

Inserting clip art

To insert clip art you use the *Clip Art* task pane.

- In Word 2003, click *Insert, Picture, Clip Art*.
- In Word 2007/2010, click *Insert, Clip Art*.

Figure 10.2, see page 134 shows how to use the task pane.

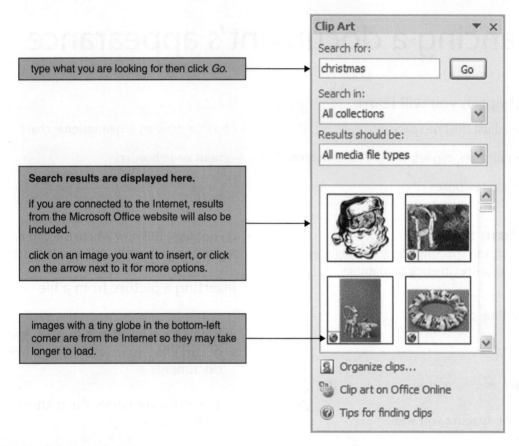

type what you are looking for then click *Go*.

Search results are displayed here.

if you are connected to the Internet, results from the Microsoft Office website will also be included.

click on an image you want to insert, or click on the arrow next to it for more options.

images with a tiny globe in the bottom-left corner are from the Internet so they may take longer to load.

Figure 10.2 Using the *Clip Art* task pane.

Repositioning an image

To reposition an image, just drag it to another location. To move the image a tiny amount in a particular direction, click on its border and then tap the arrow keys while pressing *Ctrl*.

Resizing an image

To resize an image click on it and use the sizing handles that appear (see Figure 10.3).

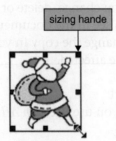

sizing hande

Figure 10.3 The sizing handles.

Here is how you use the sizing handles:

- The left and right handles change the width.
- The top and bottom handles change the height.

- The corner handles change the height and width together while maintaining the original proportions.

Formatting images

In order to format an image you must first click on it. Then you use the facilities that your version of Word provides in order to format the image.

To format images in Microsoft Word 2003 you can use the *Picture* toolbar shown in Figure 10.4.

Word 2007 and 2010 do not have a *Picture Toolbar*. Instead you use the *Picture Format* tab (see Figure 10.5) on the Ribbon.

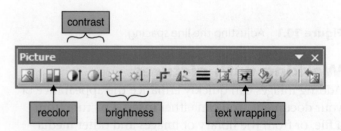

contrast

recolor   brightness   text wrapping

Figure 10.4 The *Picture* toolbar in Word 2003.

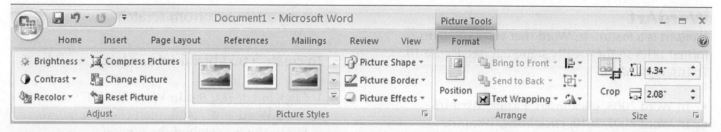

Figure 10.5 The *Picture Format* Tab in the Word 2007/2010 Ribbon.

Text wrapping

Normally where you can put an image is limited by the default text wrapping option. You can adjust the text wrapping to allow text to flow around the image, giving you a lot more freedom to move the image around.

To change the text wrapping, click the *Text Wrapping* button and choose an option.

Here are some key wrapping styles:

- *In Line With Text* – this is the default (not much positioning flexibility) The image is treated like any other character in the line, so that the text does not flow around it.
- *Tight* – text flows around the image, giving you a lot of flexibility with where you can put the image
- *Behind Text* – text flows over the image; use this option for watermarks.

Watermarks

A watermark is a faded image or piece of text that appears in the background of a page. The process of inserting a Watermark depends on what version of Word you are using.

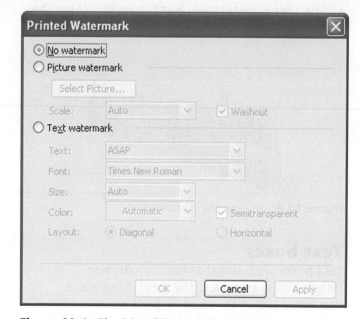

Figure 10.6 The Printed Watermark window.

Word 2007/2010

To insert a watermark in these versions:

1 Click the *Page Layout* tab, then *Watermark*.
2 For a text watermark, select the one you want from the list.
3 For a picture watermark, click *Custom Watermark...* and then choose the appropriate options from the *Printed Watermark* window.

If you want to use an image on a **single** page, you can insert it as a normal image, change its wrapping to *Behind Text* and then recolor it using the *Washout* option.

Word 2003

To insert a watermark in Word 2003:

1 Click the *Format* Menu, then *Background*, then *Printed Watermark...*
2 Choose whether you want a picture or a text watermark in the *Printed Watermark* window (see Figure 10.6).
3 In the case of the former, click the *Select Picture...* button then choose a file from on your computer.
4 For a text watermark you can choose the text, font, colour etc.
5 Click *OK* when you are done.

WordArt

WordArt is a feature in Word that you can use to format titles so they really stand out (see Figure 10.7). To insert *WordArt*:

- In Word 2003, click *Insert, Picture, WordArt.*
- In Word 2007/2010, click *Insert, WordArt.*
- Choose the style you want from the several options available.
- Then type the text you want to appear. (Alter the font and size if necessary.)

Figure 10.7 An Example of WordArt.

Text boxes

Text boxes are boxes that can contain text, images and even tables. The great thing about text boxes is that they can be positioned anywhere on the page, making them great for labelling images.

Putting existing text in a text box

If you have existing text that you want to put in a text box:

1 Select it.

2 Click *Insert, Text Box*. If you are using Word 2007/2010, click *Draw Text Box* in the *Insert* tab of the Ribbon.

Creating a text box from scratch

To create a text box from scratch:

1 Click *Insert, Text Box* in Word 2003. If you are using Word 2007/2010, then click *Draw Text Box* in the *Insert* tab of the Ribbon.

2 If a drawing canvas appears (see Figure 10.8), press the *Delete* key to get rid of it.

Create your drawing here.

Figure 10.8 Drawing canvas.

3 Draw the text box on the document. You can then type inside the text box.

You can drag the text box to move it; use the handles to resize it; or click on the border then press the *Delete* key to delete it.

Formatting text boxes

If you want to format a text box (e.g., to remove the borders or to change the colour of its background) you use the *Format Text Box* window.

To format a text box:

1 Right-click on the border of the text box.

2 Click *Format Text Box*.

3 Make the desired changes.

- If you want to remove the borders, click the arrow for the *Line Color* combo box and choose *No Color* (see Figure 10.9).
- To change the text box background colour, use the *Fill Color* combo box.

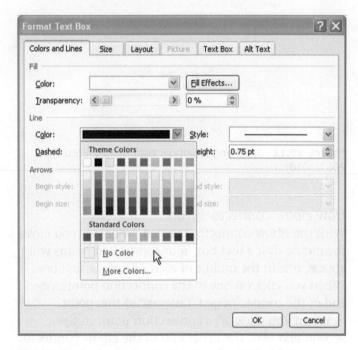

Figure 10.9 Removing the borders from a text box.

> **tip**
>
> If you are using Word 2007 or 2010, you can also use the *Text Box* formatting tab of the Ribbon (which only appears when you click on the text box).

Organisational charts

Text boxes may also be used to construct organisational charts such as the one shown in Figure 10.10.

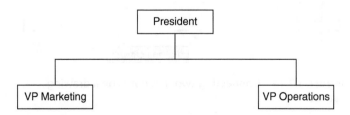

Figure 10.10 A simple organisational chart.

> **tip**
>
> You can also use Word's built-in tools to construct organisational charts. These may be accessed in Word 2003 via the *Drawing* toolbar or in Word 2007/2010 by clicking the tab in the Ribbon, then *Insert, SmartArt*.

Using the drawing canvas

When combining several drawing elements into a single entity, as is the case with an organisational chart, it is best to group them in a single drawing canvas (see Figure 10.13 on page 138).

If you are using Word 2003, a drawing canvas is automatically created when you go to insert a drawing element such as a text box, shape or line. When you go to add another drawing element, it will get placed on the selected drawing canvas.

> **In Word 2007 and 2010, you have to manually add a drawing canvas. To do so:**
>
> 1 Click the *Insert* tab of the Ribbon, then *Shapes*, then *New Drawing Canvas*.
>
> 2 Drag the mouse across the document to draw the canvas.

When you draw items on a drawing canvas they are automatically grouped together, so if you move the canvas, all the items on it will move together.

Connecting the boxes in an organisational chart

An organisational chart is simply a group of interconnected text boxes on the same drawing canvas. Drawing the text boxes is no problem – the tricky part is connecting them. The best way to do so is by using elbow connectors.

> You can sometimes use other connectors. But the elbow connector is the best one to use in most situations.

To insert an elbow connector in Word 2003:

1 Click the *AutoShapes* button on the *Drawing Toolbar*. (If your drawing toolbar is hidden, display it by clicking *View, Toolbars, Drawing*).

2 Click the *Connectors* item.

3 Click the icon for the elbow connector (see Figure 10.11).

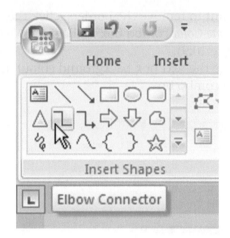

Figure 10.12 Inserting an elbow connector (Word 2007/2010).

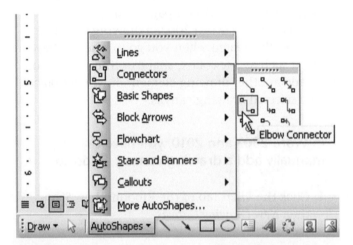

Figure 10.11 Inserting an elbow connector (Word 2003).

How elbow connectors work

With the elbow connector selected, whenever you move the mouse over a text box, four connection points will appear, one in the middle of each side of the text box. When you click on one of the connection points, one end of the connector gets 'fastened' to that point.

When you click on a connection point in the second text box, the other end of the elbow connector gets fastened to that connection point. The two text boxes are now joined together and even if you move them they will stay connected.

To delete a connection, click on it then press the *Delete* key.

To insert an elbow connector in Word 2007/2010:

Either:

1 Use the Drawing tab of the Ribbon (see Figure 10.12)

2 Or click Insert, Shape then choose the elbow connector from under the Lines section

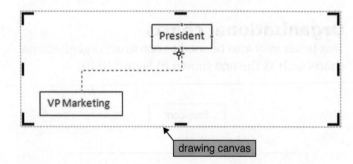

Figure 10.13 Connecting two text boxes on a drawing canvas.

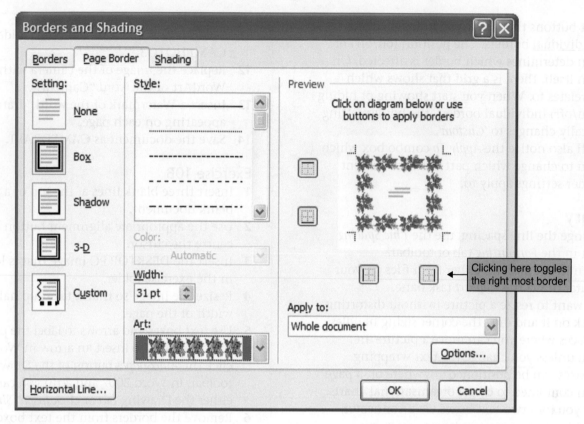

Figure 10.14 Adding a page border.

Page borders

In order to put borders around pages, you use the *Page Border* tab of the *Borders and Shading* windows, shown in Figure 10.14. This can be accessed as follows:

- In Word 2003, click *Format, Borders and Shading,* then switch to the *Page Borders* tab.
- In Word 2007/2010, switch to the *Page Layout* tab of the Ribbon, then click the *Page Borders* button.

This window can be a bit difficult to understand; I find that it helps to look at each of the three sections of the window separately:

Left section

In the leftmost section of the window, you choose a setting as follows:

- Click on *'Box'* if you want to have all four sides of the page with the same border.
- Click on *'None'* if you do not want to have a page border.

- Click *'Custom'* if you do not want all four sides of the page to have a border, or you want the sides to have different borders.

Middle section

In the middle section you can change the style, colour or width of the border. If you want to have a fancy border like the one seen inside Figure 10.14, you can choose one of the options from the *Art* combo box.

When you change the style, width or colour of a custom border, it has no visible effect. Instead, these changes are applied to any borders you add in the *Preview* section <u>from that point onwards</u>.

Right section

The rightmost section is dominated by the *Preview* of the page border. Around the preview are some very important buttons that allow you to toggle (turn on/off) <u>individual</u> borders. The position (on/off) of the button determines which border is affected. On the button itself, there is a grid that shows which border it relates to. When you start showing or hiding (border on/off) individual borders, the border setting automatically changes to '*Custom*'.

You will also notice the *Apply To* combo box which allows you to change which part of the document these border settings apply to.

Summary

- To change the line spacing, use the *Line Spacing* button in the *Formatting* tab or toolbar.
- You can insert pictures either from files on your computer or via the *Clip Art* task pane.
- If you want to resize a picture (without distorting it), click on it and drag the corner sizing handles.
- The places where you can move a picture are limited unless you change the text wrapping.
- Text boxes can be positioned anywhere on a page or even combined to create organisational charts.
- When you join two text boxes via a connector, they will remain connected even when you reposition them on the drawing canvas.

Review exercises

Exercise 10A

1 Retrieve the CAMERAS1 file from the exercise folder.
2 Change the line spacing of the <u>entire</u> document to 1.5.
3 Choose a picture of a camera from the clip art and insert it at the top of the document.
4 Resize the image so that it takes up about three-quarters of the width of the page.
5 Change the image to greyscale.
6 Save it in your class folder as CAMPHOTO1.
7 Try to drag the image to the centre of the first page. Then change the text wrapping to Square and try again.
8 Change the image to a watermark.
9 Save it in your class folder as CAMPHOTO2.
10 Put a blue 2¼ pt dotted border around each page.

11 Save the document in your class folder as CAMPHOTO3.
12 Replace the image of the camera with WordArt of the word "Cameras".
13 Insert a Watermark of the word "draft" appearing on each page.
14 Save the document as CAMPDRAFT.

Exercise 10B

1 Insert three blank lines at the top of a new blank document.
2 Use the appropriate alignment button to centre the cursor.
3 Insert the DESKTOP PC image that is located in the exercise folder.
4 Resize the image so that it takes up half the width of the page.
5 Use text boxes and arrows to label the parts of the computer. To insert an arrow in Word 2003, click the *AutoShapes* button of the Drawing toolbar. In Word 2007 and 2010 you can use either the Drawing tab or click *Insert, Shapes*.
6 Remove the borders from the text boxes.
7 Save the file in your class folder as COMPUTER.

Exercise 10C

On an A5-sized page, create a menu for a fictional restaurant. Be creative with the use of fonts, colours and clip art. Put a suitable border around the page.
    Save the file in your class folder as MENU.

Exercise 10D

Reproduce the organisational charts in Figure 10.15 and save them in your class folder as ORG1 and ORG2 respectively.

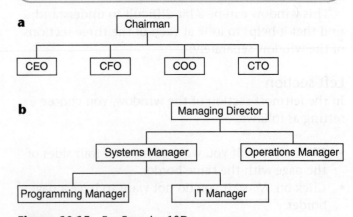

Figure 10.15 For Exercise 10D.

⑪ Working with tables

In this chapter, you will learn:

- how to create tables
- how to insert, delete and resize rows and columns

- how to merge and split cells
- how to change the cell alignment
- how to edit the table borders

Microsoft Word has a rich set of facilities for working with tables. You can create tables, merge cells, change the background and the borders and much more.

Creating a table

If you want to create a table:

- in Word 2003, click *Table, Insert, Table...*
- in Word 2007/2010, click the *Insert* tab of the Ribbon, then *Table, Insert Table...*

This will cause the *Insert Table* window to be displayed, which is shown in Figure 11.1.

Figure 11.1 The Insert Table window.

Changing the number of columns and rows

To change the number of columns and rows using the *Insert Table* window, you can:

- either click the arrows in order to increase or decrease the value
- or type the number directly into the appropriate box.

AutoFit behaviour

In the *Insert Table* window there are three *AutoFit* options:

- Fixed Column Width (default) – This makes all columns the same specific size. You can use the arrows to choose the width you want or type it in directly.
- AutoFit to Contents – This automatically adjusts the width of columns in the table based on the amount of text you type in each column.
- AutoFit to Window – This automatically resizes the table within the window of a web browser.

AutoFormat button

This button is only available in Word 2003. When you click it, it displays a list of table styles for you to choose from (see Figure 11.2 on page 142).

Changing the appearance of a table

To change the way a table looks in Word 2003:

1 Click inside the table.

2 Then click *Table, Table AutoFormat...* to bring up the *AutoFormat* window.

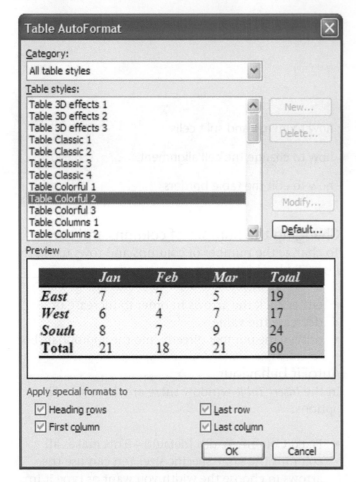

Figure 11.2 The Table AutoFormat window (Word 2003 only).

Word 2007 and 2010 have an entire tab of the Ribbon dedicated to changing the appearance of a table. The *Table Design* tab (see Figure 11.3) only appears when you click on a table.

Drawing tables

If you want to create a complex looking table, or add some lines to an existing table, you can draw the table yourself.

To start drawing a table:

- in Word 2003, click *Table, Draw Table*
- in Word 2007/2010, click the *Insert* tab on the Ribbon, then *Table, Draw Table*.

Then you drag the mouse to form the lines of the table.

To stop drawing a table, press the *Esc* key.

Changing the table layout

When you change the layout of a table, you change its <u>structure</u>. For instance, you can add rows, delete columns or merge cells.

In Word 2003, most of the table layout options are located in the *Table* menu (Figure 11.4).

Word 2007 and 2010 do not have *Table* menus. Instead they rely on the *Table Layout* tab shown in Figure 11.5.

Inserting rows and columns

To insert a row or column:

1 Click in a cell next to where you want to insert the row or column.

2 Choose the appropriate insertion option from the *Table* menu (Word 2003) or the *Table Layout* tab (Word 2007/2010).

Figure 11.3 The Table Design tab (Word 2007/2010).

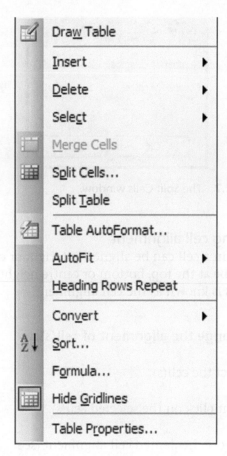

Figure 11.4 The *Table* menu (Word 2003).

Deleting Rows and Columns

To delete a row or column:

1 Click in the row or column to be deleted.

2 Choose the appropriate deletion option from the *Table* menu (Word 2003) or the Table Layout tab (Word 2007/2010).

Deleting tables

To delete an entire table:

1 Click inside the table.

2 Choose the *Delete Table* option from the *Table* menu (Word 2003) or the Table Layout tab (Word 2010).

Resizing rows and columns
If you want to resize a row or column, just drag its bottom, or right border, respectively.

Merging cells
When you merge cells you join two or more cells to form a single, larger cell.

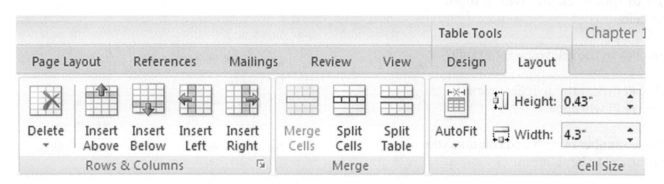

Figure 11.5 The Table Layout tab (Word 2007/2010).

To merge cells in a table:

1 Select the cells you want to merge.

2 Right-click on the selected cells and click *Merge Cells* (see Figure 11.6).

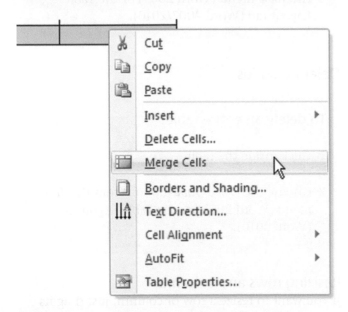

Figure 11.6 The context menu that appears when you right-click on selected cells. The *Merge Cells* item is selected.

Splitting cells

In order to split a cell into two or more smaller cells

1 Right-click in the cell you want to split.

2 Click *Split Cells...* the *Split Cells* window (Figure 11.7) will appear.

3 Type the number of rows and columns you want the cell to be split into.

4 Click *OK*.

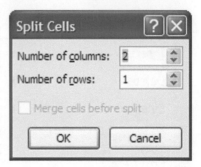

Figure 11.7 The Split Cells window.

Changing cell alignment

The text in a cell can be aligned left, right or centred, and can be at the top, bottom or centre height of the cell. This is known as the cell alignment.

To change the alignment of cell(s):

1 Select the cell(s).

2 Right-click on the selected cell(s).

3 Choose the desired cell alignment (see Figure 11.8).

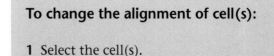

Figure 11.8 Changing the cell alignment.

Changing the alignment of the table itself

> **In order to align the table itself, as opposed to its <u>contents</u>:**
>
> 1 Position the mouse pointer in the top left corner of the table.
>
> 2 Click the *four-headed arrow* that appears.
>
> 3 Click an *alignment button* (the same ones you normally use to align text).

Modifying table borders

Whether you want to modify the borders of certain cells in the table, or the entire table itself, you can use either the *Border* buttons or the *Borders and Shading* window. Just be sure to select the cells or table first.

Using the Border button

The border button is a special sort of combo box that allows you to turn on/off individual borders.

If you are using Word 2003, the border button is on the *Formatting* toolbar. In Word 2007/2010, you can find it on either the *Table Design* tab or the *Home* tab of the Ribbon.

When you click the *arrow* of the combo box, you will see a list of the borders for the selected cell(s) or table. Each of these acts like a switch, with coloured backgrounds indicating which ones are turned on. Figure 11.9 shows how you would remove the left border in Word 2003.

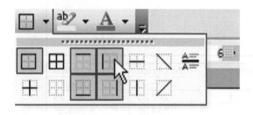

Figure 11.9 Removing the left border in Word 2003.

Using the Borders and Shading window

You can also use the *Borders* tab of the *Borders and Shading* window (see Figure 11.9) which works just like the *Page Border* tab. To access it, right-click on the table then click *Borders and Shading*.

> Be sure to change the *Apply To* option to indicate whether the changes are to be made to individual cells or the entire table.
>
> If you want to change the background colour of the table, you can switch to the *Shading* tab and change the *Fill Color*.

Summary

- The *AutoFormat* window (in Word 2003) and the *Table Design* tab (in Word 2007/2010) can be used to change the style of the table.
- If you want to insert/delete rows, columns or the table itself you can use the *Table* menu in Word 2003 or the *Table Layout* tab in Word 2007/2010.
- You can use the *Border* button or the *Borders and Shading* window to change table borders.

Review exercises

Exercise 11A

Recreate the following table then make the specified changes.

Country	2009	2010
Barbados	20,000	23,000
Guyana	38,000	36,000
Trinidad and Tobago	50,000	45,000

1 Above the row for Trinidad and Tobago, insert the following data:

Jamaica   100,000   104,000

2 After the column for Country, insert a column for the year 2008 and put some random values for each country.

3 Remove all borders from the table except the outside border around the table itself.

4 Right align all the numerical figures, except for the years.

5 Put all the headings in bold.

6 Resize the columns so that they are not any wider than necessary.

7 Use one of Word's built-in table formats to change the appearance of the table.

8 Save the document as TABLE1 in your class folder.

9 Reformat the table as a plain table.

10 Delete the row for Guyana.

11 Insert a row to the top of the table and type the word 'Year' at the second cell.

12 Merge last three cells of the top row, then centre the word 'Year' across the resulting cell.

13 Save the document as TABLE2 in your class folder.

Exercise 11B
Recreate the table in Figure 11.10 and save it as TABLE3 in your class folder.

Exercise 11C
Recreate the table in Figure 11.11 and save it as TABLE4 in your class folder.

Region	Zone	Men		Women	
		2009	**2010**	**2009**	**2010**
St. Lucy	LA1	1,000	1,020	1,050	1,051
	LA2	1,531	1,600	1,700	1,702
St. John	JO1	999	1,013	1,024	1,065
	JO2	833	900	902	918

Figure 11.10 For Exercise 11B.

Figure 11.11 For Exercise 11C.

12 Laying out documents

Vertically centring text

Before we look at the more complex ways to lay out a document, let us first look at how you centre text vertically on a page. This comes in handy when you are typing poems. In order to do so, you use the *Page Setup* window, which you can access by:

- In Word 2003, clicking *File*, then *Page Setup*
- In Word 2007/2010, clicking the *Page Layout* tab, then clicking the *More Options* button to the bottom of the *Page Setup* section.

In the *Page Setup window*, click the *Layout* tab then change the *Vertical Alignment* option from *Top* to *Centre*.

Why you need tabs

In electronic document preparation and management (EDPM), being able to precisely lay out a document is crucial. Trying to do so using spaces (by pressing the space bar) is an exercise in frustration. Look at the text in Figure 12.1. Spaces have been used to separate the page numbers from the topics.

Topic	Page
Introduction	1
Why you need programmers	1
Constants and variables	2
Reading input from the user	3
Outputting information for the user	4
Functions and procedures	5

Figure 12.1 A table of contents laid out using spaces.

You do not have to look at the example too long to see what is wrong. The page numbers are jagged – as is

usually the case when you try laying out a document using spaces – which gives this table of contents an unprofessional look.

Figure 12.2 shows the same table of contents but using tabs. Note the difference.

Topic	Page
Introduction	1
Why you need programmers	1
Constants and variables	2
Reading input from the user	3
Outputting information for the user	4
Functions and procedures	5

Figure 12.2 A table of contents laid out using tabs.

How tabs work

Usually, when you press the *Tab* key the cursor advances to the next half-inch point on the ruler. In Figure 12.3, the cursor is already past the half-inch marker, so when the *Tab* key is pressed, it will move to the one-inch marker.

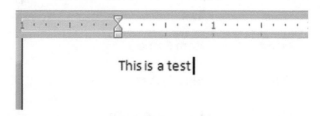

This is a test

Figure 12.3 How tabs work.

But suppose you wanted finer control over the positioning of the text. For example, what if you wanted to put page numbers at the 3¼-inch marker? You might be tempted to tab to the 3-inch marker then use spaces for fine tuning. This is a not a good idea because you are back to laying out text with spaces and the associated disadvantages.

The preferred method is to set a tab stop.

Tab stops

Tab stops allow you to control where the cursor goes when you press the *Tab* key. If, as in Figure 12.4, you click at the 3¼-inch marker on the ruler, you will set a tab stop at that position. If you were then to press the *Tab* key, the cursor would jump straight to the 3¼-inch position where the tab stop was set.

Using the ruler to set tab stops

To the left of the ruler is a button that determines the type of tab stop that will be set the next time you click on the ruler. The default type is the <u>left tab</u>, but you can change this by clicking on the button.

If a region is selected when you are setting tab stops, the tab stops will only apply to that region. Otherwise, they will apply to all the text you type below that point in the document.

tip

You can drag a tab stop to a new position on the ruler. But you have to be careful that you do not inadvertently create a new one instead.

Removing a tab stop using the ruler

You can remove a tab stop by simply dragging it off of the ruler.

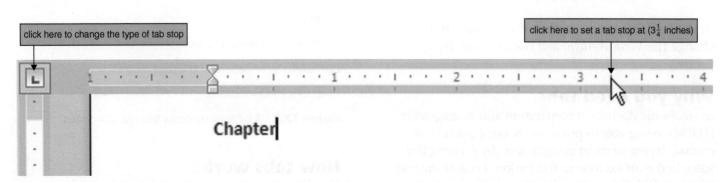

click here to change the type of tab stop

click here to set a tab stop at ($3\frac{1}{4}$ inches)

Chapter

Figure 12.4 Using the ruler to set a tab stop.

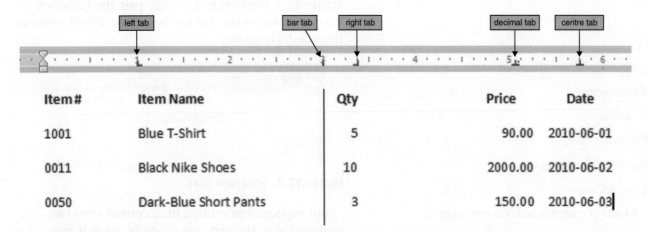

left tab   bar tab   right tab   decimal tab   centre tab

Item#	Item Name	Qty	Price	Date
1001	Blue T-Shirt	5	90.00	2010-06-01
0011	Black Nike Shoes	10	2000.00	2010-06-02
0050	Dark-Blue Short Pants	3	150.00	2010-06-03

Figure 12.5 Types of tab stops.

Types of tab stops

Earlier, I said that there were different types of tab stops. Figure 12.5 shows the available types. Each type has a different icon so you can identify it on the ruler.

Notice the position of each tab stop in relation to the text typed under it. For example, when you go to a right tab and start typing, the text is shifted around so that the tab stop is always on its right.

With decimal tabs (which look like centre tabs with decimal points to the right) the numbers are aligned so that the decimal point is placed in line with the tab stop. This comes in handy when you are lining up lists of numbers.

Bar tabs cause a bar | to be placed on each line, forming a vertical line.

Using the Tabs window to set tab stops

If you double-click on the ruler, the Tabs window appears (see Figure 12.6). This window gives you even more control over the tab stops.

If the place where you double-click does not already have a tab stop, one is created there before the *Tabs* window is opened.

To add tabs using this window:

1 Type the required position in the *Tab stop position* box.

2 Choose the type of tab.

3 Click the *Set* button.

To clear all the tabs, click the *Clear All* button.

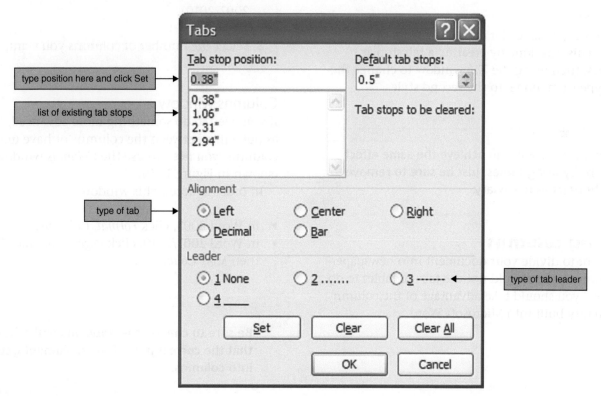

Figure 12.6 The Tabs window.

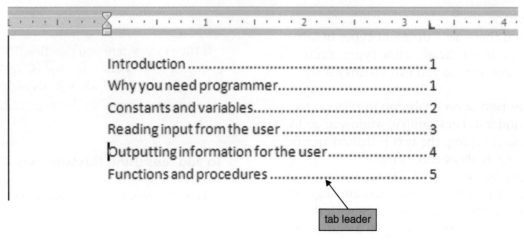

Figure 12.7 Using tab leaders.

tab leader

If you only want to erase a particular tab:

1 Select the entry for that tab.

2 Click *Clear*.

Tab leaders

In Figure 12.7, a tab leader appears in front of each number. This was done by creating a tab stop at 3.5 inches, then using the *Tab* window to change the *Leader* type from 'none' to the second style.

In many cases you can achieve the same effect as tabs by using tables. Just be sure to remove the borders as necessary.

Creating columns

If you want to divide your document into newspaper-type columns, you should not use tabs or tables to do so. Instead you should take advantage of the column functionality built into Microsoft Word.

Figure 12.8 Columns button.

The easiest way to create columns is to:

1 Select the text.

2 Click the columns button (see Figure 12.8) from the *Standard* toolbar (in Word 2003) or the *Page Layout* tab of the Ribbon (in Word 2007/2010).

3 Select the number of columns you want.

Columns window

If you need to do something more advanced, such as put a line between the columns or have unequal columns, you need to use the *Columns* window (shown in Figure 12.9).

In order to access this window:

- in Word 2003, click *Format*, *Columns...*
- in Word 2007/2010, click *Page Layout* tab, *Columns*, then *More Columns...*

Be sure to change the *Apply To* combo box so that the correct part of the document gets put into columns.

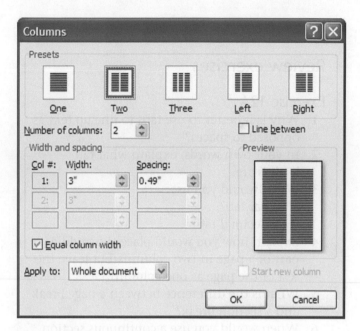

Figure 12.9 The Columns window.

Manually inserting breaks

You can use breaks to divide a document into sections or to force text on to a new page or column.

To insert a break in your document:

- in Word 2003, click *Insert, Break…*, then select the type of break
- in Word 2007/2010, switch to the *Page Layout* tab of the Ribbon, click *Breaks*, then select the type of break.

Page breaks

A page break tells Microsoft Word where to end one page and begin a new one. Word automatically inserts page breaks for you when you type too much text to fit on one page. These types of page breaks are called 'soft breaks'.

However, there are times when you may want to <u>force</u> text to be on a new page, such as when you reach a new chapter in a book. To do so, rather than pressing the *Enter* key multiple times, it is better to insert a manual (or hard) page break.

You can manually insert a page break by pressing *Ctrl + Enter*.

Section breaks

Section breaks allow you to divide a document into different sections. Why would you want to do this? When a document is divided into sections, you can make changes to the layout of one section without affecting the others.

For instance, you may want the last page of the document to be landscape but want the rest to be in portrait orientation. Here you would insert a *next page section break* as shown in Figure 12.10.

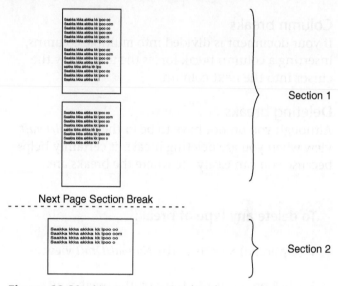

Figure 12.10 Next page section break.

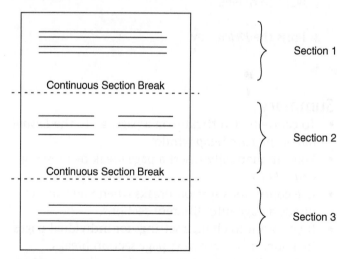

Figure 12.11 Dividing a page with continuous section breaks.

Or you may want <u>part</u> of a page to be in two columns. Here, *continuous section breaks* would be used to separate that part from the rest of the page, as in Figure 12.11. Unlike the other types of section breaks, continuous breaks allow you to start a new section in the middle of a page without forcing the text on to the next page.

If you select part of a page and change it to two columns, Word automatically inserts continuous section breaks around it for you.

Column breaks
If your document is divided into multiple columns, inserting a column break forces the text below the cursor into the next column.

Deleting breaks
Although you do not have to be in the *Normal/Draft* view when you are deleting breaks, it certainly helps because you can easily see where the breaks are.

To delete any type of break:

1 (Optional) Switch to the *Normal/Draft* view.

2 Click on, or just in front of, the break you want to delete.

3 Press the *Delete* key.

Summary
- To centre text vertically on a page, go to the *Layout tab* of the *Page Setup* window.
- You can manually insert a page break by pressing *Ctrl + Enter*.
- Use continuous section breaks when you want to divide a page into different sections.
- If you want to change settings for individual pages in a document, use next page section breaks.
- Column breaks force the text that follows to go into the next column.
- When removing breaks it is best to switch to the *Normal/Draft* view so you can see them.

Review exercises

Exercise 12A
1 Why is it better to use tabs to line up text as opposed to spaces?
2 In your own words, explain what tab leaders are.
3 When would you use:
   a a bar tab?
   b a decimal tab?
4 Explain how you would place the middle part of a page in two columns(but leave the rest of the page as one column).
5 What is the difference between a page break and a section break?
6 When would you use a continuous section break as opposed to a next page section break?
7 When would you insert a column break?
8 Which view is best for removing breaks?
9 Type a short paragraph about yourself in a new document then centre it on the page. Close the document without saving it.

Exercise 12B
Recreate Figure 12.5. Save it as TABS1 in your class folder. Then recreate it using a table and save the result as TABTABLE.

Exercise 12C
1 In a new document:
   a Use the Tab window to insert tab breaks at 1.1", 2.3" and 3.45".
   b Change the last tab break to 3.75".
   c Remove the second tab break.
2 Close the document without saving changes.
3 Recreate the table of contents in Figure 12.7. Save it as TABS2 in your class folder.

Exercise 12D
Open the CAMERAS1 file from the class folder, then:
1 Insert manual page breaks before the Ultra-Zoom section.

2 Insert a next page section break before the Summary section.

3 Change the orientation of the last page to Landscape.

4 Save the file in your class folder as CAMERAS2.

5 Switch to the Normal/Draft view. Notice that you can see the breaks you inserted in this view.

6 Remove the breaks that you inserted.

7 Switch back to the Page Layout view.

8 Insert continuous section breaks before the Ultra-Compact and Summary sections.

9 Click in one of the Point-and-Shoot paragraphs.

10 Switch the section to two columns.

11 Save the file in your class folder as CAMERAS3.

Exercise 12E

Open the BARGAINS2 file from the exercise folder then make the following changes:

1 Place the entire document apart from the main titles, chart and key in two columns.

2 Insert column breaks before the headings 'What are the benefits?' and 'About Us'.

3 Switch to the Normal/Draft view. Notice that continuous section breaks have automatically been inserted for you.

4 Switch back to the Page Layout view.

5 Fully justify the text in the columns.

6 Save the file in your class folder as BARGAINS3.

13 Headers, footers and page numbering

In this chapter, you will learn:

- about headers and footers
- how to insert different headers and footers on selected pages
- how to use Word's page numbering feature

Headers and footers

When you look at a publication such as a book, magazine or even a report, you will probably see some information like its title or the date it was published at the top of each page. That is what is known as a **header** because it is at the head – or top – of the page. Naturally, if the information is at the bottom of the page, it is called a **footer** (see Figure 13.1).

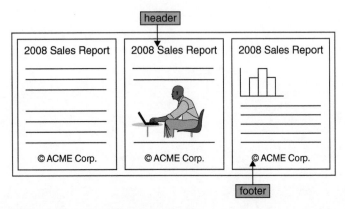

Figure 13.1 Headers and footers.

The Header and Footer view

If you want to create or edit headers and footers you have to switch to the *Header and Footer* view. You can do so by:

- double-clicking on an existing header/footer
- or clicking *View, Header and Footer* (Word 2003)
- or clicking the *Insert* tab, *Header*, then *Edit Header* (Word 2007/2010).

The Header and Footer toolbar (Word 2003)

In Word 2003, when you view a header or footer, the *Header and Footer* toolbar, shown in Figure 13.2, will be automatically displayed.

The Header Design tab (Word 2007/2010)

When you view a header in Word 2007 or 2010, the Ribbon will automatically switch to the *Header Design* tab (see Figure 13.3).

Figure 13.2 The Header and Footer toolbar.

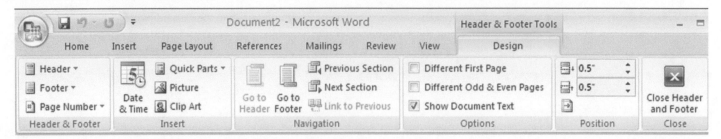

Figure 13.3 The Header Design tab of the Ribbon.

Switching from the header to the footer

By default, when you switch to the *Header and Footer* view, you will be viewing the header. In order to view the footer:

- either scroll down to the bottom of the page (simple but works)
- or click the *Go to Footer* button. In Word 2003 it says '*Switch between Header and Footer*'.

Closing the Header and Footer view

To close the *Header and Footer* view:

- either double-click anywhere outside the header or footer box
- or click the *Close* button in the *Header and Footer* toolbar or the *Header Design* tab.

Inserting a header or footer

In order to insert a header or footer:

1 Switch to the *Header and Footer view*.

2 Type the header or footer in the designated area (see Figures 13.4 and 13.5).

3 Close the *Header and Footer* view.

The header or footer will appear on all pages unless you specify otherwise.

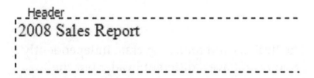

Figure 13.4 Inserting a header in Word 2003.

Formatting the header or footer

A header or footer is just ordinary text. This means that you can do all the usual formatting e.g., making it bold, changing its alignment or changing the font.

Figure 13.5 Inserting a header in Word 2007/2010.

Advanced options

Having a different first page

Sometimes you do not want a header or footer on the first page. For example, you do not normally have them on a cover page. In other cases, you may want to use a different header or footer on the first page. In both of these cases you would select the *Different First Page* option.

To have a header/footer appear on every page except the first:

1 Insert the *header* or *footer* as normal.

2 Turn <u>on</u> the *Different First Page* option as described below.

To enable the *Different First Page* option in Word 2003:

1 Click the *Page Setup* button (see Figure 13.6, on page 156) on the *Header and Footer* toolbar.

2 Switch to the *Layout* tab of the window that appears.

3 Put a check mark next to the *Different First Page* option (see Figure 13.7, on page 156).

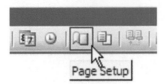

Figure 13.6 The *Page Setup* button.

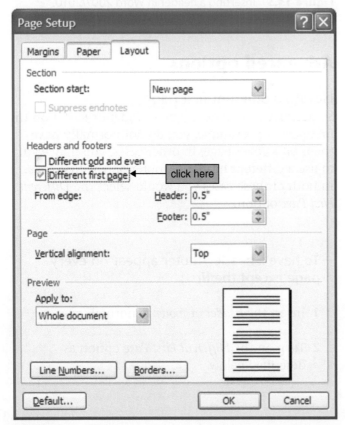

Figure 13.7 Enabling the *Different First Page* option (Word 2003).

Figure 13.8 Enabling the different First Page (Word 2007/2010).

The header and footer boxes will now say *'First Page Header'* and *'First Page Footer'* to show you that there is a different first page.

Having a different header on part of the document

To have a different header (or footer) on part of your document:

1 Put that part of the document in a separate section (if it is not already) using section breaks.

2 Click in that section and switch to the *Header and Footer* view.

3 Turn off the *'Link to Previous'* option 🔲 in the *Header and Footer* toolbar (Word 2003) or the *Header Design* tab (Word 2007/2010).

To enable the *Different First Page* option in Word 2007/2010:

1 Switch to the *Header Design* tab.

2 Put a check mark in the *Different First Page* box which is located in the *Options* section (see Figure 13.8).

The headers and footers operate independently so you can have a different header but the same footer as the rest of the document.

Page numbering

You can get Microsoft Word to automatically number your pages for you. The way it does this is by inserting a special kind of header (or footer).

To number pages in Word 2003:

1 Click *Insert, Page Numbers*.

2 Choose the position of the page numbers (either Top of page or Bottom of page).

3 Choose the alignment of the (*Left, Right, Centre* etc.)

4 (Optional) If you do not want to show the page number on the first page, uncheck the 'Show number on first page' box.

5 Click the *OK* button.

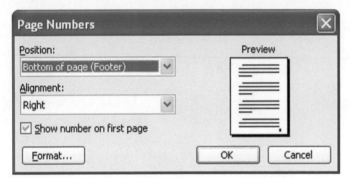

Figure 13.9 Inserting page numbers in Word 2003.

Word 2007/2010

Inserting page numbering in the newer versions of Word is completely different.

To number pages in Word 2007/2010:

1 Switch to the *Insert* tab of the Ribbon.

2 Click the *Page Number* button.

3 Select whether you want the numbers to go to the Top of page or bottom of page.

4 From the resulting submenu, choose the page numbering style you want to use. For example, if you wanted to insert the page numbers in the centre, you would choose the 'Plain Number 2' style.

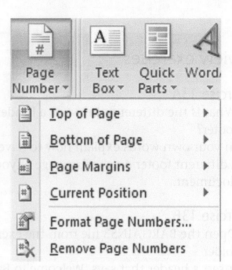

Figure 13.10 Inserting page numbers in Word 2007/2010.

 tip

As you can see from Figure 13.10, there are also options to remove the page numbers and format them.

Summary

- Double-clicking an existing header or footer will put you in the header or footer view respectively.
- To exit the header/footer view, double-click anywhere else in the document.
- If you want to have a different header or footer on the first page, you have to tick the *Different First Page* option.
- If you want part of the document to have its own header or footer, surround it with section breaks to place it in its own section, and turn off the '*links to previous*' option.
- Page numbers are special types of headers and footers.

Review exercises

Exercise 13A

1 What is the difference between a header and a footer?
2 In your own words explain how to have a different footer on the first page of your document.

Exercise 13B

1 Open the BARGAINS3 file from the exercise folder.
2 Insert a header that says 'Welcome to Bargain Shopper™' in the centre of each page. Put it in Verdana font, make it bold and underline it.
3 Insert page numbers at the bottom-centre of each page.
4 Save the file in your class folder as BARGAINS4.

Exercise 13C

1 Open the CAMERAS3 file from the exercise folder.
2 Insert page numbers at the bottom centre of each page.
3 Insert a header that says 'Choosing the Right Camera for You' on the top left of each page. Put it in a dark green 13pt Century Gothic font. Put it in italics as well.
4 Insert a page break at the top of the document.
5 Type the words 'Digital Camera' on the first line of the first page, in a size 72 font.
6 Insert the image stored in the SLR file underneath the words 'Digital Camera' and resize it so it takes up a quarter of the page.
7 On the first page only, change the header to 'All About Digital Cameras' and remove the page numbers.
8 Save the file in your class folder as CAMERAS4.

14 Using the mail merge feature

Why use mail merge?

Suppose you wanted to mail out 100 invitations to a wedding. The invitations would be almost identical. Each would have information such as:

- the name of the couple being married
- the date, time and location of the wedding.

In fact, the only difference between the invitations would be the name of the person(s) being invited. To do personalised letters like this, you can use the mail merge feature found in Microsoft Word. It combines a <u>data file</u> with a **main document** and produces personalised **form letters** as illustrated in Figure 14.1.

The data file

The data file (sometimes called a <u>recipient list</u>) is a database containing the personalised data, e.g., the name and address for each recipient. In Figure 14.1 the data source has two fields: FirstName and LastName.

The main document

The main document is a special Word document that acts as a template from which the personalised letters are generated. It contains placeholders for the fields in the data file to indicate where the personalised data is to be inserted. The placeholders are put in special angled brackets to distinguish them from the normal text that is common to each letter.

The form letters

When you perform the mail merge shown in Figure 14.1, you will get a document containing three letters – one for each recipient. None of them will actually contain the words '«FirstName»' or '«LastName»'. Instead the first letter will say 'Dear Frank Smith', the second will say 'Dear Barry Jacks', and so on.

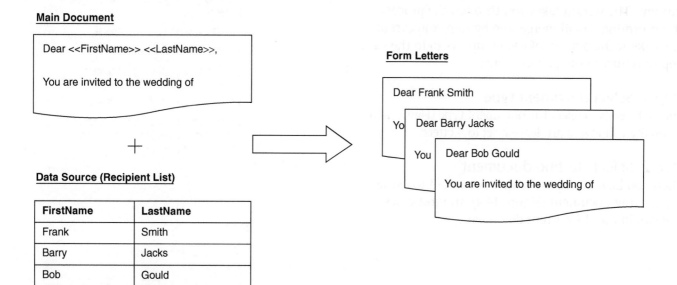

Main Document

> Dear <<FirstName>> <<LastName>>,
>
> You are invited to the wedding of

+

Data Source (Recipient List)

FirstName	LastName
Frank	Smith
Barry	Jacks
Bob	Gould

Form Letters

> Dear Frank Smith
>
> Dear Barry Jacks
>
> Dear Bob Gould
>
> You are invited to the wedding of

Figure 14.1 How the mail merge feature works.

Using the Mail Merge wizard

The easiest way to perform a mail merge in Microsoft Word is to use the *Mail Merge* wizard. To start this wizard:

- in Word 2003, click *Tools, Letters and Mailings, Mail Merge...*
- in Word 2007/2010, click on the *Mailings* tab in the Ribbon, *Start Mail Merge*, then *Step By Step Mail Merge Wizard...* (see Figure 14.2).

Figure 14.2 Starting the *Mail Merge* wizard in Word 2007/2010.

The task pane containing the *Mail Merge* wizard (see Figure 14.3) will appear to the right of the window. The wizard takes you through the process of performing a mail merge step by step. You can use the links at the bottom of the wizard to go to the next step or return to the previous one.

Step 1 Select document type
The first step is to select the document type (Figure 14.3). Normally you would just leave it set to 'Letters'.

Step 2 Select starting document
Then you have to choose which document to use as the starting document (Figure 14.4). In most cases you would use the current document.

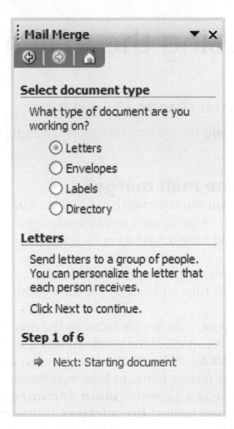

Figure 14.3 Selecting the document type in the *Mail Merge* wizard task pane.

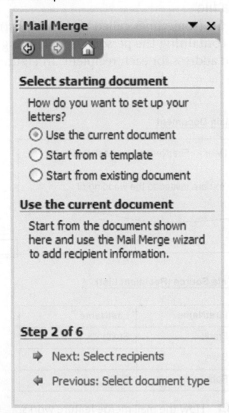

Figure 14.4 Select starting document in the *Mail Merge* wizard.

Step 3 Select recipients

At this point you choose the data source, which normally contains information about the intended recipients of the letters. You would:

- either use an existing list
- or type a new list from scratch.

Using an existing list

You would use this option if you want to use information from a list that you created during a previous mail merge.

When the '*Use an existing list*' option is selected, the *Browse* button is displayed (see Figure 14.5). Click on it to bring up an *Open* window so you can select the list you want to use.

> By default the *My Data Sources* folder is shown in the *Open* window so you may need to switch to the one containing your data source.

Figure 14.5 Using an existing list in the *Mail Merge* wizard.

Typing a new list

If you have not already created a data source, or want to use information not in any existing data source, you will have to type a new one from scratch.

Switch to the '*Type a new list*' option and then click the *Create...* button (see Figure 14.6).

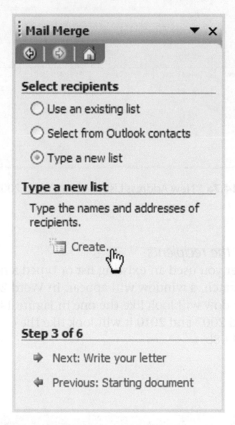

Figure 14.6 Typing a new list.

Depending on whether you are using Word 2003 or 2007/2010, a window will appear that looks like the one in Figure 14.7a (Word 2003) or Figure 14.7b (Word 2007/2010).

Although the two windows look different, they work roughly the same way:

- Click *Customize* if you want to add, remove or rename the fields.
- Type the information for a recipient in the spaces provided.
- Click *New Entry* when you want to add another recipient.
- Click *Delete Entry* to delete the current recipient.
- Click *Close* or *OK* when you are done.

When you finish entering the data, you will be asked where to save it and what to call it.

Figure 14.7a New Address List window (Word 2003).

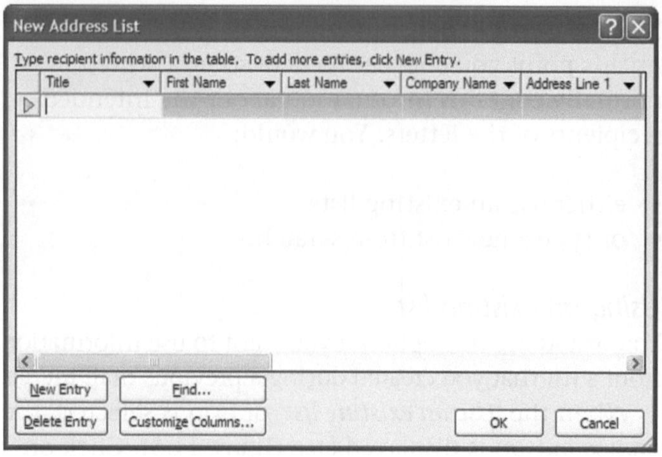

Figure 14.7b New Address List window (Word 2007/2010).

Editing the recipients

Whether you used an existing list or typed a new one from scratch, a window will appear. In Word 2003, this window will look like the one in Figure 14.8a. In Word 2007 and 2010 it will look like the one in Figure 14.8b.

It shows you the contents of the data source and allows you to select which recipients you actually want to send the letter to. By default all the recipients in the list are selected so you would normally click *OK*. But if you don't want to send a letter to a particular recipient, just remove the tick from next to his/her name.

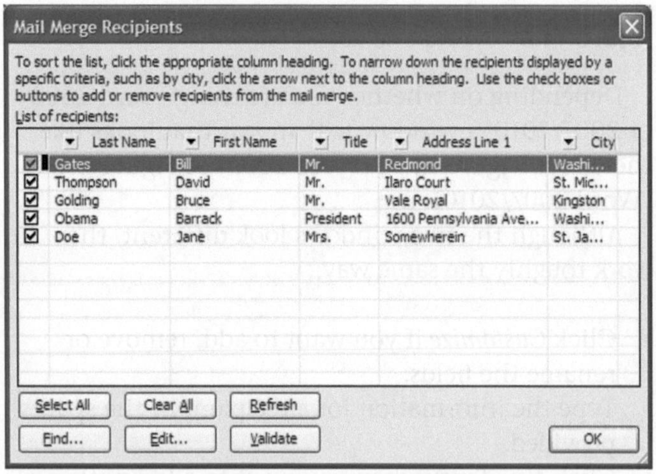

Figure 14.8a *Mail Merge* Recipients (Word 2003).

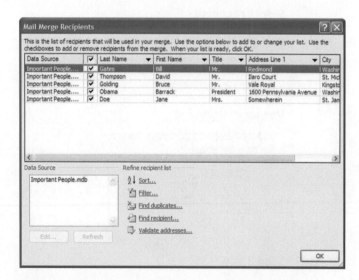

Figure 14.8b *Mail Merge* Recipients (Word 2007/2010).

Step 4 Write your letter

The next and most important step of the *Mail Merge* wizard is to write the actual letter (the main document). For the parts that are to appear in every letter, you type the same way that you would type a normal Word document. But be sure to insert merge fields (using the special angled brackets) where you want the recipients information to go.

To insert a merge field:

1 Click the *More Items* link in the *Mail Merge* wizard (see Figure 14.9).

2 From the *Insert Merge Field* window, select the name of the field you want to insert (see Figure 14.10).

3 Click the *Insert* button.

4 Close the window when you are done.

You can insert more than one field at a time but they have to be side by side.
If you manually type the name of the field in angled brackets it will not work.

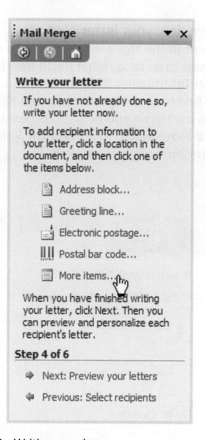

Figure 14.9 Writing your letter.

Figure 14.10 Inserting a merge field.

Step 5 Preview your letter

At this point in the *Mail Merge* wizard, you can preview your letter to see what it will look like with a recipients information filled in. Here you would normally fine-tune the spacing between fields.

You can use the >> and << buttons near the top of the *Mail Merge* wizard to preview the letter for the next or previous recipient respectively.

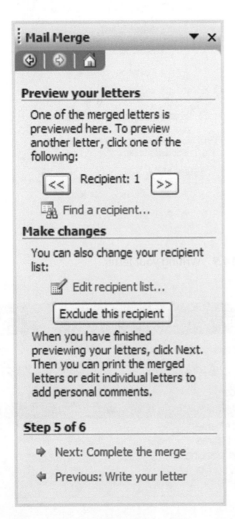

Figure 14.11 Preview your letters.

Step 6 (final step) Complete the merge

If you want to print the letters straight away you would click *Print*. But normally, you would:

1 Click the *Edit individual letters...* option from the *Mail Merge* wizard (see Figure 14.12).

2 Click OK when the *Merge* to *New Document* window (Figure 14.13) appears.

Figure 14.12 Completing the merge.

Figure 14.13 Merge to New Document window.

The computer will then generate the (personalised) form letters and insert them into a new Word document.

Summary
- You can use the mail merge feature to generate personalised letters for a mailing list.
- Mail merging combines a main document with a recipient list to produce personalised form letters.
- The main document is a sort of template which contains the content that will appear in every letter as well as merge fields indicating where the personalised data is to be inserted.
- The data source or recipient list contains fields for the recipients personalised data such as the name and the address.

Review exercises

Exercise 14A
1 In your own words, explain the mail merge process, making sure you use the following terms:
   a main document
   b data source
   c fields
   d form letters
2 Suppose your company wants to send personalised letters to its clients. Should your company name, address and telephone number be fields in the data source? Justify your answer.

Exercise 14B
Using the following main document (which you will save as FRIEND CONTRACT), generate personalised letters to eight of your friends. Be sure to sign your name at the bottom. Save the form letters as CONTRACT LETTERS and the data source as MY FRIENDS.

«FirstName» «LastName»
«Address»
«Parish»

Dear «FirstName»,

After careful consideration I have decided to renew your friend contract for yet another year. As my friend, you will be entitled to:

- a shoulder to lean on
- free advice (even when you do not want it)
- lots of good times

Please do not abuse this privilege.

Yours sincerely,

Exercise 14C
Generate personalised letters to people in your MY FRIENDS data source, inviting them to an event you are hosting.
   Save the main document as EVENTMAIN and the resulting form letters as EVENTLET.

Exercise 14D
Perform a mail merge using the main document and data source Figure 14.14, page 166. Save the result as WEB3LET.

Main document for Exercise 14D (save as SEMINAR)

CaribWeb Corporation
123 Roebuck Street
St. Michael
http://www.caribwebcorp.
com

«Title» «FirstName» «LastName»
«JobTitle»
«Company»

Dear «Title» «LastName»

You are no doubt familiar with the tremendous impact that the Internet has had in the first decade of the 21st century. With the introduction of Web 2.0, Internet browsing became a more tolerable, even pleasant experience. Users can reasonably expect interfaces that provide the majority of the functionality found in traditional desktop applications.

But now it is time for the Web to stop playing catch up. Now is the time for the web to *surpass* desktop applications. See how you can bring «Company» into Web 3.0 territory. Register now for our seminar entitled 'Web 3.0 – Are We There Yet?' which will be streamed live via our website on Tuesday, February 1, 2011. Visit our website for further details.

Corey Webb

Technology Evangelist
CaribWeb Corporation.

Data source for Exercise 14D (save as EXECUTIVES)

Title	FirstName	LastName	JobTitle	Company
Mr.	Steve	Jones	CEO	Melon
Mrs.	Patty	Smith	Senior Partner	Smith and Associates
Miss.	Indra	Ryan	President and CEO	Drinks Co
Mr.	Bill	Brown	Chairman	Computer ware

Figure 14.14 For exercise 14D

15 Printing

In this chapter, you will learn:

- how to print normal documents
- how to see a preview of what the printed document will look like

- how to print envelopes
- how to print labels

Previewing the document

Before you print a document, you should look at a *Print Preview* to see what the document will look like when it is printed.

'Why can't I simply look at the Print layout?' you may be wondering. Well, the *Print Preview* shows you <u>exactly</u> what the printed document will look like, including things you may not see in the *Print Layout* such as:

- whether or not a table has any borders
- whether any parts of your document are being 'cut off' the page.

If you want to preview the printed document in:

- Word 2003: click *File, Print Preview*
- Word 2007: click the *Microsoft Office* button, then *Print*, then *Print Preview*
- Word 2010: click *File*, then *Print*

Previewing in Word 2010

Previewing in Word 2010 needs a special mention because Office 2010 introduces a new *Print* section in the *Backstage* view. This new section combines the print preview with basic print options. You can see how this looks in Figure 15.1 on page 168.

As you can see, in the middle panel of the window there are settings to adjust things like the number of copies, what pages to print, the page size and orientation and even the printer to be used. For even more options, you can click the *Printer Properties* link.

In the right-hand panel, you can see the print preview. You can use the arrows at the bottom to preview pages other than the current one.

Printing the document

When you are finished previewing a document, you click the *Print* button. In Word 2010 the document will print right away, but if you are using Word 2003 or 2007, the *Print* dialog box (Figure 15.2 on page 169) will be displayed instead. When you are ready to print, click on *OK*.

> **tip**
>
> You can quickly print documents in Word 2003 by clicking the icon of the printer in the Standard toolbar.

Changing the number of copies

In the *Print* dialog box you can change the number of copies to be printed. If you are using Word 2010, you would change the number of copies in the *Print* section of the *Backstage* view.

Printing the entire document

By default, when you click the *Print* button (either from the *Print* dialog or the *Print* section in the *Backstage* view), Word will print the entire document.

Printing selected pages

If you only want to print some of the pages in the document, you can type the page numbers in the *Pages* box. You can use ranges as well. For example, you can type '1–4, 7' which would tell the computer to print pages 1, 2, 3, 4 and 7.

Printing envelopes

To print names and addresses on envelopes, you have to open the *Envelopes and Labels* window (see Figure 15.3 on page 169).

Figure 15.1 The Print section in Word 2010.

To open this window:

- in Word 2003, click *Tools, Letters and Mailings, Envelopes and Labels*
- in Word 2007 and 2010, click the *Mailings Tab*, then click the *Envelopes* button.

Here is how you use this window to print on an envelope:

1 Click on the *Delivery Address* box and type in the person's address.

2 If you want to include a return address, click in the *Return Address* box and type the address.

3 If you want to change the envelope size or the font:

- click the *Options* button
- choose the *Envelope Options* tab in the window that appears
- make the desired changes
- click the *OK* button.

4 Click the *Print* button.

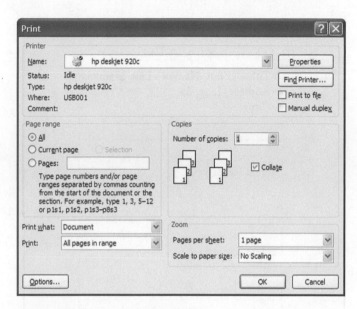

Figure 15.2 The Print dialog box.

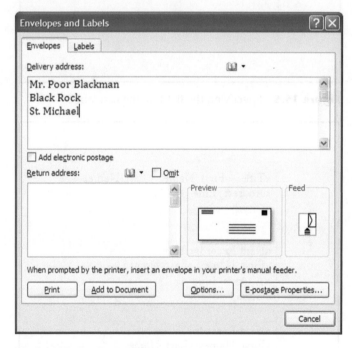

Figure 15.3 The Envelopes and Labels window.

Printing labels

The approach you use to print labels depends on whether you are typing them individually or printing them via the mail merge feature.

Printing labels individually

If you want to print a single label or repeat it for an entire page:

- In Word 2003, click *Tools, Letters and Mailings, Envelopes and Labels*.
- In Word 2007 and 2010, click the *Mailings* tab then click the *Labels* button.

This will cause the *Envelopes and Labels* window to be displayed with the *Labels* tab selected (see Figure 15.4).

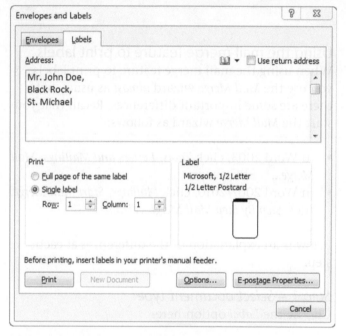

Figure 15.4 Printing individual labels.

In this window, you then:

- Type the text you want to appear on the label.
- Choose whether you want to print an entire page or a single label. If you choose the latter option, you have to indicate what row and column the label is in.
- Click the *Options …* button and change the vendor and product number to match the type of labels you are printing on (if necessary).
- Click *Print*.

Microsoft Word has the product numbers of the different types of labels that the most popular vendors sell. This information tells Word the size and positioning of the labels, as well as how many are on a page. If you have the wrong type selected, the text will not line up properly on the labels.

If the brand you are using is not listed, you can manually specify the settings or search online to find the closest match from among the list.

Using the mail merge feature to print labels

When using the mail merge feature to print labels, you use the *Mail Merge* wizard *almost* as usual, but there are some important differences. Recall that you start the *Mail Merge* wizard as follows:

- in Word 2003, click *Tools, Letters and Mailings, Mail Merge...*
- in Word 2007/2010, click *Mailings, Start Mail Merge,* then *Step By Step Mail Merge Wizard...*

Below is an explanation of the differences at each step.

Step 1 – Select document type
Choose the *Label* option here.

Step 2 – Select starting document
Click *Label Options...* and select the vendor and product number of your labels.

Step 3 – Select recipients
Use an existing list or type one yourself, just like you would do for any other mail merge.

Step 4 – Arrange your labels
This is the trickiest step, so pay careful attention!

In the space for the *first label*, specify the fields you want to appear on the labels (see Figure 15.5) by clicking *More Items...* This will act as a template for the other labels as long as you remember to follow the instruction below.

Click the *Update All Labels* button so that the fields are propagated to the other labels (see Figure 15.6).

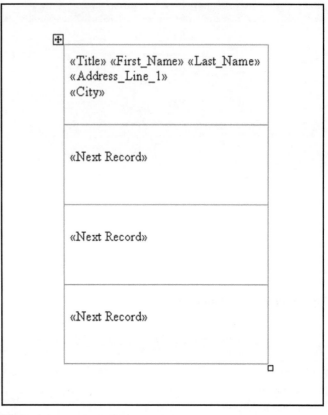

Figure 15.5 Specifying the fields in the first label.

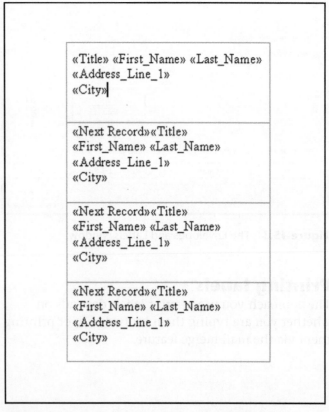

Figure 15.6 After the fields have been propagated.

tip

The <<Next Record>> field is a special field telling Word to put another record on the same page

Step 5 – Preview your labels

If you do not see multiple labels on a page in your preview, chances are you need to go back to the previous step and click the *Update All Labels* button.

Step 6 – Complete the merge

Click Print... to print your labels.

Summary

- In Word 2003 and 2007, you can use *Print Preview* to see what a document will look like when it is printed.
- In Word 2010, you can change the print settings and view a preview using the Print section in the *Backstage* view.

- If you want to print an individual envelope or label, you use the *Envelopes and Labels* window.
- You can also use the mail merge feature to print labels (but do not forget to click the *Update All Labels* button!).

Review exercises

Exercise 15

1 Open the WEB3LET file from the exercise folder.
2 Preview what the document will look like when it is printed. Be sure to preview all the pages, not just the first page.
3 Print two copies of the first three form letters.
4 Print an envelope and a label addressed to:

Mrs. Patty Hewes
Senior Partner
Hewes and Associates

5 Using the mail merge feature, print labels addressed to 10 of your classmates.

16 Microsoft Excel basics

In this chapter, you will learn:

- about the Microsoft Excel interface
- how to enter data in Excel, and change it later
- the difference between labels and values
- how to work with rows, columns, worksheets and workbooks

Introduction

Microsoft Excel is an example of a general-purpose software application known as a **spreadsheet**. Spreadsheet programs allow you to work with large amounts of numerical data, making it easy to manipulate the figures and to perform calculations on them. One really useful feature is that when you change a value, any figures that reference that value are automatically recalculated. Additional features include charts, Auto fill and sorting.

The Microsoft Excel interface

After working with Microsoft Word, the Excel interface (see Figure 16.1) might come as a bit of a shock. But once you understand how the various components are related, you will be up to speed in no time. And it does not hurt that the basic functionality is the same whether you are using Excel 2003, 2007 or 2010.

Worksheets

The majority of the Excel interface is taken up by what looks like a giant table known as a **worksheet**. An Excel document is known as a **workbook** and normally contains three worksheets. You can switch between worksheets using the *worksheet tabs*. In Figure 16.1, the current worksheet is Sheet1.

Active cell

The active cell in an Excel worksheet has a heavy border around it and its address is displayed in the *name box*. In Figure 16.1 the active cell is A1.

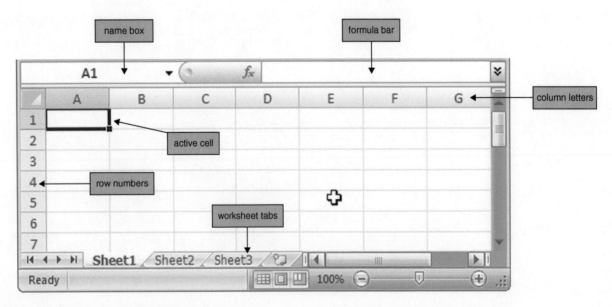

Figure 16.1 The Microsoft Excel interface.

Cell addresses

You will see a series of letters going across the top of the worksheet. These letters are used to refer to specific columns. The first column is column A, the second is column B, etc.

To the left of the spreadsheet are the row numbers.

A cell's address is given by its column letter and its row number. The column letter always comes first. So the second cell in the first row is B1 and the fourth cell in the third row is D3.

Formula bar

To the right of the *Name* box is the *formula bar*. Here you can enter a formula or change the data in the current cell.

Moving around a worksheet

You can use any of the keyboard shortcuts (e.g., the arrow keys, *Page Down*, *Home*) that you learned in Chapter 6 (see Table 6.1) to move around a spreadsheet. You can also:

- click on a cell to make it active
- press *Ctrl+G* to open the *Go To* box (Figure 16.2), then type the address of the destination cell.

Figure 16.2 Using the *Go To* window to go to cell Z36.

Entering data

To enter data in a cell, go to that cell, click in it, and type the data. In order to let Excel know when you are finished entering data in the cell, do any of the following:

- Press the *Enter* key (which will take you down to the next row).
- Press an arrow key.
- Press the *Tab* key (which will take you to the next column).
- Click on another cell.
- Click the *Enter* box on the formula bar.

If you are entering the data row by row, press the *Tab* key after you finish each cell. If you are entering the data column by column, press the *Enter* key after you finish each cell.

Automatic completion

Sometimes when you type in a cell, Excel will automatically complete the text for you.

In Figure 16.3, you can see that when you start typing 'Pencils', Excel thinks you are typing 'Pens' again and automatically completes the word for you. To accept an automatic completion, press the *Enter* key. If you do not want the completion, simply ignore it and continue typing.

	A
1	Item
2	Pens
3	Pens
4	

Figure 16.3 Automatic completion of text in Excel.

Modifying data

Replacing the contents of a cell

To replace the contents of a cell, click once on the cell then type the new data.

Making minor adjustments

You can make minor adjustments to a cell either by editing it in place or by using the formula bar.

To edit a cell in place:

1 Double-click on the cell or click on it and press the *F2* key. The cursor will start flashing in the cell indicating that it is being edited.

2 Make the necessary changes.

To edit a cell using the formula bar:

1 Click on the cell.

2 Click in the formula bar and make the necessary changes.

When you start editing a cell, a cross and a tick appear to the left of the formula bar (see Figure 16.4). To cancel the change, click the cross or press the *Esc* key. To accept the change, press the *Enter* key or click the tick.

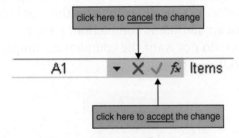

Figure 16.4 Editing a cell in Excel.

Values versus labels

Data in Excel can be placed into two broad categories – values and labels. <u>Values</u> are numbers that can be used in calculations. <u>Labels</u> are usually used to identify rows, columns or values. Labels are usually made up of letters but may contain numbers and symbols, for example '424-5662'.

In Figure 16.5, the labels are formatted in red to distinguish them from the values.

	A	B	C	D
1	Items	Jan	Feb	
2	Books	30	45	
3	Pencils	21	35	
4	Rulers	20	25	
5	Erasers	50	30	
6				

Figure 16.5 Values (in black) and labels (in red).

Labels are automatically aligned to the <u>left</u>. Values are automatically aligned to the <u>right</u>.

Sometimes you will want certain types of numbers to be formatted as labels, e.g., years. Here are some reasons why:

- so that you can have 0s in front – if you try to enter the ID '001' (without the quotes), for example, Excel will get rid of the zeros unless you format it as a label
- because you will not be using them for calculations
- so that Excel will recognise them as headings.

In order to illustrate the last point, consider Figure 16.6. Here, the years have been formatted as labels since they are meant to be column headings. If they were left as values, Excel would be confused and this could cause problems later on when sorting or creating charts.

To format a number as a label, put an apostrophe (') in front, like this: '2008.

	A	B	C	D
1		2008	2009	2010
2	Maths	45.8	56.2	59.1
3	English	60.4	66.2	66.1
4				

Figure 16.6 Numeric labels.

Working with workbooks

Creating a new workbook

If you want to create a new workbook:

- in Excel 2003, click *File, New*, then click *Blank Workbook* from the task pane
- in Excel 2007, click the Microsoft Office button, click *New*, then click *Create* in the window that appears
- in Excel 2010, click *File, New*, then click the *Create* button to the right of the *Backstage* view.

Inserting a new worksheet

Sometimes you need more than three worksheets in your workbook.

> **To insert a new worksheet:**
>
> 1 Right-click on the tab of the worksheet that you want the new sheet to appear <u>in front of</u>.
>
> 2 Click *Insert…*
>
> 3 Click *OK* in the dialog box that appears.

In Figure 16.7, the new sheet would be inserted in front of Sheet1. The first new sheet you insert will be called Sheet4, the next Sheet5, and so on.

28	Insert...
29	Delete
30	Rename
31	Move or Copy...
32	View Code
33	Protect Sheet...
34	Tab Color ▶
35	Hide
36	Unhide...
37	Select All Sheets
38	

H ◀ ▶ H **Sheet1** / Sheet2 / Sheet3

Figure 16.7 Inserting a new worksheet.

Renaming a worksheet

> **To rename a worksheet:**
>
> 1 Right-click on the tab of the worksheet that you want to rename.
>
> 2 Click *Rename*.
>
> 3 Type the new name of the sheet.

Deleting a worksheet

> **To delete a worksheet:**
>
> 1 Right-click on its tab.
>
> 2 Click *Delete*.

Working with rows and columns

Resizing rows and columns

> **To change the size of a column:**
>
> 1 Position the mouse pointer over the line to the right of the column <u>heading</u>. The cursor should turn to a double-headed arrow.
>
> 2 Hold down the left mouse button and drag the mouse to the right to widen the column (or to the left if you want to make it narrower).

You can resize a row using a similar method.

> Any time a cell contains ##########, it means that the column is not wide enough to display the full number. In a situation like that you just have to widen the column.

In the example in Figure 16.8, the Unit Cost heading looks like it has gone into column D. But if you click inside cell D1, you would realise that this is not the case. The column just needs widening. So you would drag the column separator to the right.

Figure 16.8 Resizing a column.

Inserting rows and columns

To insert a row above a particular row:

1 Right-click on that row.

2 Click *Insert*.

tip

If you select multiple rows before you click *Insert*, then you will insert multiple rows at one time.

You can insert columns using a similar method.

Deleting rows and columns

In order to delete a row or a column:

1 Right-click on the column letter or row number.

2 Click *Delete*.

Summary

- Spreadsheet software is used to manipulate numeric data.
- By default, a workbook consists of three worksheets.
- A cell address consists of a column letter followed by a row number (e.g. A1).
- The Formula Bar displays the formula of the currently selected cell.
- To modify the contents of a cell, double-click on it or click in it and press F2.
- Values are numbers that are based on calculations.
- Labels are used to identify rows, columns or values.
- To format a number as a label, put an apostrophe (') in front of it.
- If a cell contains ######## signs, it needs widening.

Review exercises

Exercise 16A

1 List three features found in Spreadsheet software.
2 Explain the difference between:
   a A workbook and a worksheet.
   b A value and a label.
3 Tanisha is puzzled because many of the cells in her spreadsheet are displaying number signs. Suggest the most likely cause and solution.

Using the 'spreadsheet' in Figure 16.9:

4 What is the value in **a** cell B2 and **b** cell C5?
5 In which cell is **a** the word 'Barbados' and **b** the figure '150,000'?

	A	B	C
1	Country	2007	2008
2	Barbados	20,000	22,000
3	Barbuda	350,000	348,000
4	Jamaica	200,000	190,000
5	Trinidad	150,000	140,000

Figure 16.9 For Exercises 16A and 16B.

Exercise 16B

1 Type the data in Figure 16.9 in a new worksheet. (Do not include the column letters or the row numbers.)
2 Change 'Barbuda' to 'Puerto Rico'.
3 Add the words '& Tobago' after 'Trinidad'. Widen the column as necessary.
4 Insert a row for the island Antigua, between the Barbados and Puerto Rico rows. It has figures of 12,000 in 2007 and 13,000 in 2009.
5 Insert a row for St. Kitts above the one for Jamaica. Under the 2007 and 2009 columns place '9,000' and '9,500' respectively.
6 Insert a column for the year 2008 in the appropriate position. Make up some figures to put under the column.
7 Convert the years to labels.
8 Save the file as COUNTRIES.

Exercise 16C

1 Open the MOVIES file from the exercise folder.
2 Insert a new worksheet before Sheet1 and rename it 'Directors'.
3 Type the following information in the Directors sheet.

Movie	Director
The Fast and the Furious	Rob Cohen
Jurassic Park	Steven Spielberg
Star Wars	George Lucas
The Incredibles	Brad Bird
King Kong	Peter Jackson
Terminator 2	James Cameron
Face/Off	John Woo
Saving Private Ryan	Steven Spielberg
The Lion King	Roger Allers
Spiderman 2	Sam Raimi

Movie	Director
The Matrix	The Wachowskis
Scream	Wes Craven
Titanic	James Cameron
The Godfather	Francis Ford Coppola
The Last Samurai	Edward Zwick
Friday After Next	Marcus Raboy
The Lord of the Rings: The Return of the King	Peter Jackson
ET: The Extra-Terrestrial	Steven Spielberg
The Mask of Zorro	Martin Campbell
Gladiator	Ridley Scott
Minority Report	Steven Spielberg
Shrek	Andrew Adamson
Pirates of the Caribbean: Dead Man's Chest	Gore Verbinski
Finding Nemo	Andrew Stanton
Independence Day	Roland Emmerich

4 Rename Sheet1 as 'Movies'.
5 Insert a sheet called 'Temp' between the Directors and Movies worksheets.
6 Save the file in your class folder as MOVIES2.
7 Delete the 'Temp' worksheet.
8 Switch to the 'Movies' tab.
9 Insert a column to the left of the Distributor tab.
10 Copy the director names from the 'Directors' worksheet and paste them in the column you just inserted.
11 Widen the columns with the numbers so that all the digits are visible.
12 Reverse the order of the Directors and Movies worksheets.
13 Save the file in your class folder as MOVIES3.

⑰ Formatting spreadsheets

In this chapter, you will learn:

- how to select data on a spreadsheet
- how to format figures and adjust the number of decimal places
- how to wrap text
- how to do oblique headings
- how to add and remove cell borders

Formatting in Excel

You should already know how to do basic formatting such as making text bold or changing the font. We will not go over that again here. Instead, we will look at formatting options specific to Microsoft Excel.

Selecting data

Whether you want to format a single cell or a group of cells (known as a range), the first step is to select it. The easiest way to do this is with the mouse.

Selecting a single cell

To select a single cell, just click on it or use one of the other methods to go to that cell. When you select a cell, you make it the active cell.

Selecting multiple cells

Selecting multiple cells is a little more difficult.

To select multiple cells:

1 Move the mouse to the top left cell of the region you want to select.

2 Make sure the cursor is a fat white cross (see the 'Before' image in Figure 17.1).

3 Drag the mouse to the bottom right cell of the region you want to select (see the 'After' image in Figure 17.1). The selected region will be highlighted except for the active cell which will remain white.

> **tip**
>
> This also works if you start at the bottom right and go towards the top left.

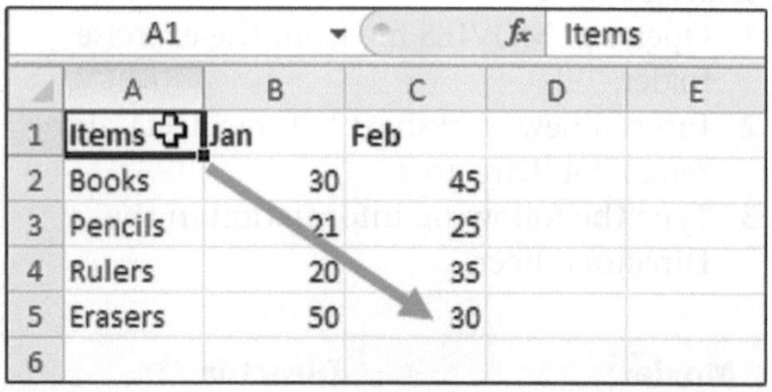

Before

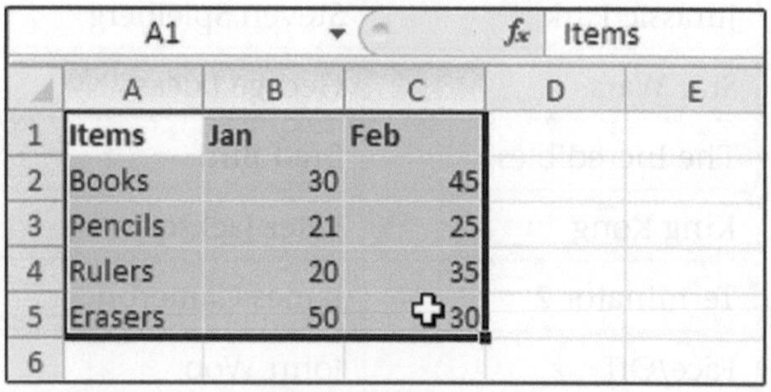

After

Figure 17.1 Selecting adjacent cells.

Selecting cells from non-adjacent regions

> **To select cells from two or more non-adjacent regions:**
>
> **1** Select the first region.
>
> **2** Hold down the *Ctrl* key and select the next region.
>
> **3** Repeat the previous step until all the regions are selected.

Let us look at the example in Figure 17.1 again. Suppose you only wanted to select the cells in the *Items* and *Feb* columns. We do not do a normal selection because that would include the *Jan* column as well. To select just the two columns, you first select the *Items* column. Then, while holding down the *Ctrl* key, you select the *Feb* column (see Figure 17.2).

Figure 17.2 Selecting non-adjacent regions.

Selecting entire rows and columns

To select an entire row or column simply click on its address heading as in Figure 17.3.

Figure 17.3 Selecting an entire column.

Selecting the entire spreadsheet

To select the entire spreadsheet, click the *Select All* button (where the column and row headings meet).

Figure 17.4 Selecting the entire spreadsheet.

Using the Formatting buttons

On the *Formatting* toolbar or the *Home* tab of the Ribbon, there are various buttons you can use to format data and cells. You are familiar with some of them already so I will just cover the new ones in Table 17.1.

Table 17.1 Formatting buttons in Excel.

If you want to...	Use these buttons
Change the vertical alignment	
Merge the selected cells and centre the data	
Decrease or increase the number of decimal places respectively	
Add or remove borders	
Format as currency, a percentage or with a comma	

The % formatting option is meant to be used to format decimal numbers like 0.25. When you click the % button, it automatically multiplies the number by 100 and adds the % sign at the end. So 0.125 would become 12.5%.

Using the *Format Cells* window

If there is not a formatting button that does what you want, you may have to use the *Format Cells* window instead.

> **To format cells using the *Format Cells* window:**
>
> 1 Select the cells.
>
> 2 Right-click on the selection, then click *Format Cells...*
>
> 3 Make the formatting changes, then click *OK*.

The Number tab

The Number tab of the *Format Cells* window (see Figure 17.5) allows you to change the way that data is presented within the cells. To the left-hand side of the *Number* tab is a list of categories that you can choose from. When you choose a category, options related to that category will be displayed on the right-hand side of the window.

Table 17.2 explains some of the categories.

Table 17.2 Number tab categories.

Category	What it does
General	Removes the formatting from the data.
Number	Sets the data as a value and gives you various ways to format a number.
Text	Formats the data as a label.
Date	Formats the data as a date; you can choose from several predefined formats.
Custom	Allows you to specify the format, e.g. 'yy/mm/dd'.

The Alignment tab

If you want to wrap the text in a cell, change its alignment or orientation, you can use the *Alignment* tab of the *Format Cells* window (see Figure 17.6).

Figure 17.5 The *Format Cells* window (*Number* tab).

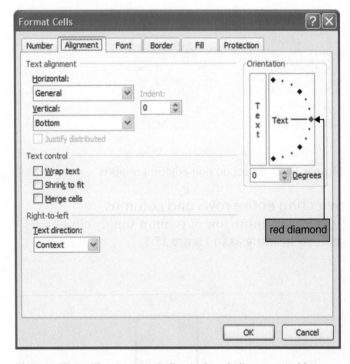

Figure 17.6 The *Format Cells* window (*Alignment* tab).

Wrapping text

Wrapping text allows long headings to take up multiple rows (see Figure 17.7).

To wrap text in a cell:

1 Go to the *Alignment* tab of the *Format Cells* window.

2 Place a tick next to the *Wrap Text* option.

	A	B
1	**WRAP TEXT**	
2		

Figure 17.7 Wrapped text.

Oblique headings

You can also use the *Alignment* tab to do oblique headings like those in Figure 17.8.

To format oblique headings:

1 Go to the *Alignment* tab of the *Format Cells* window.

2 Change the orientation of the text by dragging the red diamond in the *Orientation* section (see Figure 17.6) or by typing in the angle directly.

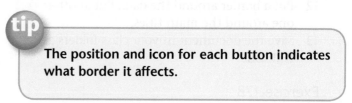

Figure 17.8 Oblique headings.

The Borders tab

Although spreadsheets look like they have borders around the cells, these will not show on a printout. You have to add borders in manually. An easy way to do so is via the *Border* button in the *Home* tab or *Formatting* toolbar. But if you want more control, you have to use the *Border* tab of the *Format Cells* window (see Figure 17.9).

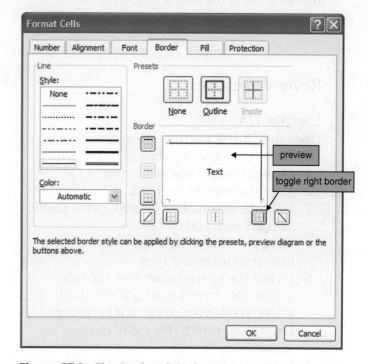

Figure 17.9 The *Border* tab in the *Format Cells* window.

Adding or removing borders

You can use the buttons on the right of the *Border* tab to turn borders on or off. You can choose from one of the presets at the top or use the toggle buttons around the preview to turn individual borders on and off.

tip

The position and icon for each button indicates what border it affects.

On the left of the *Border* tab you can change the style and colour of the border lines. Note that changes to the border lines only affect the borders you turn on from that point onward.

Summary

- Whenever you are trying to select (or highlight) cells using the mouse, make sure that the mouse cursor is a fat white cross.
- To open the *Format Cells* window, right-click on the selected cells, then click *Format Cells...*
- You can wrap text or turn it at an angle via the *Alignment* tab of the *Format Cells* window.

Review exercises

Exercise 17A

Open the CRUISE file from the exercise folder then make the following changes:

1 Change the font size of the data to 13.
2 Align the years to the right.
3 Make the destinations be bold, in the Comic Sans MS font, and in italics.
4 Make the column headings bold and dark blue, then underline them.
5 Format the figures (apart from the years) so that they have a comma and no decimal places. (Widen the columns if necessary.)
6 Insert three rows to the top of the spreadsheet.
7 Merge and centre the heading 'Caribbean Cruise Visitors' across the three columns.
8 Change its font to Arial Black, size 18.
9 In cell B1, type the text 'For 2007–2008'.
10 Merge and centre the heading across the spreadsheet.
11 Change its font to Verdana, size 14.
12 Put a border around the data. Put another one around the main titles.
13 Save the document in your class folders as CRUISE2.

Exercise 17B

Open the MOVIES3 file from the exercise folder and do the following:

1 Format the IMDB ratings to one decimal place.

2 Format the 'Cost' and 'Gross' columns to have a $ and no decimal places.
3 Change the font of the spreadsheet to Georgia.
4 Make the movie names dark blue.
5 Make the headings bold and green.
6 Format the spreadsheet to have all dark-blue borders.
7 Rotate the column headings so that they are at an angle of 45 degrees.
8 Insert two rows at the top of the spreadsheet.
9 Centre the heading 'Movie Profits and Ratings' across the top of the spreadsheet in Verdana font, size 36.
10 Save the file as MOVIES4.

Exercise 17C

Reproduce the invoice in Figure 17.10. The font used for the top part of the invoice is Century Gothic, whereas the font used in the table is Comic Sans MS.

Save the file as ACME.

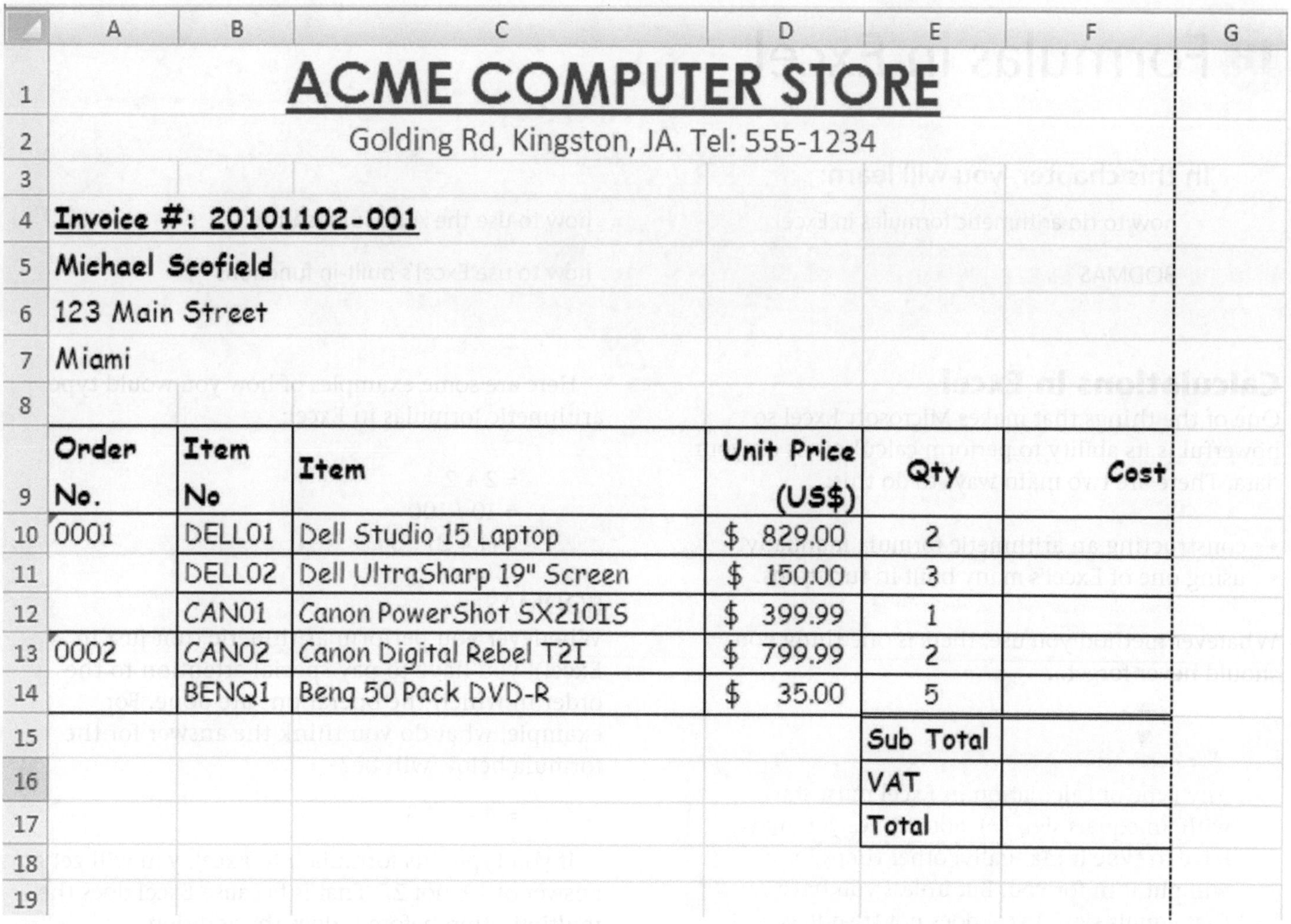

	A	B	C	D	E	F	G
1			ACME COMPUTER STORE				
2			Golding Rd, Kingston, JA. Tel: 555-1234				
3							
4	Invoice #: 20101102-001						
5	Michael Scofield						
6	123 Main Street						
7	Miami						
8							
9	Order No.	Item No	Item	Unit Price (US$)	Qty	Cost	
10	0001	DELL01	Dell Studio 15 Laptop	$ 829.00	2		
11		DELL02	Dell UltraSharp 19" Screen	$ 150.00	3		
12		CAN01	Canon PowerShot SX210IS	$ 399.99	1		
13	0002	CAN02	Canon Digital Rebel T2I	$ 799.99	2		
14		BENQ1	Benq 50 Pack DVD-R	$ 35.00	5		
15					Sub Total		
16					VAT		
17					Total		
18							
19							

Figure 17.10 For Exercise 17C.

18 Formulas in Excel

In this chapter, you will learn:

- how to do arithmetic formulas in Excel
- BODMAS
- how to use the *AutoSum* feature
- how to use Excel's built-in functions

Calculations in Excel

One of the things that makes Microsoft Excel so powerful is its ability to perform calculations on your data. There are two main ways to do this:

- constructing an arithmetic formula manually
- using one of Excel's many built-in functions.

Whatever method you use, there is one thing you should never forget...

Any type of calculation in Excel <u>must</u> start with an equals sign (=). Sometimes you may have to type it manually; other times Excel will put it in for you. But unless you have that equals sign, Excel does not treat it as a calculation.

Arithmetic formulas

An arithmetic formula is one that uses one or more of the arithmetic operators: addition, subtraction, multiplication and division.

If you look on your keyboard, you will see there is not a division sign. To divide, you use the forward slash (/). The multiplication sign is the asterisk (*).

Here are some examples of how you would type arithmetic formulas in Excel:

$$= 2 + 2$$
$$= 10 / 100$$
$$= (1 + 3) * 5$$

BODMAS

Whenever you perform arithmetic (not just in Excel), you have to pay special attention to the order in which the operations are done. For example, what do you think the answer for the formula below will be?

$$= 4 + 5 * 3$$

If you type this formula into Excel, you will get an answer of 19, not 27. That is because Excel does the multiplication <u>before</u> it does the addition.

But how do you know the order in which the operations will be done? That is where BODMAS comes in. It is an acronym for:

<u>B</u>rackets
<u>O</u>rder (indicies e.g., to the power of)
<u>D</u>ivision, <u>M</u>ultiplication
<u>A</u>ddition, <u>S</u>ubtraction

The further up the list an operation is, the higher its priority. So for instance, brackets have the highest priority, meaning that any operations inside brackets will be performed first. Similarly, multiplication has a higher priority than addition, which explains why it was done first in the example.

What about operations that are on the same line, such as division and multiplication? Since these have the same priority, it does not matter what order they are done in. So they are usually done from left to right. So in this formula, 10 is multiplied by 2 then divided by 4:

$$= 10 * 2 / 4$$

tip

You can use brackets to change the order of operations. If you wanted 4 to be added to 5 and <u>then</u> have the result (9) be multiplied by 3, you could use the formula:

= (4 + 5) * 3

Using cell references in arithmetic formulas

The previous examples were a bit unrealistic since it is fairly rare to see numbers in Excel formulas. Instead, the formulas normally contain the addresses of the cells containing those numbers. (These addresses are called <u>cell references</u>.) That way, when the value in the cell changes, you do not need to redo the formula.

Figure 18.1 shows how you would do this. In *D2*, the formula tells the computer 'take whatever is in *B2* and add it to *C2* then put the result here'. When the *Enter* key is pressed, the value 75 will be placed in *D2* (obtained by adding 30 to 45).

SUM		▼	⊗ ✕ ✓ *fx*	=B2 + C2	
	A	**B**	**C**	**D**	**E**
1	**Items**	**Jan**	**Feb**	**Total**	
2	**Books**	30	45	=B2 + C2	
3	Pencils	21	25		
4	Rulers	20	35	cell reference	
5	Erasers	50	30		
6					

Figure 18.1 Cell references in a formula.

If you were to change the value in cell *C2* to 20, the <u>value</u> in cell D2 would automatically change from 75 to 50 (30 + 20), although the formula itself has not been changed.

tip

To see the formula used to obtain the value in a cell, just click on the cell. The formula will then be displayed in the formula bar.

Each cell reference (or range of cell references) in a formula is displayed in the same colour as the cell(s) it refers to. When you are typing a formula, you do not need to type the cell addresses manually. Instead, you can click on the cell(s) in question and the address(es) will be automatically inserted into the formula.

Using Excel functions

Excel has a wealth of functions that can do everything from finding an average to calculating compound interest. We will only cover a handful here, which you can see in Table 18.1.

The two most important things to know about Excel functions are:
• you must put an = sign in front (this cannot be stated often enough!)
• they always have brackets at the end, containing any parameters that the function needs.

Table 18.1 Examples of Excel functions.

Function	What it does	Examples
Sum	Adds up the values in the cell range(s)	=sum(B2, B3, B4, B5) =sum(B2:B5) =sum(B2:B5, C2:C5)
Average	Finds the average	=average(B2:C5)
Max	Find the maximum	=max(B2:C5)
Min	Finds the minimum	=min(B2:C5)
CountA	Counts all the data in the cell range(s)	=counta(A2:B5)
Count	Counts the numbers in the cell range(s)	=count(A2:B5)
Today	Inserts the current date	=today()

Let us look at the Sum function first. You use this function like this:

=sum(whatever it is you want to add up)

In the first example in the table, the Sum function is used to add up the values in four cells: B2, B3, B4 and B5. Notice that when you have multiple cell references, you separate them by commas.

The second example shows a shorter way to perform the same calculation. The cell range B2 to B5 is used. (The colon (:) means 'to'.) In this case using the cell range is not much shorter, but if you wanted to add up, say, 100 numbers, it would be much more convenient.

As you can see in the third example, you can have multiple ranges once they are separated by commas.

The other functions work the same way, except for the *Today* function, which does not take any parameters.

Entering functions

If you are comfortable with cell addresses, you can simply type in the function by hand. If you are not, you can use the mouse to select the cells. For example, suppose you wanted to find the average of the January figures in Figure 18.1 and put it in cell B6.

To find the average:

1 Click in cell B6.

2 Type: =sum(

3 Select the January figures using the mouse. Excel will insert the range B2:B5 after the bracket.

4 Type) and press the *Enter* key to complete the function.

As you start typing the function, Excel will give you information about it (see Figure 18.2).

SUM		▾	× ✓ *fx*	=sum(	
	A	B	C	D	E
1	Items	Jan	Feb		
2	Books	30	45		
3	Pencils	21	25		
4	Rulers	20	35		
5	Erasers	50	30		
6		=sum(			
7		SUM(number1, [number2], ...)			
8					
9					

Figure 18.2 Entering a function.

Using the *AutoSum* feature

If you have difficulty working with functions, you can get Excel to enter the function for you by using the *AutoSum* feature.

To use *AutoSum*:

1 Click the cell where you want the answer to appear.

2 Click the *AutoSum* button Σ. If you want to insert a function other than *Sum*, click the arrow next to the *AutoSum* button and choose the function from the list.

3 Make sure the correct range is selected. If it is not you will have to select it manually.

4 Press the *Enter* key to accept the function.

Excel will put in the = sign in for you so this is one of the few times you do not have to.

Summary

- All calculations in Excel <u>must</u> start with an = sign.
- Division and multiplication operations are done before addition and multiplication, unless brackets are used.
- Excel formulas normally contain cell addresses as opposed to using the actual values within the cells.
- You can manually type out Excel functions like =Average() or you can use the *AutoSum* feature to insert them automatically.
- A colon in a range means 'to'. So A1:B5 means 'cells A1 to B5'.

Review exercises

Exercise 18A

1 What is the result of this calculation: =20 – 8 * 2? How would you rewrite this formula so that the subtraction is done first?

2 State what is wrong with each of these formulas, and then write them correctly.

   a =B1 * 2G
   b A3 + A4
   c =SUM(C2 to C5)
   d =AVERAGE()
   e =MAX(A6:D6

3 Write the function that inserts today's date.

Exercise 18B

1 Open the ACME file from the exercise folder.
2 Insert formulas to do the calculations. (Hint: For the VAT formula use '=cell address * 15%'.)
3 Save the file in your class folder as ACME2.

Exercise 18C

1 Open the MOVIES5 file from the exercise folder.
2 Fill in the formulas at the bottom of the spreadsheet.
3 Resave it in your class folder as MOVIES5.

⑲ Copying formulas and data

In this chapter, you will learn:

- how Excel copies calculated values
- how to use the *AutoFill* feature
- how to use the Paste Special feature
- about absolute cell references and why they are necessary
- errors commonly encountered when performing calculations in Excel

Copying non-calculated data in Excel

Copying data in Excel works the way you would expect – provided that it is not the result of a calculation. You can use the copy and paste techniques that we covered in earlier chapters. This applies to labels as well as values that you have typed in manually.

How Excel copies calculated values

Copying calculated values is a bit trickier because of the way Excel works. When you try copying a value that is the result of a calculation, Excel does <u>not</u> copy the value. Instead, <u>it copies its formula changing it to reflect the new location</u>.

Consider the example in Figure 19.1a.

	D2	▾		f_x	=SUM(B2:C2)	
	A	B	C	D	E	
1	Items	Jan	Feb	Total		
2	Books	30	45	75		
3	Pencils	21	35			
4	Rulers	20	25			
5	Erasers	50	30			

Figure 19.1a   Copying formulas (part A).

Suppose we copy the calculated value from cell D2 to cell D4. You might expect that cell D4 will now contain the value 75. But remember, Excel copies (and adjusts) the formula, not the calculated value.

Looking at Figure 19.1b, we can see that Excel puts the formula =SUM(B4:C4) in the new location. This is similar to the original formula – but the parameters

have been adjusted. How does Excel come up with the new parameters?

	D4	▾		f_x	=SUM(B4:C4)	
	A	B	C	D	E	
1	Items	Jan	Feb	Total		
2	Books	30	45	75		
3	Pencils	21	35			
4	Rulers	20	25	45		
5	Erasers	50	30			
6						

calculated using adjusted formula

Figure 19.1b   Copying formulas (part B).

Because the new location is two rows down from the old one, Excel increases the addresses in the formula by two rows.

If you want to copy the <u>old</u> formula to a new location, go into the *Formula* bar and copy it to the new cell. When you <u>cut and paste</u> a calculated value, Excel <u>moves the formula</u> to the new location (without trying to adjust it).

The *AutoFill* feature

AutoFill is one of my favourite Excel features. It allows you to quickly copy formulas as well as many other useful tasks.

Using the *AutoFill* feature to copy formulas

If you have a formula that you want to copy to adjoining cells, here is what you do:

1 Select the cell containing the formula you want to copy.

2 Position the mouse over the tiny black square (called the handle) in the bottom right-hand corner of the cell. The mouse pointer should change to a <u>thin black cross</u> (see Figure 19.2a).

3 Hold down the left mouse button and drag the cross across or down (see Figure 19.26).

4 Release the mouse button.

a

	A	B	C	D	E
	D2			f_x =B2+C2	
1	Items	Jan	Feb	Total	
2	Books	30	45	75	
3	Pencils	21	25		
4	Rulers	20	35		
5	Erasers	50	30		
6					

b

	A	B	C	D	E
	D2			f_x =B2+C2	
1	Items	Jan	Feb	Total	
2	Books	30	45	75	
3	Pencils	21	25		
4	Rulers	20	35		
5	Erasers	50	30		
6					

Figure 19.2 AutoFilling formulas. **a** position the mouse over the tiny black square, **b** hold down the left mouse button and drag in the desired direction.

When you release the mouse, Excel automatically fills in the formulas in the adjusted cells. But remember, when Excel copies formulas, it adjusts the cell

references. Fortunately, this is exactly what we want in this case, as you can see in Figure 19.3.

tip
You can also drag the handle to the left or upwards, depending on your needs.

	A	B	C	D
	D5			f_x =B5+C5
1	Items	Jan	Feb	Total
2	Books	30	45	75
3	Pencils	21	35	56
4	Rulers	20	25	45
5	Erasers	50	30	80
6				
7				

Figure 19.3 The result of AutoFilling the formula.

AutoFilling other things

The *AutoFill* feature is not limited to formulas. It can also be used to produce multiple copies of labels or even fill in the months of the year. You will see this, and more, in Exercise 19b.

The *Paste Special* feature

There are some occasions where you are not interested in the formulas used to generate values, but instead want to copy the values themselves. You can do all this and more via the *Paste Special* feature.

To use *Paste Special*:

1 Copy some data.

2 Right-click on the new location.

3 Click *Paste Special*.

4 Choose one of the options from the *Paste Special* window (shown in Figure 19.4). For example, if you want to copy the cell values but not the underlying formulas, you would select the *Values* option.

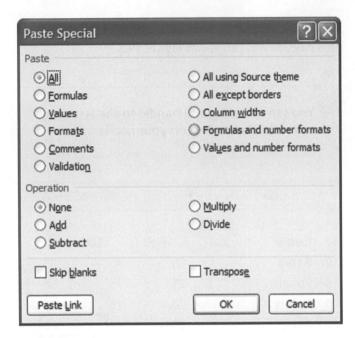

Figure 19.4 The *Paste Special* window.

If you are using Excel 2010, you do not even have to open the *Paste Special* window. Instead, you can click one of the paste options in the context menu (see Figure 19.5).

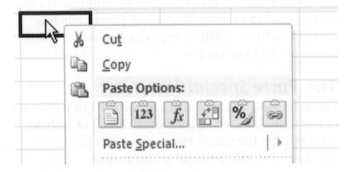

Figure 19.5 Excel 2010 Paste Options.

Absolute cell references

What is an absolute cell reference?
So far, all the formulas that you have done have used **relative cell references**. These are cell references that do not contain a dollar sign ($). For example, in the formula =MIN(A2:B2), the A2 and B2 are relative cell references.

An **absolute cell reference** is one that has a dollar sign in front of <u>both</u> the column and the row, e.g. A2.

A **mixed cell reference** is one that has a dollar sign in front of <u>either</u> the column or the row, e.g. $A2 or A$2.

So what is the big deal about the dollar sign? Think of it as meaning 'do not change'. Remember that normally, when you copy a formula to a new location, Excel adjusts the rows and the columns in that new location. By using the dollar signs, you can tell Excel 'do not change this address when you copy the formula'.

Table 19.1 explains the different types of cell references.

Table 19.1 Types of cell references and what they mean.

Cell reference	What it means
A2	When the formula is copied, both the row and the column can change
$A2	Do not change the column (A) cell reference. However, the row can change
A$2	Do not change the row (2) cell reference. However, the column can change
A2	Do not change the row or the column cell reference; in other words, fix the cell reference in formula so it does not change

Inserting an absolute reference
To insert an absolute reference, you can:

- either manually type in the dollar signs
- or press the *F4* key – Excel will automatically put in the dollar signs around the current address in the formula.

If you press the *F4* key more than once, Excel will toggle through the different types of references.

Why we need absolute cell references
To understand why we need absolute cell references, consider Figure 19.6, where we are using Excel to calculate percentages. Remember that in order to find a percentage we divide the number by an overall total.

First we calculate and format the percentage for Books (Figure 19.6a). Notice that we are dividing by D6 (the overall total). It looks correct so we copy it down to the other rows (Figure 19.6b).

We have a problem. Why do we have those errors? Looking at the formula in cell E3 reveals the problem (Figure 19.6c). The formula is =D3/D7. But are we not supposed to be dividing by D6?

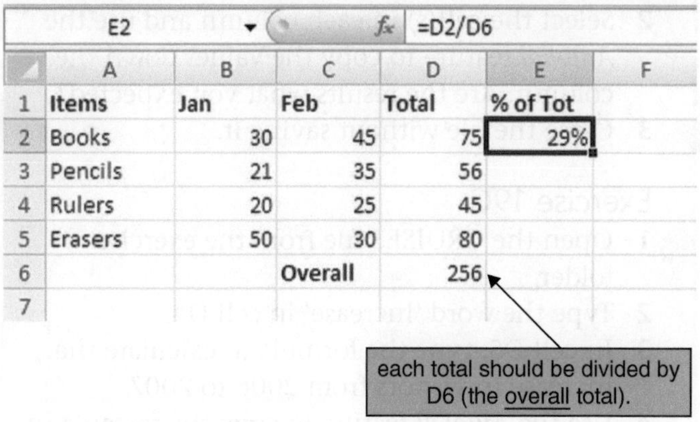

Figure 19.6a Why we need absolute references (part A).

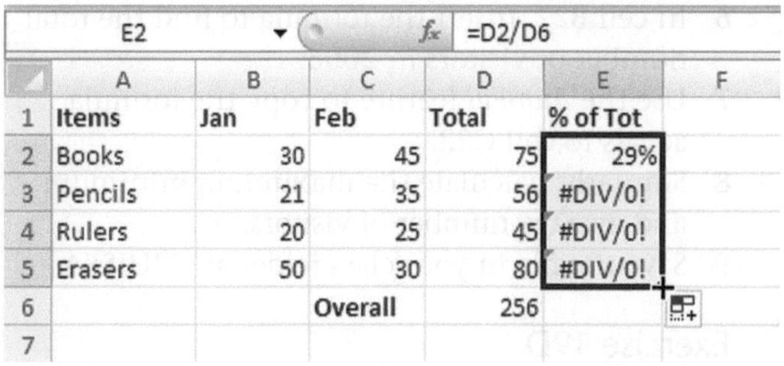

Figure 19.6b Why we need absolute references (part B).

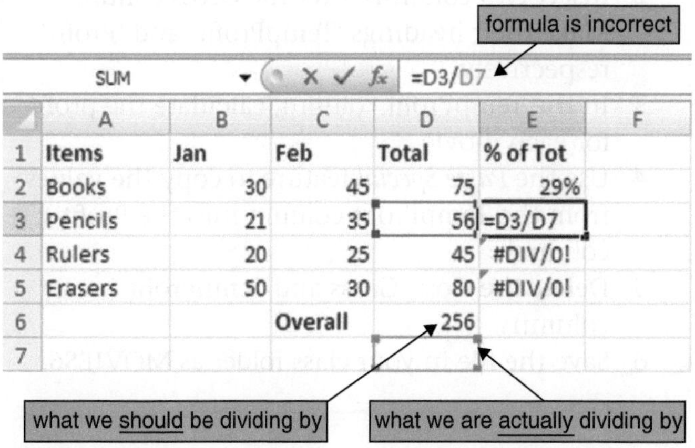

Figure 19.6c Why we need absolute references (part C).

What happened is that when we copied down the formula, Excel increased its row numbers. This is what Excel normally does, but we do not want this behaviour in this case.

How do we solve it? We use an absolute cell reference to the overall total like this: =D2/D6. Now when we copy down the formula, the D6 part remains fixed as we can see in Figure 19.6d.

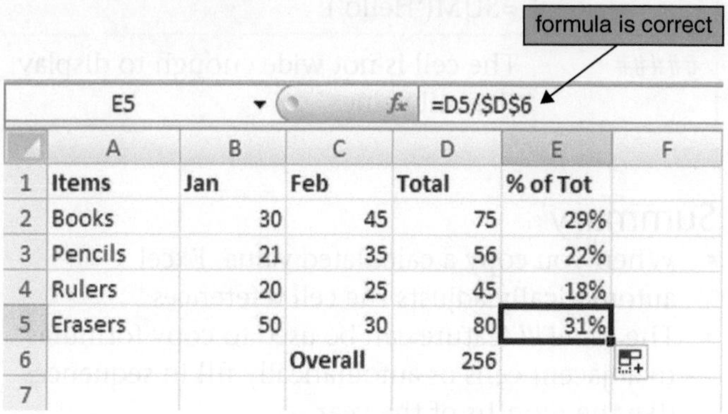

Figure 19.6d Why we need absolute references (part D).

tip

If a formula seems to be correct but when you copy it you get an error message like #DIV/0! or #VALUE!, you probably need to use an absolute reference. A list of common Excel error messages is given in the next section.

Error messages

If Excel encounters an error in a formula, instead of putting a result in the cell, Excel displays an error message. You can easily recognise these error messages since they all start with # sign.

Table 19.2 lists the most common ones.

Table 19.2 Common error messages in Excel.

Error	Meaning
#DIV/0	You have attempted to divide by zero
#NAME?	Excel does not recognise a name used in the formula. This usually happens when you misspell a function name, e.g., =AVG() instead of =AVERAGE()

Table 19.2 continued Common error messages in Excel.

Error	Meaning
#REF!	The formula references an invalid cell
#VALUE!	An operator or function has been used with incorrect arguments, e.g. =SUM('Hello')
#####	The cell is not wide enough to display the full value

Summary

- When you copy a calculated value, Excel automatically adjusts the cell references.
- The *AutoFill* feature can be used to copy formulas to adjacent cells or automatically fill in sequences like the months of the year.
- If you just want to copy values (and not the underlying formulas) you can *Paste Special*.
- If you encounter error messages like #DIV/0 or #VALUE! when you copy a formula, you probably need to use an absolute reference.
- To make a cell reference absolute, press *F4* when typing it or manually put a $ in front the column and the row.
- When you copy formulas, the absolute cell references remain fixed.

Review exercises

Exercise 19A

1 Explain how, after typing a formula at the beginning of a row, you can quickly copy the formula across to the rest of the cells in that row.

2 Which of these is the correct way to write an absolute cell reference to cell B2?
   a B2
   b B$2
   c B2$
   d B2
   e $B2

3 How would you resolve the following errors?
   a ######
   b #NAME?
   c #VALUE!

Exercise 19B

1 Open the *AUTOFILL* file from the exercise folder.

2 Select the cell(s) in each column and use the *AutoFill* feature to copy the values down the column. Are the results what you expected?

3 Close the file without saving it.

Exercise 19C

1 Open the CRUISE3 file from the exercise folder.

2 Type the word 'Increase' in cell D4.

3 In cell D5, type the formula to calculate the increase in visitors from 2006 to 2007.

4 Use the *AutoFill* feature to copy the formula in cells D6:D20.

5 Type the word 'Total' in cell A22.

6 In cell B22, insert the formula to find the total number of visitors in 2006.

7 Use the *AutoFill* feature to copy the formula across to cell C22.

8 Similarly, calculate the maximum, minimum and average number of visitors.

9 Save the file in your class folder as CRUISE4.

Exercise 19D

1 Open the MOVIES4 file from the exercise folder.

2 Insert two columns after the Gross column. Make their headings 'TempProfit' and 'Profit' respectively.

3 In the TempProfit column, calculate the profit for each movie.

4 Use the *Paste Special* feature to copy the values from the TempProfit column into the Profit column.

5 Delete the Cost, Gross and TempProfit columns.

6 Save the file in your class folder as MOVIES6.

As an experiment, try redoing the exercise without using a TempProfit column. So you would place the formulas to calculate the profit directly in the Profit column, then delete the Cost and Gross columns. What happens?

Exercise 19E

1 Open the POPULATION file from the exercise folder.
2 In cell A13 type the word 'Total'.
3 Calculate the total population in cell B13.
4 In C4, type '% of Tot'.
5 In column C, calculate the percentage that each island's population is of the overall total. You will need to use <u>absolute addressing</u>.
6 Format the percentages with a % sign and one decimal place.
7 In cells A2, B2 and D4, type 'Growth Rate', '5%' and '2012 Estimate' respectively.
8 In cell D5, type the formula '=B5+B2*B5'.
9 Use the *AutoFill* feature to copy the formula for the other countries. Identify and correct the problem.
10 Format the estimates with commas and no decimal places.
11 Save the file as POPULATION2.

20 Sorting data

In this chapter, you will learn:

- the correct way to sort data
- how to sort by multiple columns

Pitfalls when sorting data

Sorting data is not difficult once you know how to do it correctly. Unfortunately the 'obvious' way to sort data – by selecting the columns you want to sort by and clicking *Sort* – can lead to corrupt data. That is why you need a chapter dedicated to sorting. Throughout the chapter we will be working with the data in Table 20.1.

Table 20.1   Data for Chapter 20.

ID	FirstName	LastName	Salary
HC	Horatio	Caine	$15,000.00
JA	John	Alleyne	$2,500.00
JB	John	Brown	$4,000.00
LC	Lisa	Cuddy	$10,000.00
MS	Michael	Scofield	$8,000.00
TA	Tonya	Alleyne	$3,000.00

The *Sort* buttons

If you just want to sort the data within a single column, you can use the *Sort* buttons. In Excel 2003, you can find the *Sort* buttons towards the right of the *Standard* toolbar (see Figure 20.1). In Excel 2007/2010, the *Sort* buttons are hidden under the *Sort and Filter* button to the right of the Ribbon's *Home* tab (Figure 20.2).

Figure 20.1   The *Sort* Buttons (Excel 2003).

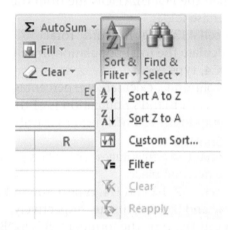

Figure 20.2   The *Sort* Buttons (Excel 2007/2010).

Although these buttons have the letters A and Z on them, they do not just refer to sorting text data alphabetically. They will also sort numbers and dates.

Sorting by one column

To sort by one column:

1 Click a cell inside the column (but do <u>not</u> select the column).

2 Click one of the *Sort* buttons.

Figure 20.3a shows what the data looks like when it is correctly sorted in descending order by *ID*. Notice that when one part of the row (in this case the ID) moves, the rest of the row moves with it. Thus, the integrity of the data is preserved.

Figure 20.3b shows how it might look if it were sorted incorrectly (e.g., if you selected the ID column before sorting). If you look at the IDs you will see that the IDs have moved but the rest of the row has not, thus corrupting your data.

	A	B	C	D	E
1	ID	FirstName	LastName	Salary	
2	TA	Tonya	Alleyne	$3,000.00	
3	MS	Michael	Scofield	$8,000.00	
4	LC	Lisa	Cuddy	$10,000.00	
5	JB	John	Brown	$4,000.00	
6	JA	John	Alleyne	$2,500.00	
7	HC	Horatio	Caine	$15,000.00	
8					

Figure 20.3a Data correctly sorted by descending ID. A single cell *within* the ID column is selected *before* sorting.

	A	B	C	D	E
1	ID	FirstName	LastName	Salary	
2	TA	Horatio	Caine	$15,000.00	
3	MS	John	Alleyne	$2,500.00	
4	LC	John	Brown	$4,000.00	
5	JB	Lisa	Cuddy	$10,000.00	
6	JA	Michael	Scofield	$8,000.00	
7	HC	Tonya	Alleyne	$3,000.00	
8					

Figure 20.3b Data <u>incorrectly</u> sorted by descending ID. The *whole* column was selected *before* sorting.

Disadvantages of using the *Sort* buttons

Although the sort buttons are very convenient, they have some disadvantages:

- They should not be used to sort by more than one column.
- They have trouble sorting data that has a total row directly underneath.

The *Sort* window

The *Sort* window gives you total control over how your data is sorted. It allows you to sort by multiple columns even if their sort orders are different. Unfortunately, the *Sort* windows in Excel 2003 (Figure 20.4) and later versions (Figure 20.5) are very different. The figures explain how to use each *Sort* window.

Excel 2003

The *Sort* window in Excel 2003 can be accessed by clicking the *Data* menu, then *Sort*.

Excel 2007/2010

If you are using Excel 2007 or 2010, the *Sort* window can be accessed by switching to the *Home* tab, clicking *Sort and Filter*, then clicking *Custom Sort...*

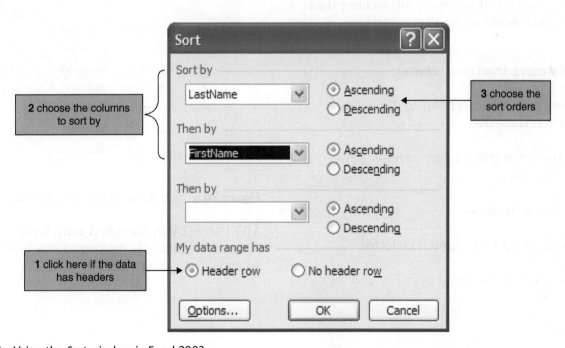

Figure 20.4 Using the *Sort* window in Excel 2003.

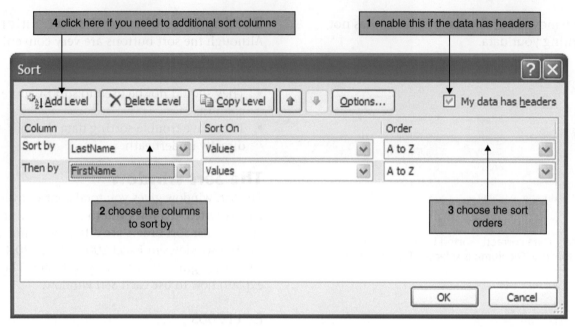

4 click here if you need to additional sort columns

1 enable this if the data has headers

2 choose the columns to sort by

3 choose the sort orders

Figure 20.5   Using the *Sort* window in Excel 2007/2010.

If the *Headers* option is not enabled, when you go to select the columns, you will see A, B, C etc.

Sorting by more than one column

The following method allows you to sort by more than one column and it works under all circumstances.

To sort by more than one column:

1 Remove any blank rows between the column headings and the data.

2 Select the entire table of data (excluding any summary rows).

3 Open the *Sort* window.

4 Ensure the *Header* row option is selected.

5 Choose the fields you want to sort by and the sort order.

6 Click *OK*.

If you sort by two columns, the first column is called the <u>primary field</u> and the second one is called the <u>secondary field</u>. In Figure 20.6, *LastName* is the primary field and *FirstName* is the secondary field. So in the cases where two people have the same last name, Excel then sorts them by their first names.

	A	B	C	D
1	ID	FirstName	LastName	Salary
2	JA	John	Alleyne	$2,500.00
3	TA	Tonya	Alleyne	$3,000.00
4	JB	John	Brown	$4,000.00
5	HC	Horatio	Caine	$15,000.00
6	LC	Lisa	Cuddy	$10,000.00
7	MS	Michael	Scofield	$8,000.00
8				

Figure 20.6   Sorting by two columns or fields.

The correct way to select data before sorting

Figure 20.7 illustrates the correct way to select data when you are going to sort it.

ID	FirstName	LastName	Salary
HC	Horatio	Caine	$15,000.00
JA	John	Alleyne	$2,500.00
JB	John	Brown	$4,000.00
LC	Lisa	Cuddy	$10,000.00
MS	Michael	Scofield	$8,000.00
TA	Tonya	Alleyne	$3,000.00
		Total Salary	$42,500.00

do not include summary rows like the total

Figure 20.7 The correct way to select data before sorting.

Summary

- When using the *Sort* buttons to sort by a column, do <u>not</u> select that column. Instead, click a <u>cell</u> in the column, then use the *Sort* button.
- If you want to sort by more than one column, use the *Sort* window.
- When selecting data before sorting, select all the columns of the table but do not include summary rows like the total.

Review exercises

Exercise 20A

1 Open the CLIMATE file from the exercise folder.
2 Use the *Sort* buttons to sort the months so that the month with the highest rainfall is at the top.
3 Save the file in your class folder as CLIMATE1.
4 Sort the months by hours then by temperature. The hours should be in ascending order whereas the temperature should be in descending order.
5 Save the spreadsheet in your class folder as CLIMATE2.

Exercise 20B

1 Open the MOVIES6 file from the exercise folder.
2 In row 29, calculate the average movie profit and rating.
3 Use the *Sort* buttons to sort the movies by descending rating. What happens?
4 Click the *Undo* button and use the *Sort* window instead to sort the movies by descending rating.
5 Save the file in your class folder as MOVIES7.
6 Use the *Sort* window to sort by year then by profit. Both should be in descending order.
7 Save the file in your class folder as MOVIES8.
8 Sort by the distributor then by the movie title. Both should be in alphabetical order.
9 Save the spreadsheet in your class folder as MOVIES9.

㉑ Charts

In this chapter, you will learn:

- how to select data to be displayed in charts
- how to modify the charts
- how to create charts

Types of charts

One of the key aspects of Microsoft Excel is the way it allows you to visualise data using charts. Figures 21.1, 21.2 and 21.3 are examples of the most common types of chart.

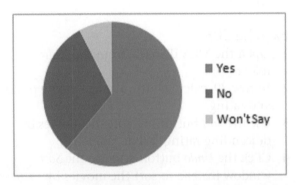

Figure 21.1 A pie chart is best for showing percentages.

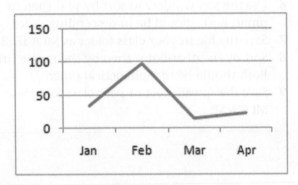

Figure 21.2 A line chart is great for showing trends.

Components of a chart

Before you can master plotting charts, you need to know the components of a chart. Figure 21.4 illustrates some of these components.

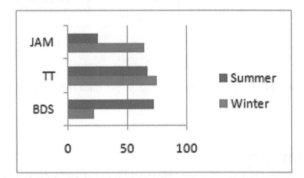

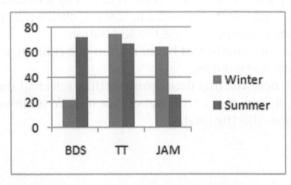

Figure 21.3 Bar and column charts are good for comparisons.

Axes

You should be already familiar with chart axes from mathematics. But Excel calls them the <u>category</u> and <u>value axes</u> as opposed to the *x* and *y* axes. The category axis is normally the horizontal axis.

In bar charts the axes are switched around so the vertical axis is the category axis and the horizontal one is for the values. Pie charts have no axes at all.

Series

Each set of values plotted on a chart is known as a **series**. In Figure 21.4 there are two series: one for the January values and one for the February values.

Legends

A **legend** in a chart serves a similar function to a key on a map. It tells you what colour represents a given series or slice of a pie.

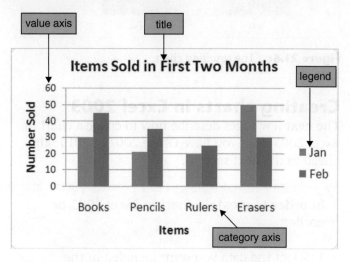

Figure 21.4 The main components of a chart.

Selecting the data you want to plot

The first step of plotting a chart is always to select the data. In many cases, this is actually the trickiest part.

If the areas you have to select are disconnected you will have to use the *Ctrl* key.

Selecting data for a pie chart

This is the easiest one. You simply select the values you want to plot as well as their corresponding labels.

In Figure 21.5a we have selected the data needed to plot the names of the items and the number sold in January. In this case the items (A2:A5) are acting as the labels. The data being plotted in this chart (the series) are in the columns.

Figure 21.5b shows how you would select the data if you wanted to plot the number of erasers sold in each month. In this case the months are acting as the labels. Since the values are going across, we say that the series are in rows.

	A	B	C
1	Items	Jan	Feb
2	Books	30	45
3	Pencils	21	35
4	Rulers	20	25
5	Erasers	50	30
6			
7			

Figure 21.5a Selecting data for a pie chart (series in columns).

	A	B	C
1	Items	Jan	Feb
2	Books	30	45
3	Pencils	21	35
4	Rulers	20	25
5	Erasers	50	30
6			
7			

Figure 21.5b Selecting data for a pie chart (series in rows).

Note that the 50 is included in the selection, but it is displayed in white because it is the active cell.

Selecting data for a bar, column or line chart

The way you select the data for these types of chart depends on how many sets of <u>values</u> (i.e. series) you are going to plot.

Plotting one series

If you are plotting <u>one</u> series, you select the data the same way you would for a pie chart.

Plotting two or more series

If you are plotting <u>more than one</u> series, you will need to include the column/row heading as well so that Excel knows how to label them in the legend.

In Figure 21.6a, we are plotting two series, the figures for Jan and Feb. Therefore, we also include the three column headings: Items, Jan and Feb. This is the selection that was used to plot Figure 21.4.

In Figure 21.6b we are plotting the number of books and erasers sold each month. We need to use the row headings for the legend so they are selected as well. The resulting chart is shown in Figure 21.6c.

	A	B	C
1	Items	Jan	Feb
2	Books	30	45
3	Pencils	21	35
4	Rulers	20	25
5	Erasers	50	30
6			
7			

Figure 21.6a   Plotting two series in a column chart (part A).

	A	B	C
1	Items	Jan	Feb
2	Books	30	45
3	Pencils	21	25
4	Rulers	20	35
5	Erasers	50	30
6			

Figure 21.6b   Plotting two series in a column chart (part B).

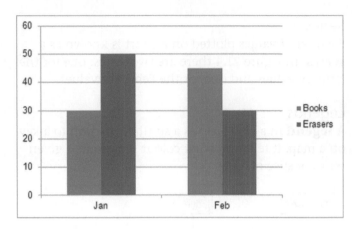

Figure 21.6c   The resulting chart.

Creating charts in Excel 2003

The next few pages describe how to create a chart in Excel 2003, so if you have Office 2007 or 2010 skip ahead to the next section.

In order to create a chart in Excel 2003 or earlier:

1 Select the data you want included in the chart.

2 Click the *Chart Wizard* icon in the Standard toolbar. (Or click *Insert, Chart...*)

3 Follow the steps in the wizard that appears. Each step is covered below.

Step 1 Select chart type

The first thing you are asked to do is select a chart type (Figure 21.7). To do so:

- Select the type of chart on the left (e.g. pie).
- Then select the subtype on the right (e.g. what type of pie chart).

tip

You can get an idea of how your data will look with the selected type by clicking the big button near the bottom of the window.

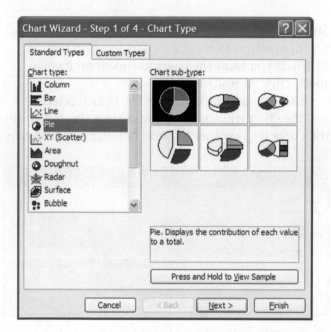

Figure 21.7 Chart wizard step 1 (chart type) in Word 2003.

Step 2 Chart source data

Here you are given a preview of how the chart will look (see Figure 21.8). If the preview looks right then click the *Next* button. Otherwise:

- If you realise the incorrect data was selected, click the *Collapse* button and reselect the data.
- If the preview looks 'wrong' but the right data is selected, try changing whether the series is in rows or in columns.

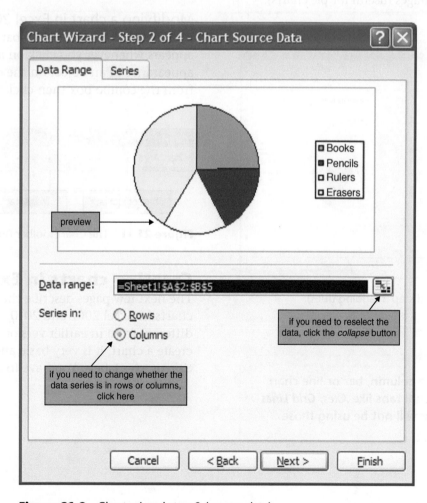

Figure 21.8 Chart wizard step 2 (source data).

Step 3 Select the chart options

This is the step where most of the work is done (see Figure 21.9). Fortunately most of the options are pretty straightforward. Table 21.1 explains how you would use each tab.

Table 21.1 Chart option tabs in Excel 2003.

Tab	How to use it
Titles	Type in the title for the chart. If the chart is not a pie chart, you can type in the axes labels as well.
Legend	If you want to hide the legend (e.g. if it just says Series 1), uncheck the *Show Legend* box.
Data labels	Tick *Value* if you want to show the data values on the chart. Tick *Percentage* if you want to show percentages (useful for pie charts).

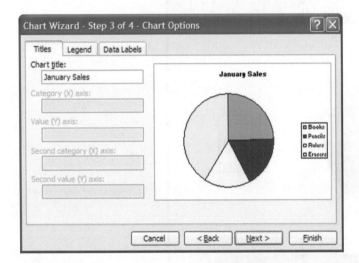

Figure 21.9 Chart wizard step 3 (adding titles).

> **tip**
>
> If you are creating a column, bar or line chart you will see additional tabs like *Axes*, *Grid Lines* and *Data Table*. You will not be using those.

Step 4 Choose the chart location

The final step is to choose a chart location (Figure 21.10). If you want the chart to appear on its own sheet, click '*As new sheet*'.

Otherwise, leave the '*As object in*' option selected and the chart will appear in the current sheet. You can then drag it to another location or resize it as necessary.

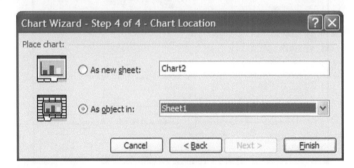

Figure 21.10 Chart wizard step 4 (chart location).

Modifying a chart in Excel 2003

In Excel 2003, the *Chart* toolbar (Figure 21.11) appears whenever you click on a chart. To change the appearance of an object on the chart, select the object from the combo box then click the *Format* button.

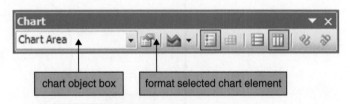

Figure 21.11 The Chart toolbar (Excel 2003).

Creating charts in Excel 2007/2010

The next few pages describe the process of creating charts in Excel 2007 and 2010, which is much different from in earlier versions. When you first create a chart, it is very basic and does not include a title or axes labels. You have to add them later.

To create a chart in Excel 2007/2010:

1 Select the data you want included in the chart.

2 Switch to the *Insert* tab of the Ribbon.

3 Choose the type of chart you want (see Figure 21.12).

4 Customise the chart.

5 Choose the location of the chart.

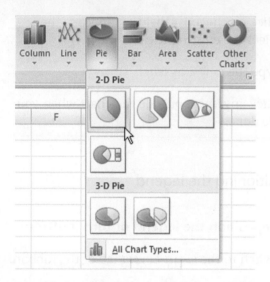

Figure 21.12   Creating a pie chart in Excel 2007/2010.

Whenever a chart is selected in Excel 2007/2010 – as happens immediately after you create a chart – three chart tabs appear to the right of the Ribbon. The Table 21.2 explains what each tab is for.

Table 21.2   Chart tabs in Excel 2007/2010.

Chart tab	What it allows you to change
Design	The location of the chart and how it looks in general, e.g. its colour scheme
Layout	Whether the chart has a title or axes labels as well as the position of the legend
Format	The appearance of individual objects on the chart

Changing the chart location in Excel 2007/2010

To change whether the chart is on the current sheet (default) or its own sheet:

1 Click on the *Chart Design* tab of the Ribbon.

2 Click the *Move Chart* button (located at the far right; see Figure 21.13).

3 Choose the desired option from the dialog box that appears.

Figure 21.13   *Move Chart* button.

Changing the chart layout in Excel 2007/2010

Although you can manually add chart objects like titles, it is much easier to choose from one of Excel's predefined chart layouts (see Figure 21.14).

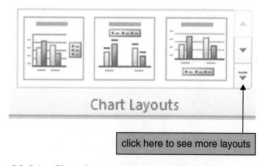

click here to see more layouts

Figure 21.14   Chart layouts option in 2007/2010.

To choose a predefined chart layout:

1 Switch to the *Chart Design* tab of the Ribbon.

2 Choose a layout.

Then it is just a matter of editing the title, axes labels etc.

Adding a title to an Excel 2007/2010 chart

To add a title to a chart:

1 Switch to the *Chart Layout* tab of the Ribbon.

2 Click the *Chart Title* button.

3 Click the *Above Chart* option (see Figure 21.15).

4 Click on the title that appears, then select the existing text.

5 Type the new title.

6 Click anywhere outside the chart when you are done.

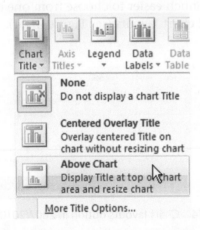

Figure 21.15 Adding a chart title in 2007/2010.

Adding an axis label in Excel 2007/2010

To add an axis label to the chart:

1 Switch to the *Chart Layout* tab of the Ribbon.

2 Click the *Axis Titles* button.

3 Choose which axis you want to label.

4 Choose where to display the axis label (see Figure 21.16).

5 Click on the axis label that appears, then select the existing text.

6 Type the new axis label.

7 Click anywhere outside the chart when you are done.

Repositioning the legend

To reposition the legend or turn it off/on:

1 Switch to the *Chart Layout* tab of the Ribbon.

2 Click the *Legend* button.

3 Choose the appropriate option.

Adding data labels

To add data labels, for example to display percentages on a pie chart:

1 Switch to the *Chart Layout* tab of the Ribbon.

2 Click the *Data Labels* button.

3 Click Label *Options* (see Figure 21.17).

4 Select the options that you want.

5 Click *Close*.

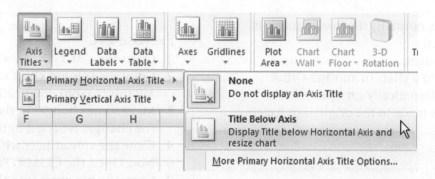

Figure 21.16 Adding an axis label.

Figure 21.17 Adding data labels.

Copying charts

If you want to copy a chart (e.g. so that you can paste it into Microsoft Word):

1 Click on the <u>background</u> of the chart.

2 Click the *Copy* button.

Excel 2003 does not allow you to copy a chart by right-clicking on it.

When you right-click in another Office program in order to paste the chart, you have the option of either pasting a copy of the chart or a link to the chart. If you do the latter, any changes made to the chart in Excel will be updated in Microsoft Word.

Summary
• In Excel 2003, you use the *Chart* wizard to create charts.
• In Excel 2007 and 2010, you use the *Insert* tab to create a skeleton chart then use the *Chart Layout* and *Chart Design* tabs to add things like titles.
• The legend on a chart is a 'key' that tells you what each colour represents.

- The category axis is normally the horizontal axis, except in bar charts.
- Pie charts have no axes.
- If you paste a link to a chart in another Office program, it will automatically get updated to reflect any changes made to the original in Excel.

Review exercises

Exercise 21A
1 Open the CRUISE4 file from the exercise folder.
2 Create a pie chart showing the 2006 cruise arrivals for:
   - Antigua and Barbuda
   - Aruba
   - the Bahamas
   - and Barbados.

   The chart should be displayed to the right of the data on the same sheet and its title should be '2006 Cruise Arrivals'. Display the percentages.
3 On a new sheet called 'Comparison', insert a column chart that compares the 2006 and 2007 arrivals for the Bahamas, Barbados and St. Lucia. Give the chart and its axes suitable titles. Include a legend which indicates what year each series represents.
4 Save the file in your class folder as CRUISE5.

Exercise 21B
1 Open the CLIMATE file from the exercise folder.
2 On a new sheet called 'Rainfall', insert a line graph that shows the rainfall for each month. Give it a suitable title and label the axes. Hide the legend.
3 Underneath the data, insert a bar chart that shows the temperature for Jan, Apr, Jul and Oct. Hide the legend, label the axes and give it a suitable title.
4 Save the file in your class folder as CLIMATE3.

Exercise 21C
1 Open the CRUISES file.
2 Copy the column chart and paste it into a new Microsoft Word document (but not as a link).
3 Make some changes to the original chart. Are the changes reflected in the Word document?
4 Close the spreadsheet without saving.
6 Now Open the CLIMATE3 file.
7 Copy the bar chart into the Word document as a link.
8 Make some changes to the bar chart in Excel. Has the chart in the Word document been updated?
9 Close both files without saving.

22 Printing

In this chapter, you will learn:

- how to set the print area
- how to preview what you are about to print
- how to force the spreadsheet to print on one page
- how to centre the spreadsheet on a page
- how to insert headers and footers

Print area

The print area is the part of the spreadsheet that would be printed if you clicked *Print*. Normally Excel will simply print all the data on the sheet, but by setting the print area you can control which part gets printed.

Setting the print area

To set the print area:

1 Select the range that you want printed.

2 Click *File* (or the *Page Layout* tab in 2007/2010), *Print Area, Set Print Area*.

Clearing the print area

If you clear the print area, Excel will go back to printing the entire spreadsheet.

To clear the print area:

1 Click File if you are using Excel 2003 or Page Layout if you are using Excel 2007/2010.

2 Click *Print Area, Clear Print Area*

Print preview

Before you print a spreadsheet, you should preview it in order to see what it will look like when it is printed and how many pages it will take.

In order to get a *Print Preview*:

- in Excel 2003, click *File, Print Preview*
- in Excel 2007, click the *Microsoft Office* button, then *Print*, then *Print Preview*
- in Excel 2010, click *File*, then *Print*.

Previewing in Excel 2010

Previewing in Excel 2010 is different from the previous versions of Excel. Office 2010 combines the print preview with basic print options in a new *Print* section (shown in Figure 22.1). As you can see, this section is located in the *Backstage* view.

In the middle panel of the window there are settings where you can adjust things like the number of copies, which pages to print, the page size and orientation and which printer to use. For even more printer options, you can click the '*Printer Properties*' link.

The right-hand panel shows you the print preview. You can use the arrows at the bottom to preview other pages apart from the current one. In Figure 22.1 you can see that page 1 is currently being previewed and that there are 6 pages.

Printing the document

When you have finished previewing, you can click the *Print* button. In Excel 2010 the print area will be printed right away. If you are using Excel 2003 or 2007, the *Print* dialog box will be displayed instead. In this case, you would make sure the settings are to your liking, then click *OK*.

The *Page Setup* window

The *Page Setup* window, shown in Figure 22.2, allows you to change a variety of settings to do with the layout of the spreadsheet.

Opening the Page Setup window

If you are previewing the spreadsheet, you can easily access the *Page Setup* window by clicking (Page) Setup ....

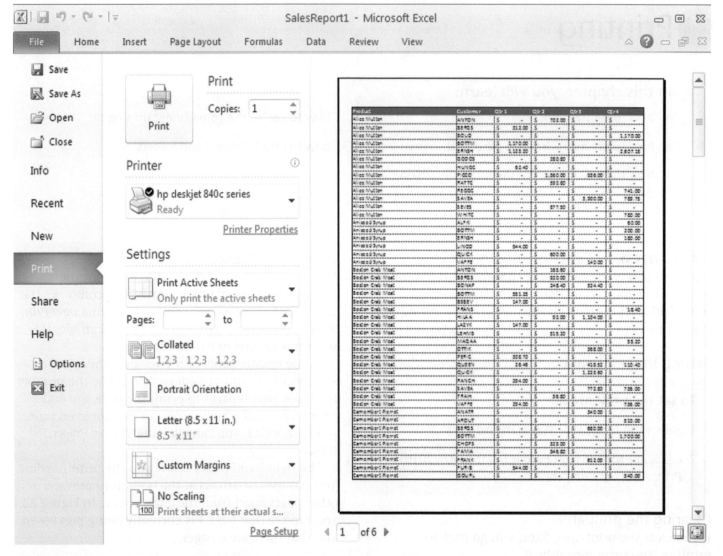

Figure 22.1 The Print section in Excel 2010.

The *Page Setup* window is also accessible:

- in Excel 2003, by clicking *File*, *Page Setup*
- in Excel 2007/2010, by selecting the *Page Layout* tab, then clicking the *More Options* button in the *Page Setup* group (see Figure 22.3).

Most (but not all) of the options in the *Page Setup* window can be found in the *Page Layout* tab of the Ribbon. And if you are using Excel 2010, you can find many of them in the *Print* section of the *Backstage* view.

Table 22.1 explains what each tab in the *Page Setup* window does.

Table 22.1 Page Setup tabs.

Tab	Why you would use it
Page	To change the orientation; to fit a spreadsheet onto one page
Margins	To change the margins; to centre the spreadsheet on the page
Header/Footer	To add a header or a footer
Sheet	To show gridlines or repeat rows

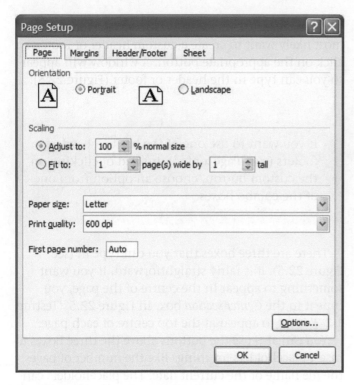

Figure 22.2 The *Page Setup* window.

If the columns in your spreadsheet are extremely wide, fitting the spreadsheet on one page will make the text very tiny. You should make the columns as narrow as possible before using this option.

Centring the spreadsheet on the page

If you want to centre the spreadsheet on the page:

1 Open the *Page Setup* Window.

2 Go to the *Margins* tab.

3 Place ticks in the two centre boxes at the bottom of the window.

4 Click *OK*.

Fitting the spreadsheet on a certain number of pages

The *Page* tab of the *Print Setup* window has an option you use if you want to fit the spreadsheet on one page (or any number of pages). Excel will resize the text and the graphics to suit. If you want to fit it on one page, make sure this option is selected and that it is set to fit to 1 page wide and 1 page tall.

Headers and footers

To set headers and footers in Excel you have to first go to the *Header/Footer* tab (Figure 22.4). To do so:

* either open the *Page Setup* window and click on the *Header/Footer* tab
* or, if you are using Excel 2003, click *View, Header and Footer*.

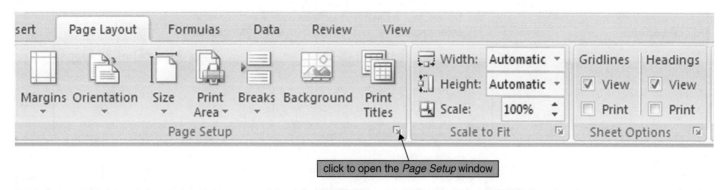

Figure 22.3 Opening the *Page Setup* window in Excel 2007/2010.

Figure 22.4 The Header/Footer tab.

Once you are in the Header/Footer tab, you will most likely want to create a custom header or footer, so click on the appropriate button. A window will appear so you can type in the header or footer (Figure 22.5).

> If you want to use one of the built-in headers or footers (e.g. 'Page x of y'), instead of clicking on the custom button, choose an option from one of the combo boxes.

There are three boxes that you can type in (see Figure 22.5). It is fairly straightforward. If you want something to appear in the centre of the page, you type it in the *Center section* box. In Figure 22.5, 'Testing 1-2-3' is set to appear at the top centre of each page.

You can also use the buttons above the three boxes to insert placeholders for things like the number of pages, the file name or the current date. The placeholders can be recognised by the '&' in front them. In Figure 22.5, placeholders have been used to insert 'Page 1 of 3', 'Page 2 of 3', etc. on the top right of each page.

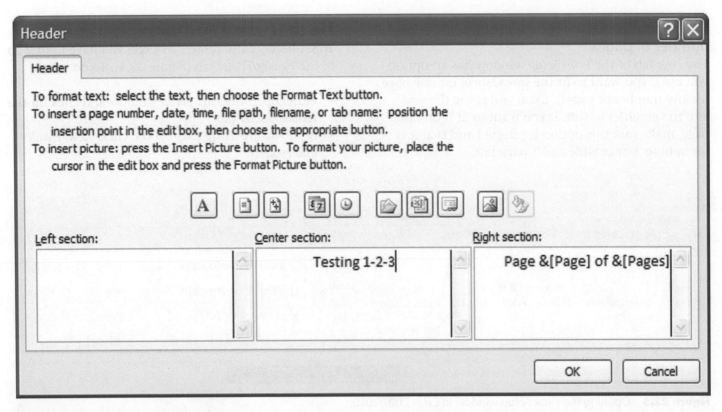

Figure 22.5 Typing a custom header.

Summary

- Setting the print area allows you to specify which part of the spreadsheet will be printed.
- You should use the *Print Preview* window (or the *Print* section of the *Backstage* view if you are using Excel 2010) to preview a spreadsheet before you print it.
- The option to fit a spreadsheet on one page is in the *Page* tab of the *Page Setup* window.
- The option to centre a spreadsheet on a page is in the *Margins* tab of the *Page Setup* window.
- You can insert custom or built-in headers and footers via the *Header/Footer* tab of the *Page Setup* window.

Review exercises

Exercise 22

1 Open the CRUISE5 file from the exercise folder.
2 Print Sheet1 in landscape orientation on one page. Is the text really small? How can you correct that?
3 Change the print area so that the chart at the right of Sheet1 is not printed.
4 Close the file without saving.

23 Microsoft® PowerPoint basics

In this chapter, you will learn:

- how PowerPoint should be used
- about the PowerPoint interface
- how to add, delete and reorder slides
- how to view a slideshow

Introduction

Microsoft PowerPoint, which is part of Microsoft Office, is the most commonly used presentation software in the world. Presentation software allows you to create slideshows that can be used:

- as teaching tools during lectures and training sessions
- to present reports (in business meetings, in class, etc.)
- to illustrate points made during speeches
- to enhance sales pitches.

Presentation software contains features like animations, slide transitions and sound effects to help keep your audience's attention. But it should be used to <u>supplement</u> what the speaker is saying. What do I mean by that?

- You should not be reading from the slides.
- Your slides should not be packed with text – they should only contain the <u>main</u> points you are talking about.
- The slides should have some pictures or charts to illustrate what you are talking about.

The PowerPoint interface

Let us look at the main components of the PowerPoint interface. PowerPoint 2007 is shown in Figure 23.1, but the elements are the same in all versions of PowerPoint.

Current slide

The most prominent element of the PowerPoint interface is the current slide, which takes up most of the middle of the window.

List of slides

To the left of the window there is a panel that lists the slides in the slideshow. By default, the *Slides* tab is selected in this panel, but you can switch to the *Outline* tab by clicking on it. The *Slides* tab shows thumbnails of the slides in the presentation.

Here is how you use the <u>Slides</u> tab:

- to switch to a particular slide just click on its thumbnail
- to select multiple slides use the *Shift* or *Ctrl* keys.

The Notes box

Near the bottom of the window is a third panel called the Notes box. This is a place where you can type notes for the current slide. These notes do not appear on the slide itself.

Differences from Microsoft Word

Working with presentations requires a different mindset to working with Word documents. The main difference is that PowerPoint uses slides instead of pages. The most important thing to remember is this:

You can not type directly onto slides – you have to use text boxes.

Creating a new blank presentation

Whenever you first open PowerPoint, it automatically creates a blank presentation for you to work with (usually called Presentation1). However, if you need to do so manually, it is simple:

- In PowerPoint 2003, click *File*, *New*, then click *Blank Presentation* from the task pane. Or click the *New* icon in the *Standard* toolbar.

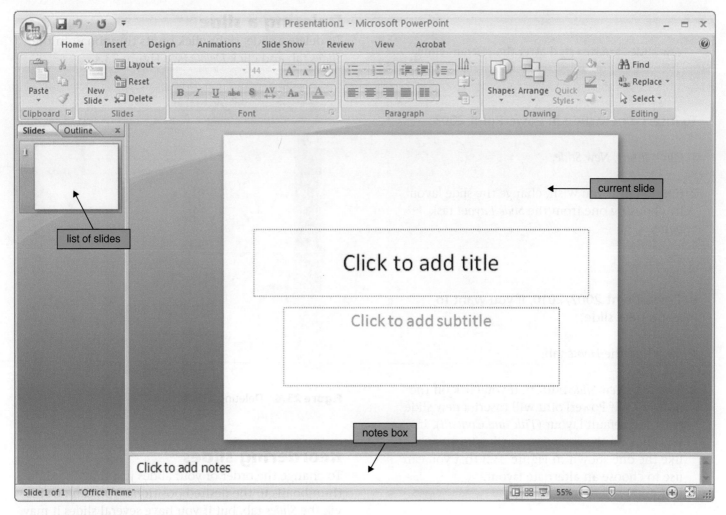

Figure 23.1 The PowerPoint 2007 interface.

- In PowerPoint 2007, click the Microsoft Office button, click *New*, then click *Create* in the window that appears.
- In PowerPoint 2010, click *File, New*, then click the *Create* button.

A new blank presentation contains only one slide – the Title Slide (see Figure 23.2). On it there are two placeholder text boxes – one for the title and one for the subtitle.

When you click in one of the text boxes, the placeholder text disappears, allowing you to insert some text of your own.

Adding a new slide
Regardless of what version of PowerPoint you are using, when you add a new slide you have the option of using the default slide layout or choosing another

one. (We will talk more about slide layouts in a little while.)

Figure 23.2 The title slide.

New slides are inserted <u>after</u> the current slide.

To insert a new slide in PowerPoint 2003:

1 Click *Insert, New Slide*.

2 (Optional) If you wish, change the slide layout by choosing one from the *Slide Layout* task pane.

In PowerPoint 2007/2010, if you want to insert a new slide:

1 Switch to the *Home* tab.

2 Click the *New Slide* button. If you click on the button itself PowerPoint will insert a new slide with the default layout (*Title and Content*). If you click on the arrow, you will get a menu like the one shown in Figure 23.3 that you can use to choose an alternate layout.

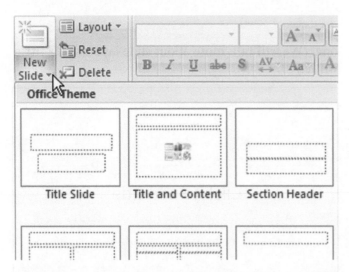

Figure 23.3 Inserting a new slide in PowerPoint 2007/2010.

Deleting a slide

To delete a slide, right-click on its thumbnail in the *Slides* tab and click *Delete* (see Figure 23.4).

Figure 23.4 Deleting a slide.

Reordering slides

To change the order of your slides just drag the slide thumbnails to the desired positions. You can do this via the *Slides* tab, but if you have several slides it may be easier to reorder them via the *Slide Sorter*.

To switch to the *Slide Sorter* view, click *View, Slide Sorter*.

Figure 23.5 shows the third slide being repositioned so that it will now be the second slide. Notice a couple of things:

- The mouse pointer has a little rectangle at the bottom. Whenever you see this icon, you are in the process of dragging an item to a new location.
- The vertical line indicates where the slide will go.

If you want to get back to the default view, click *View, Normal*.

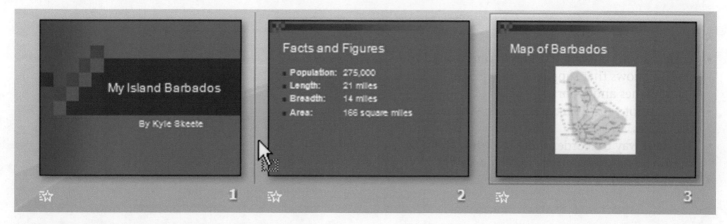

Figure 23.5 Reordering slides via the *Slide Sorter* view.

Viewing a slideshow

When you have finished creating your presentation you will want to see what it looks like as a slideshow.

To view a slideshow, click *View, Slideshow* or press the *F5* key.

Some slideshows are designed to automatically advance to the next slide. (You will learn how to do this in Chapter 26). Others require you to manually go from one slide to the next.

There are several ways you can go to the <u>next</u> slide:

* click the left mouse button
* press the *Enter* key
* press the right or down arrow.

You can go to the <u>previous</u> slide by pressing the left or up arrow on your keyboard.

Navigation controls

If you move the mouse during a slideshow, a semi-transparent overlay will appear at the bottom left-hand corner of the screen, as shown in Figure 23.6.

Here is what each item in Figure 23.6 does:

1 Goes to the previous slide.

2 Allows you to change the current annotation settings. You can make the mouse pointer behave like a pen or highlighter, change the colour and more.

3 Displays a menu from which you can jump to a particular slide, pause the slideshow, and get help on what keys do what during the slideshow. Note that you can get this same menu by right-clicking on the slide.

4 Goes to the next slide.

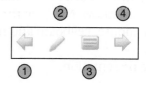

Figure 23.6 The navigation controls.

Keyboard shortcuts

Table 23.1 gives some additional keyboard shortcuts you may find useful.

Table 23.1 Keyboard shortcuts in Microsoft PowerPoint.

In order to...	Press
End the slideshow	*Esc*
Go to a particular slide	The number for that slide, followed by *Enter*
Erase annotations from the screen	*E*

Summary

- Presentation software like PowerPoint is used to do slideshows that supplement speeches, lectures, sales pitches and reports.
- You cannot type directly on slides; you have to use text boxes.
- The best way to reorder slides is to drag them to their new positions using the *Slide Sorter*.
- To view a slideshow press the *F5* key.

Review exercises

Exercise 23A

1 List four uses of presentation software.
2 Give four features found in Presentation software.
3 Open the ISLAND file from the exercise folder.
4 Use the scroll bar on the right to scroll through the different slides.
5 Use the *Slides* tab to return to the first slide.
6 Switch to the *Outline* tab to see what it looks like, then switch back to the *Slides* tab.
7 View the slideshow. Navigate through it by using the mouse, keyboard and navigation controls.
8 Close the presentation.

Exercise 23B

1 Open the ISLAND file from the exercise folder.
2 Interchange the second and third slides.
3 Delete the fourth slide.
4 Save the file in your class folder as ISLAND1.

Exercise 23C

1 Create a new blank presentation.
2 In the appropriate placeholder, insert the title 'All About Me'. Put your name as the subtitle.
3 Add the following slides and fill in the appropriate information:

   - My Family.
   - My Hobbies.
   - My Favourite Things.

4 Insert a slide after the title slide called 'Words that Best Describe Me'.
5 Save the presentation as MYSELF.

24 Slide layouts

Changing the layout

PowerPoint provides multiple layouts that you can use in your slides. These layouts have placeholders where you can insert text or various media.

You can change the layout of a slide at any time. When you change a slide's layout, you don't erase the material you already have on the slide. Instead, the material is repositioned to fit the new layout.

To change the layout of a slide:

1 Right-click on the slide's thumbnail in the Slide tab.

2 Click (*Slide*) Layout.

3 Choose the layout you want. In PowerPoint 2003, you have to do so from the task pane (see Figure 24.1).

Choosing the right layout

You can divide the slide layouts into two broad categories: text layouts and content layouts. Text layouts are straightforward – you just click in the text box and replace the placeholder text with some text of your own.

Content layouts require a bit more work. But the good thing about them is that they allow you to insert different types of media – tables, pictures, clip art, charts and video clips.

Table 24.1 explains when to use a particular layout.

Using content layouts

Each content layout has a cluster of icons that you can click to insert different types of media. PowerPoint 2003 has slightly different icons to those in 2007/2010 but very similar functionality (see Figure 24.2).

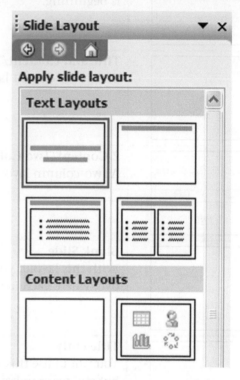

Figure 24.1 Changing slide layout in PowerPoint 2003.

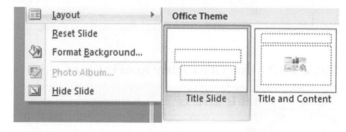

Figure 24.2 Changing slide layout in PowerPoint 2007/2010.

Table 24.2 lists what clicking each content icon in Figure 24.3 will insert.

We will only cover inserting pictures and clip art. If you want to insert a table or chart it is often easier to copy it from another Microsoft Office program than to create one in PowerPoint.

Table 24.1 Choosing the right layout

	Title Slide Use this layout on the first slide of your presentation. Give the title of the presentation and a subtitle or the name of the presenter.
	Section Header (PowerPoint 2007/2010 only) You should use a section header slide to let the audience know whenever a new section is beginning.
	Title and Content/Title and Text This is the default layout for any new slides that you add.
	2 Content/Two Column Text A two-column layout is a good way to show or compare two items.
	Blank Slide With this layout, you will have to add each item manually but you have full control over where each item on the slide goes.
	Title Only You would use this layout if you want to manually position information on the slide but still want to have a title that is consistent with the rest of the slides.

Table 24.2 Using the content icons in Figure 24.3.

Icon	What it inserts
1	Table
2	Chart
3	Clip art
4	Picture from on file on your computer
5	Smart chart/diagram
6	Media clip, e.g. video, sound

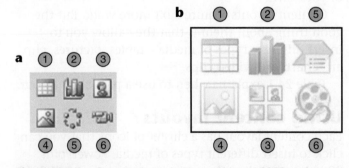

Figure 24.3 Content icons in PowerPoint. **a** 2003 and **b** 2007/2010.

Inserting clip art

When you click on the *Clip Art* content button in a slide, it will open the *Clip Art* task pane. You can also show the *Clip Art* task pane (see Figure 24.4) by clicking:

- *Insert, Picture, Clip Art...* (in PowerPoint 2003)
- *Insert, Clip Art* (in PowerPoint 2007/2010).

Inserting a picture

In order to display the dialog box that allows you to insert a picture from a file on your computer:

- either click the *Picture* content button on the slide
- or click *Insert, Picture* (from file).

Once you have inserted a picture you can drag it to another location or use the picture handles to resize it (Figure 24.5).

Figure 24.5 Using the picture handles to resize a picture.

Summary

- In PowerPoint 2007 and 2010 you can change the slide layout by right-clicking on the slide.
- In PowerPoint 2003 you have to go through the *Slide Layout* task pane.
- Content slides have icons that you can click to insert media like pictures and clip art.

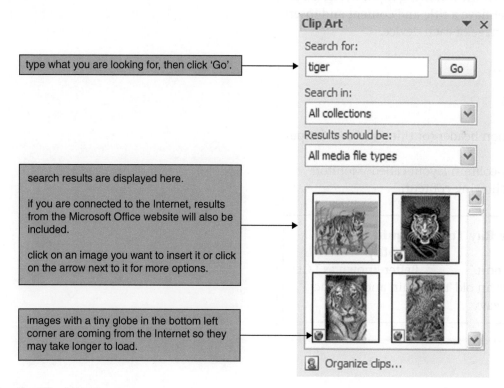

type what you are looking for, then click 'Go'.

search results are displayed here.

if you are connected to the Internet, results from the Microsoft Office website will also be included.

click on an image you want to insert it or click on the arrow next to it for more options.

images with a tiny globe in the bottom left corner are coming from the Internet so they may take longer to load.

Figure 24.4 Using the *Clip Art* task pane.

Review exercises

Exercise 24

1 Create a new blank presentation.
2 In the title slide, add the title 'Computer Hardware'. Put 'Basic Stuff You Should Know' as the subtitle.
3 Add a new slide. Put its title as 'Types of Hardware'. Mention the following types:

> - Central Processing Unit (CPU)
> - Input Devices
> - Output Devices
> - Storage Devices

4 Add a section header for 'Input Devices'. If you are using PowerPoint 2003 use a title slide instead.
5 Add slides for the following input devices. Use layouts that have a title and content and insert a clip art image of each device.

- Keyboard
- Mouse
- Joystick.

6 Add a section header (or title slide) for 'Output Devices'.
7 Add a two-column layout called 'Monitors'. Add the following content.

Cathode Ray Tube	Liquid Crystal Display
CRT for short	Better known as LCD
Looks like an old TV	Thin and compact
Big and heavy	

8 Add a title and content slide called 'Printers' and add the following points:

- **Dot-Matrix** – uses a ribbon
- **Inkjet** – uses ink
- **Laser** – uses a laser and toner
- **Thermal** – uses heat.

9 Save the presentation in your class folder as HARDWARE.

25 Themes

Introduction

Let's face it, the presentations that we have created so far have looked a bit dull. Fortunately, PowerPoint comes with a set of themes (design templates) that can be used to make a presentation look more interesting. Each one has been carefully designed so that the background and the text go well together.

Figure 25.1 New presentation (PowerPoint 2003).

In PowerPoint 2003 'themes' are called 'design templates'. I will use the terms 'design template' and 'theme' interchangeably.

Creating a new presentation that uses a theme

Creating a new presentation based on a theme requires a few more steps than one from a blank document.

To create a new presentation from a design template in PowerPoint 2003:

1 Click *File, New...*

2 Click '*From Design Template*' from the task pane (see Figure 25.1).

3 Select the template you want (see Figure 25.2).

Figure 25.2 Choosing a design template (PowerPoint 2003).

Figure 25.3 Creating a new presentation from a theme in PowerPoint 2007.

To create a new presentation from an installed theme in PowerPoint 2007:

1 Click the *Microsoft Office* button.

2 Click *New*.

3 Click *Installed Themes*.

4 Select the theme you want to use (see Figure 25.3).

5 Click the *Create* button at the bottom of the window.

The steps in PowerPoint 2010 are slightly different:

1 Click the *File* tab.

2 Click *New*.

3 Click *Themes*.

4 Select the theme you want from the list (see Figure 25.4).

5 Click the *Create* button.

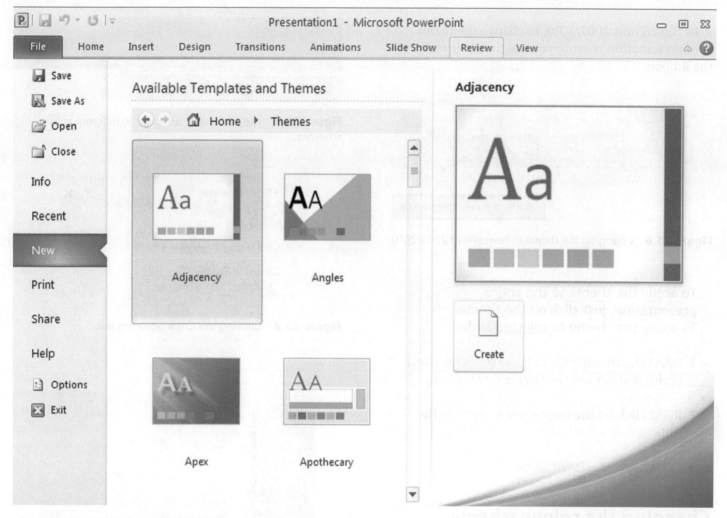

Figure 25.4 Creating a new presentation from a theme in PowerPoint 2010.

Changing the design template or theme

If you do not like your presentation's design template (or if it does not have one), you can always change it later.

In PowerPoint 2003, there is a task pane dedicated to changing the design template (the same one you use when creating a new presentation from a design template). You can access it by clicking *Format, Slide Design...*

When you position the mouse pointer over a design, you will see an arrow appear to its side. If you click on it, you will see the list of options (Figure 25.5). Choose the option that suits your particular situation.

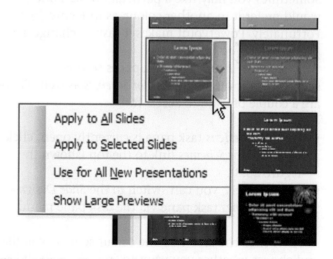

Figure 25.5 Changing the design template in PowerPoint 2003.

In PowerPoint 2007/2010, to change the theme your presentation is using you use the *Design* tab of the Ribbon.

Figure 25.6   Changing the theme in PowerPoint 2007/2010.

To apply the theme to the <u>entire</u> presentation, just click on the theme. To apply the theme to <u>selected</u> slides:

1 Select the thumbnails of those slides (to select multiple slides use the *Shift* or *Ctrl* button).

2 Right click on the theme you want from the ribbon.

3 Click *Apply to Selected Slides*.

Changing the colour scheme

Sometimes you may like a particular design but would prefer it in another colour, as in Figure 25.7. Fortunately, PowerPoint makes it easy to change a presentation's colour scheme.

PowerPoint 2003 loves task panes so not surprisingly it has one for *Color Schemes* as well. There are a couple of ways to access it.

- If a *Slide Designs* task pane is currently open, click on the *Color Schemes* link to the top (shown in Figure 25.8).
- Alternatively, you can switch to the *Slide Design – Color Schemes* task pane via the task pane menu.

Then click the arrow by the colour scheme you like and choose whether you want to apply it to all slides (see Figure 25.9).

Figure 25.7   The same slide using three different colour schemes.

Figure 25.8   Clicking the Color Schemes link.

Figure 25.9   Changing the colour scheme in PowerPoint 2003.

As expected, PowerPoint 2007 and 2010 take a Ribbon-based approach.

To change the colour scheme in PowerPoint 2007/2010:

1 Switch to the *Design* tab.

2 Click on the *Colors* button (Figure 25.10).

3 Click on the colour scheme you want.

If you only want to apply the scheme to selected slides, right click on the colour scheme and choose 'Apply to Selected Schemes'.

The current scheme has an orange box around it. So in Figure 25.10, Apex is the current colour scheme.

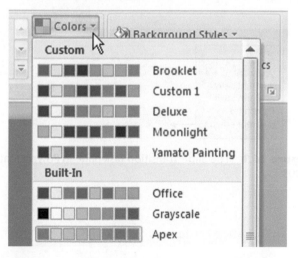

Figure 25.10 Changing the color scheme in PowerPoint 2007/2010.

Summary

- Themes (or design templates in PowerPoint 2003) allow you to enhance the appearance of your presentations.
- You can create a presentation based on one theme and change it later.
- If you like a theme but not its colour, you can change its colour scheme.
- You do not have to use the same theme and colour scheme throughout your presentation. You can apply a new theme (or colour scheme) to selected slides while having the others remain unchanged.

Review exercises

Exercise 25

1 Open the HARDWARE file.
2 Apply a design template/theme to the presentation.
3 Change the colour scheme to one of your choosing.
4 Apply a new design template/theme to the first slide only. Change <u>its</u> colour scheme.
5 Save the file as HARDWARE1.
6 Create a new presentation from a design template/theme. Add a few slides with different layouts. Change the colour scheme and save the file as TEMPLATES.

26 Slide transitions

In this chapter, you will learn:

- how to add transitions to slides
- how to rehearse timings
- how to add hyperlinks to other slides

Applying slide transitions

Slide transitions allow you to control how PowerPoint moves from one slide to the next. You can make PowerPoint advance to the next slide after a number of seconds, have transition animations and more.

PowerPoint 2003 has a task pane dedicated to *Slide Transitions* which can be accessed by clicking *Slide Show, Slide Transition...* Of course you can also use the *Task Pane* menu (Figure 26.1).

In PowerPoint 2007, the *Slide Transition* options (see Figure 26.2) are part of the Ribbon's Animations tab.

In PowerPoint 2010 there is a dedicated *Transitions* tab in the Ribbon but it looks virtually the same as the image in Figure 26.2.

Transition options

Here is what the various options are for:

- Transition effects – These control how your slide appears on the screen. For example you can have a dissolve effect or make it fade from black.
- Speed – This allows you to control whether the animation occurs at a <u>Fast</u>, <u>Medium</u> or <u>Slow</u> speed.
- Sound – This makes PowerPoint play a sound as the slide appears on the screen. You can choose from the list or use a file stored somewhere else on your computer.
- Advance Slide – This allows you to control what causes this slide to advance to the next one. By default PowerPoint requires you to click the mouse or press a button to go to the next slide. But you can also make it advance automatically after a certain amount of time. In the example below, the slide will advance when you click the mouse or after 5 seconds (whichever comes first).

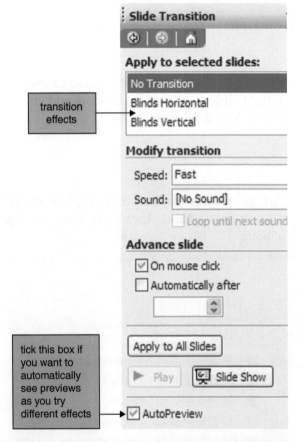

Figure 26.1 The Slide Transition task pane in PowerPoint 2003.

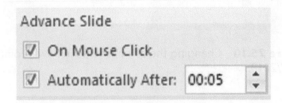

- *Apply to All* – Click this button if you want to apply these settings to all the slides in the show.

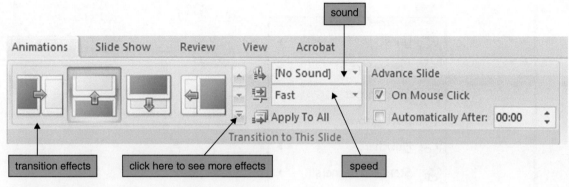

Figure 26.2 Slide transition options in PowerPoint 2007.

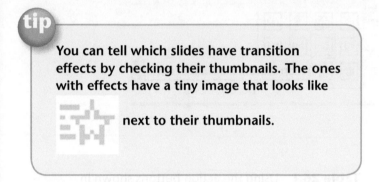
Rehearsing timings

This is a very useful feature, especially if your presentation is accompanying a speech or has to be a certain length.

Here is how it works. You rehearse your presentation while looking at a slide. All the while there are two timers going – one that lets you know how long you have spent on the current slide and another that tells you the total time that has elapsed.

When you are ready to go to the next slide, you click the *Next* button. When you have finished, PowerPoint asks you if you want to keep the new slide timings. If you click *Yes*, PowerPoint will update your slide transitions so that the slides automatically advance according to the rehearsed timings.

To access this feature (regardless of what version of PowerPoint you are using):

1 Click *Slide Show*.

2 Click *Rehearse Timings*.

The first slide of the presentation will be displayed full screen, with the *Rehearsal* window on top.

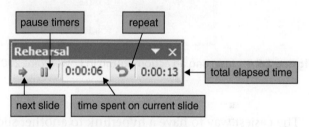

Figure 26.3 The Rehearsal Window.

Let me explain the parts of the window that are not self-explanatory:

- *Pause Timer* – Click this once to pause both timers. Click it again to start them back.
- *Repeat* – This allows you to start over the current slide and resets the timers to suit. The first timer gets reset to 0:00:00 whereas the total elapsed time gets rolled back to whatever it was when you first got to this slide.

 The rehearsed timings can also affect your custom animations. We will talk more about custom animations in the next chapter.

Inserting hyperlinks

Much like hyperlinks in web pages allow you to go from one page to another, you can use hyperlinks in PowerPoint presentations to allow a user to navigate from one slide to the next.

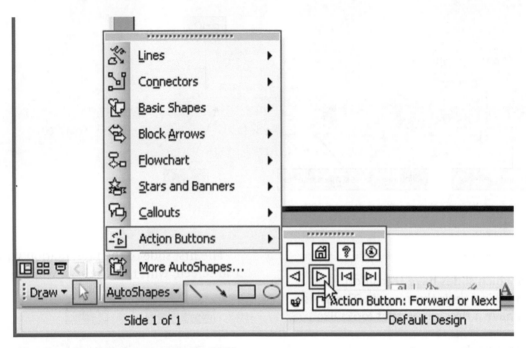

Figure 26.4 Inserting an action button in PowerPoint 2003.

The easiest way to have a hyperlink to another slide is by inserting an action button on the slide.

To add an action button to a slide:

- In PowerPoint 2003, click the *AutoShapes* button in the *Drawing* toolbar, click *Action Buttons*, then choose a button from the list (see Figure 26.4).

- In PowerPoint 2007/2010, click *Insert, Shapes* then click one of the action buttons at the bottom of the list that appears (see Figure 26.5).

Figure 26.5 Action buttons.

Each action button that you see in Figure 26.5 has a specific purpose, detailed in Table 26.1. We are only going to be using the first five.

Table 26.1 Using the action buttons shown in Figure 26.5.

Button	Which slide it is normally used to link to
1	The previous slide
2	The next slide
3	The first slide in the presentation
4	The last slide in the presentation
5 (Home button)	The home slide (which is normally – but not always – the first slide in the presentation)

After you choose an action button, you then draw it on the slide by dragging the mouse. When you release the mouse button the *Action Settings* window (Figure 26.6) will appear. You can change the hyperlink in this window if you like but normally you would just click *OK*.

Figure 26.6 *Action Settings* window.

tip

You can edit or remove an action button's hyperlink by right-clicking on it and choosing the appropriate option.

Review exercises

Exercise 26

1 Open the file HARDWARE1 from the exercise folder.
2 Add a dissolve effect to <u>all</u> the slides and have each slide automatically advance after 5 seconds.
3 Apply a fade effect to the title slide as well as the slides with the section headers (*Input Devices, Output Devices*). These slides should automatically advance after 2 seconds.
4 Save the file in your class folder as HARDWARE2.
5 At the bottom of each slide, add hyperlinks to take you to the next, previous and home slides (where applicable).
6 Use the *Rehearse Timings* feature to set timings for the slides. Pretend that you are talking to the class about these various devices.
7 Save the file in your class folder as HARDWARE3.

Summary

- To adjust slide transitions use the *Slide Transition* task pane or the *Animations* tab of the Ribbon.
- You can configure slides to advance automatically after a certain time and have transition effects.
- You can use the rehearse timings feature to make sure presentation takes a certain amount of time.
- PowerPoint has a variety of action buttons that you can easily use to insert hyperlinks to other slides.

27 Custom animations

In this chapter, you will learn:

- how to add and remove custom animations
- how to make animations start automatically
- how to delay animations by a certain amount of time

Custom animations are similar to transition effects except that they work on the individual elements on a slide instead of the slide itself.

In a surprising change, PowerPoint 2003 and 2007 use the same interface to add custom animations, whereas PowerPoint 2010 introduces a new one.

Categories of effects

PowerPoint has four categories of animation effects.

- Entrance – In these effects the object is hidden at first but then animates into view.
- Emphasis – These emphasise objects that are currently on the screen by changing their size or colour, by making them flicker, etc.
- Exit – These effects make objects on the screen disappear.
- Motion Paths – These move an object that is already on the screen to another position along a straight line, curve or custom path.

Of these four types, we will be using only the Entrance effects. The rest are more difficult to use effectively.

Using custom animations in PowerPoint 2003 and 2007

PowerPoint 2003 and 2007 use the same interface when it comes to custom animations – the *Custom Animation* task pane. If it is not currently being displayed, you can see it by clicking:

- *Slide Show, Custom Animation...* (if you are using PowerPoint 2003).
- *Animations, Custom Animation* (if you are using PowerPoint 2007).

It is one of the more complicated parts of PowerPoint, but it helps if you think of it as being divided into four sections (see Figure 27.1).

Adding a custom animation

To add a custom animation in PowerPoint 2003/2007:

1 Select the element you want to animate, e.g. a picture or paragraph.

2 Click the *Add Effect* button.

3 Choose an effect from one of the four categories (see Figure 27.2). The effect that you choose gets added to the list of custom animations for the slide.

4 Change the settings for the effect to suit your needs.

Removing or switching custom animations

To remove an animation or switch to another one in PowerPoint 2003/2007:

1 Select the animation from the list.

2 Use the *Remove* or *Change* buttons respectively.

Making the animation start automatically

When you are playing the slideshow, you normally have to click the mouse to start an animation. To get the animations to start automatically, you change the settings in the *Start* combo box. These settings are explained in Table 27.1.

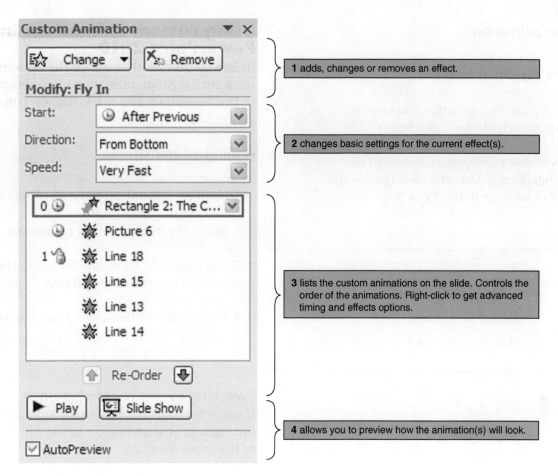

Figure 27.1 The *Custom Animation* task pane (with effects already added).

1 adds, changes or removes an effect.

2 changes basic settings for the current effect(s).

3 lists the custom animations on the slide. Controls the order of the animations. Right-click to get advanced timing and effects options.

4 allows you to preview how the animation(s) will look.

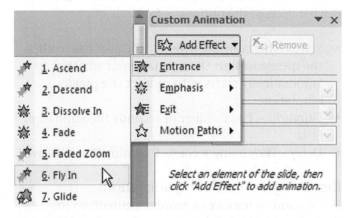

Figure 27.2 Adding an entrance effect in PowerPoint 2003 or 2007.

Table 27.1 Options in the *Start* animation combo box.

Option	When the animation will start
Start On Click	When the user clicks the mouse or presses Enter
Start With Previous	At (roughly) the same time as the previous animation
Start After Previous	After the previous animation has completed

Delaying an animation

To delay a custom animation:

1 Right-click on the animation you want to delay, then click *Timing...* (see Figure 27.3).

2 In the window that appears, switch to the *Timing* tab (Figure 27.4) and then change the number of seconds in the *Delay* box.

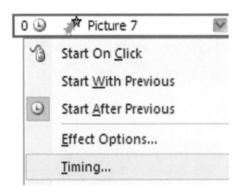

Figure 27.3   Changing the timing.

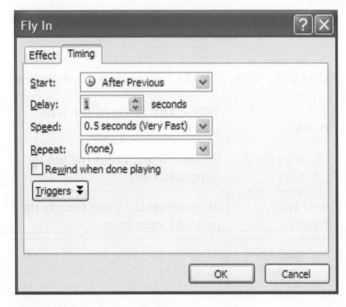

Figure 27.4   Timing settings.

Using custom animations in PowerPoint 2010

In PowerPoint 2010, many of the options to work with custom animations have been moved to the *Animations* tab of the Ribbon (shown in Figure 27.5).

Adding an animation

To add an animation in PowerPoint 2010:

1 Select the item you want to animate.

2 Click the *Add Animation* button in the Animations tab of the Ribbon.

3 Choose the desired effect from the list that appears (shown in Figure 27.6).

Switching to another animation

If you want to switch to another animation, you can just click on that animation in the Animation group of the *Animations* tab.

Adjusting the timing

If you want the animation to start automatically, change how long it lasts or how much it is delayed, you use the *Timing* group of the *Animations* tab. Here is what each of the options is for:

- Start – This controls whether the user has to click the mouse to start the animation or whether it automatically starts with or after the previous animation.
- Duration – The number of seconds the animation lasts.
- Delay – How many seconds the animation is delayed.

Removing or reordering animations

If you want to remove or reorder animations in PowerPoint 2010, it is best to use the *Animations* pane. That way you can see the list of current animations.

As you can see from Figure 27.7, the *Animations* pane is like a trimmed down version of the *Custom Animations* task pane found in PowerPoint 2003 and 2007.

Figure 27.5 PowerPoint 2010 *Animations* tab.

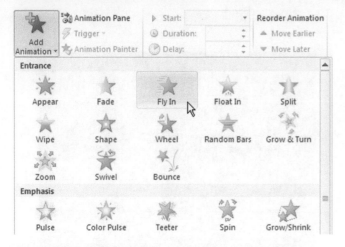

Figure 27.6 Adding an animation in PowerPoint 2010.

Figure 27.7 *Animations* pane (PowerPoint 2010).

To remove an animation:

1 Select it in the list.

2 Press the *Delete* key.

To reorder an animation:

1 Select it.

2 Click the *Reorder* buttons.

Summary

- PowerPoint has four categories of effect but you will normally use only the *Entrance* effects.
- To add animations you use the *Custom Animations* task pane in PowerPoint 2003/2007 or the *Animations* tab on the Ribbon in PowerPoint 2010.
- To make animations start automatically, use the *Start After Previous* or *Start With Previous* options, then adjust the delay.
- You can use the *Reorder* buttons in the *Custom Animations* task pane or the *Animations* pane (in PowerPoint 2010) to change the order of animations.

Review exercises

Exercise 27

1 Open the HARDWARE2 file from the exercise folder.
2 Add some custom animations. Each one should start after a delay of 0.5 seconds.
3 View your handiwork.
4 Save the file as HARDWARE3.

28 The slide master

In this chapter, you will learn:

- how the slide master works
- how to insert headers and footers
- how to insert slide numbers

In PowerPoint there is a special slide called the **slide master**. Anything you put on this slide will appear on all the other slides. For instance, if you need a company logo to automatically appear on every slide, you would put it on the slide master. This is how PowerPoint does things like footers, slide numbers and even design templates – it just modifies the slide master accordingly.

Viewing the slide master

In order to view the slide master:

- in PowerPoint 2003, click *View, Master, Slide Master*
- in PowerPoint 2007 and 2010, click *View, Slide Master*.

You can see what a slide master looks like below. If you are not using a theme it is normally blank, as in Figure 28.1. Otherwise, it is formatted with the background, bullet style and colours of your theme (Figure 28.2).

Figure 28.1 Blank *Slide Master*.

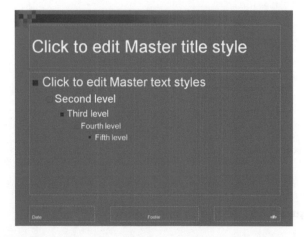

Figure 28.2 The *Slide Master* for the Island presentation.

PowerPoint 2007 and 2010 have multiple slide masters – one for each slide layout in addition to an overall slide master. But the concept is the same.

Editing the slide master

The first things you will notice about the slide master are the placeholders. For example, at the top of Figure 28.2, you can see a box that says 'Click to edit Master title style'. This is not normal text, because otherwise you would see it on all your slides. It is the placeholder for the title. Any changes you make to its appearance (e.g. underlining it) will be passed on all your slide titles.

You can edit the slide master in virtually the same way you would edit any other slide. You can change the font and colour, change the background, etc.

Closing the *Master* view

To close the *Master* view and return to the view you were in before, you have to click the *Close Master View* button.

Footers

You can add footers to your slides via the slide master or the *Header* and *Footer* window.

To add a footer via the slide master:

1 Open the slide master.

2 Click in the footer placeholder at the bottom.

3 Type the text you want as the footer.

If you prefer, you can use the *Header* and *Footer* window (Figure 28.3). To open it:

- in PowerPoint 2003, click *View, Header* and *Footer...*
- in PowerPoint 2007 and 2010, click Insert, Header & Footer...

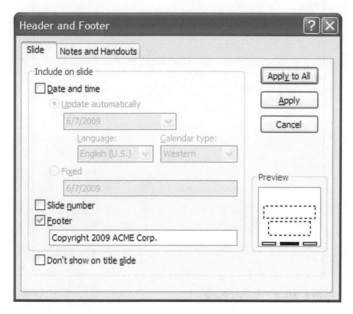

Figure 28.3 *Header* and *Footer* window.

To add the footer via the *Header* and *Footer* window:

1 Tick the footer box.

2 Type the footer.

3 Click *Apply to All*.

Inserting slide numbers

To insert numbers on your slides:

1 Click *Insert, Slide Numbers*.

2 When the *Header* and *Footer* box appears, tick the *Slide Number* box.

3 Click the *Apply to All* button.

A slide number is a special kind of footer, so it will get added to the slide master.

Summary

- What you put on the slide master gets displayed on every slide.
- Headers and footers are put on the slide master.
- Slide numbers are special footers that are added to the bottom of the slide master.
- On the slide master there are placeholders which, although they do not appear on every slide, allow you to change the formatting of things like the slide titles.

Review exercises

Exercise 28A

1 What is the slide master used for?
2 If placeholders do not appear on every slide, then why do you need them?

Exercise 28B

1 Open the HARDWARE2 file from the exercise folder.
2 Open the slide master.
3 Underline the title.
4 Close the Master view. When you view your slides you should see that all of their titles are underlined.
5 Add the name of your school as a footer.
6 Insert slide numbers.
7 Save the file in your class folder as HARDWARE4.

29 Printing

In this chapter, you will learn:

- how to add notes to your slides
- how to print as well as how to preview what will be printed
- how to change the printing options

Why print?

After you have prepared your presentation and rehearsed the timing, your presentation is ready for viewing. Normally, the presentation is shown to the audience via a laptop that is connected to a projector. So what could you possibly need to print?

Well, for starters, you may want to print handouts of your presentation to give to people in your audience. But, more importantly, you will probably want to print out your slide notes so that you can refer to them while you are doing the presentation.

Slide notes

I mentioned earlier that you can type notes in the *Notes* box at the bottom of the Slide view (Figure 29.1). You can also use the *Notes* page (Figure 29.2). Just click *View, Notes Page.*

Click to add notes

Figure 29.1   *Notes* box.

Printing in PowerPoint 2003 and 2007

Before you print something in PowerPoint 2003 or 2007, you should use the *Print Preview* option to see what it will look like. To access the *Print Preview*:

- in PowerPoint 2003, click *File, Print Preview*
- in PowerPoint 2007, click the Microsoft Office button, point at *Print* then click *Print Preview*.

At the top of the *Print Preview* is either the *Print Preview* toolbar (if you are using PowerPoint 2003; see

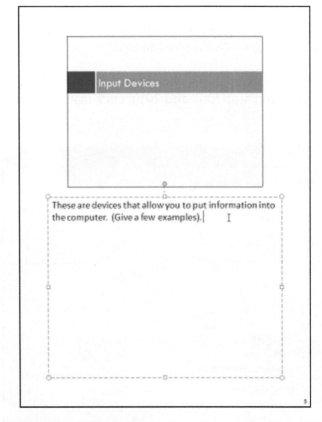

Figure 29.2   *Notes* Page.

Figure 29.3) or the *Print Preview* tab (PowerPoint 2007; Figure 29.4).

Table 29.1 explains what each option does.

Print What box

Before you print, choose what you want to print via the *Print What* combo box. In addition to being able to print slides and notes pages, you can choose among several handout options that allow you to fit multiple slides on a page.

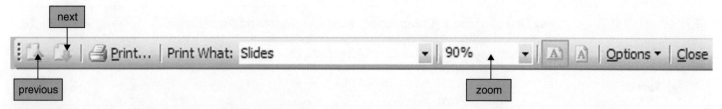

Figure 29.3 Print Preview toolbar (PowerPoint 2003).

Figure 29.4 *Print Preview* tab (PowerPoint 2007).

Table 29.1 *Print Preview* buttons.

Button	What it does
Next/ Previous	Goes to the next or previous slide
Print	Opens the Print dialog
Options	Allows you to set options such as whether you are going to print in grayscale or colour
Print What	Enables you to choose whether to print slides, handouts or notes pages
Zoom	Allows you to zoom in or out of the preview
Close	Closes the print preview

Print dialog (PowerPoint 2003 and 2007)

Once you are satisfied with the preview, click the *Print* button. The *Print* dialog box (Figure 29.5) will be displayed. Adjust the options to suit your needs then click the *OK* button to print.

 You can also open the Print Dialog by clicking File (or the Microsoft Office button) then *Print*.

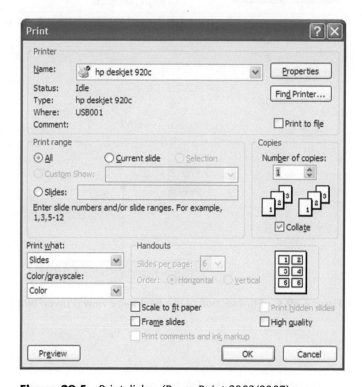

Figure 29.5 *Print* dialog (PowerPoint 2003/2007).

Printing in PowerPoint 2010

Like all the other Office 2010 programs, PowerPoint 2010 combines the *Print Preview* and *Print Options* windows into a single *Print* section in the *Backstage* view (see Figure 29.6).

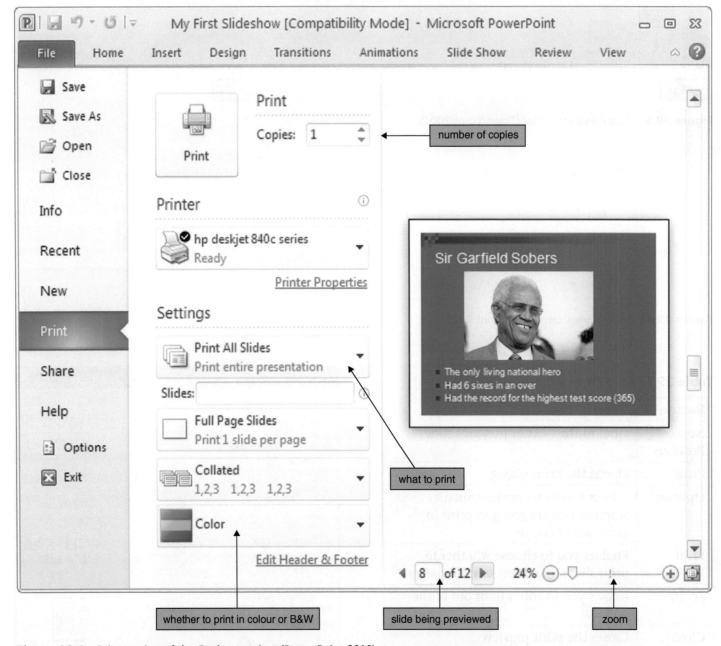

Figure 29.6 *Print* section of the *Backstage* view (PowerPoint 2010).

To see this, click the *File* tab, then click *Print*. Most of the options you would want to change such as what to print, the number of copies, and so on, can be changed in this section. But if you need to change things like the print quality, click the *Printer Properties* link.

When you are ready to print, click the big *Print* button at the top left.

Summary

- To add notes to your slides you can either type them in the *Notes* box at the bottom of the window, or use the *Notes* page.
- You can opt to print slides, handouts or notes pages in colour or in black and white.
- You should preview what you are going to print before you print it.

Introduction to Microsoft Access

In this chapter, you will learn:

- some of the features of Database Management Systems
- how to open database objects
- how to create and save a new database and open an existing one

Features of database management systems

A Database Management System (DBMS), such as Microsoft Access, is a piece of software that allows you to efficiently store, retrieve and manipulate data stored in database tables. More specifically, a DBMS allows you to:

- Create tables.
- Enter records into the tables.
- Retrieve the records from the tables.
- Establish relationships between the tables.
- Perform queries on the stored data (e.g. 'What are the names of the students who are doing English?').
- View reports on the data.

I will show you how to do the first three in Microsoft Access; the rest are beyond the scope of this course. In EDPM, you will only really use Microsoft Access to manage mail-merge data files (which happen to be stored using database tables).

Of course, you can also manage mail-merge data files in Microsoft Word.

Databases

Simply put, a database is a collection of related data, organised into tables. A table contains rows of data known as **records**. Each column of the table corresponds to a particular field, or piece of information about an item.

Let us look at an example. Suppose you own a business and want to store information about your customers. It would make sense to have a database with a customers table in it. What kind of information about your customers would you store? Here are a few suggestions:

- the customer's first and last name
- his/her address (and parish)
- their telephone numbers (home, work and mobile)
- since when has the person been a customer.

All of these would be fields in your table. Each row in the table would correspond to a customer's record.

In addition to the Customers table, you may also want to have an Orders table. Although these are two different tables, they are both recording information pertaining to the business. So it would make sense to have them in the same database.

Although a lot of the information stored in a database could also be stored in spreadsheets, databases are <u>much</u> more efficient when it comes to storing and retrieving data.

Creating a new database

Unlike other Microsoft Office programs you cannot just open Microsoft Access and start typing. It does not automatically create a blank database for you to work with. Instead, you have to create one yourself.

Access 2003

To create a new database in Access 2003:

- Click *File*, *New...*
- Click the *Blank Database...* option from the top of the Task Pane.
- In the dialog box that appears, go to the location where the new database is to be stored and type the name you want to call it.
- Click the *Create* button.

Access 2007/2010

To create a database in the newer versions of Access:

- Click the *Microsoft Office* button (or the File tab)
- Click *New*
- Make sure the Blank Database option is selected.
- In the right side of the window, where it says 'File Name:' click the folder icon.
- In the dialog box that appears, type the name of the file and choose the location where it will be stored.
- Change the file type to the 2002–2003 (*.mdb) format.
- Click the *OK* button.
- Click the *Create* button.

From Access 2007, the (*.accdb) file type is the default database format. Unfortunately, previous versions of Access cannot read this format. For that reason, whenever you are creating a new database, change the file type to (*.mdb).

When you first create a database, Access 2007 and 2010 will automatically create a blank table for you to type in information. Close this table. We will be using a different method to create tables.

Opening database objects (Access 2003)

At the heart of the Access 2003 is the Database Window (see Figure 30.1) where you work with the various types of database objects.

The Database Window only displays one type of object at a time. You use the buttons on the left side

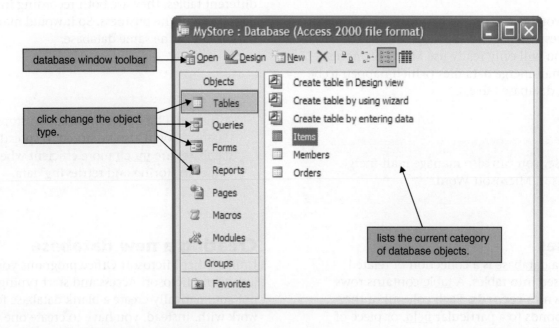

Figure 30.1 The Database Window (Access 2003).

of the window to switch to another type of object. The right part of the window shows you a list of the current type of item.

To open an item, either double-click it or select it, then click the *Open* button in the Database Window Toolbar.

Opening database objects (Access 2007/2010)

Instead of a Database Window, a list of the objects in the database is shown in a panel to the left of the main Access window. These objects are organised by type and by default, only the tables are shown (See Figure 30.2). However, you can click the down arrow in the top right-hand part of the panel to change to another object type.

In order to open a database object, simply double-click on it.

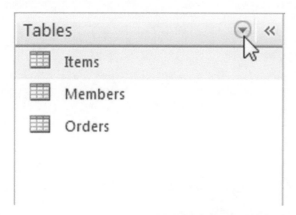

Figure 30.2   List of Database Tables (Access 2007/2010).

Saving a database

Unlike other Microsoft Office products, Access automatically saves any changes you make to your data. But if you want to save a database object at any time:

- Click *File* (or the Microsoft Office button)
- Click *Save*.

Opening an existing database

In order to open an existing database:

- Click *File* (or the Microsoft Office button)
- Click *Open*
- Go to the folder that contains the file then double-click on the file.

Sometimes when you open a file, Microsoft Access will display a security warning. The appearance of the warning depends on the Access Version.

Security warnings in Access 2003

In Access 2003, the security warning will pop up in a window similar to the one in Figure 30.3. When this happens, just click the *Open* button.

Security warnings in Access 2007/2010

Figure 30.4 shows what the security warning looks like in Access 2007 (the one in 2010 is similar). If you get this message, then certain types of content in the database will be disabled. We will not be working with this type of content so you can safely ignore the security warning.

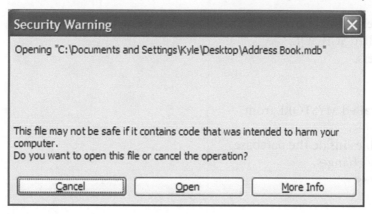

Figure 30.3   Security Warning in Access 2003.

Figure 30.4   Security Warning in Access 2007/2010.

Summary

- A DBMS is a program that allows you to efficiently store, query and manipulate data stored in database tables.
- A database is a collection of related tables.
- Each row in the table is a record and each column in a table corresponds to a particular field of data.
- To open a database object, make sure that type of object is being displayed then double-click on the one you want to open.

Review exercises

Exercise 30A

1 List five features that Database Management Systems normally provide.
2 By use of an example, explain the relationship between tables, fields and records.
3 Suppose you wanted to create a table that records information about the courses offered at a university. Suggest four fields that should be included in this table.
4 ACME Corporation Inc. wants to store its employee information in a database. What are some of the fields ACME might want to keep track of in its Employee table?

Exercise 30B

1 Open Microsoft Access.
2 Create a database called SCHOOL.
3 Close Microsoft Access.

Exercise 30C

1 Open the database called MYSTORE from your exercise folder.
2 Open each of the tables inside the database but do not make any changes.
3 Close Microsoft Access.

31 Entering and editing data

In this chapter, you will learn:

- how to move around a table
- how to enter data into a table
- how to edit data in a table
- how to widen the columns in the table

In Microsoft Access, when you open a table (e.g. by double-clicking its name from the list of objects), the table is opened in the Datasheet View (see Figure 31.1). This view allows you to add and edit information in your table.

Moving around the datasheet

Since a datasheet is like a giant table, you can click in a particular cell if you want to type new data or edit existing data.

If there is too much information to show on the screen at one time, Access will display one or both scrollbars. You can use the horizontal scroll bar to view additional columns or the vertical scroll bar to view additional rows.

You can also move around by using the keyboard or clicking the *Navigation* buttons.

Navigation buttons

At the bottom left of each datasheet are navigation buttons. These allow you to move from one record to the next and even add new records. You can also type the number of a record in the Current Record box and press *Enter*.

The Current Record box also tells you how many records are in your table. In Figure 31.2 there are 6 records and the current record is #3.

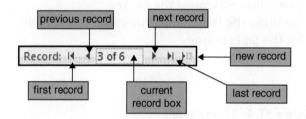

Figure 31.2 The Navigation buttons.

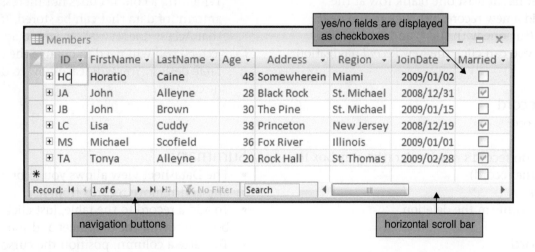

Figure 31.1 The datasheet view.

Editing data

Each cell in the table corresponds to a field in the record. If you click inside the field, the cursor will start flashing inside the chosen field so you can edit its data. Once you start editing a field, Access will display an icon of a pencil to the left of the margin indicating that changes are being made to the record (see Figure 31.3).

	ID ▾	FirstName ▾	LastName ▾	Age ▾
⊞ HC	Horatio	Caine	49
⊞ JA	John	Alleyne	29
⊞ JB	John	Brown	31
⊞ LC	Lisa	Cuddy	39
⊞ MS	Michael	Scofield	37
⊞ TA	Tonya	Alleyne	21

Figure 31.3   Editing a Field.

If you are editing a field, but want to revert to what it previously was, press the *Esc* key.

To undo the last change you made to the table, click the *undo* button.

Figure 31.4   *Undo* Button.

Adding a new record

Each datasheet has at least one blank row at the bottom. To add a new record just click in the next available row (the one with the *) and start typing. Alternatively, you can click the *New Record* navigation button.

Deleting a record

To delete a record:

* Right-click on record's row header (the gray box to the left of the record)
* Click *Delete*
* Click *Yes* to confirm the deletion.

Saving a record

Microsoft Access automatically saves a record when you go to another one. But if you want to force Access

to save the changes immediately, you can click the *Save* button.

Figure 31.5   *Save* Button.

Widening a column

To change the width of a column:

* Position the cursor over the line to the right of the column header (see Figure 31.4).
* Drag the cursor to the right if you want to widen the column. If you want the column to be narrower, drag it to the left.

	CID ▾	IDNo ▾	FirstName ▾
	0001	6002110000	Horatio
	0004	6911110000	Lisa
	0005	7205040000	Michael
	0003	7712310000	John
	0002	8001010000	John
	0006	8804010000	Tonya

Figure 31.6   Resizing a column.

Widening a column does not increase the amount of data that can be stored. If you find that Access does not allow you to add any more letters, you will need to change the underlying table design. You will learn how to do so in the next chapter.

Summary

* The Datasheet view allows you to browse tables and add/remove records from it.
* To add a record to the table, just click inside the bottom row of the datasheet and start typing.
* To resize a column, position the cursor to the right of the column header and drag to the right or the left.

Review exercises

Exercise 31

1 Open the MYSTORE database from your exercise folder.
2 Open the Members table and:
   a Widen the columns as necessary.
   b Add information for 10 new members.
   c Change Lisa Cuddy's age from 39 to 41, her status from not married to married and her last name to House.
   d Change Michael Scofield's address to Miami, Florida.
   e Close the table. If it asks you whether to save changes to the layout, click *Yes*.
3 Open the Items table and:
   a Add information for 10 new items.
   b Change the price of the Bravia to $1,966.49
   c Change the description of the Canon Powershot camera to say 'Powershot SX30IS Compact Digital Camera'
   d Widen the columns as necessary.
   e Change the Windows 7 version from Home Premium to Professional and the price to $350.00.
   f Delete the records for QuickBooks and the Samsung LCD TV.
   g Close the table. If it asks you whether to save changes to the layout, click *Yes*.

32 Creating and modifying tables

In this chapter, you will learn how to:

- create tables using the design view

- use the design view to add, delete and modify fields

Creating a table

We have already looked at how to enter data into existing tables, now let us look at how to create some of our own. Access provides a variety of ways to create tables, but we will always create tables using the Design View.

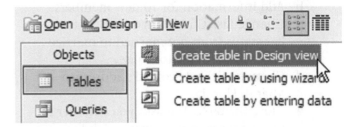

Figure 32.1 Creating a table in Access 2003.

Access 2003

To create a table in Access 2003:

- Switch to the Tables section of the Database Window.
- Double-click the *Create table in Design View* option.

Access 2007/2010

To create a table in Access 2007 or 2010:

- Click the *Create* tab of the ribbon
- Then click the *Table Design* button.

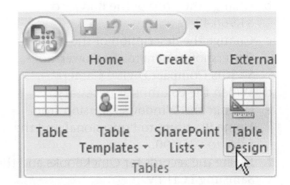

Figure 32.2 Table Design Button (Access 2007/2010).

The table design window

Regardless of what Access version you are using to create the table, the Table Design window will be displayed. It looks complicated, but it helps to think of it as being divided into three main sections.

The first part – the top of the window – displays a list of the fields, their data types and their descriptions. In Figure 32.3, there are 4 fields: MID, ItemNo, Qty and OrderDate.

The second part – the bottom left of the window – displays the field properties for the <u>currently selected field</u>. In our example, since the MID field is currently selected, the field properties that you see are for that field. If you want to see the settings for another field, you have to click on it.

Finally, at the bottom-right of the window is an explanation of what the <u>currently selected field property</u> does. Information about the Field Name property is currently being displayed since that is what is currently selected.

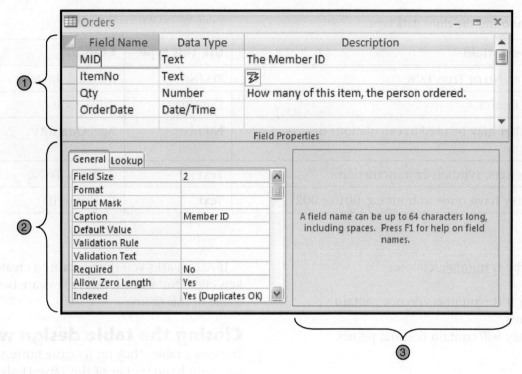

Figure 32.3 The Table Design Window.

Creating fields

Although there are several properties that you *could* set, the way you typically create a field is:

1 Type the field name.
2 Choose an <u>appropriate</u> data type.
3 Set the field size (if necessary).
4 Set the format (if necessary).
5 Set the maximum number of decimal places, if necessary.

Field name

The first thing you have to do is to type in the field name in the next available row. Although field names may be up to 64 characters, most are pretty short. Having spaces in your field names is generally considered a bad practice, so instead of First Name, say FirstName.

Data type

When you first create a field, it is automatically set to type Text. If your field is not going to be storing text, you should change this to the <u>appropriate</u> type of data for your field. This is very important for two reasons:

1 To makes sure that the user is not allowed to enter the wrong type of data. For instance, if you left the age field as type Text, nothing is stopping the user from entering something like 'ABC' or 'hello' for the age.
2 The data type affects what you are able to do with the data. For instance, if the type is <u>Number</u> or <u>Currency</u> you can perform calculations on it.

Choosing the right data type

The following 'cheat sheet' on the next page helps you choose the right data type for your field.

Field size

If the data type is <u>text</u>, set the field size to the <u>maximum</u> number of characters you want to allow in that field.

Table 32.1 Choosing the right data type.

The data in your field	Use this type	Example
Can only be Yes/No or True/False	Yes/No	Married, InStock
Are monetary figures	Currency	Price, Cost
Are numbers that may be used in calculations or comparisons	Number	Age, Quantity
May contain letters, symbols or punctuation	Text	Address, TelNo
Are IDs that may have zeros in front e.g. 001 or 002	Text	CustomerID

If the data type is <u>number</u>, choose:

- <u>Long Integer</u> if the numbers do not contain decimal points.
- <u>Double</u>, if they *will* contain decimal points.

Format

The Format Property controls the way the information is displayed in the Datasheet view.

If the data type is Date/Time, either:

- Choose a format from the list.
- Or type yyyy/mm/dd (all lowercase) if you want a 4 digit year followed by a 2 digit month, followed by a 2-digit day.

If the data type is a number:

- Choose fixed if you want a fixed number of decimal places.
- Choose percentage if the number is a percentage.

Decimal places

If the data type is <u>Number</u> or <u>Currency</u>, choose the maximum number of decimal places to be displayed, or leave it as Auto if you want the computer to decide for you.

Saving the table design

To save table design:

- Click the *save* icon (the tiny blue disk at the top of the window).
- Type the name you want to give to the table and click *OK*.

If Access asks you if you want to create a primary key, click 'No' since primary keys are beyond the scope of this course.

Closing the table design window

To close a table, click on its close button (X) in the top-right hand corner of the Table Design Window. If there are any unsaved changes, Access will ask you whether you want to save them.

Renaming a table

To rename a table:

- Go to the list of tables in your Database.
- Right-click on the table you want to rename.
- Click *Rename*.
- Type the new name of the table.
- Press ENTER.

How to modify your table design

After you have created your table, you might need to go back and make changes. For example, you may want to add or field, or may have discovered that a field size is not big enough.

If you want to go back to your table design to make changes:

- Right-click on its name in the list of tables.
- Click *Design View*.

Inserting fields

If you are inserting the field to the bottom of the list, you just click inside the first available row and

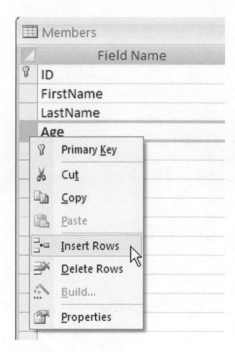

Figure 32.4 Inserting a Field.

start typing. If you want to insert a field <u>in between</u> existing ones:

- Right-click on the row header to the left of an existing field.
- Click *Insert Rows*.

The new row will be inserted <u>before</u> the row you right-clicked on.

Deleting fields

To delete a field:

- Right-click in the row and click *Delete*.
- Click *Yes* when the confirmation box pops up.

Changing field properties

You can change a table's field properties in the Design view, even after you have entered data into the table. However, you should exercise caution when changing the field size and the field type because you run the risk of losing data.

Anytime you reduce the size of a field, when you go to save the database, Access will warn you that data may be lost even though that might not be true in *your* case. If you are confident your field size is big enough, you can ignore the warning.

Summary

- The Datasheet view allows you to browse tables and add/remove records from it.
- To add a record to the table, just click inside the bottom row of the datasheet and start typing.
- To resize a column, position the cursor to the right of the column header and drag to the right or the left.

Review exercises

Exercise 32A

1 Create a database called ADDRESS BOOK in your class folder.
2 In that database create a table which stores the following information about each contact:
   - First name and Last name
   - Address and Parish
   - Age
   - Birth-Date
   - Gender
   - His or her age
   - The home and work telephone numbers
   - The gender
   - Whether or not he/she is married.
3 Make sure you use the correct field names and sizes.
4 Save the table as CONTACTS.
5 Enter information for 10 contacts in the table.

6 Change the information for the third and fourth contacts to John Doe and Jane Doe, who are married to each other. John was born on July 3rd 1980 and his work telephone number is 555-0000. Jane was born on May 11th 1981 and her work telephone number is 555-1111. Their home telephone number is 555-2222.

Exercise 32B

1 Open the SCHOOL database from your exercise folder.

2 Create tables (with appropriate fields) to store information about the Students, Teachers and Courses offered at a fictitious private school. Here are a few suggestions for fields you could put in the tables:
- The relevant names.
- A CourseID.
- A brief description of what the course entails.
- What date the course begins.
- How much the course costs.
- How many years the teacher was teaching.
- Any other fields you deem necessary.

3 Add 5 records to each table.

Exercise 32C

1 Open the MYSTORE database from your exercise folder.

2 Change the structure of the Members table as follows:
   a Delete the Age field.
   b Add a text field to store each member's telephone number.
   c Change the format of the JoinDate field to yyyy-mm-dd.

3 Add telephone numbers for each of the members.

4 Change the structure of the Items table as follows:
   a Change the width of the Description to 50.
   b Add a field called DutyFreePrice.
   c Change the field name Department to Category.

5 Add Duty-Free prices to all of the items.

Document preparation

Part 4

1 Choosing the right paper

In this chapter, you will learn:
- about the different types of paper
- some of the standard paper sizes

Types of paper

Chances are you do not give a lot of thought to the type of paper you print documents on; you just use what is in the printer. But using the correct type – and size – paper is essential if you want your documents to have a professional look.

There are many types of paper, each of which is used for a particular purpose. Table 1.1 describes the different types as well as their uses, and Figure 1.1 shows some of them.

Table 1.1 Types of paper and their uses.

Type	Description	Primary uses
Bond	Thick, uncoated paper that is very durable and has a high quality	Letterheads and business forms
Onionskin	Translucent (partially see through) paper that is thin and light but relatively strong	With carbon paper for making duplicates; airmail; to reduce weight when large numbers of records are being printed
Flimsy	Very thin, low quality paper that is much more opaque than onionskin paper	Draft quality documents; pages in bibles
Carbon	Thin paper that is coated 'underneath' with a dark, waxy, pigment	Placed between two sheets of paper, to duplicate what is typed on the top sheet on the paper underneath
Stencil	Tough, white, translucent paper that is covered in wax	To create master sheets used in risographs; by artists to create design templates
Copy	White paper that is pretty light and does not curl easily, making it suitable for use in copiers	For copying documents and in laser printers; general purpose office use
NCR (no carbon required) paper	Multipart paper, where the bottom of each intermediary sheet is coated in a special dye and the top is coated with clay that reacts to the dye	As an alternative to carbon paper
Index	Smooth, stiff paper that is fairly inexpensive and not particularly thick	Post cards, greeting cards and business reply cards
Cover paper	Stiff, fairly heavy type of paper	Presentation covers, greeting cards and business cards

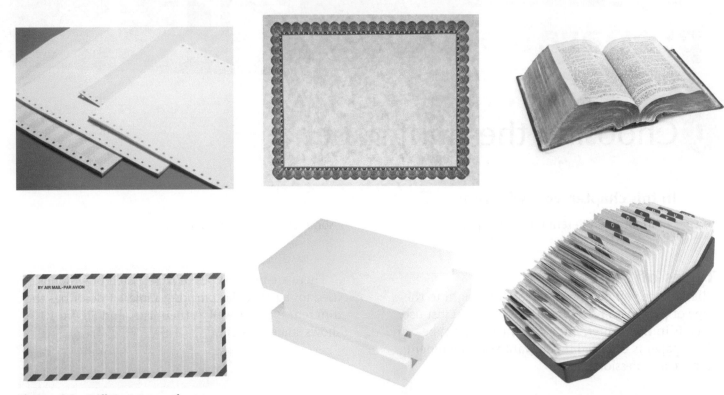

Figure 1.1 Different types of paper.

Orientation

In the Microsoft Word section, we briefly looked at the two paper orientations – portrait and landscape (see Figure 1.2). In portrait orientation, which is what you are used to, the sides of the paper are <u>longer</u> than the top and bottom. In landscape orientation the opposite is true; the paper is turned so that the sides are <u>shorter</u> than the top and bottom.

Whether you use portrait or landscape orientation depends on the nature of the document. For example, legal documents are normally printed in portrait since they are long but not very wide. In contrast, brochures and wide tables are usually printed landscape.

Paper sizes

As you can see from Table 1.2, paper comes in many different sizes. The most common ones are highlighted.

 There are also <u>customised sizes</u> where the paper is cut to specific dimensions.

A series

The international standard for paper size is the A series (A0, A1, A2 etc.). Each size is twice as big as the one following it in the series. So for instance, if you fold an A4 sheet of paper in half along its longest side and then cut along the fold, you would get two A5-sized sheets (see Figure 1.3).

this is portrait orientation

this is landscape orientation

Figure 1.2 Portrait orientation vs. landscape orientation.

Table 1.2 Standard paper sizes.

System	Size	Dimensions, width × height (mm)
North American	Letter	216 × 279 (8.5 × 11 in)
	Legal	216 × 356 (8.5 × 14 in)
International Standard (ISO)	A0	841 × 1189
	A1	594 × 841
	A2	420 × 594
	A3	297 × 420
	A4	210 × 297 (8.3 × 11.7 in)
	A5	148 × 210
	A6	105 × 148
	A7	74 × 105
	A8	52 × 74
	A9	37 × 52
	A10	26 × 37

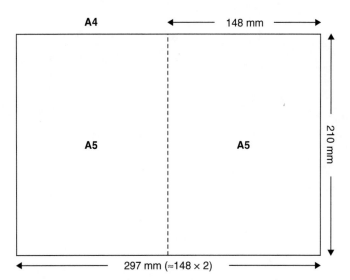

Figure 1.3 The relationship between the A4 and A5 sizes.

Of the A series, the size used the most in the office environment is the A4 size. However, since the Letter size is so similar, it is often used as an alternative to A4 paper.

Choosing the correct paper size

Choosing the correct paper size is just as important as choosing the type. If someone sends a very short document on a huge piece of paper, it looks unprofessional. Table 1.3 gives the recommended paper sizes and orientation for various types of documents.

Table 1.3 Recommended paper sizes and orientation for various types of documents.

Type of document	Paper size	Orientation
Agenda	A4	Portrait
Agenda (short)	A5	Landscape
Brochures	A4; Legal for larger brochures	Landscape
Debit and credit notes	A5; A6 for small ones	Landscape
Flyer	A4	Either
Invitation	A5 or A6	Either
Invoices	A4	Portrait
Legal documents	Legal or A4	Portrait
Letters	A4; A5 for short letters	Portrait
Manuscripts	A4	Portrait
Memoranda	A5	Either
Memoranda (long)	A4	Portrait
Menus	A4; A5 for small ones	Portrait
Minutes	A4	Portrait
Newsletters	A4	Portrait
Notices	A4	Portrait
Plays	A4	Portrait
Poems	A4; A5 for short poems	Portrait
Programmes	A4	Portrait
Reports	A4	Portrait
Specifications	A4	Portrait
Tabular work	A4	Landscape

Summary

- The type of paper is determined in large part by the thickness, strength, transparency and the coating (if any).
- The two most common systems for paper sizes are the A series (the international standard) and the North American. Custom sizes are also available.
- A good rule-of-thumb for paper sizes is: use Legal or A4 for legal documents, A5 for short documents and A4 for the rest.
- Most documents are done in portrait orientation; landscape is usually reserved for wide documents and brochures.

Review exercises

Exercise 1

1. Give a use of each of the following types of paper.
   a Cover
   b Index
   c Bond
   d Copy
   e Stencil
2. What is the difference between:
   a flimsy paper and onionskin paper?
   b onionskin and stencil paper?
3. In your own words, explain how carbon paper is used.
4. What is the relationship between A1 and A0 sized paper?
5. When would you use custom paper sizes?
6. Why do you sometimes need to use landscape orientation? List three types of documents for which this type of orientation is recommended.
7. When would you use A5 paper instead of A4 paper? List three types of documents that are typed on this size paper.

② Envelopes

In this chapter, you will learn:

- about the different envelope types and sizes
- which envelope size to use for a particular size of paper

Categorising envelopes

Envelopes may be categorised in several ways. For instance, they may be categorised by:

- their quality
- the size and position of the flaps
- whether or not they have a window
- their purpose.

Quality

The same way you have types of paper, some of which are of a higher quality than others, you have different quality envelopes.

Bond

If you need an envelope suitable for holding bond paper, why not use a bond envelope? Like its paper counterpart, a bond envelope is durable and high quality.

Manila

Manila envelopes are made of strong, relatively thick paper and, depending on who you ask, are light brown or beige in colour (see Figure 2.1). The colour is so distinctive that other types of envelopes which have a similar colour are also called manila envelopes.

They are usually large enough for full-sized documents to be placed in them without folding and are often designed so they can be reused. Reusable manila envelopes come in two forms:

- those with a flexible two-pronged metal clasp
- those with a string and button mechanism.

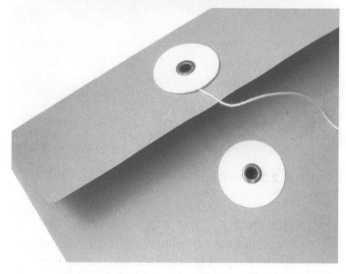

Figure 2.1 Manila envelopes.

Padded

These envelopes are padded with either bubble wrap or recycled material in order to protect their contents. Because of the additional padding, they are bulkier than regular envelopes and do not sit flat even when they are empty.

If you want to send fragile items like CDs via mail, a padded envelope is the best type to use.

Flaps

As you can see from Figure 2.2, the flap is the part of the envelope that you fold. It normally has adhesive on the edges which allows you to seal the envelope. Depending on the position of the flap, an envelope may be categorised as:

- open end – in these, the flap is along the shorter part of the envelope (like the manila envelopes in Figure 2.1)
- open side – the flap is along the longer part of the envelope (like in Figure 2.2).

Envelope flaps may be commercial style (as in Figure 2.2), pointed (i.e. look like triangles), or rectangular.

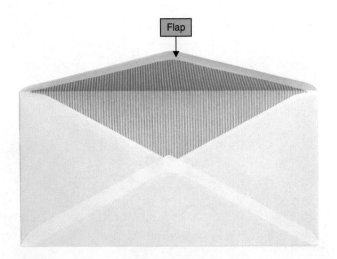

Figure 2.2   The flap of an envelope.

Windows

Some envelopes have rectangular windows which allow you to see part of the document inside (see Figure 2.3). The window is positioned so that if a letter is folded correctly, you can see the recipient's address, saving you the time and trouble of printing it on the outside of the envelope.

Purpose

An envelope's shape, size and even weight may make it suited for a specific purpose. Let us look at a few examples.

Figure 2.3   An envelope with a window.

Banker

A banker envelope is an open-side envelope with a commercial style flap. It is used to send invoices, bills and business documents.

Catalogue

A catalogue envelope is a large open-end envelope which makes it easy to insert magazines, reports and catalogues without folding them.

Baronial

These are the open-side envelopes with pointed flaps used for greeting cards.

Airmail

Airmail envelopes, as you can see from Figure 2.4, have a very distinctive red, white and blue design. They are also very light which is vital for items that are transported by aeroplane.

Figure 2.4   An airmail envelope.

Envelope sizes

C series

The same way you have the A series for paper sizes, you have the C series for envelope sizes, as shown in Table 2.1. As with the A series, the higher the number, the smaller the dimensions, with a C4 envelope being twice as big as a C5.

> The C series envelopes are large enough to hold the corresponding A series paper size without folding it. For instance, a C4 envelope can hold an A4 sheet of paper without having to fold it. This also means that it can hold an A3 sheet if it is folded in half.

B series

The B series of envelopes is designed to hold C series envelopes. Table 2.2 lists the sizes in this series.

Other sizes

Of the sizes given so far, the C6/5 size (also called C65) is used the most for business correspondence. Two popular alternatives are the DL (110×220 mm) and the Size 10 (105×241 mm) envelopes.

Summary

- Envelopes come in different qualities.
- An envelope may be categorised as open end or open side depending on whether the flap is on the shorter side of the envelope or not.
- A C series envelope can hold an equivalent A series sheet of paper.

Table 2.1 C series envelope sizes.

Size	Dimensions, width × height (mm)	Used to hold
C3	324 × 458	A3 page (without folding) or A2 page (folded in half)
C4	229 × 324	A4 page (without folding) or A3 page (folded in half)
C5	162 × 229	A5 page (without folding) or A4 page (folded in half)
C6/5 C65	114 × 229	A4 page (folded in thirds)
C6	114 × 162	A6 page (without folding), A5 page (folded in half) or A4 page (folded in quarters)
C7/6	81 × 162	A5 page (folded in thirds)
C7	81 × 114	A7 page (without folding), A6 page (folded in half) or A5 page (folded in quarters)

Table 2.2 B series envelope sizes.

Size	Dimensions, width × height (mm)	Used to hold
B4	250 × 353	C4 envelope or A4 page (without folding)
B5	176 × 250	C5 envelope, A5 page (without folding) or A4 page (folded in half)
B6	125 × 176	C6 envelope, A6 page (without folding), A5 page (folded in half) or A4 page (folded in quarters)

- A B series envelope can hold an equivalent C series envelope.
- C6/5, DL and Size 10 commercial style envelopes are the types most commonly used for business correspondence.

Review exercises

Exercise 2

1 Explain the difference between an open-end and an open-side envelope.
2 What is the advantage of using an envelope with a window?
3 If you had to send a DVD by mail, what type of envelope would you put it in? Why?
4 Explain the difference between the two types of reusable manila envelopes.
5 What type of envelope would you use to send a magazine? What qualities make it suitable for this task?
6 Describe an airmail envelope.
7 What is the difference between a B series and a C series envelope?
8 Give five different envelope sizes that can be used to hold A5 paper.
9 Can you use a DL or Size 10 envelope to hold A4 paper? Justify your answer.

3 Typing manuscripts and reports

In this chapter, you will learn:

- the difference between manuscript and typescript
- some guidelines for typing manuscripts
- types of headings
- some common abbreviations
- how to type reports

What is a manuscript?

A **manuscript** is a handwritten or roughly typed document that has not yet been typed up professionally. When a manuscript is typed out professionally, it is known as a **typescript**. Some of the things the typist or secretary would do with the manuscript are:

1 Format it according to accepted professional standards.
2 Make changes as directed.
3 Correct any spelling or grammar errors.
4 Expand abbreviated words.

Typing manuscripts

When you are typing manuscripts, use A4 paper with portrait orientation unless directed otherwise. Leave a clear line space after paragraphs.

Word 2003 and 2007/2010 take different approaches to paragraph spacing. In Word 2003, when you press the *Enter* key, it takes you to a new *line* so you have to press *Enter* again to get one clear line space. In the newer versions, pressing *Enter* takes you to a new *paragraph*, automatically inserting one clear line space.

tip

If you want to go to a new line in Word 2007/2010 (without inserting a clear line space) hold down the *Shift* key when pressing *Enter*. Alternatively you can choose the *No Spacing* style from the *Home* tab of the Ribbon.

Formatting guidelines

Up to this point, we have not worried too much about the correct way to type up documents – the main emphasis was learning the computer techniques. This section gives a list of general typing guidelines you should strive to follow when producing documents.

Margins

Unless you have been instructed otherwise or are planning to get the typescript bound, set all the margins to 1".

If the typescript is to be bound, add at least an additional half inch to the margin on the side where it is to be bound in order to compensate for the space required by the binding process. For example, if the manuscript is going to be bound on the left, and the left margin would normally be 1", set it to at least 1.5" instead.

Line spacing

The line spacing used depends on the type of document being typed. For instance, academic papers normally use double-line spacing. You should also use double-line spacing when you are typing a draft to make it easy for correction symbols (see Chapter 4) to be inserted.

When typing the final copy, be sure to use the line spacing indicated by the writer of the manuscript.

Blocked layout versus indented layout

When typing, you may be asked to use a blocked layout or an indented layout. We will learn more about these in the coming chapters but in general:

- With a blocked style layout, everything is aligned to the left.
- With an indented style layout, things may be centred or aligned to the right and the first line in each paragraph is indented.

There is also a semi-blocked layout which combines features of the two layouts.

Spacing

After sentences
Leave two spaces after the end of each sentence. For example:

> Hey! How are you? I'm doing fine. Say hi to your mum for me.

After commas
Leave a single space after a comma.

Before and after colons (:)
You put one space after a colon, but none before it. For example:

> There are five vowels: a, e, i, o and u.

Parentheses (also called brackets)
As you can see from the heading above, you do not leave a space after an opening parenthesis or before a closing parenthesis.

Quotation marks
Do not leave a space after an opening quotation mark or before a closing quotation mark. For example:

> It is often said "If you fail to prepare, prepare to fail".   (right)
> It is often said "If you fail to prepare, prepare to fail".   (wrong)

Do not confuse single quotes with apostrophes. Apostrophes are used to denote ownership (e.g. Andrea's house) or contractions (e.g. can't or won't) and do not have a space before *or* after them.

Ellipsis
An ellipsis (or …) is used to show that something, for example a part of a quote, has been omitted. You

normally leave a space before <u>and</u> after an ellipsis, unless it is at the beginning or end of a quote, in which case the normal rules for quotation marks apply.

You can have a full stop directly after an ellipsis, in which case you would write four dots ….

For example:

> A wise man once said that love is "… patient … kind (and) … keeps no record of wrongs"
>
> "… can't hear you … breaking up …. call me …."

Numbers
Never begin a sentence with a number. Instead, type it out in words. When numbers have more than three digits, groups them in threes, starting from the right. These groups are separated by a space or a comma.

Consistency is important. Also, the digits after a decimal point are not included in the count.

Here are a few examples:

- 123 (no grouping necessary)
- 1,234
- 1 234 (using a space instead)
- 1,234,567,890
- 123.45678 (no grouping necessary)
- 1,234.58

Fractions
You use the slash (/) when typing fractions e.g. 3/4 or 1/8. Notice that there is no space before or after the slash.

Units
When using the abbreviations for units e.g. m for metre or kg for kilogram, do not put an s or a full stop after the unit. So 9 mm is correct whereas 9 mms and 9 mm. are incorrect.

Punctuation styles
There are two main styles of punctuation: <u>full punctuation</u> (also called closed or standard punctuation) and <u>open punctuation</u>.

The difference between the two is that open punctuation omits any cosmetic punctuation marks whereas with full punctuation they are included. For instance, when using open punctuation, commas and full stops are excluded:

- After name titles and initials e.g. Mr J Doe instead of Mr. J. Doe.
- When typing abbreviations and acronyms e.g. USA instead of U.S.A.
- From dates and times.
- From numbers (apart from the decimal point) e.g. 1 000 000 instead of 1,000,000.
- After the complimentary close in a letter such as Yours sincerely.

As you would expect, open punctuation is quicker to type.

> With open punctuation, ordinal numbers like 1st, 2nd, 3rd and 24th are not used in dates. For example, you would type July 23 instead of July 23rd.

Headings

Headings are used to organise documents into logical sections which are much easier to digest than a big blob of text. There are different levels of headings, with each level of heading formatted so it is less prominent than the one before it. So for instance, a first level heading is usually larger than a second level one.

Headings are usually distinguished from regular text by:

1 Their position e.g. centring them, putting above or putting them to the left of the text.
2 By making them larger than regular text.
3 By underlining them, putting them in boldface, italics, capital letters or a combination thereof.

> **A quick and easy way to make text a heading is to use one of Microsoft Word's built-in styles. You just select the one you want from the formatting toolbar (Word 2003) or the *Home* tab of the Ribbon (Word 2007 and 2010).**

Main heading (first level)

The **main heading** or title is found at the top of the entire document, and of all the headings it has the largest font. For further emphasis it may be typed in bold, CLOSED CAPS or S P A C E D   C A P S and/or underlined.

It may be left aligned (e.g. with block layouts) or centred (e.g. indented or semi-blocked layouts).

Subheading (second level)

Underneath the title is the **subheading** which provides additional information about the topic covered in the document.

It is placed immediately underneath the main heading (with the same alignment) but formatted so it is slightly less prominent. It may be in Title Case or CLOSED CAPS.

Section heading (third level)

Each section of the document normally has a corresponding heading, called (unsurprisingly) the **section heading**. These headings may be typed in CLOSED CAPS or in Title Case and may also be bold and/or underlined.

Most section headings are **shoulder headings** that are found above the first paragraph of the section. But there are also paragraph headings and margin headings, which are positioned on the same line as the start of the paragraph.

Paragraph heading: A paragraph heading is actually part of the paragraph itself so it is left aligned or indented depending on the layout used. In order to distinguish the heading from the rest of the paragraph, it is usually put in bold with a colon after it.

Marginal Heading | A **marginal heading** (also called a <u>side</u> heading) is positioned to the left of the paragraph, possibly inside the left margin itself. It is used in documents like plays and programmes. If you want a marginal heading like this one, press *Tab* after the heading. Then adjust the hanging indent using the Ruler.

Common abbreviations

Table 3.1 gives the meaning of abbreviations that you will encounter frequently when you are typing manuscripts.

Table 3.1 Common abbreviations and their meaning.

Abbreviation	Meaning
&	and
+	and
a/c	account
A4 L	A4 Landscape Orientation
A4 P	A4 Portrait Orientation
approx	approximately
appt	appointment
bec	because
bn	been
bus	business
cd	could
Co	Company
CV	curriculum vitae
def	definitely
diff	difference
Dirs	Directors
dls	double line spacing
Dr Sir	Dear Sir
ea	each
esp	especially
ex	exercise
f	for
f/t	full-time
ffy	faithfully
fig	figure
fr	from
hv	have
inc	incorporated
info	information
intl	international
mfr	manufacturer
misc	miscellaneous
mtg	meeting
opp	opportunity
p	page or pages

Abbreviation	Meaning
p.a.	per annum
p/t	part-time
pl	please
pp	page or pages
ps	postscript
q & a	question and answer
recd	received
sh	shall
shd	should
sls	single line spacing
s-ly	sincerely
st	street or saint
t	the
tbl	table
th	that
tls	triple line spacing
v	very or versus
VP	Vice President
w	with
w/o	without
wh	which
wl	will
wrt	with reference to
wt	weight
yrs	yours

Written reports

A written report is a document intended to inform the reader about research findings, progress made in a project, or an event that occurred.

The layout of a report depends on its type, how formal it is, as well as the requirements of the organisation for which you are preparing it.

Informal reports

For an informal report, the general structure is as follows:

- A main heading at the top of the first page containing the title of the report, the author's name and the date it was written.
- A brief introduction.
- The body of the report.
- The conclusion.

Formal Reports

For some reports such as academic reports or research reports, the structure is a lot more formal. The typical layout is as follows:

- Title page.
- Table of Contents (for long reports).
- Abstract.
- Introduction.
- The body of a report.
- Conclusion (including any recommendations).
- References or Bibliography.
- Appendix.

Title page

A title page is a page placed at the beginning of the report which includes:

- The title of the report.
- The name of the author, as well as the school or department.
- The date it was prepared.

Abstract

An abstract is a concise summary (at most 200 words) of the report which is placed before the introduction. Therefore it must be done after the report is finished. An abstract includes:

- The motivation of the research.
- A brief description of the methods used.
- An outline of the results and what conclusions can be drawn from them.

Shown below is a fictional abstract.

It is a common for students to listen to music while studying. Thompson (2005) suggests that this actually impairs their ability to concentrate. Students from the University of the West Indies were tested to see what the impact listening to various types of music had on their ability to perform a series of exercises. It was found that the effect on concentration depends on the type of music. Students got the lowest scores while listening to Dub and Calypso music. However, when students listened to Classical, R&B or Jazz music there was actually an improvement in their scores. A follow-up study will be done to see if these trends hold across a larger age range.

Introduction

The introduction of a research report defines the problem, stating the reason why the research was done.

Body

The body of the report typically contains:

- A review of previous research that is relevant to yours.
- A detailed explanation of the research methodology, including a description of how the sample was obtained.
- A discussion and analysis of the results, including Figures, Charts and Tables as appropriate.

References and bibliography

It is extremely important to cite any external sources you used while preparing your report, by means of a list of references or a bibliography. Part 5, Chapter 5 explains how to do so using the APA style. You can also visit http://owl.english.purdue.edu for an in-depth explanation of how to do academic writing.

Appendix

At the end of the report you normally have an appendix which includes a sample of any survey forms used, as well as the data you compiled.

Additional guidelines

Here are some additional tips you should follow when preparing reports:

- Label any figures, charts and tables included in the report so you can refer to them by number e.g. 'see Figure 5.1'.
- Write out an abbreviation in full the first time it is mentioned unless it is a ubiquitous term such as CD-ROM. For example: 'Electronic Document Preparation and Management (EDPM)'.
- Define any terms with which the reader may not be familiar.

Summary

- When a manuscript is typed out professionally, the result is called a typescript.
- Type manuscripts on A4 paper with 1" margins and portrait orientation and leave a clear line space after paragraphs unless instructed otherwise.
- Full punctuation is the type we normally use. With open punctuation, extraneous punctuation is removed.

- The types of headings are: main headings, subheadings, section headings, shoulder headings, paragraph headings and margin headings.
- A level one heading is usually bigger than a level two, which in turn is bigger than a level three.
- A report is a document written with the intent of informing the user and has a different layout depending on whether it is formal or informal.
- An abstract is a concise summary of a formal report.

Review exercises

Exercise 3.A

1 In your own words, what is the difference between a manuscript and typescript?
2 List <u>four</u> things the typist is expected to do when typing the manuscript.
3 List the <u>four</u> different types of headings.
4 Give one similarity between a paragraph heading and a side heading.
5 Explain the difference between open and standard punctuation. Give examples of both.
6 Match these types of headings to the heading levels:

Paragraph heading	Level 1
Main heading	Level 2
Shoulder heading	Level 3
Section heading	Level 4
Subheading	Level 5

7 What is the recommended number of spaces after:
  a A question mark.
  b A comma.
  c A full-stop at the end of a sentence.
  d A colon.
8 Rewrite the following using the correct spacing
  a " Help me! "he shouted.
  b My whole family(including me) has long hair.
  c 10,9,8...1
  d "... and that's the end of the news .... enjoy the rest of your ...."
9 Rewrite the following address using open punctuation:
  a Dr. Jeremy Bentham,

  b 1,234 Main Street,
  c Kingston,
  d Jamaica.
  e Dec. 21st, 2012.
10 What do the following abbreviations mean:
  a A5 P
  b yrs s-lry
  c fr
  d hv
11 Suppose you were asked to do an informal report about the rising cost of living for your class. Write an example of what the main heading would look like.
12 In your own words explain what an abstract is.
13 What type of section heading is used in the manuscript in Figure 3.1?

Exercise 3.B
Type the text given in Figure 3.1 on A4 paper, paying special attention to the manuscript rules mentioned in this chapter. Use an Arial Black size 28 font for the title. The subheading should be bold, in italics and in Times New Roman size 18. All section headings should be in the Arial font and be made bold. Expand all abbreviations apart from the units of measurement.

Exercise 3.C
Type the document in Figure 3.2 on A4 paper.

Exercise 3.D
Prepare a report on any of the topics below. Be sure to include images, charts and tables where appropriate in order to enhance the effectiveness of your report.

1 The Health Risks Associated with Computers
2 Literacy rates in the Caribbean
3 The Impact of Diabetes on the Caribbean
4 The Decline of the Sugar (or Banana) Industry
5 The Growth of the Tourism Industry
6 The World's Largest Oil Producers
7 The World's Richest Men and Women
8 The Top 10 Grossing Movies
9 The Wealthiest Sports Teams
10 How the 100 m Record Has Fallen

Units of Measurement
Making Sense of All the Numbers

Introduction

It is sometimes difficult to mk sense of all t different measurements th are out there. Ea type of measurement has its own unit and although there are stds, it seems like countries switch between them randomly. T aim of this doc is to give you a better understanding of t different units.

Different Systems

There are three main sys in use : t metric sys (t intnl std) , t US customary sys & t Imperial Sys. T latter two are vry similar.

Weight

T std unit of wt is t kilogram (kg). However, most ppl are familiar with wts in pounds (lbs). 1 kg = 2.0246 lbs.

Length

T std unit of length is t metre (m) but there are a no of prefixes th can be used w them. T tbl below explains what ea prefix means.

Prefix	Meaning
milli	1/1000
centi	1/100
deci	1/10
kilo	1,000

T US and Imperial Sys take a different approach to lengths as shown in t tbl below.

Length	Metric Equiv
1 inch (in)	2.54 cm
1 foot (ft) = 12 in	0.3048 m
1 yard (yrd) = 3 ft	0.9144 m
1 mile (mi) = 1,760 yd	1,609 m

Conclusion

Th is just a fraction of t many units th are out there. There are def many others. Hope this helps!

Figure 3.1 Manuscript for Exercise 3.B

Browser Wars Part 2

Can Internet Explorer Make a Comeback?

From humble beginnings in 1995, Microsoft Internet Explorer reached its peak in popularity between 2002 and 2003, with a staggering 95% market share[1]. But such days are a distant memory. Each year sees its market share getting further eroded, as browsers like Mozilla's Firefox and Google's Chrome nip at the former giant's heels. Once the pinnacle of browsing technology, Internet Explorer is now the subject of almost-universal ridicule throughout the technology community. Now Microsoft is looking to reverse this negative momentum with Internet Explorer 9.

The Original Browser Wars

One cannot talk about Internet Explorer's fall without mentioning how it came to prominence in the original browser wars. Internet Explorer wasn't always the world's most popular web browser. In the 90s the distinction belonged to Netscape Navigator, a browser which introduced many of the features we take for granted today such as download progress indicators. So complete was Netscape's dominance that few gave the young upstart out of Redmond any chance of taking the crown.

For years Microsoft had neglected the Internet, and Netscape took advantage of that opportunity, its name becoming synonymous with web browsing. But then came the infamous Internet Tidal Wave memo[2], the one that changed the face of web browsing forever. No less a figure than one William Gates III had realised there might be something to this Internet thing after all and set the sights of the World's largest software company squarely on Netscape's browser.

Netscape never knew what hit it. A sleeping giant had been awoken and updates were fast and furious. Microsoft had two aces up its sleeve. First of all, it happened to have a little operating system that was installed on almost every PC. So naturally, it started bundling Internet Explorer with Windows. And secondly it had deep enough pockets to do the

---

[1] Source: Wikipedia.org
[2] http://www.justice.gov/atr/cases/exhibits/20.pdf

Figure 3.2 Page 1 of 2   Manuscript for Exercise 3.C

unthinkable (at that time) – give away its web browser completely free. Netscape, on the other hand, actually needed to make money from its browser.

By its 3rd version, Internet Explorer was roughly equivalent with Netscape in terms of features. By version 4.0, it had pulled ahead, both in terms of features of users. By the time Internet Explorer 6 came around, the once ubiquitous Netscape was deemed dead and buried.

The Challengers to Internet Explorer's Throne

Having conquered the Web, Microsoft rested on its laurels from 2001 to 2006. But people were becoming increasingly frustrated with Internet Explorer. Many a virus was able to exploit IE's security holes. So Mozilla began promoting the Firefox browser as a safer alternative, with unprecedented extensibility to boot, the technology world took notice. For the first time since the mid 90s, Microsoft had a credible David to its aging Goliath.

But Firefox isn't the only browser Microsoft has to worry about. Here are some of the others:

Opera: This Norwegian browser actually pioneered several features such as tabbed browsing but because of its licensing model, never really caught on.

Safari: Apple's browser is the default on its popular consumer hardware devices including the iPod, iPhone and iPad.

Chrome: Google's offering prides itself on two things: speed and simplicity. Having the backing of the most powerful web company doesn't hurt either.

Microsoft's Comeback Bid

Although Internet Explorer 7 and 8 were massive improvements over the version 6.0, Microsoft's market share has continued to decline. In the 2 or so years it takes for Microsoft to release a new version of IE, its competitors are able to release several updates. Microsoft is trying to be more agile with its development with version 9, releasing frequent updates and involving the web development community at an unprecedented (for Microsoft anyway) level. It says its new browser will be faster and follow the latest HTML standards.

But will it be enough? I am not certain. But one should never count a sleeping giant out.

Figure 3.2 Page 2 of 2 Manuscript for Exercise 3.C

④ Correction symbols

In this chapter, you will learn the different correction symbols you might encounter when typing manuscripts

Marking up corrections

Often, you will be asked to make corrections to a manuscript. The person on whose behalf you are typing the document will use correction symbols to tell you what changes need to be made. A correction is usually – but not always – indicated in two places.

- A mark in the body of the document identifies where the change needs to be made.
- An instruction, usually in the margin but sometimes in the document itself, provides additional information pertaining to the correction.

Instructions may also be written in plain English. In such cases, they should done in such a way that they will not be confused with the document itself, e.g. by drawing circles or balloons around them.

Insertion and deletion

Inserting text
The insertion symbol ⋀ is used to show where text is to be inserted. The text to be inserted may be indicated in the margin or with an arrow. You can also use the universal insertion character, the caret ^.

Inserting a space
To tell the typist to insert a space, show where the space is to go with the insertion symbol and place a # sign in the margin.

Deleting text
Cross out any text to be deleted. The word 'Delete' or one of these deletion symbols ૭ ૭ ૪ may be placed in the margin as well.

Deleting spaces
If you want the space between two words to be deleted or 'closed up', put an arc above and below the space like this:

brides⁀maid

Additionally, you may write the words 'close up' in the margin.

Example: insertion and deletion

Before

close up
⋀ (match)

demolished
Barcelona ~~beat~~ Real Madrid in the football yesterday ~~evening~~. The result was never in any doubt since Barcelona was the team.

superior

After

Barcelona demolished Real Madrid in the football match yesterday. The result was never in any doubt since Barcelona was the superior team.

Paragraphs

New paragraphs

In order to signal a new paragraph, place [or // where the new paragraph is to start and put 'NP', 'Para' or ¶ in the margin.

Joining paragraphs

If two paragraphs are to be joined, draw an S-shaped line from the end of the first paragraph to the beginning of the second and put any of the following in the margin: 'Run on', 'Run in' or 'No ¶'.

This is the first paragraph here and undeneath is the second.

Run on

However, this paragraph is to be joined to the one above.

Indentation

If you want a paragraph indented, place an] next to the part of the paragraph to be indented and put the word 'Indent' in the margin.

If you no longer want a part of a paragraph indented, draw a [next to the part where the indentation is to be removed and put the word 'Flush' in the margin.

Example: Marking up paragraphs

Before

Indent] *Staff members have been using the*
flush [*Internet at work.*
No ¶
¶ *Desist from this practice.*[*Thanks for your cooperation.*

After

Staff members have been using the Internet at work. Desist from this practice.

Thanks for your cooperation.

Moving text

When you want text moved, the easiest way is to circle the text and indicate with an arrow where the text is to go.

Transposing

However, sometimes you want to change the order of words or sentences. This is known as <u>transposing</u>. Suppose you had the phrase 'sound and safe' and wanted to switch the words 'sound' and 'safe'. The way you would show this is as follows:

The result is 'safe and sound'.

You can also transpose text vertically:

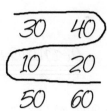

becomes

10   20

30   40

50   60

You should also put the word 'trs.' in the margin to make the instruction clearer.

Capitalisation

Table 4.1 explains how to indicate changes in capitalisation.

Table 4.1   Indicating changes in capitalisation.

If you want	Write this in the margin	And...
lowercase	lc	Strike through the letters to be made lowercase or put a <u>single line</u> underneath each one.
UPPERCASE	UC, CAPS or Closed Caps	Put <u>two lines</u> underneath the letters to be put in uppercase.
Initial Caps	Ini Caps	Put <u>two lines</u> underneath the <u>first</u> letter of each word.
SPACED CAPS	SC or Sp Caps	Put <u>three lines</u> underneath the letters.

Closed caps is the same thing as regular caps.

Example: Capitalisation

Before

Sp Caps <u><u>OPENING HOURS</u></u>

lc The store will be open from 8 A.M.
UC to 6 p.m. during the <u>xmas</u> holidays.
Ini Caps <u>m</u>erry <u>c</u>hristmas to <u>a</u>ll!

After

OPENING HOURS

The store will be open from 8 a.m.
to 6 p.m. during the XMAS holidays.
Merry Christmas to All!

Formatting

The abbreviations 'bf', 'ital' and 'U/S' are used when you want text put in **boldface**, *italics* or <u>underscored</u> (underlined). You usually put them in the margins but they can also be put near the text that is to be formatted.

In order to identify the text to be formatted, you underline it.

Example: Formatting text

Before

U/S <u>Formatting Text</u>
bf Formatting text is a <u>great</u> way to
ital emphasise it (<u>make it stand out</u>).
bf U/S A single line may contain <u>multiple</u>
<u>formatting</u> options.
(bf) (ital)

After

<u>Formatting Text</u>
Formatting text is a **great** way to
emphasise it (*make it stand out*).
A single line may contain <u>**multiple**</u>
formatting options.

Lining Up Text

If you want to line up text vertically, you draw two vertical parallel lines next to it.

Example

Before

10 ‖ 20
30 ‖ 40
50 ‖ 60

After

$$10 \quad 20$$
$$30 \quad 40$$
$$50 \quad 60$$

Miscellaneous

Unintelligible words

Handwritten scripts are difficult to understand, especially if the writer's handwriting is terrible (like mine). If you think that the typist may have difficulty with a word, underline it then write the word in the margin in ALL CAPS enclosed in dashed box.

> Although the word in the margin is written in CAPS, the typist is to type the word in the same case as the surrounding text.

Stets

A **stet** is used to cancel a deletion or correction.

> **If you no longer want a correction to be made:**
>
> 1 Underline the text you want to remain unchanged using a dotted line.
>
> 2 Put the word 'Stet' above or beside the text. Alternatively, you can insert a tick with a circle around it in the margin.

Writing out words in full

When people are writing scripts, they use abbreviations in order to save time. To tell the typist to write out a word in full, circle it and write the words 'in full' next to it.

Example

Before

Congratulations
stet
I am extremely pleased with the
[PERFORMANCE] performance of this dept for the last
month. *in full*
✓ Looking (fwrd) to even better results
next month!

After

Congratulations
I am extremely pleased with the
performance of this department
for the last month.
Looking forward to even better
results next month!

Summary

- Correction symbols may be placed near the site of the correction or in the margins.
- Additional instructions that are given in plain English should be circled.
- If you want to cancel a correction or deletion instruction you can use a stet.

Review exercises

Exercise 4A

1 Explain in your own words what each of the following instructions means.
   a Close up
   b Closed Caps
   c Run on
   d Ini Caps
   e NP

f Stet
g Flush
h ¶
i lc

Exercise 4B

Write down this (abbreviated) passage, then add the correction symbols as directed.

CHOOSING A COMPUTER
With the no. of computers out there, choosing a computer can be a very challenging task. And with the introduction of Net books and devices like Apple's ipad, this decision has become even more difficult. The first thing you have to do is ask yourself, "how am I going to use this computer?". If portability is a major concern, then you need a Notebook, Netbook or something similar. Otherwise, a desktop is a better bet since they are cheaper.

Add correction symbols or instructions for the following:
1 Put the heading in initial caps, underline it and centre it.
2 Spell out the word 'no.' (in the first line) in full.
3 Delete the space between the words 'Net' and 'books'.
4 Capitalise the p in 'ipad'.
5 The part with 'The first thing …' should start a new paragraph.
6 Delete the word 'major'.
7 Insert the word 'usually' before the word 'cheaper'.

Exercise 4C

Write down this (abbreviated) passage, then add the correction symbols as directed.

Getting an Email Address

Don't have an email address? Don't worry, getting one is very easy.

There are a number of free email providers out there. The most popular one is Windows Live Hotmail. The steps

in the signup process are usually as follows.

Agree to the rules and conditions and that's it!

Go to the Hotmail.com.

Open your web browser.

Click Sign Up.

Fill in your information.

Choose an email address.

Type the letters shown in the captcha.

Add correction symbols or instructions for the following:
1 Put the heading in spaced caps using a size 20 Arial font.
2 Remove the indentation from the first line.
3 Delete the word 'very' from the first sentence.
4 Join the second paragraph to the end of the first one.
5 Add the text '(or Hotmail for short)' after 'Windows Live Hotmail'.
6 Insert a space in the middle of the word 'signup'.
7 Put the word 'usually' in italics.
8 Number the steps using Roman numerals.
9 Switch the order of the second and third steps.
10 In the line that says 'Click Sign Up', make the words 'Sign Up' bold.
11 In the line where it says 'Choose an email address', insert the word 'available' between 'an' and 'email'.
12 Capitalise the word 'captcha'.
13 Move the line that says 'Agree to the rules…' to the bottom of the list.
14 Cancel the deletion of the word 'very' from the first sentence.
15 Align these steps vertically.

Exercise 4D

Type the manuscript shown in Figure 4.1 on A4 paper making the changes as indicated. Use a line spacing of 1.5.

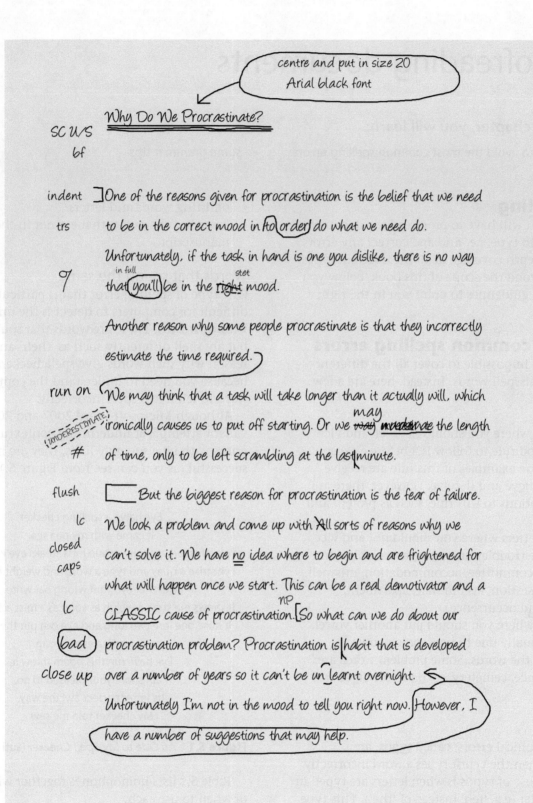

Figure 4.1 Manuscript for Exercise 4D.

5 Proofreading documents

In this chapter, you will learn:

- how to avoid the most common spelling errors
- some grammar tips

Proofreading

As a typist, you will have to proofread the documents you are asked to type, i.e. find and correct any errors. While an in-depth coverage of all the different types of errors is beyond the scope of this book, below you will find a few guidelines to point you in the right direction.

Avoiding common spelling errors

Obviously it is impossible to cover all the different ways people misspell words. Instead, here are a few common ones.

- Putting 'ie' where you should have 'ei' and vice versa. A good rule to follow is 'i before e except after c'. Some examples of this rule are rec<u>ei</u>ve, bel<u>ie</u>ve, ach<u>ie</u>ve and dec<u>ei</u>ve. However, there are a few exceptions to this rule, such as prot<u>ei</u>n and s<u>ei</u>ze.
- Doubling letters where you should not and vice versa. Some troublesome words are: Caribbean, tomorrow, committee, accommodation, misspell, skilful, possession, accumulate, apartment, occasion and occurrence.
- Putting 'a' where you should put another vowel. This is normally due to how some people pronounce the words. Some problem words are: independ<u>e</u>nce, cem<u>e</u>tery, coc<u>o</u>nut, priv<u>i</u>lege and irrel<u>e</u>vant.

Typos

Some typographical errors, called <u>typos</u>, are introduced when the typist types a word incorrectly. A common cause of typos is when letters are typed in the wrong order (e.g. 'teh' instead of 'the'). This type of error is called a **transposition error.**

Other types of typos are:

- typing the wrong letter or number

- omitting words and letters
- inserting characters that are not in the original manuscript.

Words that sound the same

One type of spelling error that is particularly difficult for computers to detect is the misuse of **homophones**. These are words that sound the same but are spelt differently such as 'their' and 'there'. The reason why such words give spellcheckers trouble is because you need to understand the <u>context</u> of the word to tell if it is spelt incorrectly.

Although Microsoft Word 2007 and 2010 make valiant attempts at underlining contextual spelling errors with blue squiggly lines, they are not always successful (as you can see from Figure 5.1).

Eye halve a spelling checker
It came with my pea sea.
It plainly marks four my revue miss steaks eye kin knot sea.
Eye strike a <u>quay</u> and type a word and weight for it to say
Weather eye yam wrong <u>oar</u> write.
It shows me strait a weigh as soon as a mist ache is maid.
It nose bee <u>fore</u> two long and eye can put the error rite.
<u>Its rare lea ever wrong.</u>
Eye have run this poem threw it,
I am shore your pleased to no.
Its letter perfect awl the way.
My checker told me sew.

Figure 5.1 *An Ode to My Spell Checker* (author unknown).

Table 5.1 lists homophones together with examples of when to use each.

Table 5.1 Common homophones and examples of their use.

Homophones	Examples of their use
Aid Aide	The World Bank gave Greece billions of dollars in <u>aid</u>. The President's <u>aide</u> went to fetch him some coffee.
Aisle Isle	The bride's father to walked her down the <u>aisle</u>. '<u>Isle</u>' is short for 'island'.
Altar Alter	At the front of a church you can find the <u>altar</u>. The seamstress needed to <u>alter</u> the dress.
Bare Bear Beer	He dug the hole with his <u>bare</u> hands. I can't <u>bear</u> the thought of that. Let's go to the pub after work and grab a <u>beer</u>.
Board Bored	The teacher wrote the homework on the <u>board</u>. The students look <u>bored</u>.
Bread Bred	A loaf of <u>bread</u>. The past tense of 'breed' is '<u>bred</u>'.
By Buy Bye	Your shoes are <u>by</u> the door. I need to <u>buy</u> a new watch. Tim forgot to tell his grandmother <u>bye</u>.
Check Cheque	You need to <u>check</u> the pressure in your tyres. Can I write you a <u>cheque</u>?
Cell Sell	He stared gloomily through the bars of his prison <u>cell</u>. Laura wanted to <u>sell</u> her car.
Cent Scent Sent	A quarter is twenty-five <u>cents</u>. The <u>scent</u> of her perfume. Mother <u>sent</u> me to the store to buy some groceries.
Cite Sight Site	You should <u>cite</u> any sources that you use. Someone who is blind no longer has his <u>sight</u>. The workers stood on the <u>site</u> of the new building.

Homophones	Examples of their use
Coarse Course	Another word for 'rough' is '<u>coarse</u>'. Phillip is currently doing an IT <u>course</u>.
Colonel Kernel	A <u>colonel</u> is a position in the army. A <u>kernel</u> of popcorn.
Compliment Complement	Sarah blushed when the man gave her a <u>compliment</u>. Peanut butter and jelly <u>complement</u> each other well.
Core Corps	The <u>core</u> of an object is in its middle. The marine <u>corps</u>.
Cue Queue	Many people can not smile on <u>cue</u>. He had to wait in the <u>queue</u> for hours.
Currant Current	A <u>currant</u> is a dried fruit placed in cakes. Electric <u>current</u> is flowing through the wires.
Deer Dear	She looked like a <u>deer</u> in headlights. <u>Dear</u> John.
Discrete Discreet	'<u>Discrete</u>' is a word meaning 'separate and distinct'. Be <u>discreet</u> when dealing with sensitive matters.
Die Dye	Unfortunately, everybody has to <u>die</u>. She wanted to <u>dye</u> her hair purple.
Ensure Insure	<u>Ensure</u> that the gas is turned off. You should <u>insure</u> your car before driving it.
Fair Fare	Life is not <u>fair</u>. He did not have any bus <u>fare</u>.
Feat Feet	Usain Bolt's 100 m record was an incredible <u>feat</u>. You must learn to stand on your own two <u>feet</u>.
Flour Flower	<u>Flour</u> is one of the main ingredients of a cake. A rose is her favourite type of <u>flower</u>.

Homophones	Examples of their use
Forth Fourth	'Lazarus, come <u>forth</u>!' April is the <u>fourth</u> month in the year.
Jeans Genes	She was wearing a tight pair of <u>jeans</u>. DNA contains a number of <u>genes</u>.
Knew New	He <u>knew</u> the answer to that question. Look at my brand <u>new</u> car!
Gorilla Guerrilla	A <u>gorilla</u> is an animal in the monkey family. The insurgents practised <u>guerrilla</u> warfare.
Groan Grown	The patient <u>groan</u>ed in pain. Little Timmy is all <u>grown</u> up now!
Hair Hare Here	Most people in the Caribbean have black <u>hair</u>. Have you heard the story of the <u>hare</u> and the tortoise? Come <u>here</u>! Now!
Heel Heal	Her shoe <u>heel</u> came off when she was running. Some wounds take a long time to <u>heal</u>.
Hours Ours	He waited in line for 3 <u>hours</u> to get a ticket. That dog is not one of <u>ours</u>.
Hole Whole	There is a <u>hole</u> in my bucket. Jamario ate the <u>whole</u> cake by himself.
Knight Night	He was her <u>knight</u> in shining armour. The <u>night</u> was very dark since there was no moon.
Laps Lapse	An 800 m is two <u>laps</u> around the track. She had a brief <u>lapse</u> in concentration.
Mail Male	The postman delivers the <u>mail</u>. On the form indicate whether you are <u>male</u> or female.
Maize Maze	<u>Maize</u> is another word for corn. She got lost in the <u>maze</u>.

Homophones	Examples of their use
Meat Meet	Chicken, pork and lamb and all types of <u>meat</u>. I would love to <u>meet</u> Halle Berry.
Naval Navel	The term '<u>naval</u>' has to do with the sea. Another word for '<u>navel</u>' is 'bellybutton'.
None Nun	That is <u>none</u> of your business. A <u>nun</u> wears a black and white gown called a habit.
Overseas Oversees	Caribbean residents like to travel <u>overseas</u>. The supervisor <u>oversees</u> the workers.
Pail Pale	'<u>Pail</u>' is another word for bucket. You need to get a tan. Your skin looks very <u>pale</u>.
Pain Pane	The <u>pain</u> from the burn on her hand was intense. The <u>pane</u> of glass fell and broke.
Peak Peek Pique	He climbed to the <u>peak</u> of the mountain. My neighbour loves to <u>peek</u> through her curtains. He is trying his best to <u>pique</u> her interest.
Peer Pier	Do not give in to <u>peer</u> pressure. There are no ships at the <u>pier</u>.
Plain Plane	That dress design is quite <u>plain</u>. '<u>Plane</u>' is short for 'aeroplane'.
Pole Poll	That telephone <u>pole</u> is about to fall down. The latest <u>poll</u> has the DLP party winning.
Pray Prey	Even if you do not go to church, you should <u>pray</u> daily. The lion was on the lookout for its <u>prey</u>.
Principal Principle	The headmaster of a school is also called the <u>principal</u>. It is a matter of <u>principle</u>.

Homophones	Examples of their use
Rain Reign Rein	The clouds were grey because it was about to <u>rain</u>. The Queen's <u>reign</u> was over 50 years. The jockey held the <u>reins</u> of the horse tightly.
Ring Wring	She lost her wedding <u>ring</u>. Sometimes I just want to <u>wring</u> his neck!
Red Read	The Trinidadian flag is <u>red</u>, white and black. Tom <u>read</u> ten books last month.
Role Roll	Each member of the team should know his <u>role</u>. You are on a <u>roll</u> today.
Scene Seen	That was my favourite <u>scene</u> in the whole movie. I have not <u>seen</u> you in ages!
Seam Seem	The <u>seam</u> of his pants. Things are not always what they <u>seem</u>.
Sees Seas Seize	She wants to buy every pair of shoes that she <u>sees</u>. Sinbad sailed the Seven <u>Seas</u>. To <u>seize</u> something is to take a hold of it or grab it.
Stair Stare	He ran up the stairs one <u>stair</u> at a time. It is rude to <u>stare</u> at people.
Stake Steak	The farmer hammered the <u>stake</u> into the ground. Americans love to eat <u>steak</u>.
Stationary Stationery	When something is <u>stationary</u> it is not moving. Pencils and rulers are examples of <u>stationery</u>.
Steel Steal	<u>Steel</u> is a very strong metal. Thou shalt not <u>steal</u>.
Storey Story	They lived in a two-<u>storey</u> house. My son's favourite <u>story</u> is The Three Little Pigs.

Homophones	Examples of their use
Their They're There	The word '<u>their</u>' is used to show ownership. Instead of saying 'they are' you can say '<u>they're</u>'. Don't stand up here. Go over <u>there</u>.
Threw Through	He <u>threw</u> the ball into the air. Stop making me jump <u>through</u> hoops.
Vain Vane Vein	Their efforts were in <u>vain</u>. A wind-<u>vane</u> tells you the direction of the wind. A <u>vein</u> is a blood vessel.
Waist Waste	Tom is so slim that his pants has a 32-inch <u>waist</u>. What a <u>waste</u> of time!
Weather Whether	The <u>weather</u> has been very bad recently. I do not know <u>whether</u> to laugh or cry.
Wear Where	I do not know what to <u>wear</u> tonight. Home is <u>where</u> the heart is.

Grammar tips

Correct punctuation and capitalisation

When you are proofreading what you have typed, be sure to check for correct punctuation and capitalisation. Here are some of the things to look for:

- full-stops missing from the end of sentences
- common letters after full-stops
- names and places that do not start with a capital letter (although they should)
- missing commas
- missing quotation marks.

Subject and verb agreement

Be sure to use singular verbs (those which end in s or es) with singular subjects and plural verbs with plural subjects. For example:

- She <u>sings</u> in the shower every morning. (singular verb)
- They <u>sing</u> in the church choir. (plural verb)

But it is not always that simple. Here are a few tricky cases where singular verbs are used:

- Henry, along with his brothers, <u>goes</u> fishing every Saturday.
- Either her mother or her father <u>was</u> European.
- Neither John nor Mary <u>is</u> at school today.

Common pitfalls

- Confusing the words its and it's. It's is short for 'it is' whereas its is used to denote ownership. So it is incorrect to say 'The dog wagged it's tail'.
- Putting an apostrophe in words like yours and ours.
- Saying 'would of', 'should of' or 'could of' (incorrect) instead of 'would have', 'should have' or ' could have' (correct).
- Saying 'between you and I' (incorrect) instead of 'between you and me' (correct).
- Writing 'alot' (incorrect) instead of 'a lot' (correct).
- Using 'less' where you should use 'fewer'. You should use 'fewer' whenever you are talking about something that can be counted. So it is incorrect to say 'I had less visitors today than yesterday'.
- Constantly switching between tenses.

Summary

- Be sure to watch out for misspelt words, especially those due to transposition errors and confusing words that sound the same.
- Watch your subject and verb agreement.
- Be on the lookout for missing punctuation marks and incorrect capitalisation.

Review exercises

Exercise 5A

1 What is a transposition error? Give two examples.

2 Give three other types of typos.
3 What is a homophone? Give three sets of examples.
4 Correct the spelling errors (if any) in these words (feel free to use your computer's spell-check feature):
   a relieved
   b tommorow
   c skilful
   d Carribean
   e cematary
   f appart
   g defanite
   h accommodate
   i committee
5 Each one of these sentences contains at least one grammatical error. Rewrite each sentence correctly.
   a I should of paid more attention in English class.
   b Neither Kyle nor his sister were anywhere to be found.
   c The lion might of found it's cubs.
   d Its really easy to make mistakes when you were typing.
   e There was alot of sugar in the container.
   f Between you and I I'm glad that he didn't win the race.
   g Have you read Call of the Wild she asked.

Exercise 5B

Type the following passage, correcting any spelling and grammar errors.

```
i wanted to cell my car so i put an
add in the newspaper a man who new me
saw the add called me and oferred to
by it we arranged to meat after work
but when he arrived he wanted to paid
with a check although i said i was only
taking cash what a waist of my time
the hole thing has me vrey frustrated
especially sense its not the first time
something like thta had happen to me
the man wants to meet again tomorow i
prey that this time the meeting wont
be in vane
```

6 Letters and memos

Memoranda

A memorandum (memo for short) is a short letter used for inter-office communication. Memoranda (plural) are typically used to inform members within an organisation about policy changes as well as problems which need addressing.

Memos are generally pretty short and so can be put on A5 paper using portrait or landscape orientation. However, for longer memos use A4 paper in portrait orientation since it is preferable to have the memo on one page instead of two. Use 1" margins and single spacing unless directed otherwise and leave a clear line space between paragraphs.

There are three main layouts used for memoranda: the blocked layout (see Figure 6.1a on page 280) and the indented layout (Figure 6.1b on page 281) and the semi-blocked layout (Figure 6.1c on page 282). Notice the differences in the positions of the following:

- the word 'Memorandum'
- the date
- the reference number
- the subject
- the first line of each paragraph

Reference number

The reference number near the top of the memo is optional. It is used to make it easier to refer to a particular memo.

Enclosure notation

The enclosure notation is only used if attachments are being sent with the memo. If one attachment is being sent write 'Enc'. Write 'Encs.' if multiple items are being sent with the memo.

Signing

A memo does not need to be signed but the writer's name or initials may be placed at the bottom. In the latter case, the writer's initials are in capital letters followed by a slash and the typist's initials in lowercase (if one was used).

tip

To insert the horizontal rule near the top of the memo:
- **In Word 2003, click *Format, Borders* and *Shading* then click the *Horizontal Rule* button.**
- **In Word 2007 and 2010, click the *Borders* button on the *Home* tab, then click *Horizontal Line.***

Typing blocked layout memo

With a blocked style memo, everything is aligned flush against the left margin except:

- The names of the writer, recipient(s) and people to whom the memo are addressed.
- The reference number.
- The subject.
- And the date.

Press the *TAB* key once after the word SUBJECT is typed and then type the subject. Then use tabs to put the rest of the items mentioned above in line with the subject. For some items, two tabs may be necessary. For instance you may have to place two tabs after the word 'TO'. Of course, you could avoid having to press TAB multiple times by setting a Tab Break instead.

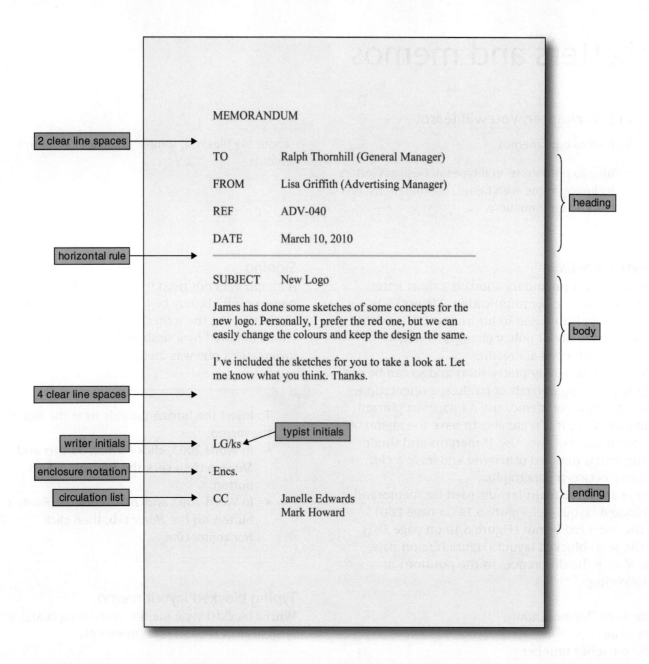

Figure 6.1a Memorandum with blocked layout.

The following labels appear pointing to the memorandum:

- 2 clear line spaces
- horizontal rule
- 4 clear line spaces
- writer initials
- enclosure notation
- circulation list
- typist initials
- heading
- body
- ending

MEMORANDUM

TO   Ralph Thornhill (General Manager)

FROM   Lisa Griffith (Advertising Manager)

REF   ADV-040

DATE   March 10, 2010

SUBJECT   New Logo

James has done some sketches of some concepts for the new logo. Personally, I prefer the red one, but we can easily change the colours and keep the design the same.

I've included the sketches for you to take a look at. Let me know what you think. Thanks.

LG/ks

Encs.

CC   Janelle Edwards
            Mark Howard

Typing an indented layout memo

In the body of an indented style memo, indent the first line of each paragraph by pressing the *TAB* key once.

Centre the word MEMORANDUM and the line containing the subject.

Use the tab key to line up the date and the reference number with the To and From fields as shown in Figure 6.1b.

Typing a semi-blocked layout memo

If you compare Figures 6.1a and 6.1c (see page 282), you will see that for the most part, a semi-blocked layout memo looks the same way as one with a blocked layout. The difference is that the word MEMORANDUM is centred and the subheadings To, From, Ref and Date are right-aligned.

MEMORANDUM

TO: Lisa Griffith (Advertising Manager)   DATE: March 12, 2010

FROM: Ralph Thornhill (General Manager)   REF: GEN-038

SUBJECT: Re: New Logo

You're right, the style used in the red logo does look better. However, I'd prefer a more subtle shade since the red is quite bright. *trs. 3* ¹

Ask James to do the Logo using two other shades of red, one darker and one paler. ²

lc

RT/ks

Figure 6.1b Memorandum with indented layout.

To right-align the subheadings:

- Type the memo as if you were doing a blocked style memo.
- Select the rows for the subheadings TO, FROM, REF and DATE
- Insert a *Right Tab Break* in line with the end of the word SUBJECT.
- Put the cursor in front of each of the subheadings then press the *TAB* key once.

Continuations

Even though you normally make every effort to fit a memo on a single page, sometimes this is impossible. In such cases you put a continuation containing the page number, recipient's name and the date, on each page after the first.

As you can see from Figure 6.2 on page 283, the way the continuation is written depends on the layout used. The Figure also illustrates different ways you can write the page numbers.

When a memo overflows to another page, make sure you do not have part of a paragraph on one page and the other part on the next page.

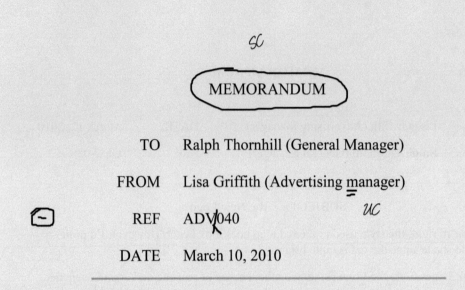

MEMORANDUM

TO   Ralph Thornhill (General Manager)

FROM   Lisa Griffith (Advertising manager)

REF   ADV040

DATE   March 10, 2010

SUBJECT   New Logo

James has done some sketches of some concepts for the new logo. Personally, I prefer the red one, but we can easily change the colours and keep the design the same.

I've included the sketches for you to take a look at. Let me know what you think. Thanks.

LG/ks
Encs

CC   Janelle Edwards
        Mark Howard

Figure 6.1c   Memorandum with semi-blocked layout.

Blocked

-2-

TO: Ralph Thornhill

DATE: March 10, 2010

Let me once again thank everyone involved for their support with the new logo. I look forward to seeing it in production soon.

1 clear line space

2 clear line spaces

Indented

(2)

TO: Ralph Thornhill   DATE: March 10, 2010

        Let me once again thank everyone involved for their support with the new logo. I look forward to seeing it in production soon.

Semi-Blocked

2

TO   Ralph Thornhill   DATE   March 10, 2010

Let me once again thank everyone involved for their support with the new logo. I look forward to seeing it in production soon.

Figure 6.2 Continuations for the different memo layouts.

Business letters

Business letters are more structured than ordinary letters as you can see from Figure 6.3. This letter has a <u>fully-blocked</u> layout (also called a block layout).

Figures 6.4 (on page 286) and 6.5 (on page 287) show additional layouts (the indented and semi-blocked layout respectively).

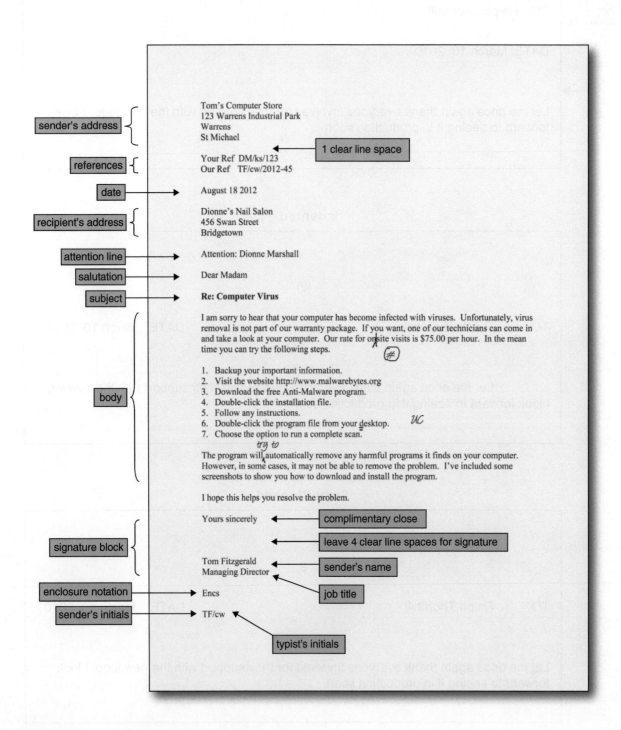

Figure 6.3 A (fully) blocked letter with an enumeration.

Near the top of the business letter, there may be two references, one referring to a letter that is being responded to (Your ref) and one for the current letter (Our ref).

When writing the complimentary close, the second word starts with a lowercase letter e.g. 'Yours sincerely', 'Yours faithfully' or 'Yours truly' (more informal).

Like with memos, if there is an attachment being sent with the letter, the word 'Enc' is put to the bottom of the letter. Also, if copies are being sent, the circulation list (CC) may be put underneath.

Paper size
Normally you use A4 paper with portrait layout and 1" margins. However, if you are typing a short letter, you may put it on A5 paper.

Fully blocked layout
This is the simplest layout since everything is simply aligned to the left of the page (see Figure 6.3).

Indented layout
In this layout (see Figure 6.4), the first line of every paragraph is indented with a tab, the subject is centred and the following items are positioned on the right of the page:

- The address information for the sender and the date the letter was typed.
- The complimentary close and the signature block (including the sender's job title).

> For cosmetic reasons, you usually use a left tab stop to position the items on the right of the page.

Semi-blocked layout
The semi-blocked layout is almost a hybrid between the blocked layout and the indented layout. For starters, the date is aligned to the right. In addition, the following information may either be positioned to the right or start from the centre of the page:

- The address of the sender.
- The complimentary close.
- The signature block (including the sender's job title).

If they start from the centre of the page like in Figure 6.5, a left tab stop is used. The rest of the information is aligned to the left.

Addresses
If a sender's address is included, it goes above the address of the intended recipient. Do not include the name of the sender or his/her title (since they appear in the signature block).

The country is normally omitted (from both addresses) when sending letters locally, but if it is present it may be capitalised.

Letterheads
A letterhead like the one on top of Figure 6.6a on page 288 may be used in place of the sender's address. Actually, it is *expected* that business letters come with a letterhead (and on high quality paper such as bond paper).

The letterhead should contain the name of the company, the address and any contact information such as the telephone number, fax number, e-mail address and/or website. It may also include the company logo.

The letterhead is normally centred at the very top of the first page.

Letters with continuations
As with memos, you try to get letters on one page, wherever possible. However in the event that your letter goes over to multiple pages (i.e. has continuations), here are a few guidelines you should follow:

1 The letterhead should only be on the first page.
2 All pages after the first page should contain:
   - The page number.
   - The name of the person the letter is addressed to.
   - And the date.

> This is so that if a page gets detached, one would still know which letter it came from. You should leave at least one inch of space at the top of the page before typing this information and two clear line spaces after it.

Figure 6.6a on page 288 shows a letter with a continuation which also includes a table.

Tom's Computer Store,
123 Warrens Industrial Park,
Warrens,
St. Michael.
August 18, 2012.

Your Ref: DM/ks/123
Our Ref: TF/cw/2012-45

Dionne's Nail Salon,
456 Swan Street,
Bridgetown.

Attention: Dionne Marshall

Dear Madam,

bf

Re: Computer Virus

I am sorry to hear that your computer has become infected with viruses. Unfortunately, virus removal is not part of our warranty package. If you want, one of our technicians can come in and take a look at your computer. Our rate for on-site visits is $75.00 per hour. In the mean time you can try the following steps.

1. Backup your important information.
2. Visit the website http://www.malwarebytes.org
3. Download the free Anti-Malware program.
4. Double-click the installation file.
5. Follow any instructions.
6. Double-click the program file from your Desktop.
7. Choose the option to run a complete scan.

The program will try to automatically remove any harmful programs it finds on your computer. However, in some cases, it may not be able to remove the problem. I've included some screenshots to show you how to download and install the program.

I hope this helps you resolve the problem.

Yours sincerely,

Tom Fitzgerald
Managing Director

Encs.

TF/cw

Figure 6.4   The same letter with indented layout (and standard punctuation).

Tom's Computer Store,
123 Warrens Industrial Park,
Warrens,
St. Michael.

August 18, 2012.

Your Ref: DM/ks/123
Our Ref: TF/cw/2012-45

Dionne's Nail Salon,
456 Swan Street,
Bridgetown.

Attention: Dionne Marshall

Dear Madam,

Re: Computer Virus *bf*

I am sorry to hear that your computer has become infected with viruses. Unfortunately, virus removal is not part of our warranty package. If you want, one of our technicians can come in and take a look at your computer. Our rate for on-site visits is $75.00 per hour. In the mean time you can try the following steps.

1. Backup your important information.
2. Visit the website http://www.malwarebytes.org
3. Download the free Anti-Malware program.
4. Double-click the installation file.
5. Follow any instructions.
6. Double-click the program file from your Desktop.
7. Choose the option to run a complete scan.

The program will try to automatically remove any harmful programs it finds on your computer. However, in some cases, it may not be able to remove the problem. I've included some screenshots to show you how to download and install the program.

I hope this helps you resolve the problem.

Yours sincerely,

Tom Fitzgerald
Managing Director

Encs.

TF/cw

Figure 6.5   The same letter with a semi-blocked layout (and standard punctuation).

WS

St. Francis Anglican Church
Faith Road, Castries
Tel: 555-PRAY

Ref: CW/ls/com045

June 30th, 2012.

The Manager,
Computer Training Centre,
#16 Silicon Valley,
Castries.

Attention: Ellis Bissette

Dear Sir,

Computer Training

As you may be aware, the St. Francis Anglican Church has been very active in the Castries community, particularly when it comes to educating underprivileged young people. To date, over one thousand children, teenagers and young adults have benefited from our programs.

NP Our latest venture is a Computer Training program, where young adults would cover the following topics:

As the leading computer training centre in St. Lucia, we believe that your company is the best one to undertake such training. We know you have a rich tradition of generosity and truly believe that ours is a worthy cause. That is why we are asking if you would be able to train ten students free of charge or at a discounted rate.

- Computer Basics
- Keyboarding
- Introduction to Microsoft Office
- Document Preparation

Name	Age	Tel. No.	Preferred Times
Paul Smith	21	555-0000	Anytime in the morning
Sera-Lee Frederick	20	555-1000	Tuesday and Thursday evenings
Amelia Auguste	19	555-2000	Anytime
Matthew White	22	555-3000	Monday and Wednesday evenings
Brian Gill	24	555-4000	Anytime
Natalie Monsdesir	18	555-5000	Mornings
Shawn Walcott	20	555-6000	Evenings
Amanda Baptiste	21	555-7000	Anytime
Angelique Richards	25	555-8000	Tuesday and Thursday evenings
Venessa St. Rose	28	555-9000	Saturdays

Figure 6.6a   A two page letter with a table (blocked layout).

- 2 -

Mr. Ellis Bissette

June 30th, 2012.

These are young people who are having difficulty making ends meet. Most of them don't have jobs, and those that do get paid next to nothing, so they wouldn't otherwise be able to afford computer courses.

The table above lists the names of the young people and the times they prefer to come. Some have young children and as a result, would only be able to come certain days. These names were submitted both by numbers of the community as well as members of the congregation.

Help us help these young people. Looking forward to hearing from you,

Yours In Christ,

Claude Williams (Rev.)
Priest in Charge

/ls

Figure 6.6a *(Continued)*

Indented

(2)

Mr Ellis Bissette June 30 2012

The table above lists the names of the young people and the times they prefer to come. Some have young children and as a result,

Semi-Blocked

2

Mr Ellis Bissette June 30 2012

The table above lists the names of the young people and the times they prefer to come. Some have young children and as a result, would only

Figure 6.6b Continuations for indented and semi-blocked layouts.

Letters with enumerations

If a letter has enumerations (numbered lists), you should leave a clear line space before the first item in the list and after the last item in the list. Use single-line spacing unless instructed otherwise.

The best way to insert an enumeration is to use Word's bullets and numbering feature. By default it will automatically indent the numbers, which is fine for letters typed using an indented layout.

For blocked (including semi-blocked) letters, however, you should highlight the entire list then click the *remove indent* button until the numbers are flush against the left margin.

Figures 6.4–6.6 show letters with enumerations.

Letters with insets

You can inset long quotes, enumerations and even tables from the margins in order to set them apart from the surrounding text. In order to do so you can adjust the left and right indents in the Ruler bar depending on whether you want to insert from the left, right or both margins.

The enumerations in Figure 6.4 and 6.5 are inset from the left margin. When you inset, you normally do so by 0.5" from the left and right margins.

Letters with tables

When including a table inside a letter, you should leave <u>at least</u> one clear line space before and after the table so that it does not appear as if it is squeezed on to the other surrounding text.

Circular letters

A **circular letter** (a letter that will be sent to several people) is written differently from a normal letter. This is because all the recipients are getting the same letter, information such as the recipient's name and address is either written in a generic fashion or left out so it can be filled in later.

For example, you might say 'Dear Sir or Madam' (since you do not know whether the person receiving the letter is going to be male or female). Some other examples are:

- Dear Valued Customer
- Dear Employee
- Dear Parent/Guardian

A Mail Merge Letter is a special type of circular letter

If you have a standard letter that may be sent on different days, some or all of the date may be omitted. For instance you may type the year and the month, but the day will be filled in later when the letter is sent out.

Circular letters with tear-offs

Sometimes letters come with a part at the bottom that you are to fill in, cut-off and send back (Figure 6.7). It is usually indicated by a dotted line, indicating where you are supposed to cut.

Have you ever heard the expression 'sign on the dotted line'? Well dotted lines and underscores are used to show where the person is supposed to fill-in the information. But these lines should be long enough to accommodate people with large handwriting. For the same reason there should be <u>at least</u> one clear line space above the line.

How to fold a business letter

Business letters are typically typed on A4 paper and placed in a C6/5, DL or Size 10 envelope. As a result they should be folded in (roughly) <u>thirds</u> as shown below Figure 6.8.

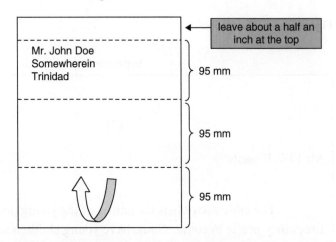

Figure 6.8 How to fold a business letter.

The exact measurements are not critical. What is important is that you start folding from the bottom and that you leave a part at the top that the recipient will be able to use when he/she is taking the letter out of the envelope.

Summary

- If an attachment is sent with the memo or letter, the word 'Enc.' is put at the bottom.

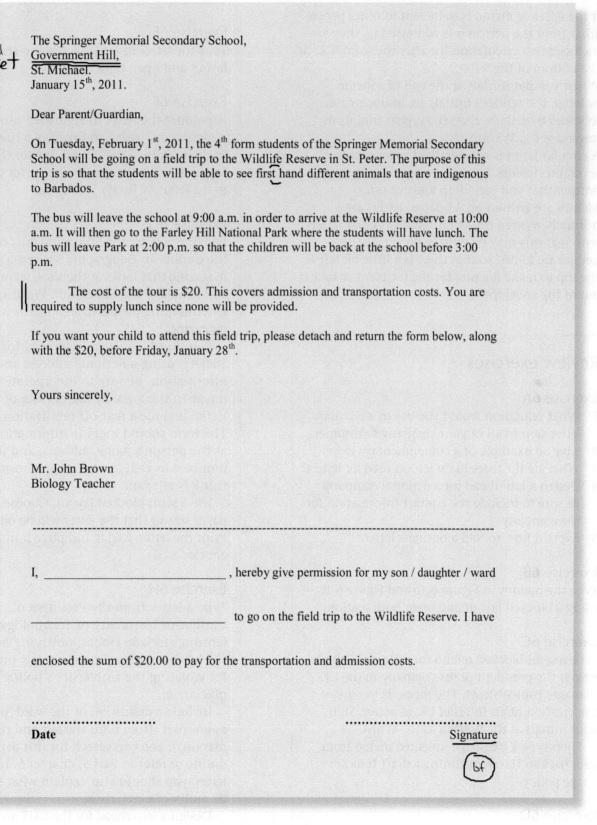

The Springer Memorial Secondary School,
Government Hill,
St. Michael.
January 15th, 2011.

[handwritten margin note: Closed, stet, caps]

Dear Parent/Guardian,

On Tuesday, February 1st, 2011, the 4th form students of the Springer Memorial Secondary School will be going on a field trip to the Wildlife Reserve in St. Peter. The purpose of this trip is so that the students will be able to see first hand different animals that are indigenous to Barbados.

The bus will leave the school at 9:00 a.m. in order to arrive at the Wildlife Reserve at 10:00 a.m. It will then go to the Farley Hill National Park where the students will have lunch. The bus will leave Park at 2:00 p.m. so that the children will be back at the school before 3:00 p.m.

The cost of the tour is $20. This covers admission and transportation costs. You are required to supply lunch since none will be provided.

If you want your child to attend this field trip, please detach and return the form below, along with the $20, before Friday, January 28th.

Yours sincerely,

Mr. John Brown
Biology Teacher

I, _____ , hereby give permission for my son / daughter / ward

_____ to go on the field trip to the Wildlife Reserve. I have

enclosed the sum of $20.00 to pay for the transportation and admission costs.

....
Date   Signature

[handwritten note: bf]

Figure 6.7   A circular letter with a cut-off (top and bottom cropped).

- If the letter or memo is to be sent to other people apart from the person it is addressed to, they are included in a circulation list after the word 'CC' at the bottom of the letter.
- When you put initials at the end of a memo or letter, the sender's initials are in uppercase, followed by a slash, then the typists initials in lowercase e.g. WS/mp.
- A circular letter is a generalised letter sent to several recipients. Some have a section at the bottom that you can fill in and cut-off.
- Memos are written on A5 paper; letters are normally written on A4 (although circular letters with tear-offs may be written on legal paper).
- Letters are folded so that there is a little bit left at the top to make it easier for the recipient to take it out of the envelope.

Review exercises

Exercise 6A

1 What salutation would you use in a circular letter sent to all of your company's customers.
2 Give an example of a complimentary close.
3 What are the three main layouts used for letters?
4 Design a letterhead for a fictional company. Be sure to include the contact information for the company.
5 Explain how to fold a business letter.

Exercise 6B

Type the memos in Figure 6.1b and Figure 6.1c using a blocked layout and open punctuation.

Exercise 6C

Type a semi-blocked memo from Harry Nicholls who is the president of his company to the I.T. manager Paul Walcott. The memo is to request the creation of an Internet Usage policy. Sign your initials at the bottom as the typist.

Then type a two-page indented memo from Paul back to Harry, outlining a draft Internet Usage policy.

Exercise 6D

Type the letter from Figure 6.3 on A4 paper using closed (standard) punctuation.

Exercise 6E

Type the letter in Figure 6.6 using an indented layout and open punctuation.

Exercise 6F

Reproduce the letter in Figure 6.7 using open punctuation. Insert an image of a tiny scissors in the middle of the dotted line for the tear-off form. (Tip: Set the text wrapping for the image to 'In Front of Text'.)

Exercise 6G

Imagine you are the Editor-in-Chief of the Caribbean Geographic Society, a magazine that looks at the sites, scenery and people of the Caribbean. Write a circular letter inviting people to sign up for your magazine.

You should create a letterhead for the Society, using a fictional address and contact information. Be sure to incorporate a suitable image in the logo. At the bottom of the letter, include a tear-off registration form. The form should include information such as the person's name, address, and telephone numbers as well as any other information you think is relevant.

Use a semi-blocked layout. Choose a suitable paper size so that the letter will be on one page. Print the letter, fold it and place it in a suitable envelope.

Exercise 6H

Type a letter from the President of the Caribbean University of Technology, John jennings to Jane Hobbs, notifying her that she has been placed on academic probation for violating the University's policy on plagiarism.

Include a definition of the word 'plagiarism' as an inset (from both the left and right margins). You can search for this definition online or refer to Part 5, chapter 5. In the letter, you should also explain what she did to be guilty of plagiarism.

Design a letterhead for the CUT and put it to the top of the letter. Type the letter on A4 paper and make up any addresses you need.

In response to the letter in Figure 6.6a, Mr. Ellis Bissette has agreed to train the students (at a discounted rate) and has drafted a letter for you to type in reply (see Figure 6.9). Type the letter using a full blocked layout, on A4 paper, inserting a letterhead for the Computer Training Centre.

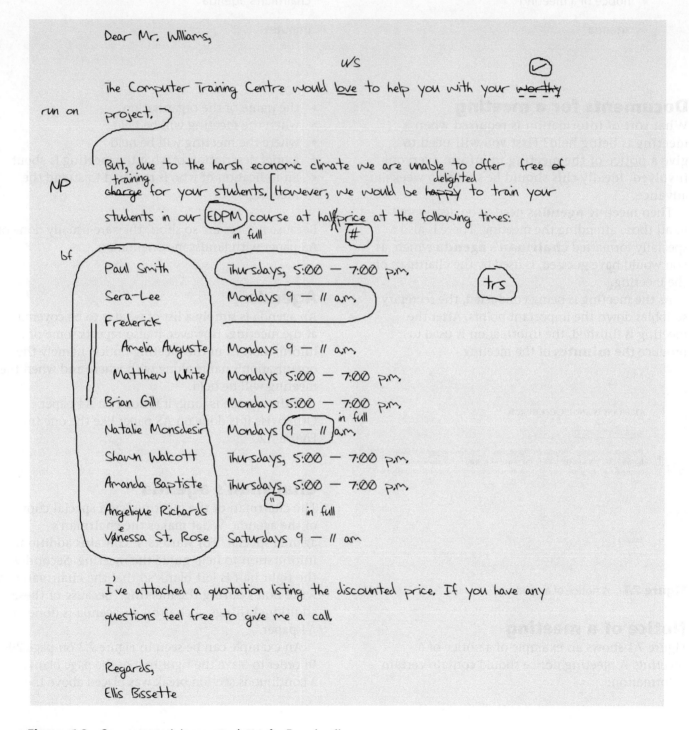

Dear Mr. Williams,

The Computer Training Centre would love to help you with your ~~worthy~~ project.

But, due to the harsh economic climate we are unable to offer free of charge training for your students. However, we would be delighted to train your students in our EDPM course at half price at the following times:

Paul Smith — Thursdays, 5:00 – 7:00 p.m.
Sera-Lee — Mondays 9 – 11 a.m.
Frederick
Amelia Auguste — Mondays 9 – 11 a.m.
Matthew White — Mondays 5:00 – 7:00 p.m.
Brian Gill — Mondays 5:00 – 7:00 p.m.
Natalie Monsdesir — Mondays 9 – 11 a.m.
Shawn Walcott — Thursdays, 5:00 – 7:00 p.m.
Amanda Baptiste — Thursdays, 5:00 – 7:00 p.m.
Angelique Richards
Vanessa St. Rose — Saturdays 9 – 11 am

I've attached a quotation listing the discounted price. If you have any questions feel free to give me a call.

Regards,
Ellis Bissette

Figure 6.9 Computer training centre letter for Exercise 6I.

7 Committee documents

In this chapter, you will learn about the documents used in connection with meetings:

- notice of a meeting
- agenda

- chairman's agenda
- minutes

Documents for a meeting

What sort of information is required when a meeting is being held? First you will need to give a <u>notice of the meeting</u> to inform everyone involved. Ideally this should be sent two weeks in advance.

Then meeting **agendas** need to be distributed to all those attending the meeting. There is also a specially formatted **chairman's agenda** which, as you would have guessed, is used by the chairman of the meeting.

As the meeting is being conducted, the secretary scribbles down the important points. After the meeting is finished, the information is used to produce the **minutes** of the meeting.

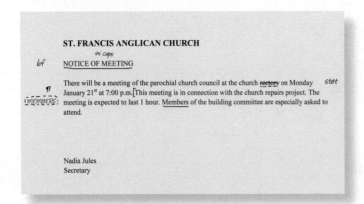

Figure 7.1 A notice of a meeting.

Notice of a meeting

Figure 7.1 shows an example of a notice of a meeting. A meeting notice should contain certain information:

- the name of the organisation
- when the meeting will be held
- where the meeting will be held
- a brief description of what the meeting is about
- an indication of who is required to attend the meeting.

Because notices are so short, they are usually done on A5 paper with landscape orientation.

Agenda

An agenda is simply a list of what is to be covered at the meeting. However, it also repeats some of the information from the meeting notice, namely the organisation's name along with where and when the meeting will be held.

If the agenda is long, it is done on A4 paper. Otherwise it is done on A5 paper like the one in Figure 7.2.

Chairman's agenda

The chairman of the meeting has a special copy of the agenda. What makes the chairman's agenda special? For starters, it contains additional information to help guide the meeting. Secondly, the right half is left blank so that the chairman can write notes during the meeting. Because of these additional things, a chairman's agenda is done on A4 paper.

An example can be seen in Figure 7.3 on page 296. In order to leave the right half of the page blank, a continuous section break was placed above the

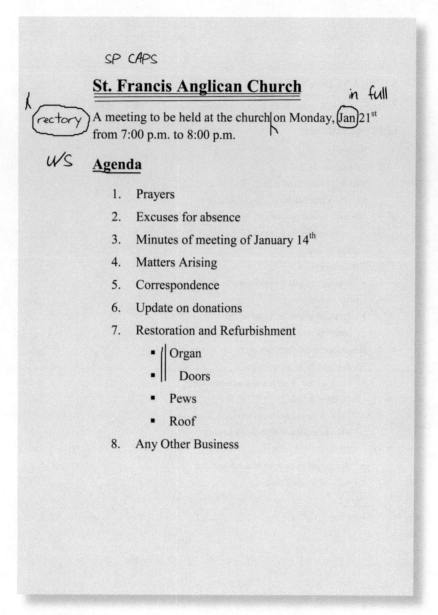

Figure 7.2 An agenda set on A5 paper.

heading 'Chairman's Agenda' and a large right margin was used for the rest of the document. A left margin of 0.5" was used in order to provide some additional space.

Minutes

The minutes of the meeting are a record of what happened during the meeting. They are normally typed on A4 paper using single line spacing. Figure 7.4 shows the minutes for our imaginary meeting. There is usually a section for each item on the agenda.

Obviously you should give some indication as to which meeting the minutes were taken from. This information is put at the top of the minutes. Underneath that goes a record of who was present and who was absent from the meeting.

When you are reporting what someone said at the meeting, you use their title if they have one. For example, 'The Chairman stated that ...' or 'The Treasurer remarked that...'.

At the end of the meeting there is usually time for Any Other Business (AOB), which is when one would discuss items that were not on the agenda.

ST. FRANCIS ANGLICAN CHURCH

A meeting to be held at the church rectory on Monday, January 21ˢᵗ from 7:00 p.m. to 8:00 p.m.

Chairman's Agenda

1. Prayers
2. Excuses for absence
   - Mr. Timothy Leon is ill.
   - Ms Yvette Mathurin is out of the island.
3. Minutes of meeting of January 14ᵗʰ
   - To be read by the secretary.
4. Matters Arising
5. Correspondence
   - Secretary to read the letter from the Bishop.
6. Update on donations
   - Treasurer to give an update on the donations received so far for the month.
7. Restoration and Refurbishment
   - Ask what to do about the organ.
   - Frank's Hardware has offered to replace the doors for free.
   - The new pews have been completed. They will be installed on Wednesday January 23ʳᵈ.
   - Need to get an estimate as to how much it will cost to repair the roof.

in full
8. (AOB)
9. Closure

Figure 7.3   A chairman's agenda set on A4 paper.

MINUTES OF THE MEETING

of the St. Francis Parochial Church Council

Held at the Church Rectory on January 21st at 7:00 p.m.

PRESENT

Rev. Claude Williams	(Chairman)
Mrs. Nadia Jules	(Secretary)
Ms. Patricia Baptiste	(Treasurer)
Mr. Martin Isidore	(Church Warden)
Mr. Patrick Edward	(Church Warden)
Mrs. Claudette Wilson	(Council Member)
Mrs. Cheryl Edward	(Council Member)

ABSENT

Mr. Timothy Leon	(Council Member)
Ms Yvette Mathurin	(Council Member)

1. **PRAYERS**

   The meeting was called to order at 7:04pm, by the Chairman, Reverend Griffith. Mrs. Claudette Wilson said the opening prayer.

2. **ABSENSES**

   The Chairman apologised for the absence of Mr. Timothy Leon who was ill and Miss Yvette Mathruin who was out of the island.

3. **MINUTES OF THE PREVIOUS MEETING**
   The minutes of the meeting held on January 14th were read by the Secretary. They were adopted by Mr. Patrick Edward and seconded by Mrs. Claudette Wilson.

4. **CORRESPONDENCE**

   A letter from the Bishop was read by the Secretary which gave permission for additional repairs to be made to the church.

5. **UPDATE ON DONATIONS**

   The Treasurer informed Council that $5,000 in donations was received so far for the month. Of that, $3,000 came from Dr. Gregory Paul. The Chairman expressed the need to write a formal letter of thanks to Dr. Paul.

6. **RESTORATION AND REFURBISHMENT**

   6.1 **Church Organ:** The Chairman expressed concern about the state of the church organ and asked for suggestions as to what should be done about it. Mr. Isidore suggested

Figure 7.4 page 1 of 2   Minutes of a meeting set on A4 paper.

Summary

- The notice of the meeting contains information about where and when the meeting will be held and who is expected to attend.
- The agenda (a list of what is to be covered at the meeting) is circulated before the meeting.
- The chairman has his/her own agenda with additional information to be discussed at the meeting and a space on the right-hand side for notes.
- Minutes usually contain information about where and when the meeting was held, who was present and absent, and what happened during the meeting.

that it should be repaired, but Mr. Edward suggested that a new organ should be purchased, because the organ was very old and repairs might be expensive.

The Chairman suggested that estimates of the cost of a new organ as well as the cost to repair the existing one be obtained so that an informed decision could be made.

6.2 **Doors:** The Chairman stated that the Frank's Hardware had offered to replace the doors for free and that a letter should be sent to them, thanking them for their generosity. He thanked Mr. Patrick Edward for his role in securing the deal.

6.3 **New Pews:** The Chairman informed council that the new pews had been completed and would be installed on Wednesday, January 23rd.

Mrs. Edward expressed surprise at how quickly the pews were completed and wondered about the quality of the work. Mr. Isidore assured her that he had seen the pews and that they were of a very high quality. The Chairman was in agreement.

Roof: The Chairman voiced the need to get an estimate of the cost to repair the roof. He said that although the cost would most likely be high, it was necessary since the roof was in very bad condition. All the members of the Council agreed that something needed to be done soon.

Mr. Edward promised to obtain some estimates before the next meeting.

7. **A.O.B**

7.1 The Secretary informed Council that she had successfully completed a course in EDPM. The Chairman offered his congratulations and urged her to keep up the good work.

7.2 The Secretary said that the course was a good one and suggested that the Church offer the course for free to deserving young people. The Chairman said that this was a good idea but that it needed to be discussed further at the next meeting.

8. **CLOSURE**

The Chairman called the meeting to a close at 7:50 p.m. with a prayer and the singing of the hymn 555 from Hymns Ancient and Modern.

....

Nadia Jules   **Claude Williams**
(Secretary)   (Chairman)

....

Date   **Date**

Figure 7.4 page 2 of 2

Review exercises

Exercise 7A
Type the committee documents shown in this chapter using suitable paper sizes.

Exercise 7B
For a fictional company, create committee documents for a meeting to be held at a time of your choosing.

8 Simple display documents

- programmes
- menus
- invitations
- flyers

Programmes

A programme such as the one in Figure 8.1 provides information about the times of various events. In addition, it usually lists the venue. Programmes are normally done on A4 paper.

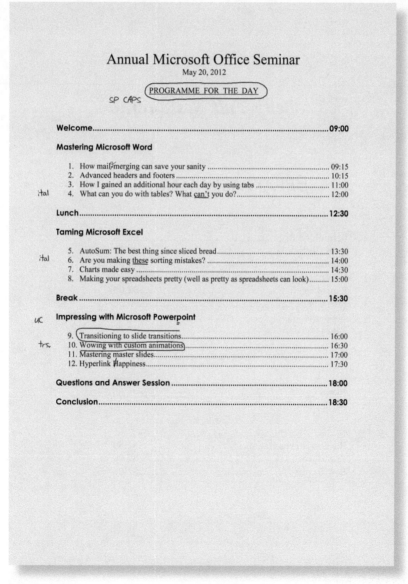

Figure 8.1 A programme set on A4 paper.

As you can see, a programme is essentially a table of contents, but with times instead of page numbers. Therefore, you use similar techniques when preparing one. You add a <u>right tab</u> at the right edge of the page, and add leaders so you can get the dotted lines from the items to the times.

Menus

When you are producing a menu for a restaurant or a special event, the aim is to make it as visually pleasing as possible. Instead of boring Times New Roman, fancy fonts like Monotype Corsiva or other script fonts are used. In addition, colour and images should be <u>effectively</u> utilised to make the menu even more appealing.

'Effectively' is the key word since people tend to go overboard, especially when it comes to colour. No more than three different colours and three different fonts should be used. The sample menu in Figure 8.2, which was done on A5 paper, adheres to these rules.

When you are inserting an image, be sure to change the text wrapping to 'in front of text' or 'behind text', so that you can freely move the image without it pushing the text around.

Usually the menu lists the prices of the different dishes, but in certain cases such as buffet (self-serve all you can eat) menus, no prices are given. In the latter case, the menu is usually centred. The menu also lists the name and location of the restaurant, hotel or event.

Figure 8.2 A menu set on A5 paper.

Invitations

When you are creating an invitation to an event, you need to be sure to include the relevant information such as:

- the type of event
- the time, date and location
- the name of the bride and groom (for a wedding)
- the required dress (formal, semi-formal, elegantly casual, etc.)
- whether or not one needs to RSVP.

The invitation is usually centred on an A5 portrait or A6 landscape piece of card or paper. Sometimes a cursive font is used to give the invitation an elegant look.

Invitations with menus

Depending on the type of event, the invitation may be combined with the menu. In such a case, the invitation would be placed above the menu, on A4 paper as in Figure 8.3.

Figure 8.3 An invitation with a menu set on A4 paper.

Flyers

You no doubt have seen flyers used to promote events such as suppers, cake sales, fetes and parties. Those flyers are done on A4 or larger paper with large fonts so they can be big enough to be seen. In order to make them stand out, they are usually colourful with large images or several small ones.

Like an invitation, a flyer needs to contain certain information. What is being promoted should be displayed (prominently) along with where and when it will be held, the items being sold or the services being provided.

Any text that you need to be able to position precisely you will have to put in a text box. As with a menu, you should pick a few fonts and colours and stick to them.

In Figure 8.4 *WordArt* is used to make the 'Healthy Hearts 2012' stand out from the rest of the text. To insert *WordArt*, click *Insert, Picture, WordArt* in Word 2003 or simply *Insert, WordArt* in Word 2007/2010.

Figure 8.4 A flyer set on A4 paper.

WordArt should be used sparingly since it often clashes with existing text.

Summary
- You use right tabs with leaders when creating programmes.
- Programmes and flyers are normally done on A4 paper. Menus are done on either A4 or A5 paper. Invitations are done on small-sized card or paper (e.g. A6 landscape) unless they are combined with menus.
- Change the text wrapping of images to in front of or behind text if you want to be able to move them without affecting the text in the document.
- Place text in textboxes when you need to be able to position it precisely.

Review exercises

Exercise 8A
Type the programme in Figure 8.1. The font used for the items in bold such as 'Welcome', 'Lunch' etc. is Century Gothic.

Exercise 8B
Create an invitation for a fictional wedding on A6 landscape paper.

Exercise 8C
Reproduce the invitation with a menu in Figure 8.3. Three fonts were used:

- Verdana.
- Script MT Bold.
- Century Gothic.

All the items in CAPS were done in small caps which you can enable via the Font Window. You can access this window by clicking *Format Font* in Word 2003. If you have a later version of Word, switch to the Home tab of the Ribbon and click the *More Options* button of the Font Group.
 All images are clip-art images which are automatically installed with Microsoft Word. If you prefer, you can insert images that you download from the Internet.

Exercise 8D
Create a menu for a fictional restaurant on A5 paper. Be sure to add a suitable page border.

Exercise 8E
Use the information from Figure 8.4 to create another flyer for the Healthy Hearts event. Use no more than one *WordArt* image.

9 Advanced display documents

In this chapter, you will learn about the following advanced displays:

- flowcharts
- organisation charts
- newsletters
- brochures

Flowcharts

A <u>flowchart</u> is a graphical tool used to illustrate a procedure or a process. It consists of a series of shapes that are connected via arrows which indicate the order in which the steps are to be done. Figure 9.1 gives a brief rundown of what the different shapes are used for.

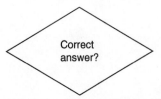

Start

Rounded rectangles or ovals are used to indicate the beginning or the end of the process.

Turn on the computer

Rectangles are used to show the different steps.

Correct answer?

Any time a choice has to be made, you put it in a decision box like the one above.

Figure 9.1 Flowchart shapes and what they mean.

In order to insert these shapes into your document, you either use the *AutoShapes* option in the *Drawing Toolbar* (Word 2003) or click *Insert, Shapes* (Word 2007/2010).

I strongly recommend putting them in a Drawing Canvas. Doing so:

- makes it easy to connect the shapes using the arrows

- allows you to move the flowchart as one object instead of several individual shapes.

In Word 2003, the Drawing Canvas is automatically created when you first insert a shape. In Word 2007/2010 it has to be manually created by clicking *Insert, Shapes, New Drawing Canvas*.

To connect the shapes in the flowchart you should either use regular arrows or elbow arrow connectors (which are handy when doing certain types of decision boxes).

Figure 9.2 shows an example of a flowchart.

Organisation charts

If you read Chapter 10 in the Microsoft Word part of this book, you should already know how to create organisation charts like the one in Figure 9.3. In any case, the process is very similar to that used to create a flowchart.

Newsletters

Creating a newsletter like the one in Figure 9.4 on page 306 requires a variety of techniques.

- The title was done using WordArt.
- An item of clipart was used as the main graphic.
- A header was inserted at the top of the page.
- A page number was inserted at the bottom of the page.
- The M in 'My Fellow Collegians' was done using a drop cap.
- A continuous section break was inserted beneath the image so that...
- The bottom section of the page could be put into two columns without affecting the rest of the document.

Newsletters are usually done on A4 paper with portrait orientation.

Signing up for an Email Address

```
┌──────────────┐
│    Start     │
└──────────────┘
       │
       ▼
┌──────────────────────┐
│ Go to www.hotmail.com│
└──────────────────────┘
       │
       ▼
┌──────────────────────┐
│   Click Sign-Up      │
└──────────────────────┘
       │
       ▼
┌──────────────────────┐
│ Fill in your name and│
│      birth-date      │
└──────────────────────┘
       │
       ▼
┌──────────────────────┐
│ Choose an email address│◄───┐
│    and password      │    │
└──────────────────────┘    │
       │                    │
       ▼                    │ No
    ╱────────╲              │
   ╱ Invalid? ╲─────────────┘
    ╲────────╱
       │ Yes
       ▼
┌──────────────────────┐
│ Choose a secret question│
└──────────────────────┘
       │
       ▼
┌──────────────────────┐
│ Type the answer to that│
│      question        │
└──────────────────────┘
       │
       ▼
┌──────────────────────┐
│ Type the text in the image│◄──┐
└──────────────────────┘    │
       │                    │ No
       ▼                    │
    ╱────────╲              │
   ╱ Correct? ╲─────────────┘
    ╲────────╱
       │ Yes
       ▼
┌──────────────────────┐
│   Accept Agreement   │
└──────────────────────┘
       │
       ▼
┌──────────────┐
│     Done     │
└──────────────┘
```

Figure 9.2 An example of a flowchart.

ST. JOHN'S SECONDARY SCHOOL

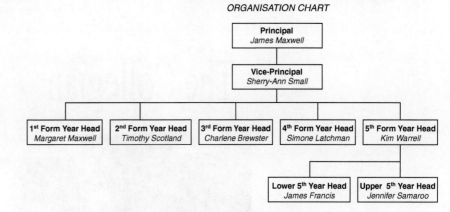

ORGANISATION CHART

Figure 9.3 An example of an organisation chart.

To create a drop cap:

1 Click inside the paragraph.

2 In Word 2003, click *Format, Drop Cap...*
In Word 2007/2010 click *Insert, Drop Cap.*

3 Select the Dropped Option.

Brochures

Creating a brochure uses similar techniques. Legal-sized or A4 paper is normally used in landscape orientation. A brochure uses both sides of a <u>single</u> sheet of paper.

For a four-page brochure, you need to create a two-page document that is divided into two columns (see Figure 9.5 on page 306). Each page of the document corresponds to a side in the brochure, and each column of that page, corresponds to a page in the brochure. The brochure is folded along the dotted line.

Figure 9.6 on page 307 shows how to lay out a six-page brochure, like the one in Figure 9.7 on page 308.

Use left and right margins of 0.5".
You can use a Column Break to force text into another column.

The Collegian, Issue #13. September 2012

The Collegian

Letter from the Editor

My fellow Collegians, another school year is upon us, and I for one am excited.

There are many questions on my mind – good questions mind you. "Will the Lions repeat as Under-20 Football Champions?", "Can our athletes continue to dominate at the Inter-Collegiate Sports?" and "What will the debating team do for an encore?".

run on

NP

I don't know the answers to these questions, but I look forward to finding out/I also want to extend a Collegian welcome to the 200 new students joining us here at Queen's College. You'll soon find out what the other students

(fully justify)

know already, that this is the best school in the island!

↩— The Collegian family is also growing. Joining us are: **Matthew Franklyn** (Graphics Editor), **Janelle Sobers** (Writer) and **Shane Trotman** (Website ⟨Admin⟩). We look forward *in full* to great things from them soon.

Speaking of websites, we'll be officially launching our website later this month. You can see a preview at **www.the-collegian.com**. Feel free to let us know what you think. We'll try our best to incorporate whatever feedback you provide.

That's all for now. Thanks for reading,

Clarke Kent

1

Figure 9.4 An example of a newsletter set on A4 paper.

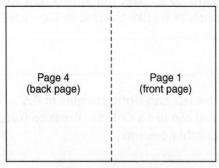

Side 1: Outside of the brochure

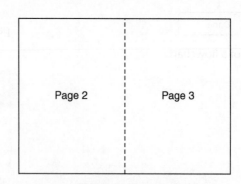

Side 2: Inside of the brochure

Figure 9.5 How to lay out a four-page brochure.

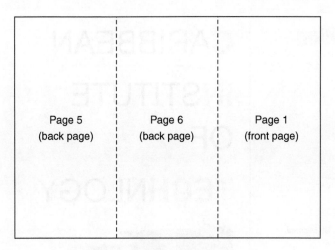

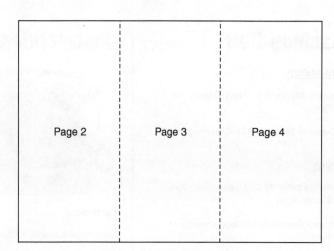

Side 1: Outside of the brochure   **Side 2:** Inside of the brochure

Figure 9.6 How to lay out a six-page brochure.

Printing brochures

To print a brochure:

1 Click inside the first page of the document (the first side of the brochure).

2 Print with the Current Page option selected.

3 Put back in the <u>same</u> sheet of paper, with the <u>printed side face down</u>.

4 Click inside the second page of the document.

5 Print with the Current Page option selected.

Summary

- To create a flowchart or an organisation chart, create a new drawing canvas and draw the various shapes. Connect them using arrows or elbow (arrow) connectors.
- Brochures and newsletters are both printed on A4 paper but brochures are printed in landscape orientation.
- You print both sides of a brochure on the same sheet of paper. Use the Print Current Page option to print one side at a time.

Review exercises

Exercise 9A
Reproduce the flowchart in Figure 9.2 on A4 paper. Use margins of 0.5". In order to centre the flowchart, change the text wrapping of the drawing canvas to square and drag the canvas to the desired location.

Exercise 9B
Type the organisation chart in Figure 9.3 on A4 paper.

Exercise 9C
Reproduce the newsletter in Figure 9.4 on A4 paper.

Exercise 9D
Use the information in Figure 9.7 on page 308 to create a brochure for the Caribbean Institute of Technology. Use A4 paper with left and right margins of 0.5".

Teaching Staff

MATHEMATICS

- **Nicole Alleyne** (B.Sc. Hons. University of Waterloo)

- **Cameron Persaud** (B.Sc. Queen's University)

PHYSICS

- **William Smith** (M.Sc. Massachusetts Institute of Technology)

- **Shawn Graham** (B.Sc. Hons. University of Miami)

- **Daniel Faraday** (B.Sc. Cambridge University)

- **Michael Scofield** (B.Sc. Harvard University)

COMPUTER SCIENCE

- **Kyle Skeete** (B.Sc. Hons. Queen's University)

- **Tim Alleyne** (B.Sc. Carnegie Melon University)

- **William Gates III**

Contact Information

Location:

Our campus is located at Cave Hill, St. Michael.

Telephone Numbers:

- **Main Office:**   555-1111
- **Registration:**   555-2222
- **Library:**   555-3333
- **Gym:**   555-4444
- **Security:**   555-5555
- **Counsellor:**   555-6666

Website & Email

Our main website is www.cintech.com. However, if you'd like to request additional information, send an email to: info@cintech.com.

CARIBBEAN INSTITUTE OF TECHNLOGY

"Always Looking Forward"

The CinTech Advantage

1. Teachers not Professors

At CinTech, the professors pride themselves on being teachers first. They don't lecture you. Instead they make sure each and every student grasps the concepts being taught. Classes are fun, engaging and interactive. Participation from the students is encouraged.

2. Practical Learning

A criticism levelled at most universities is that they are too theoretical and don't prepare you for the world of work. CinTech is not most universities.

From the get-go, theory is supplemented with practical learning. Industry-standard tools are used in the classrooms. Students are assigned project managers and have business meetings. Andl each student gets to intern at a leading company.

3. E-Learning+ ™

Unique to CinTech is what we call E-Learning plus. Most universities use traditional teaching methods. A few offer electronic courses. But only one, uses both.

With E-Learning+ ™, all courses are offered both in the classroom and online. Miss a class? Then view it online. Need help with a problem? Then ask the teacher in person. The choice is yours!

Degrees

Each of our degrees is a 4-year degree with an internship in the final year.

COMPUTING DEGREES

- **Software Engineering**
- **Database Architecture**
- **Network Architecture**
- **Operating System Architecture**
- **Game Creation**

OTHER DEGREES

- **Mathematics**
- **Electrical Engineering**
- **Mechanical Engineering**

Testimonials

"CinTech is a university like none other. The staff, teaching and facilities are all top notch" – James Brown

"I dropped out of my previous university, frustrated and disillusioned. A friend recommended CinTech. I was a bit skeptical at first but decided to give them a try. It was the best decision I ever made. CinTech put the joy back into learning agan" – Victoria Bentham

Figure 9.7   A six-page brochure set on A4 paper.

10 Legal documents

In this chapter, you will learn how to prepare the following legal documents:

- wills
- leases
- conveyance documents
- hire-purchase agreements
- contracts
- endorsements

Preparing legal documents

In document preparation, accuracy is always important, but with legal documents it is absolutely critical. Punctuation is kept to a minimum or avoided altogether since a misplaced comma could alter the meaning of a phrase.

If any errors are spotted after the document has been printed, you should correct them on the computer and reprint the document. If, for whatever reason, the document cannot be reprinted, <u>do not use liquid paper</u>. Instead, cross out the incorrect text and have each change initialled by each person signing the document.

The finished legal document is called the **engrossment**. There may be multiple copies of the document, called **counterparts**. In some cases, each counterpart is signed by a different party.

The examples given here are not actual legal documents. They are for illustration purposes only and so may have been significantly abbreviated or pieced together by the author.

Page setup

Type legal documents on legal size or A4 paper with the following margins:

- Top: 1.5" (or 2")
- Bottom: 1"
- Left: 1.5"
- Right: 0.5"

Body of the document

1 Use double-line spacing (unless instructed otherwise) and fully justify the text in the body of the document. (The examples in this chapter will use a line spacing of 1.5 to save space)
2 Start each new sentence on a new line. The first few words of the sentence are capitalised and may also be made bold or underlined.
3 Also capitalise the following:
   - Names of people whenever they are mentioned.
   - Connecting words like BETWEEN, HEREBY and WHEREAS.
4 Fill the space to the right of lines of text using dashes or lines (see Figure 10.1). To do so, drag a right tab to the right of the document and in the Tab Options window, change the leader to one with dashes. This is to prevent people from adding

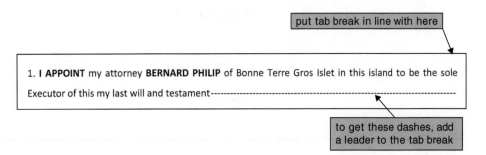

Figure 10.1 Lines of text using dashes.

information to the document after it has been signed.

Additional guidelines

Below are some additional rules you should follow when preparing legal documents:

1 Type out dates in full.
2 Type out numbers in full unless they are part of addresses.
3 Avoid using abbreviations.
4 Print on both the front and back of the paper unless instructed otherwise.

Attestation clause

According to Merriam-Webster's Dictionary of Law, an attestation clause is the clause at the end of a legal document (e.g. a Will), in which the witnesses state that 'the (document) was signed and witnessed with all the formalities required by law and which often sets forth those requirements'.

The attestation clause is the part at the bottom of the Will in Figure 10.3 that states 'SIGNED by the above ... subscribed our names as witnesses'.

Backing sheet

In addition to the legal document itself, a cover page called a **backing sheet** may be printed. This cover page allows one to ascertain the nature of the legal document, even when it is folded. Figure 10.2 shows a possible backing sheet for the Will in Figure 10.3 (the dotted lines indicate where it is to be folded).

Notice that:

• A backing sheet states the date, the nature of the document, the parties involved and (optionally) the name and address of the solicitors.
• The sheet is designed to be folded into thirds.
• The information on the backing sheet is positioned in the middle panel so that it is visible when the document is folded.

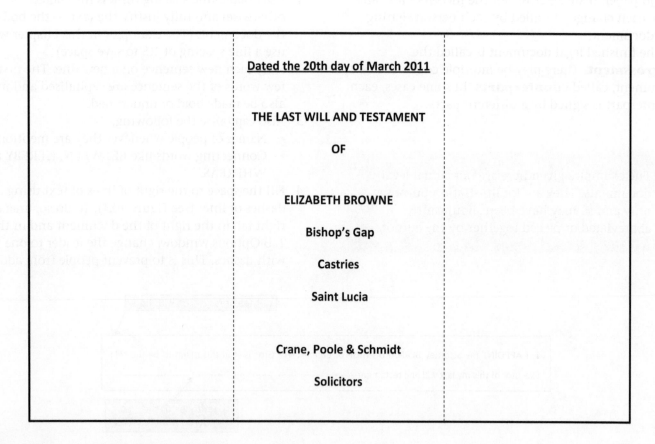

Dated the 20th day of March 2011

THE LAST WILL AND TESTAMENT

OF

ELIZABETH BROWNE

Bishop's Gap

Castries

Saint Lucia

Crane, Poole & Schmidt

Solicitors

Figure 10.2 An example of a backing sheet.

THIS IS THE LAST WILL AND TESTAMENT of me **ELIZABETH BROWNE** of Bishop's Gap in the city of Castries in this island hereby revoking all former wills and testamentary dispositions at any time heretofore made by me--

1. **I APPOINT** my attorney **BERNARD PHILIP** of Bonne Terre Gros Islet in this island to be the sole Executor of this my last will and testament--

2. **I DIRECT** that all my just debts funeral and testamentary expenses be paid as soon as conveniently possible after my death ---

3. **I GIVE AND BEQUEATH** all monies standing in my credit at my death in my bank account or other accounts with financial institutions to my two children **JEREMY BROWNE** and **TERRICIA BROWNE** to be divided equally between them--

4. **I GIVE DEVISE AND BEQUEATH** the rest of my possessions both movable and immovable wheresoever situated to my husband **RUDOLPH BROWNE** ---

IN TESTIMONY WHEREOF I the said **ELIZABETH BROWNE** have to this my Last Will and Testament set my hand this   day of   Two Thousand and Eleven-------------

SIGNED by the above named Testator the said   )
ELIZABETH BROWNE in the presence of us both)
present at the same time who at her request in   ) ....
in her presence and in the presence of each   )
other have hereunto subscribed our names as   )
witnesses   )

....
Name: Name:
Address: Address:

Calling/Description: Calling/Description:

Figure 10.3   An example of a Will.

In order to prepare a backing sheet:

- Create a new document/section in landscape orientation.
- Use Word's *Columns* function to divide it into three columns.
- Insert a column break in the first column, so that the cursor gets positioned at the top of the second column.
- In the *Layout Tab* of the *Page Setup* window, change the vertical alignment to centre if you so desire.
- Then type the required information.

In <u>this</u> case, the date is <u>not</u> typed out in words.

Wills

Figure 10.3 (page 311) shows a very basic example of a Will. Notice the following:

- Any previous Wills are revoked (making them invalid).
- The <u>testator</u> is the person whose Will it is.
- The <u>executor</u> (female executrix) is the person appointed to carry out the terms of the Will and pay the funeral expenses.
- Space has been left for the day of the month to be written when the will is being signed.
- Space has also been left for information about the witnesses to be inserted such as their names and addresses.

The parties involved endorse the contents of the attestation clause by signing it.

Don't use Word's *Bullets* and *Numbering* Feature. In order to position the brackets ')' at the end of the document, you should set a *tab break*.

Leases

Figure 10.4 shows what a lease for a house might look like. In this case the words that have been capitalised have also been underlined. But they could just as easily have been put in bold.

Conveyance documents

A <u>conveyance</u> is a legal document that authorises the transfer of property from one person/party (the vendor) to another (the purchaser). Figure 10.5 on page 314 shows an example of what one might look like. Notice that the location of the piece of land (in this case) is precisely specified.

The giant bracket at the end of the document is an *AutoShape*.

Hire-purchase agreements

For a hire-purchase agreement like the one in Figure 10.6 on page 315, a schedule provides details about the goods in question, such as the cash price, hire purchase price and how the balance is to be paid. In this case a table has been used to store some of the information.

Use the *Border* and *Shading* window to remove the borders from the bottom-left part of the table. *Merge* the cells in the top row.

SAINT GEORGE'S, GRENADA

THIS LEASE is made and entered into this TWENTY SECOND day of JANUARY Two thousand and eleven BETWEEN NORMA SMITH of Upper Woburn (hereinafter called 'the Landlord') and ALWYN JONES (hereinafter called 'The Tenant') where the Landlord is the fee owner of certain real property having a street address of 123 2nd Avenue Morne Jaloux in the parish of Saint Georges (hereinafter called 'the Premises')---

NOW THIS LEASE WITNESSETH as follows --
1. IN CONSIDERATION of deposit of Four thousand dollars, the receipt and sufficiency of which is hereby acknowledged, and the covenants and obligations herein contained, the Landlord agrees to lease the Premises to the Tenant for the term of ONE YEAR from the FIRST day of FEBRUARY Two thousand and eleven to the TWENTY EIGHTH day of FEBRUARY Two thousand and twelve during which monthly payments of Two thousand dollars will paid by the Tenant to the Landlord before the TWENTY EIGHTH day of EACH MONTH---

2. IF AND WHENEVER the monthly rent hereinbefore reserved or any part thereof shall be in arrears or unpaid for the space of Fourteen days next after the day of the month hereinbefore appointed for the payment thereof the said term of One year will immediately cease and the deposit shall not be returned and the Landlord shall thereafter hold and enjoy the same rights held before the commencement of the lease without prejudice to any right of action of the Tenant in respect of any antecedent breach hereinbefore contained ---

3. IT IS HEREBY CERTIFIED that the transaction hereby effected does not form part of a larger transaction or a series of transactions between the Landlord and the Tenant --

IN WITNESS whereof the parties hereto have hereunto set their hands and seals the day and year first hereinbefore written --

SIGNED SEALED AND DELIVERED)	
by the said NORMA SMITH)	
in the presence of)	
)	
)	
....)	....
WITNESS)	NORMA SMITH
)	
SIGNED SEALED AND DELIVERED)	
by the said ALWYN JONES)	
in the presence of)	
)	
)	
....)	....
WITNESS)	ALWYN JONES

Figure 10.4 An example of a lease (top and bottom have been cropped).

BARBADOS

THIS CONVEYANCE is made the NINETEENTH day of SEPTEMBER Two thousand and twelve **BETWEEN** **DAVID WILLIAMS** of Worthing Main Road in the parish of Christ Church (hereinafter called 'the Vendor') of the one part and **KEISHA SMALL** of Rockfield in the parish of Saint Lucy (hereinafter called 'The Purchaser') of the other part ---

NOW this conveyance witnesses as follows --
IN PURSUANCE of the said Agreement and in consideration of the sum of Five Hundred and Seventy five Thousand Dollars paid by the Purchaser (the receipt of which sum the Vendor hereby acknowledges), the Vendor as Beneficial Owner **HEREBY** conveys to the Purchaser **ALL THAT** parcel of land of three acres having a frontage to Millionaire Road on the West and Boardwalk Boulevard on the North and more specifically shown and described on Plan No LOL of the layout of plots located in the City of Bridgetown for the purpose of identification only --

TO HOLD the said property unto and to the use of the Purchaser in fee simple in possession free from all encumbrances---

IN WITNESS whereof the Vendor and Purchaser have hereunto set their hands and seals the day and year first hereinabove written---

SIGNED SEALED AND DELIVERED
by the said **DAVID WILLIAMS** as and for
his act and deed in the presence of

....

Name: DAVID WILLIAMS
Address:

SIGNED SEALED AND DELIVERED
by the said **KEISHA SMALL** as and for
her act and deed in the presence of

....

Name: KEISHA SMALL
Address:

Figure 10.5   An example of a conveyance document (top and bottom edges have been cropped).

BARBADOS

THIS HIRE PURCHASE AGREEMENT made on this fourteenth day of June Two Thousand and Eleven between KITCHEN WORLD LIMITED a company incorporated and registered under the Companies Act on this island and having its registered office in the City of Bridgetown in this island (hereinafter called 'The Owner') on the one part and HENDERSON ROLLOCK of Rose Hill in the parish of Saint Peter (hereinafter referred to as 'The Hirer') on the other part---

WHEREBY the Owner in consideration of the payments made by the Hirer under this agreement agrees to let and the Hirer agrees to hire the goods described in the schedule hereto with the option of purchasing the same upon the terms and conditions hereinafter mentioned which form part of this Agreement ---

SCHEDULE TO THE FOREGOING AGREEMENT				
Item Number	Description	Qty	Serial No.	Price
513212000	Frigidaire Gas Oven FGB24T3EC RANGE	1		2346.96
			VAT	**341.48**
			Cash Price	**2618.03**
			Add H.P Charges	**1241.52**
			Total H.P. Price	**3859.55**
			Less Deposit	**(135.00)**
			Balance Payable	**3724.55**

The Balance shown is payable in thirty Monthly instalments consisting of twenty nine instalments of 125.00 and one instalment of 99.55 to be paid on the twenty eighth day of each month commencing the twenty eighth day of June Two Thousand and Eleven ---

1 THE HIRER shall pay interest at the rate of eight percent per month on all overdue instalments -----------

2 DURING the currency of this agreement the Hirer shall ensure that the Goods are kept in his possession and shall not remove them nor permit their removal without the consent in writing of the Owner from the premises specified hereinabove as the place where it is contemplated that the goods will normally be stored ---

3 THE HIRER may pay off this agreement in a shorter period and by higher monthly rentals than shown hereinbefore in which event a rebate if applicable will be granted--

4 THE HIRER certifies before signing this agreement that the goods described in the schedule are in good condition and to his satisfaction --

5 THE HIRER may put an end of this agreement by giving notice of termination in writing to any person who is entitled to collect or receive the hire rent and at the same time or prior thereto by delivering the Goods to the Owner --

6 THE HIRER must then pay any instalments which are in arrears at the time he has given notice -----------

Figure 10.6   An example of a hire-purchase agreement (top and bottom edges have been cropped).

7 IF the Hirer does not deliver the goods to the Owner at the time mentioned in paragraph five above the notice of termination will be ineffective and the agreement will remain in force ----------------------------

8 IF after Sixty Six and Two Thirds per Centum of the Hire Purchase Price has been paid for the Goods the Owner cannot recover them without the Hirer's consent unless the Owner obtains an order from the Court ---

9 WHERE LESS than Sixty Six and Two Thirds per Centum of the Hire Purchase Price has been paid for the Goods the Owner cannot recover them without the Hirer's consent unless the Owner has given the Hirer twenty one clear days written notice of its intention to do so ---

10 IF WITHIN the said period of twenty one clear days the Hirer pays to the Owner all instalments of the hire purchase price due at the date of the issue of such notice the agreement will continue in force -------

IN WITNESS THEREOF the said parties hereto have set their hands the day and year first hereinabove written---

Witness to Signature of Hirer | Signature of Hirer

....

Address:

Witness to Owner's Signature | Signature for and on behalf of KITCHEN WORLD LIMITED

....

Address:

Figure 10.6   *(continued)*

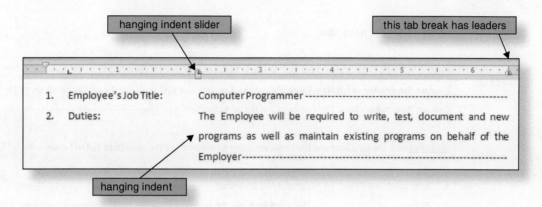

Figure 10.7 How to lay out the contract.

Employment contracts

There are several ways you can construct an employee contract – Figure 10.8 on page 318 shows just one of them. Here are some suggestions for how to lay out the document:

1 If you are using Word 2007/2010, choose the *No Spacing* style from the *Home* tab of the Ribbon. Doing so will save you a lot of stress later on.
2 Do not use Word's *Bullets* and *Numbering* feature.
3 When you are typing the terms of the agreement, set three tab breaks in the positions shown in Figure 10.7, with the one by the right margin set to show leaders.
4 If the sentence is too long to fit on one line, after you type it, drag the hanging indent slider from the left margin in line with the second tab stop.

Summary

- Type legal documents using double spacing on Legal/A4 paper with margins of top, bottom, left and right margins of 1.5", 1", 1.5" and 0.5" respectively.
- Start each new sentence on a new line with the first few words capitalised and optionally made bold or underlined.
- Do not use liquid paper on legal documents. If mistakes are spotted, reprint the documents.
- Fully justify the body of the document and fill any space to the right of sentences of text using dashes or lines.

Review exercise

Exercise 10
Prepare the legal documents shown in this chapter using appropriately-sized paper. Feel free to substitute names and addresses for the parties involved.

SAINT GEORGES, GRENADA

THIS CONTRACT OF EMPLOYMENT is made between ACMESOFT CORPORATION of Grenville St Georges (hereinafter called 'The Employer') of the one part and NATASHA SMITH of Morne Jaloux St Georges (hereinafter called 'The Employee') of the other part --

WHEREBY both the Employer and the Employee agree to the terms of the conditions stated herein -------

1.	Employee's Job Title:	Computer Programmer ---
2.	Duties:	The Employee will be required to write, test, document and new programs as well as maintain existing programs on behalf of the Employer --
3.	Hours and Days of Work:	Mondays to Fridays from 8:30 am to 5:00 pm----------------------------------
4.	Lunch:	A half hour lunch may be taken between 12:00 pm and 12:30 pm or 1:00 pm and 1:30 pm ---
5.	Duration of Contract:	From the first day of March Two Thousand and Eleven until the contract has been terminated by either the Employer or the Employee
6.	Salary:	The Employer shall pay the Employee a basic salary of Four thousand five hundred dollars per month until a three month probation period has been completed after which the basic salary shall be increased to Five thousand dollars per month--
		The Employer shall pay the Employee the salary hereinbefore mentioned by the twenty fifth day of each month ---------------------------
		IF the Employee is required to work overtime the Employee shall pay her at a rate of fifty dollars per hour or part thereof ------------------------
7.	Deductions:	The Employer shall register the Employee with the National Insurance Scheme ---
		The Employer shall deduct from the Employee's salary contributions for the National Insurance Scheme and the Inland Revenue Division according to the rates decreed by the laws of Grenada---------------------
8.	Attendance:	The Employee is expected to report for work on time and notify the Employer in advance anytime she is unable to do so -------------------------
		SHOULD the Employee be absent for more than two consecutive days she shall supply a medical certificate --------------------------------------
		IF the Employee is absent for more than two consecutive days and fails to submit a medical certificate or is late more than three times in a month she may receive a written warning -----------------------------------
9.	Termination of contract:	IF the Employee is repeatedly late or absent or continuously displays poor performance the Employer reserves the right to terminate the contract--

Figure 10.8 An example of an employment contract (top and bottom edges have been cropped).

11 Literary documents

In this chapter, you will learn how to type poems and plays

Poems

When you are typing poems, you should follow these conventions.

- Type short poems on A5 paper (and long ones on A4).

- Centre the title, put it in ALL CAPS and leave two clear line spaces before you type the poem itself.
- If it is the only item on the page, you should also centre it vertically (via the layout tab of the Page Setup window).

THE RUINED CHAPEL

By the shore, a plot of ground
Clips a ruin'd chapel round,
Buttress'd with a grassy mound;
Where Day and Night and Day go by,
And bring no touch of human sound.

Washing of the lonely seas,
Shaking of the guardian trees,
Piping of the salted breeze;
Day and Night and Day go by
To the endless tune of these.

Or when, as winds and waters keep
A hush more dead than any sleep,
Still morns to stiller evenings creep,
And Day and Night and Day go by;
Here the silence is most deep.

The empty ruins, lapsed again
Into Nature's wide domain,
Sow themselves with seed and grain
As Day and Night and Day go by;
And hoard June's sun and April's rain.

Here fresh funeral tears were shed;
Now the graves are also dead;
And suckers from the ash-tree spread,
While Day and Night and Day go by;
And stars move calmly overhead.

WILLIAM ALLINGHAM

Figure 11.1   A poem typed on A4 paper.

- Indent alternating lines that rhyme with two or three spaces (see Figure 11.2).
- Start each line with a capital letter.
- Consistently leave one or two clear line spaces between verses.
- Leave two clear line spaces before typing the poet's name (in ALL CAPS). Use a right tab to line up the rightmost part of the poet's name with the end of the longest line of the poem.

- The title is centred and placed in uppercase.
- Acts of the play are put in uppercase and numbered using uppercase roman numerals.
- Scenes are numbered with lowercase roman numerals or using normal numbers e.g. 1, 2, 3.
- Unspoken directions are put in parentheses and written in bold.
- Hanging indentation is used to type what a particular character says, as well as the unspoken directions.

Individual actor scripts

Suppose you want to type the script for an individual actor. You cannot just type that actor's lines by themselves because the actor needs to know what the other characters are saying so he will know when to speak.

Instead you type the play as before, but highlight the particular actor's lines and any cues or instructions that pertain to him. For instance, you may type them in another colour. In addition, you format that character's dialog in double-line spacing.

THE SOUL'S STORM

It struck me every day
  The lightning was as new
As if the cloud that instant slit
  And let the fire through.

It burned me in the night,
  It blistered in my dream;
It sickened fresh upon my sight
  With every morning's beam.

I thought that storm was brief, —
  The maddest, quickest by;
But Nature lost the date of this,
  And left it in the sky.

EMILY DICKINSON

Figure 11.2 A poem typed on A5 paper.

Review exercises

Exercise 11A
Type the poem in Figure 11.2 on A5 paper.

Exercise 11B
Type the play in Figure 11.3 on A4 paper.

Exercise 11C
Type a poem and extract of a play that you found on the Internet. Or, if you are feeling creative, write your own.

Plays

Figure 11.3 shows a play. Notice the following.

- Plays are typed on A4-sized paper, usually with top, left and right margins of 1", 1.5" and 0.5" respectively.

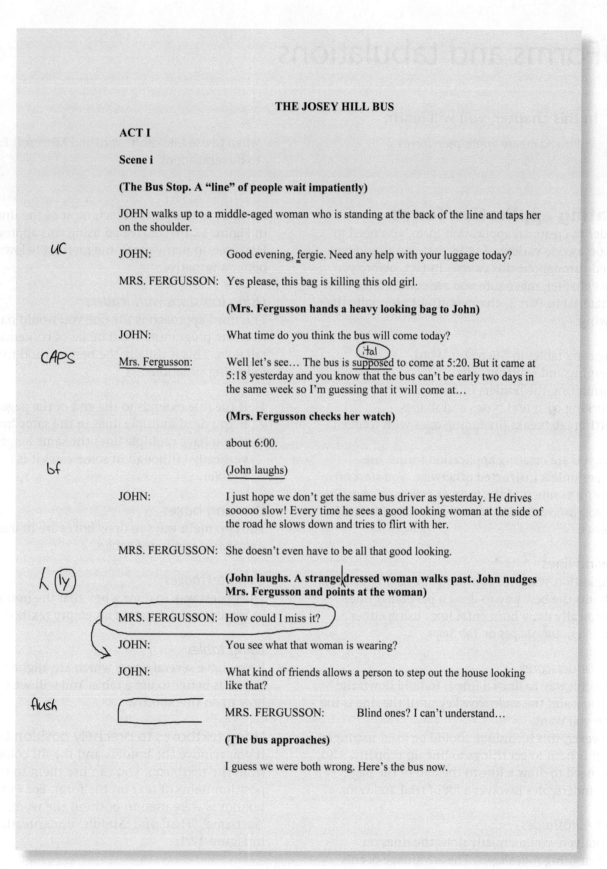

THE JOSEY HILL BUS

ACT I

Scene i

(The Bus Stop. A "line" of people wait impatiently)

JOHN walks up to a middle-aged woman who is standing at the back of the line and taps her on the shoulder.

uc

JOHN: Good evening, fergie. Need any help with your luggage today?

MRS. FERGUSSON: Yes please, this bag is killing this old girl.

(Mrs. Fergusson hands a heavy looking bag to John)

JOHN: What time do you think the bus will come today?

CAPS

ital

Mrs. Fergusson: Well let's see… The bus is supposed to come at 5:20. But it came at 5:18 yesterday and you know that the bus can't be early two days in the same week so I'm guessing that it will come at…

(Mrs. Fergusson checks her watch)

about 6:00.

bf

(John laughs)

JOHN: I just hope we don't get the same bus driver as yesterday. He drives sooooo slow! Every time he sees a good looking woman at the side of the road he slows down and tries to flirt with her.

MRS. FERGUSSON: She doesn't even have to be all that good looking.

^ (ly)

(John laughs. A strange|dressed woman walks past. John nudges Mrs. Fergusson and points at the woman)

MRS. FERGUSSON: How could I miss it?

JOHN: You see what that woman is wearing?

JOHN: What kind of friends allows a person to step out the house looking like that?

flush

MRS. FERGUSSON: Blind ones? I can't understand…

(The bus approaches)

I guess we were both wrong. Here's the bus now.

Figure 11.3 A play typed on A4 paper.

12 Forms and tabulations

Creating application forms

In order to create an application form, you need to draw on a wide variety of skills that you would have learned throughout this course. In fact, before you do this chapter, make sure you are comfortable with the material in Part 3, chapters 10–12 especially the following:

- Creating tables in Microsoft Word.
- Merging and splitting cells.
- Formatting the borders in a table.
- Working with text boxes and shapes.
- Setting tab breaks (including ones with leaders).

When you are creating application forms, use A4 paper unless instructed otherwise. You start off by typing as much of the form as you can normally, then you use various techniques to add additional elements.

Drawing lines

One question you willl constantly be asking yourself is 'what is the best way to draw a particular line?'. You typically draw horizontal lines using either *underscores*, *AutoShapes* or *Tab Stops*.

Using underscores

The easiest way to draw a line is to hold down the *SHIFT* key and the *underscore* key until the line is the length you want.

However, this technique should be used sparingly since it is hard to get things to line up properly. Also, if you need to draw a line to the end of the page, using underscores involves a lot of trial and error.

Using Autoshapes

Alternatively you manually draw the lines on the form using *AutoShapes*. The advantage of this approach is that you can use it to draw lines on any part of the page. In fact, most of the lines in Figure 12.1 were created using this approach. However, in many cases, the method below is a much better alternative.

Using tab stops with leaders

The third approach is the one you would have used to create programmes and tables of contents – using *tab stops*. This is usually the best method to use in the following situations:

1 If the line extends to the end of the page.
2 If you need multiple lines in the same 'row'.
3 If you have multiple lines the same length, aligned vertically (although in some cases it is better to use a table).

Drawing boxes

The two main ways to draw boxes are to use *AutoShapes* and to use tables.

Using textboxes

The easiest way to draw a box that the user is supposed to tick is to use an empty textbox.

Using tables

If you have several boxes which are aligned side by side, it is better to use a table. You will see exactly how to do this shortly.

Using textboxes to precisely position text

If you remove the borders and the fill colour from the textboxes, you can use them to precisely position items of text on the form. For example, textboxes were used to position the words 'Surname', 'First' and 'Middle' underneath the lines in Figure 12.1.

SECOND CARIBBEAN INTERNATIONAL BANK

APPLICATION FOR POSITION OF _____

Personal Information

Name: _____
               Surname   First   Middle

Address: _____

_____

Date of Birth: ___ / ___ / ___   Male ☐
        yyyy mm dd   Female ☐

Contact Info: _____ _____ _____
         Home Tel   Cell   Email

Marital Status: Married ☐   Divorced ☐   Single ☐

Education & Employment History

What	Where	When
Secondary		
Undergraduate		
Postgraduate		
Second Last Job		
Previous Job		

List any relevant academic qualifications:

_____

_____

_____

Figure 12.1 A job application form.

Caribbean Institute of Technology

Student Application Form

Full Name: _____
               (First Name)   (Middle Name)   (Surname)

Address: _____

_____

Birthdate: _____ / _____ / _____   **Marital Status:** Single ☐   Married ☐

Home Tel: ☐☐☐ - ☐☐☐☐   **Work Tel:** ☐☐☐ - ☐☐☐☐   **Mobile Tel:** ☐☐☐ - ☐☐☐☐

PREVIOUS SUBJECTS

Level (CSEC, CAPE, O'Level, A'Level)	Subject	Grade

COURSE INFORMATION

Name: _____

Start Date: _____ / _____ / _____   **Cost:** _____

Days: Mon & Wed ☐   Tue & Thu ☐

Time: 9:00 – 12:00 a.m. ☐   5:00 – 7:00 p.m. ☐

Signature: _____   **Date:** _____

Figure 12.2 A student application form.

Creating an application form step by step

In this section you will learn how to create the application form in Figure 12.2 on page 324 step by step.

Before we start

If you are using Office 2007/2010, select the *No Spacing Style* before you start constructing the form.

Full name

Since the line for the full name extends to the end of the page, you should create it using tabs.

1 A little to the right of the words 'First Name', set a normal *tab break* where you want the line to begin.
2 Set another *tab break* on the far right of the page by the *Right Indent* (you may need to click to the left of the right indent, then drag the tab stop across).
3 Double-click on it to open the *Tabs* window.
4 Select the second tab in the list. (Whenever you want to change the leader for a tab stop you should first make sure you have the right one selected).
5 Select Leader type number 4.
6 Click *OK* to close the window.
7 Now press the *tab* key twice (once to get to the first tab break you set, then the second time to go to the end of the page).

But so far we have just done the line. We need to put the labels under the line to tell the user what part of the name to put where:

1 Press the *Enter* key to go to the next line.
2 Change the *font* size to a small size (e.g. 8pt).
3 Use three additional *tab* stops to position the labels.

Address

Having done the line for the Full Name you should be able to do the lines for the address on your own.

Birthdate

The line for the birthdate is a one off sort of thing, so you can use underscores for this one.

Marital status

First type the text that is related to the marital status:

1 Press *tab* until you are in line with the *tab* stop you set for the Middle Name.

2 Type 'Marital Status: Single' (formatted appropriately).
3 Use another *tab* stop to position the word 'Married'.

The next question is how to do the boxes. Since they are separate boxes you can use *textboxes*:

1 Draw a textbox to the right of the word 'Single'.
2 Right-click on the border of the textbox. If you have done this correctly it should be selected but no cursor should be flashing inside.
3 Click *Copy*.
4 Right-click on a blank area of the page then click *Paste*.
5 Move the new textbox to the right of 'Married'. (Make sure they line up).

> **tip**
>
> If you select an *AutoShape* by clicking on its border, you can nudge vertically or horizontally using the *arrow* keys.

Telephone numbers

The trickiest part of this whole exercise is to do the telephone numbers. Although it may be hard to tell, this is actually a one-row table with several columns. Instead of trying to guess beforehand how many columns we need, we will take a top down approach.

First we create a table with 1 row and 3 columns (one for each type of number), like in Figure 12.3a:

Home Tel:	Work Tel:	Mobile Tel:

Figure 12.3a Starting with 3 columns.

Then we split the Home Tel cell into two parts (see Figure 12.3b on page 326):

1 Right-click inside the Home Tel cell.
2 Click *Split Cells...* .
3 Make sure that it is set to 1 row and 2 columns then click *OK*.

4 Drag the column line which is to the right of Home Tel, towards the left until it is next to Home Tel.

Home Tel:	Work Tel:	Mobile Tel:

Figure 12.3b Splitting the first column into 2.

Now we split the right half of the Home Tel section into 8 columns (7 for the digits in the telephone number and 1 for the dash).

Home Tel:				-					Work Tel:	Mobile Tel:

Figure 12.3c Home telephone number section complete.

Now repeat the above steps for the Work and Mobile Telephone numbers. When you are finished, you should have something looking like Figure 12.3d.

Home Tel:				-					Work Tel:				-					Mobile Tel:				-				

Figure 12.3d Almost done.

We *could* leave it like this, but it would definitely look better if we remove the borders from around the labels, so that it no longer looks like a single table.

Let us start by removing the borders around 'Home Tel' so we will end up with something similar to Figure 12.3e:

1 Right-click inside the cell that contains 'Home Tel'.
2 Click *Borders and Shading...* to open the *Borders and Shading* Window.
3 Switch to the *Borders* tab.
4 Change the option in the *Apply To* combo box to Cell so that any changes we make affect the current cell only.
5 Make sure the left, top and bottom borders are off in the *Preview.*
6 Then click *OK.*

Figure 12.3e Borders removed from home tel cell.

Now you have the hang of it, remove the appropriate borders for the Work Tel and Mobile Tel cells. These are slightly trickier, but when you are finished, it should look like this:

Home Tel:				-					Work Tel:				-					Mobile Tel:				-				

Figure 12.3f Final telephone number section.

Previous subjects
This is a pretty straightforward table with the left and right borders removed. You should not have too much trouble with this one.

Rest of the form
At this point you know all the techniques required to complete the rest of the form.

Tabulations
You have learned how to do tabular work such as invoices in two programs: Microsoft Word and Excel. How do you know which one to use? Here are a few rules of thumb:

- If you have to do calculations on the table, use Excel.
- If you want oblique headings, use Excel.
- Otherwise, the choice is up to you. However, if you want to create a ruled table in Excel you have to manually insert the borders; in Word, tables have borders by default.

Figure 12.4 shows an example of a table you might want to do in Microsoft Word.

Examples of tables that should be done in Microsoft Excel are financial statements like trial balances, balance sheets and profit and loss statements.

Tabulations are normally done on A4 paper. If they are very wide, the orientation should be set to landscape.

CARIBBEAN GEOGRAPHIC

New Subscribers in March, 2011

SUBSCRIPTION	NAME	ADDRESS	TELEPHONE		
			HOME	WORK	MOBILE
Monthly	Kimberley Hanely	Annette Crescent, Kingston 10,	555-1903	426-1981	655-1903
	Natasha Beard	Mapleleaf Avenue, Kingston 10	555-0981	812-1903	655-0981
	Danielle Hutchinson	Corona Crescent, Kingston 20	555-2348	892-0981	655-2348
	Daniel Franklyn	Rockland Heights, Ocho Rios	555-1890	988-0801	655-1890
	Jessica Cupid	Brooke Avenue, Kingston 20	555-8903	637-1098	655-8903
	Marguerite Clarke	Mahoe Avenue, Nightingale GroveBushy Park	555-8907	678-0981	655-8907
	James Moore	Candlelight Crescent, QueensBorough	555-1341	671-7356	655-1341
	Miglisa Humphrey	Ruthven Road, Kingston 10	555-0189	748-1951	655-0189
	Trudy Rogers	Catherine Hall, Montego Bay	555-8976	846-1010	655-8976
	Sabrina Robinson	Guava Walk, Montego Bay	555-5782	981-1091	655-5782
	Tracy Burgess	Tennyson Crescent, Kingston 20	555-8017	989-5555	655-8017
	Chris Corbin	Tucker Main Road, Campbell Hill	555-1871	771-7890	655-1871
Yearly	Britney Joseph	Felicity Crescent, Montego Bay	555-1349	987-6666	655-1349
	Cherise King	Andreas Avenue, Old Harbour	555-1341	856-7546	655-1341
	Rodney White	Hampton, Runaway Bay	555-1675	968-2010	655-1675
	Ricardo Skeete	Walkway 26 Braeton	555-6757	391-6789	655-6757
	Ryan Boyce	Norwood Gardens, Montego Bay	555-5478	456-9189	655-5478
	Dionne Marshall	Oak Road Pines of Karachi, Kingston 6	555-4892	467-8333	655-4892
	Patricia Lavine	Monticello Crescent, Spanish Town	555-8919	598-2509	655-8919
	Tamesha Phillips	Cornwall Courts, Montego Bay	555-7891	673-1001	655-7891

Figure 12.4 A table that can be done in Microsoft Word.

Invoices

Figure 12.5 shows an example of an invoice with oblique column headings. In order to fill in the Cost column, you can calculate the Cost for the first cell = Unit Price* Qty (obviously you would type the cell addresses instead of the words themselves), and then use the *AutoFill* feature to fill in the remainder of the column.

To calculate the Subtotal you add up all the costs using the *AutoSum* feature. In this example VAT is 15% so we calculate it using the formula = Subtotal * 0.15. This is then added to the Subtotal using the formula =Subtotal + VAT to give the overall total.

Bajan Garments

Building 11, Harbour Road, St. Michael
Tel: 555-9876 **Fax:** 555-7890 **Email:** sales@bajangarments.bb

Invoice Number: BG0001

Date:	September 12th, 2011
Company:	Combined Security Corporation
Address:	Suite 124,
	Warren's Business Centre,
	Warrens

Order No.	Item No	Item	Unit Price	Qty	Cost
0001	SS001	White S/S Men's Shirt	$ 36.00	20	$ 720.00
	SS002	Blue S/S Men's Shirt	$ 36.00	30	$ 1,080.00
	DD002	Navy Blue Drill Long Pants	$ 75.00	10	$ 750.00
	DD001	Black Drill Long Pants	$ 75.00	40	$ 3,000.00
	T0001	Black T-Shirt	$ 20.00	100	$ 2,000.00
	P0001	Blue Polo Shirt	$ 40.00	30	$ 1,200.00
0002	SS003	White S/S Blouse	$ 36.00	10	$ 360.00
	SS004	Blue S/S Blouse	$ 36.00	14	$ 504.00
	G0001	Black Garberdene Skirt	$ 67.00	24	$ 1,608.00
				Sub Total	$ 11,222.00
				VAT	$ 1,683.30
				Total	$ 12,905.30

Figure 12.5   An example of an invoice.

Sales receipts

As you can see from Figure 12.6, a sales receipt is very similar to an invoice. The main difference is that there is a section stating the method used to pay for the items.

Sales Receipt

BOB'S BOOKSTORE

Great Books at Better Prices

Receipt No:	20100
Date:	09/09/2011

Sold To: Ellerslie Secondary School
Black Rock
St. Michael

Payment Method:	Cash	**Cheque No:**	N/A

Qty	ISBN	Description	Unit Price	Line Total
30	0521153271	Information Technology for CSEC	$ 60.00	$ 1,800.00
10	1593345763	Viva! Primer Curso de Lengua Espanola	$ 55.00	$ 550.00
15	0521189578	Principles of Business for CSEC	$ 55.00	$ 825.00
23	0521701147	Biology for CSEC	$ 60.00	$ 1,380.00
28	0521168821	CSEC Integrated Science	$ 60.00	$ 1,680.00

Subtotal	$	6,235.00
VAT (17.5%)	$	1,091.13
Total	$	7,326.13

Figure 12.6 An example of a sales receipt.

Trial balances

A trial balance like the one in Figure 12.7, contains at least three columns:

- The name of the particular account.
- The Debits column.
- The Credits column.

An account can have a figure in the Debits column or the Credits column. The total debits and the total credits are added up and the two columns are added up and placed at the bottom of their respective columns. This can easily be done using the *AutoSum* function.

The difference between the two columns may be calculated using the formula = Debits Total − Credits Total.

Computer Training Centre
Trial Balance
As of December 31, 2010

Account Title	Debit	Credit
Accounts payable		$ 20,000.00
Accounts receivable	$ 15,000.00	
Advertising	$ 4,500.00	
Bank charges	$ 645.00	
Equipment	$ 3,260.00	
Income taxes	$ 5,000.00	
Inventory	$ 1,500.00	
Notes payable		$ 10,000.00
Notes receivable	$ 6,100.00	
Office supplies	$ 645.00	
Prepaid insurance	$ 350.00	
Rent	$ 8,000.00	
Revenue		$ 70,000.00
Travel	$ -	
Utilities	$ 5,000.00	
Wages	$ 50,000.00	
Totals	**$ 100,000.00**	**$ 100,000.00**
Difference		$ -

Figure 12.7 An example of a trial balance.

Balance sheets

Figure 12.8 shows an example of a balance sheet. Balance sheets are divided into two sides. On the left side you will find any assets the company has; on the right side you will see the liabilities + the shareholder's equity. The idea is that the totals on the two sides should be equal.

The two sides are further divided into different sections, with a total at the end of each column. Some sections may consist of only one item such as the Total Liabilities section (which simply adds the current and long term liabilities) or the Investments section.

ACME Corporation

Balance Sheet
December 31, 2012

ASSETS			LIABILITIES		
Current Assets			**Current Liabilities**		
Cash	$	5,000	Notes Payable	$	10,000
Petty Cash	$	200	Accounts Payable	$	30,000
Accounts Receivable - net	$	50,000	Wages Payable	$	15,000
Inventory	$	55,000	Interest Payable	$	4,000
Supplies	$	8,000	Taxes Payable	$	10,000
Prepaid Insurance	$	6,800	Unearned Revenue	$	69,000
Total Current Assets	$	125,000	Total Current Liabilities	$	138,000
Investments	$	30,000	**Long Term Liabilities**		
			Notes Payable	$	29,000
Property, Plant & Equipment			Bonds Payable	$	60,000
Land	$	30,000	Total Long-term Liabilities	$	89,000
Land improvements	$	10,000			
Buildings	$	200,000			
Equipment	$	300,000	**Total Liabilities**	$	227,000
Less: Accumulated Depreciation	-$	70,000			
Prop, Plant & Equipment - net	$	470,000			
			STOCKHOLDERS' EQUITY		
			Common Stock	$	150,000
Other Assets	$	10,000	Retained Earnings	$	200,000
			Less: Treasury Stock	-$	80,000
			Total Stockholders' Equity	$	270,000
Total Assets	$	635,000	**Total Liab. & Stockholders' Equity**	$	635,000

Figure 12.8   An example of a balance sheet.

Income statements

Figure 12.9 shows an example of an income statement (also known as a profit and loss statement). It is a bit tricky to understand at first. I will do my best to explain it to you.

First the Gross Profit is calculated by subtracting the cost of the goods that were sold from the Sales.

Then the Total Operating Expenses are calculated. First the Total Selling Expenses are determined by adding the Advertising and Commission (giving $8000). This figure is combined with the total Advertising Expenses to give a total of $12,000.

Next, the Operating Income ($58,000) is calculated by subtracting the Total Operating Expenses from the Gross Profit.

This figure is added to the Non-Operating Total to give the Net Profit (or Loss).

Caribbean Computers
Income Statement
For Q1 2011

Sales		$ 150,000
Cost of Goods Sold		$ 80,000
Gross Profit		$ 70,000
Operating Expenses		
Selling Expenses		
Advertising	$ 3,000	
Commission	$ 5,000	$ 8,000
Administrative Expenses		
Office Supplies	$ 2,000	
Office Equipment	$ 2,000	$ 4,000
Total Operating Expenses		$ 12,000
Operating Income		$ 58,000
Non-Operating or Other		
Interest Revenues		$ 6,000
Interest Expense		$ (600)
Total Non-Operating		$ 5,400
Net Income		$ 63,400

Figure 12.9 An example of an income statement.

Summary

- Use *Tab* stops, underscores or *AutoShapes* to draw horizontal lines on application forms.
- Use *AutoShapes* and *Tables* to draw boxes on application forms.
- Any tables that require calculations or oblique headings should be done in Microsoft Excel.

Review exercises

Exercise 12A
If you have not done so already, recreate the Student Application Form given in this chapter.

Exercise 12B
Reproduce the application form in Figure 12.1 on A4 paper. The fonts used were Times New Roman and Century Gothic. Put the Heading 'Second Caribbean International Bank' as a header.

Exercise 12C
Create an application form for the Young People's Sports Club. The form should contain (at least) the following information:

- The person's name and address.
- The telephone numbers.
- What sports they play (provide boxes for the following sports: football, cricket, basketball, tennis, netball, hockey).
- Who to contact in the event of an emergency.
- Space for them to list any medical conditions they suffer from.

Be sure to create a letterhead for the sports club.

Exercise 12D
Reproduce the tabulations in this chapter using the appropriate programs and suitably sized paper. Be sure to use the appropriate formulae for calculated figures instead of typing them manually.

Exercise 12E
Using Figures 12.5 and 12.6 as examples, create an invoice and sales receipt for a company of your choosing. Some suggestions are:

- A sporting goods store.
- A shoe store.
- An electronics store.

Type and centre them on A4 paper using a suitable orientation.

13 Technical documents

In this chapter, you will learn how to prepare two types of technical documents:

- specification documents
- bills of quantities

Page layout

For both types of document use A4 paper with 1" margins unless directed otherwise. For the Specification Document use single-line spacing as well.

Specification document

A specification document is a document which describes the technical requirements for a particular project. Although there are several types of specifications, for this course you are only required to know how to produce <u>either</u> a builder's specification or an architect's specification.

Figure 13.1 shows an <u>abbreviated</u> specification document, using information obtained from homedesigndirectory.com.au. This document shows some of the work a builder is to do in the construction of a new property.

The image below shows just one possible way to do a specification document. It consists of an introductory paragraph, the name and address of the architect and two sections (each of which is divided into multiple parts). A full specification document may be several pages long with several sections and have a table of contents.

Bill of quantities

Figure 13.2, page 336, shows an example of a Bill of Quantities. As you can see, this type of document lists the materials, parts and labour (and their associated costs) required for a particular project.

As was mentioned in the previous chapter, since this document involves several calculations, it is best to do it in Microsoft Excel. Each figure in the Value column is calculated by multiplying the quantity by the rate.

Review exercises

Exercise 13A
Reproduce the two documents in this chapter, making sure to use the appropriate Excel formulas for the Bill of Quantities.

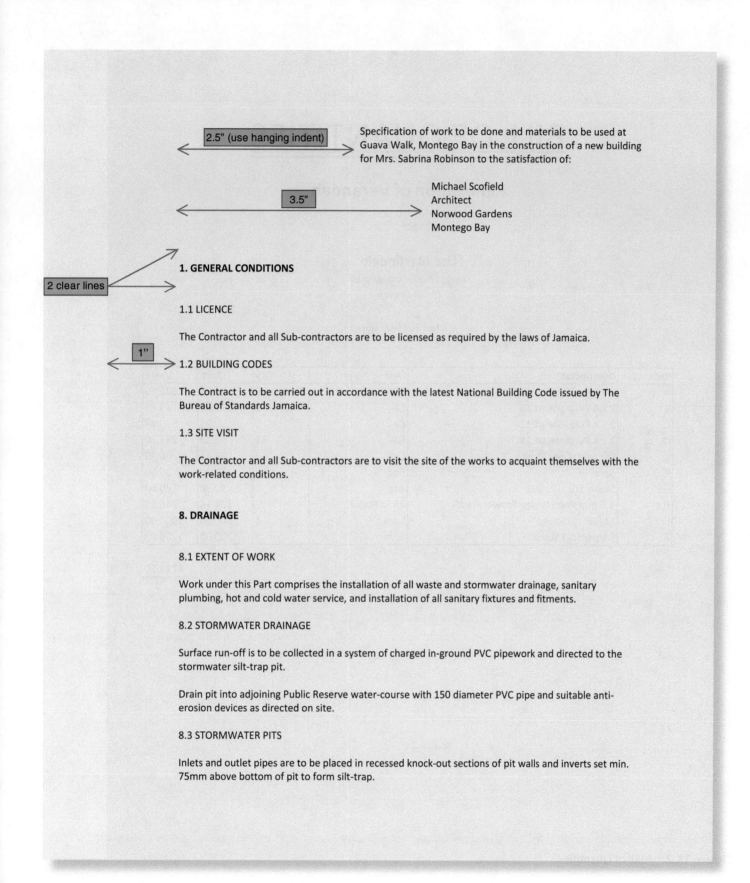

2.5" (use hanging indent)

Specification of work to be done and materials to be used at Guava Walk, Montego Bay in the construction of a new building for Mrs. Sabrina Robinson to the satisfaction of:

3.5"

Michael Scofield
Architect
Norwood Gardens
Montego Bay

2 clear lines

1. GENERAL CONDITIONS

1.1 LICENCE

The Contractor and all Sub-contractors are to be licensed as required by the laws of Jamaica.

1"

1.2 BUILDING CODES

The Contract is to be carried out in accordance with the latest National Building Code issued by The Bureau of Standards Jamaica.

1.3 SITE VISIT

The Contractor and all Sub-contractors are to visit the site of the works to acquaint themselves with the work-related conditions.

8. DRAINAGE

8.1 EXTENT OF WORK

Work under this Part comprises the installation of all waste and stormwater drainage, sanitary plumbing, hot and cold water service, and installation of all sanitary fixtures and fitments.

8.2 STORMWATER DRAINAGE

Surface run-off is to be collected in a system of charged in-ground PVC pipework and directed to the stormwater silt-trap pit.

Drain pit into adjoining Public Reserve water-course with 150 diameter PVC pipe and suitable anti-erosion devices as directed on site.

8.3 STORMWATER PITS

Inlets and outlet pipes are to be placed in recessed knock-out sections of pit walls and inverts set min. 75mm above bottom of pit to form silt-trap.

Figure 13.1 An abbreviated Specification Document.

BILL OF QUANTITIES

Renovation of Verandah

for

Lisa Martindale
Kings Court, Lodge Road
Christ Church

(Dated 2011-06-06)

Ref	Description	Unit	Qty	Rate	Value
A	2 x 6 Purpleheart 14'	Ea	5	104.58	522.90
B	2 x 6 Purpleheart 16'	Ea	1	119.85	119.85
C	2 x 4 Purpleheart 12'	Ea	9	59.93	539.37
D	2 x 4 Purpleheart 18'	Ea	11	89.30	982.30
E	Cement (Grey Stock)	Bag	2	24.15	48.30
F	Sand	Bag	3	10.30	30.90
G	Stone 1/2	Bag	2	10.30	20.60
H	1.0 mm Pearl White Trowel Plastic	65 lb Bucket	2	124.14	248.28
I	Masonry Labour	Sum	1	1000.00	1000.00
J	Carpentry Labour	Sum	1	1200.00	1200.00

4712.50

Figure 13.2 A Bill of Quantities

Document management and ethics

Part 5

1 Filing systems

In this chapter, you will learn about:

- manual and electronic filing systems
- advantages and disadvantages of each

Manual filing systems

Before the advent of computers, all filing had to be done manually. A manual filing system is one where the documents are arranged by hand into folders and stored in filing cabinets.

Even after the introduction of computers, manual systems are still very commonplace. Some companies are reluctant to make the transition to an electronic filing system for a myriad of reasons including cost, staff that are not computer literate and the amount of work involved in computerising existing records.

Advantages

Manual systems have a number of advantages over their electronic counterparts. First of all, they are still accessible in the event of a power outage. Secondly they are more secure from the point of view that physical access is required i.e. they cannot be hacked remotely.

Also, as was mentioned before, manual filing systems do not require the users to know how to use the computer. This is why many government agencies still use application forms – since they are dealing with the general public, they need to cater for the people who are not computer literate.

Disadvantages

With a manual filing system, finding a particular document can be time consuming, particularly if it is not in the correct location. Manual filing systems also take up a lot of space. Another disadvantage is that if someone has taken out a particular file, then other

people have to wait for him/her to be finished before they can view it.

Electronic filing systems

An electronic filing system is one where documents are stored in computer files and organised hierarchically into folders on electronic media. The term hierarchically is a big word that simply means that folders can be placed inside folders like in Figure 1.1.

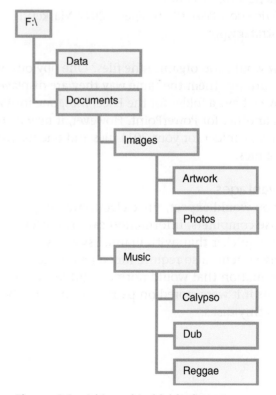

Figure 1.1 A hierarchical folder layout.

If you look closely, you can see a number of parallels between electronic filing systems and manual ones. For instance, virtual folders play the same role as physical ones and disks can be thought of as electronic filing cabinets.

Organising files electronically

In Part 1, Chapter 6, you learned how to use the My Computer tool in Microsoft Windows in order to browse, organise and manipulate electronic filing systems. Graphical User Interfaces (GUIs) like Windows make it very easy to manage electronic filing systems. For instance you could copy files from the Photos folder and paste them in the Images folder. Or you could drag the Music folder and move it (and files contained in it and its subfolders) under the Data folder instead.

Just like with manual systems, determining how best to organise your files requires some thought. You have to consider what groups of files have in common. Suppose you have the following files:

- Microsoft Excel Files – 2012 Budget.xls, 2012 Sales Targets, 2011 Budget.xls, 2011 Revenue.xls
- Microsoft Word Files – Goals for 2012.doc, Report for 2011.doc
- Microsoft PowerPoint Files – 2012 Marketing Strategy.ppt

How would you organise the files? One obvious way is to arrange them the same way they are displayed above – have a folder for the Excel files, one for Word and another for PowerPoint. However, it may be better to have a folder for your 2011 files and one for your 2012 files.

Advantages

As you would expect, since electronic filing systems utilise computers, information can be retrieved much quicker than with manual systems. Electronic filing systems also require much less space. Information that would normally fill up entire rooms if it were stored on paper, can now easily fit onto tiny disks.

Electronic filing systems also make it much easier to share and access information. If information is stored electronically, several people from all over the world can access it simultaneously. Contrast that to a manual system which would require each person to physically go to the location where the information is stored, in order to access it.

Disadvantages

The most obvious disadvantage of an electronic filing system is directly attributable to its use of computers – when the power goes out you cannot access the information. This is why some businesses maintain manual systems in addition to their electronic records.

Unfortunately, information that is stored electronically is vulnerable to hackers. Some of the ways this risk can be mitigated are described in subsequent chapters.

Summary

- Manual systems use physical documents, folders and filing cabinets whereas electronic systems use computer files and folders stored on electronic media.
- Manual filing systems are slow and require a lot of space, and make accessing information more difficult but are not affected by power outages.
- Electronic filing systems are faster, require much less space and make it convenient to access information but are vulnerable to hackers and power outages.

Review exercises

Exercise 1

1 In your own words explain the similarities and differences between manual and electronic filing systems.
2 Why do businesses, even those that are computerised, still use manual systems?
3 Give three disadvantages of manual filing systems.

4 Discuss how you would organise the files below:

- Acid and Alkalais.doc
- Admiral Nelson.doc
- Arawak.jpg
- Barbados Coat of Arms.jpg
- British Monarchs.doc
- Carib.jpg
- Caribbean Capitals.doc
- Caribbean History.doc
- Caribbean Populations.xls
- Christopher Columbus.doc
- Eye of a Storm.jpg
- Jamaican flag.jpg
- Helium atom.jpg
- Hurricane damage.jpg
- Hydrogen atom.jpg
- Napoleon Bonaparte.doc
- Laws of Gravity.doc
- Sir Isaac Newton.jpg
- World War II.doc

② Types of documents

In this chapter, you will learn:

- about various types of documents

- the difference between human-readable and machine-readable documents

- about document versioning

Source documents

Source documents are the documents on which the information was originally recorded. Examples include:

- Application forms.
- Medical record cards.
- Multiple-choice sheets.
- Payroll time cards.

For the data from source documents to be used by computers, it may need to be keyed in manually or scanned using devices such as optical mark readers and optical character readers.

Turnaround documents

A **turnaround document** is a document that has been output by a computer, then filled out and used as an input document. For instance, you may use the computer to compose and print application forms, then, once they have been completed, turn around and key back in the information. Another example of a turnaround document is a meter card used to collect readings.

Human-readable versus machine-readable documents

As you would imagine, **human-readable documents** are documents that are in a form for humans to read. With advances in natural language processing, computers are better able to recognise text in such documents but they still make mistakes (especially if the text is handwritten).

A **machine-readable document** is one where the data is encoded in a way that can easily be read by computers. The entire document does not have to be machine-readable. Usually such documents

have a *portion* that is machine-readable in addition to the human-readable part. Examples include modern passports, items with barcodes and cheques (which have magnetic ink).

Document versioning

As edits are made to a document or a file, version numbers may be used to increase traceability. The higher the version number, the more recent the document is. A version number normally consists of two parts, separated by a decimal point e.g. 1.2. The number *before* the decimal point is called the **major version number**, whereas any numbers after the point is called the **minor version number**.

The first complete version of a document is usually given a version number of 1.0. Preview versions may be given version numbers like 0.7 or 0.9 which give a rough percentage of how complete the document is. Subsequent version numbers are normally assigned depending on the magnitude of the changes. For instance, if a series of minor edits are made, the sequence of numbers may go like 1.1, 1.2, 1.3 etc. Major changes are indicated by increasing the major version number e.g. 2.0, 3.0.

One drawback of the traditional version number scheme is that there is often debate over what constitutes major or minor change. Also the version number by itself gives no indication of how up-to-date a document is. This is why some people give documents version numbers like 2011.01.25 which signify when last the document was edited.

Regardless of what method is used, the version number is usually specified in the file name and/or within the document itself. In the latter case, it might be shown in a header or footer or within the first few pages.

Summary

- Source documents are the original documents the information was recorded on.
- Turnaround documents are documents that were output from a computer and then filled out.
- Human-readable documents are those that can be read by humans; machine-readable means that only a machine can read it.
- The higher the version number the more recent the document is.
- In a version number like 1.3, the 1 and 3 are the major and minor revision numbers respectively. Major updates are indicated by increasing the major version number.

Review exercises

Exercise 2

1. Explain the relationship between a turnaround document and a source document.
2. Give four examples of source documents. Can you think of any others?
3. Give two examples of documents which have machine-readable portions.
4. In the table below, indicate when major changes were made to the document.

Release Date	Version Number
2011-01-01	0.2
2011-03-20	1.0
2011-04-01	1.1
2011-04-02	1.2
2011-04-30	2.0
2011-05-12	2.2

③ Maintaining file security and integrity

In this chapter, you will learn:

- how to restrict access to files
- how to guard against data loss
- about virus protection
- about disaster recovery

Restricting access to files

The best way to maintain file security is to restrict access to files. There are two main approaches employed – physical access restriction and software access restriction.

Physical access restriction

With physical access restriction, measures are put in place to prevent unauthorised users from gaining physical access to your files (whether electronic or manual). Documents and removable storage media may be placed in locked cabinets or vaults. Surveillance cameras, alarms and armed guards may also be used.

Software access restriction

This type of restriction deals with protecting your computer files from unauthorised users (including hackers). There are three main techniques utilised: password protection, encryption and firewalls.

Password protection

You can protect your entire computer by requiring that users enter passwords in order to log into the computer. The Microsoft Office programs also allow you to password protect individual files. If you are interested, ask your teacher to show you how to do so.

Encryption

Encryption is the process of encoding a file so that it bears no similarity to the original. A secret combination of characters called a <u>key</u> is used to tell an encryption algorithm how to encode the information. The only way the encrypted file can be read is if the <u>same key</u> is used to decrypt it. That way sensitive information can be protected from prying eyes.

Firewalls

Despite the name, a computer firewall does not have anything to do with fire. Rather, a firewall is a piece of hardware or software designed to protect your network from hackers. This is particularly important if your computer is connected to the Internet. Many antivirus programs come with built-in firewalls.

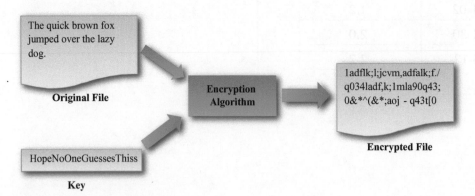

Figure 3.1   How encryption works.

Virus protection

If you are not careful your computer can become infected with a virus. Like their biological counterparts, computer viruses can quickly spread, causing a lot of damage. Some of the ways viruses can spread are:

- Via email attachments.
- When you place an infected flash drive or floppy disk into a computer.
- When you download malicious software from the Internet.

To protect against viruses, you should use special antivirus software such as Norton Antivirus or Mcafee (see Figure 3.2). These programs check your computer for files resembling *known* viruses, alerting you to their presence and giving you the option of removing them. New viruses come out all the time so it is important to keep your antivirus software up-to-date! Unfortunately, a virus may be 'in the wild' for a number of days before the antivirus manufacturer knows about it, so even if your virus guard is fully up-to-date your computer can still get infected.

To further reduce the risk of infection you should only download and open files from trusted sources.

Protecting against data loss

Data loss can occur in a number of ways apart from virus infections. It can be caused by hardware failures, information being accidentally deleted or even Mother Nature herself. Here are some ways you can protect against data loss.

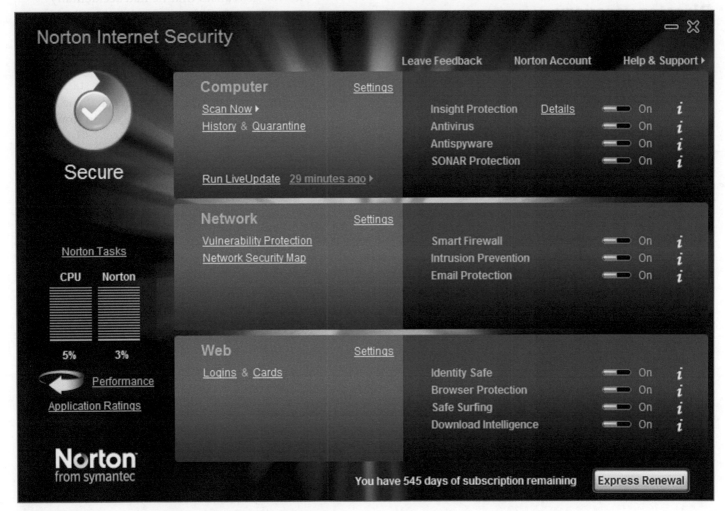

Figure 3.2 An antivirus program with a built-in firewall.

Preventing accidental deletion

There are two ways you can reduce the chance of someone accidentally deleting or overwriting your data. First, you can open the write-protect tab on floppy disks and some flash media. When this tab is open, the data on the disk cannot be altered or deleted, so someone cannot accidentally save over your data.

Secondly, you can right-click on individual files, click Properties and enable the Read-Only option. When it is turned on, people can read that file but cannot make changes to it.

Preventing damage from fire or water

In order to prevent manual records or electronic media (such as CD-ROMs or tape drives) from being damaged by fire or water, you can put them in fireproof and waterproof cabinets respectively.

Disaster recovery

Despite your best efforts, you may still lose your data, particularly as a result of a hardware failure. That is why it is important to make backups of important data at regular intervals. That way, when the unthinkable happens, you can restore your information from a recent backup. If you are lucky (and diligent) the data loss will be minimal.

When you are backing up data, store it in another location in fireproof or waterproof cabinets if possible. That way you reduce the risk of your backup being damaged as well.

Summary

- Access can be restricted to files by physical or software means.
- Passwords, firewalls and encryption help protect against unauthorised users such as hackers.
- Computer viruses are spread via infected programs, storage devices and email attachments.
- Although antivirus software reduces the risk of infection, newer viruses may slip through, especially if you do not update your antivirus software regularly.
- Backup your data regularly and if possible, store the backups at other locations.

Review exercises

Exercise 3

1 Explain the difference between the two categories of access restriction.
2 Give four ways that data loss can occur.
3 A client wants to hire you as a security consultant. Devise a strategy to help them protect their manual and electronic files.
4 Explain in your own words how encryption works.
5 Your friend has backed up some important information on a separate hard drive in his computer. Is this a good idea? Justify your answer.
6 When Shawn goes to open a file, to his horror he realises that he had accidentally overwritten it with an older version. Suggest two ways he can reduce the chance of this happening in the future.
7 Tiffany opened an email from a stranger and soon afterwards, her computer started acting 'strange,' despite the fact that she has antivirus software installed. Explain how this could happen.

4 Archiving data

In this chapter, you will learn:

- about archiving data
- about issues related to the retaining and disposal of data

Archiving data

Archiving is the process of moving files or records, which are no longer being actively used, into long term storage.

Archiving is primarily done as a means to save space. Suppose, for example, your filing cabinet is overflowing with client records, some who have not done business with the company for years. You might decide to put the former clients' records in a box and store them 'in the back' of the office, thereby freeing up valuable filing cabinet space.

You may be asking yourself, 'but why don't you just throw the old stuff out?' There are two main reasons for this. First of all, you may not be certain that you will *never* need the information again. Secondly, you may want to save the information for historical purposes.

The same concept applies to electronic documents. When you run out of disk space, you may move files that you do not currently use and store them on CDs or magnetic tape, thereby freeing up disk space. This is also a form of archiving.

Archives vs. backups

The difference between backups and archives is that with backups, *additional* copies are being kept.

Compressing the data

In order to reduce the amount of space the archived data takes up, it may be stored in some compressed form.

If the original data is in the form of physical documents, it may be scanned and stored electronically. Another approach, which is popular in libraries, is to store it on microfilm (see Figure 4.1). In this case, a snapshot is taken of the original document, and stored on a tiny piece of film. Since the film is much smaller than the sheets of paper, it saves a lot of space.

Figure 4.1 Archived documents on microfilm.

Electronic files can be compressed as well. Here, clever algorithms take advantage of the fact that most documents contain repeated data, in order to reduce the amount of disk space they take up.

Whichever method you use to compress your data, you can safely get rid of the original documents since the compressed records contain all the information found in the original. However, in order to view compressed documents, additional steps are needed, such as decompressing the file or using a special viewer.

Legal issues associated with retaining data

Companies are collecting data about you all the time. Even when you visit a website, some computer somewhere may be recording information about your browsing patterns. This is why many countries have found it necessary to introduce data privacy laws. While the letter of the law may vary depending on the country, they typically state that companies should:

1 Let you know what information they are collecting about you.
2 Let you know how long they will retain this information, <u>and dispose of the data after that time has elapsed</u>.
3 Ensure that the information they store about you is accurate.
4 Not share this information with anyone without your permission.

This is why many websites have privacy policies and why it is important to 'read the fine print.' On the flip side, there are also laws which state that you must store data for *at least* a certain amount of time. This would apply, for instance, to medical records and companies' accounting records. Similarly, some countries require Internet Service Providers to keep records of their customers' Internet activity (in case they get involved in illegal activity).

Disposing of data

Companies have to be careful when it comes to disposing of sensitive information. If they simply throw out old documents, what is to stop someone from going through the trash and finding the information? Similarly, old hard drives are treasure troves of information since there are sophisticated programs that can often recover files deleted by normal means.

This is why prudent companies shred sensitive documents, see Figure 4.2, before disposing of them and wipe their hard drives clean before selling or throwing out old equipment.

Figure 4.2 Shredding sensitive information before disposing of It.

Summary

- With backups additional copies are kept whereas with archiving, non-active records and files are *moved* into long term storage.
- If archived data is compressed to save space, it must either be decompressed or viewed with a special viewer before you can read the original data.

- Companies should let you know what personal information they are collecting about you and for how long, and should dispose of it after that time has passed.
- Laws also govern the minimum amount of time certain types of information must be kept before it can be disposed.
- It is best to shred the documents and wipe the hard drives clean when disposing of sensitive information.

Review exercises

Exercise 4

1 In your own words, explain what archiving is and why a company would want to do it.
2 List two examples of storage media on which electronic data may be archived.
3 Some Internet Marketing companies secretly compile profiles of users' Internet browsing habits and sell the information to other businesses. What privacy laws are they most likely violating?
4 Give three types of data that companies may be required by law to store for a certain amount of time.
5 To free up some storage space, a doctor is considering throwing out the medical records of patients who have not been to the office in the last 5 years. Give two reasons why this is a bad idea and suggest an alternative which will still save space.

5 Intellectual property

What is intellectual property?

We are all used to the idea of physical property. Clothes, vehicles, crops – these are all things that can be touched, things that can potentially be stolen from us. But what about something intangible like an idea, or a song – not the CD the song comes on, but the song itself? Can that be stolen as well? The answer is yes.

According to the United States Patent and Trademark Office, the term **intellectual property** refers to 'creations of the mind – creative works or ideas embodied in a form that can be shared or can enable others to recreate, emulate, or manufacture them'. Things which fall into this category are:

- literary works such as textbooks, poems or novels
- music (including the jingles you hear on the radio)
- inventions
- phrases, e.g. Nike's 'Just do it' slogan
- designs, e.g. architectural plans
- art (including logos and photographs)
- dramatic works such as plays and movies.

Intellectual property rights

People who create or produce intellectual property – such as screenwriters, authors, journalists, singers, inventors or architects – are entitled to certain rights as explained below.

Economic rights

Unsurprisingly, you have a right to be paid when someone uses your intellectual property. For instance, authors are to receive royalties from the books they write. Photographers should be compensated when their photos are used in magazines. Studios must be paid when their movies are shown in cinemas or broadcast on television. These are all examples of economic rights.

You can transfer your economic rights to another person or entity.

Moral rights

The creator of intellectual property is also entitled to a variety of moral rights which aim to protect the integrity of the work as well as the reputation of the author.

- The creator/author should be acknowledged whenever someone uses part of his work (unless he requests anonymity). So for instance, if one composer uses another's melody in her song, she should give the original composer credit. Similarly journalists should quote their sources.
- Authors should not be quoted out of context. For instance, you should not quote part of something a person wrote if it changes the original meaning. For instance, consider these two quotes:

  'I would have to be crazy to think that women don't deserve equal rights!' (Original quote)
  'women don't deserve equal rights!' (Misquote)

  By leaving out the beginning of the original quote, you unfairly paint the author in a negative light.

- Similarly, you should not attribute a quote to someone who never said it or wrote it in the first place.

Copyright

To understand what copyright is, let us look to Wikipedia, which defines it as 'the set of exclusive rights granted to the author or creator of an original work, including the right to copy, distribute and adapt the work'. Legal action may be taken against anyone who does these things without the copyright holder's permission.

Note that it must be an <u>original</u> work, which is often a point of contention. In most countries, the author/creator of the intellectual property <u>automatically</u> becomes the initial copyright holder (although he may then transfer those rights to someone else). In other countries, you are required to provide a copyright notice such as 'Copyright ©2012 ACME Corporation' in order for your work to be protected under copyright.

Merely having an idea is not enough. The copyright only applies to an implementation, written description or recording of that idea. So two distinct people can have intellectual property based on similar ideas due to differences in their implementations.

As the copyright holder, you can specify whether your intellectual property can be copied or distributed and dictate the terms. Violation of these terms is called copyright infringement.

Legal distribution of copyrighted material
The legal distribution of copyrighted material is normally done via a process like the one in Figure 5.1.

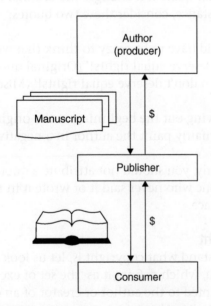

Figure 5.1 The distribution process for a book.

As you can see, there are three entities involved:

- producers or owners (e.g. artists and authors) – these maintain control over the intellectual property and are given a percentage of any profits by the distributor
- publishers or distributors – these record, film or print the material then market it or distribute it on behalf of the owner
- users or consumers – if they buy or rent the product they normally do so through the distributor instead of directly from the producer.

Even when a consumer buys a product, the creator maintains ownership of the intellectual property.

Protecting intellectual property rights
There are a number of ways people and organisations can protect their intellectual property. Some of them are outlined in this section. They mainly give you the ability to prosecute unauthorised profiting from your intellectual property rather than prevent it.

Patents
To protect an invention you can apply for a patent. If your invention is patented, you can prevent other people from producing or selling it.

Trademarks
If you want to protect a name, phrase or logo you can register it as a trademark. An R with a circle around it ® denotes a registered trademark. If the trademark is not registered, you use the ™ symbol instead.

It is illegal to use someone else's trademark to promote a company in a similar field. This is to prevent customers from confusing your company with the original. So, for instance, do not think about calling your new computer store Microsoft Computers. And despite the numerous knockoffs that seem to prove otherwise, you should not use the Nike swoosh on shoes or clothing.

Copy protection
Companies try to prevent unauthorised copying of things like music, programs and movies by

copy-protecting the media used to distribute them. This is why you are sometimes asked to enter a serial number printed on the back of a DVD case when you are installing a new program. Unfortunately, such measures only deter piracy rather than preventing it altogether.

Plagiarism

Suppose you go on the Internet and find a great article, which, as luck would have it, answers a question in an assignment. So you copy it into Microsoft Word, print it and submit it. This is an all-too-common example of plagiarism. Plagiarism is the act of presenting someone's work as your own, and is frowned upon as form of academic dishonesty.

So how do you make sure that you are not guilty of plagiarism? Let us look at some of the ways below.

Generating your own ideas

Although it sounds obvious, generating your own ideas is the best way to avoid plagiarism. Look at the data then draw your own conclusions. Put things in your own words. Be creative!

Obtaining approval to use someone's work

You should try to get someone's permission before using their work as part of your own work. Of course, if they refuse, you should not go ahead and use it anyway.

Acknowledging sources of information

You should get in the habit of acknowledging sources. There are a number of ways to do so.

- You can quote them, like this: 'As John Maxwell said, "If we're growing, we're always going to be out of our comfort zone".'
- You can include in-text citations.
- You can list them in a bibliography at the end of the publication.

Citations

Citations are used in academic documents such as term papers and research reports. There are a number of standards, but the most common one (and the one recommended by CXC) is the APA style. The APA style goes into great detail and as a result can seem a bit daunting. So here are the basics (note that all the quotes are made up).

When you are referencing a book or article, you give the author's surname, followed by the year of publication in brackets. For example, here is how you would do a direct quote:

According to Graham (2010), 'Social media platforms such as Facebook and Twitter will augment but never replace traditional means of human interaction'.

Even if you are summarising someone's work, instead of directly quoting them, you should still include a reference. For example:

Skeete (2012) presents the argument that EDPM is an easy subject to learn but a different one to master.

Gates (2009) believes that one could significantly reduce the amount of email spam by using e-stamps.

If the work you are referencing has more than one author, put all their names and the publication year in brackets for the first reference, then use 'et al.' in future references.

Everyone, no matter how poor, is entitled to legal representation (Crane, Poole & Schmidt, 2001). 'Whether a person lives or dies should not be determined by the size of his wallet' (Crane et al., 2001).

If you are referencing multiple articles the same author published in one year, you can distinguish between them by using a, b, c, etc. after the year.

Skeete (2011a) believes that traditional ways of measuring intelligence are misguided.

Skeete (2011b) proposes having tests that measure street smarts as well as book smarts.

To reference particular pages, write them like this: '(p. 100)'. For example:

Gates (2010) believes that the future of computing is in smart devices such as cell phones (p. 5). He argues that we are already seeing the transition to these smart devices (p. 100).

Writing bibliographies

In addition to in-text citations, you should include a **bibliography** (a detailed list of references) at the end of the document. Again, the recommended format is the APA style. The format of the reference depends on the type of material being referenced.

Books

When including a reference to a book, use the following format:

> Surname, First Initial. (Publication year in brackets). Book title in italics. City of publication: Publisher.

For example:

> Covey, S. (1989). *The Seven Habits of Highly Effective People*. New York: Simon & Schuster.

tip

> You can find the publication information within the first few pages of the book.

Printed articles

When typing a bibliography entry for printed articles such as newsletters or magazines, the format you should use is:

> Surname, Initial. (Date). Article title. Publication title in italics, volume # in italics (issue #), pages.

> If there is no publication date, put n.d. (for 'no date'). For newspapers omit the volume number and issue number.

For example:

> Funk, M. (2010, May). Mountain Transformed. *National Geographic, 217* (5), 34–53.

Internet

Internet articles are a bit different. In addition to the internet address (URL) of the web page, you need to say <u>when</u> you retrieved that article, since web pages may change over time. The format is:

> Surname, Initial. (Date or n.d. for no date). Article title in italics. Retrieved month day, year, from URL.

Here is an example:

> Walters, H. (2010, May 5). *How Google Got Its New Look*. Retrieved May 8, 2010 from http://www.businessweek.com/magazine/content/10_20/b4178000295757.htm

Summary

- Intellectual property encompasses creations of the mind such as written work, art, music and inventions.
- The creator of intellectual property is entitled to economic and moral rights in addition to the copyright.
- The three entities involved in the legal distribution of copyrighted material are producers, distributors and consumers.
- If you present someone's work as your own that is plagiarism. To avoid it you should acknowledge the original author by using citations or including them in a bibliography.
- The APA style is the recommended style for citations and bibliographies.

Review exercises

Exercise 5

1. In your own words, what is intellectual property?
2. What is the difference between moral and economic intellectual property rights? Give examples of breaches of both.
3. Explain what copyright is.
4. Give an example of a copyright notice.
5. What is plagiarism?

6 Give three ways you can avoid plagiarism.

7 Give an example of how you would cite a quote from three authors.

8 Write a (single) bibliography for the following:

    a Pages 163–167 of *Gray's Anatomy for Students* written by Richard L. Drake, Wayne Vogl and Adam W. M. Mitchell and published by Churchill Livingstone on October 19, 2004 in London.

    b An article called Facing Down the Fanatics which appeared in the October 2009 issue (Volume 216, No. 4) of the *National Geographic* magazine. The article was on pages 76 and 99 and was written by Michael Finkel.

    c An online article called 'Human brains excel at detecting cheaters' that was created on May 13 2010 and accessed on the same day from the URL http://arstechnica.com/science/news/2010/05/one-of-the-major-questions.ars. The article was written by Kate Shaw.

6 Work ethics

What makes a good team member?

Everyone who has been studying or working long enough has had the misfortune of working with people who are inconsiderate, annoying and unreliable. People like that are <u>terrible</u> team members! But how do you know someone is not saying that about you?

Let us look at some desirable work habits.

The ability to work without supervision

This is one of the most desired characteristics of an employee – an employee who you can give a task to do and be confident that it will be done without looking over his or her shoulder. As an employee you should not be listening out for your boss's footsteps in order to come off of Facebook or stop playing Solitaire.

If you do not have all the information you need to accomplish your task, try to acquire it. Do not wait until your boss or teacher returns to say, 'I could not do X because of Y'. If you see something that needs to be done, do it! Do not wait for your boss to tell you about it.

The ability to meet deadlines

The editors of this book will probably have a good chuckle when they see this, since I struggle a lot with this one. But students and employees alike should be able to meet deadlines. Students should strive to submit their projects and assignments on time. Employees should finish their work in a timely manner.

The biggest obstacle to meeting deadlines is procrastination. By putting things off until the last minute you are at the mercy of any technical glitches or similar problems that may crop up unexpectedly. Even though you may think you have enough time, unforeseen circumstances may leave you with less time than you had imagined.

If a problem seems too immense, break it down into a series of smaller tasks, each with a <u>realistic</u> deadline of its own. That way you would have a clearer picture of whether or not you are progressing at the required rate.

Teamwork and cooperation

If you want to improve your chances in a job interview, say that you value the importance of teamwork or mention the phrase 'team player'! The reason why teamwork is so important (and why teachers insist on those annoying group projects) is that very few things of consequence can be accomplished by flying solo.

So, inevitably, you will have to rely on other people. The way you do so will determine the success of your endeavour.

The key to good teamwork is communication and cooperation. Each member of the team must have a clear idea of what he or she is expected to do and should communicate any challenges in carrying out that task. Someone else on the team may have information that can help you. Just be sure to return the favour. Nothing frustrates other team members like someone who does not pull their own weight.

If you are assigned a task, you should make sure you keep the rest of your team updated with regards to your progress. Similarly, if you ask a team member to do something, you should make sure you follow up to see how he/she is getting through.

Recognition of diversity

Crucial to good teamwork is the recognition of the diversity of your classmates and workmates. I am not only talking about the classic examples such as race and religious beliefs. What works with one person may not work with another. You might be a night person and your teammate may be a day person. You might be comfortable giving presentations whereas your workmate may dread it. You should not only recognise diversity, you should use it to your advantage.

Courtesy

You should be polite at all times and respectful to your co-workers. This may be more difficult some days than others, especially when you have something that is bothering you, but be careful not to take it out on your peers.

If you work in an environment where you are interacting with customers, courtesy is especially important. You should strive to provide excellent customer service and you should be patient with them, even when they ask questions that seem silly on the surface.

Punctuality

You should make a special effort to be punctual – not just by getting to work or class on time, but by getting to meetings early. No one likes to be kept waiting.

Good grooming

Your school or workplace will most likely have its own policies on good grooming, so always make sure you are dressed suitably for work or school. Pants should not be too tight and skirts should not be too short. Fingernails should be kept clean and hair should be combed. Ladies should not wear outrageous hairstyles with multiple colours.

Integrity

As a student, a big part of integrity is academic honesty. Cheating is a big no-no, which is why plagiarism is so frowned upon. But integrity is a virtue that you should have, not only as a student (or employee), but as a person.

People must be able to trust you and believe what you say. Obviously this is not something that comes overnight. It has to be earned. People take note of whether you say what you mean and do what you say. This is why it is so important to be a person of your word and to be honest.

Acceptable standards of work

The work you produce should be of a high standard. It is critical that whatever documents you create, should look and sound professional. If you submit a printed document, it should not be on dirty or untidy paper. If it is folded it should be folded neatly.

Review exercises

Exercise 6
1 Why is teamwork important?
2 Give two examples of <u>bad</u> grooming.
3 List five desirable work habits. For each one, ask yourself if you possess that quality and what you can do to acquire it if you do not.

Part 6

Part 6 Practice papers and SBA guidelines

Practice papers and SBA guidelines

1 Exam and SBA tips

Breakdown of exam

Regardless of whether you are an in-school candidate or a private candidate, the EDPM examination will consist of three papers.

Paper 1

This <u>1 hour</u> paper consists of <u>10</u> questions worth <u>50 marks in all</u> and makes up <u>20% of your total marks</u>.

It is a theory paper that tests your knowledge of the concepts you should have covered in the course. For example, you may be asked questions about what type of stationery to use for certain types of documents, or to list the steps required to perform a task in Microsoft Word.

This paper will test your knowledge of material from every section of this book. However, I have listed some topics you should pay <u>special</u> attention to:

Paper 1 Checklist

Table 1.1 (on page 355) is a checklist of the topics you need to know for Paper 1.

Only after you thoroughly know these topics, should you attempt the Practice Paper 1 questions in the next chapter.

Paper 2

This <u>2 hour</u> paper consists of <u>4</u> questions worth <u>100 marks in all</u> and makes up <u>40% of your total marks</u>.

Paper 2 is a practical paper that will be done on the computer. Each question consists of a handwritten document, complete with correction symbols, which you have to type using either Word or Excel. There are also instructions that specify things like the margins, paper size, layout and punctuation style.

The instructions are usually typewritten but sometimes they are handwritten. Make sure you do not type back the instructions like some students did one year!

CXC states that the paper "will assess candidates' ability to prepare letters, tables, reports, business forms and creative displays". Historically, the most common document types you are given are:

- Manuscripts or letters written in hard to read handwriting.
- Tables which you would usually have to type in Excel.
- Brochures.

In order to prepare for this exam, I recommend doing <u>at least</u> the exercises in the following chapters:

Paper 2 checklist

Table 1.2 (on page 355) contains a list of exercises you can do to practice for Paper 2.

Once you have finished these exercises, you can attempt the Practice Paper 2 questions in Chapter 3.

Paper 3

This paper is worth <u>100 marks in all</u> and makes up <u>40% of your total marks</u>.

This paper is either in the form of a School-Based Assessment (Paper 3/1), or an alternative paper (Paper 3/2) which is compulsory for private candidates since they would not be associated with a particular school. The alternative paper is a 90 minute paper which covers the same concepts tested for in the SBA.

Table 1.1 Paper 1 checklist.

	Do You Know...	Chapter(s) in Book	✓
1	The types, advantages and disadvantages of computers?	Part 1, Ch 1	
2	The five components of a computer system?	Part 1, Ch 2	
3	When to use a particular input or output device?	Part 1, Ch 3	
4	The different ways printers can be categorised (e.g. impact, page)?	Part 1, Ch 3	
5	The different types of secondary storage media and what they are used for?	Part 1, Ch 4	
6	The icons commonly found on the Desktop?	Part 1, Ch 5	
7	The steps for creating a folder, copying/moving a file or recovering a deleted file?	Part 1, Ch 6	
8	The difference between systems and application software (and examples of each)?	Part 1, Ch 7	
9	How to care for your computer and work environment?	Part 1, Ch 8	
10	The terms associated with the World Wide Web?	Part 1, Ch 9	
11	The advantages and disadvantages of email?	Part 1, Ch 10	
12	The steps for sending an email and when to use Cc and Bcc?	Part 1, Ch 10	
13	The factors to consider when choosing a means of electronic communication?	Part 1, Ch 11	
14	The correct posture for typing?	Part 2, Ch 1	
15	The different types of productivity tools and when to use each?	Part 3, Ch 1	
16	The common features of Word Processing, Spreadsheet, Presentation and Database software?	Part 3, Chs 7, 16, 23 and 30	
17	The steps for changing the font and size of text?	Part 3, Ch 5	
18	The steps for copying, moving, finding and replacing text?	Part 3, Ch 6	
19	The common keyboard shortcuts used in Microsoft Office?	Part 3, Ch 6	
20	The different stationery types and sizes and when they should be used?	Part 4, Chs 1 & 2	
21	The different heading and punctuation styles?	Part 4, Ch 3	
22	The different correction symbols?	Part 4, Ch 4	
23	How to rewrite a paragraph, correcting common types of errors?	Part 4, Ch 5	
24	The different layouts for letters and memos?	Part 4, Ch 6	
25	The information that should be on a letterhead?	Part 4, Ch 6	
26	The advantages and disadvantages of manual and electronic filing systems?	Part 5, Ch 1	
27	The different types of documents (source, turnaround, human and machine-readable)?	Part 5, Ch 2	
28	The techniques for protecting documents and recovering from disasters?	Part 5, Ch 3	
29	The issues pertaining to retaining and disposing of data?	Part 5, Ch 4	
30	About intellectual property rights and copyright?	Part 5, Ch 5	
31	What is plagiarism and how to avoid it?	Part 5, Ch 5	

Table 1.2 Paper 2 checklist.

	I have re-done the exercises in the following chapters	✓
1	Part 3, Chapter 6 – Editing text	
2	Part 3, Chapter 8 – Helpful word processing features (Exercise 8b)	
3	Part 3, Chapter 9 – Margins and indentation	
4	Part 3, Chapter 11 – Working with tables	
5	Part 3, Chapter 12 – Laying out documents (Exercise 12b, 12c)	
6	Part 3, Chapter 15 – Printing (Exercise 15, questions 1–3)	
7	Part 3, Chapter 17 – Formatting spreadsheets	
8	Part 3, Chapter 18 – Formulas in Excel	
9	Part 3, Chapter 19 – Copying formulas and data	
10	Part 3, Chapter 20 – Sorting	
11	Part 3, Chapter 22 – Printing	
12	Part 4, Chapter 3 – Typing manuscripts and reports	
13	Part 4, Chapter 4 – Correction symbols	
14	Part 4, Chapter 6 – Letters and memos (Exercises 6.1, 6.4–6.9)	
15	Part 4, Chapter 8 – Simple display documents	
16	Part 4, Chapter 9 – Advanced display documents (Exercises 9.3, 9.4)	
17	Part 4, Chapter 12 – Forms and tabulations	

SBA format

For your SBA you will have to:

- Do 3 assignments (including a speed test), worth a total of 75 marks.
- Create a portfolio, worth a total of 25 marks.

Teachers are supposed to allocate 10% of your SBA marks for 'communication of information in a logical way using appropriate grammar'. Part 4, Chapter 5 contains several tips to help you with this.

Speed Test

For the speed test, you will be asked to type a manuscript that your teacher prepared and make the specified amendments and corrections. The typed document should adhere to established guidelines.

While you are typing the document, your teacher will be marking you on things like:

- Your accuracy.
- Whether your eyes are consistently on the copy.
- Your body posture and hand positions.
- How well you are typing.
- How organised you are.

To prepare for this speed test you should make sure you are familiar with the material in Part 2 and Part 4, chapters 3 and 4. And of course, you should be comfortable typing and editing documents in Microsoft Word.

Other assignments

For your other two assignments, you may be asked to compile, summarise and email some information and to prepare a presentation. You will be marked on your ability to:

- Use the Internet.
- Create and send emails.
- Create email contacts.
- And use your presentation software.

General criteria

Your assignments will be also marked on things like:

- Using the appropriate fonts, formatting, layout and margins.
- How attractive and creative your work is presented.

Portfolio

As part of your SBA you will be asked to prepare a portfolio which you will be able to take with you to job interviews. This portfolio should consist of a:

- Title page containing the subject (Electronic Document Preparation and Management), the exam period, your name and registration number, school and territory.
- Table of contents.
- The following elements, labelled with your name and a description of the element being demonstrated:

  a Letters:
     i Two-page indented OR blocked style letter.
     ii A circular letter or form with a tear-off slip.
  b Manuscript:
     i A report OR specification OR play (with actor's part)
  c Tabular work:
     i A ruled tabulation with a main heading and multiple oblique or vertical column headings
  d Committee documents:
     i A notice of a meeting with an agenda for a meeting.
     ii A Chairman's agenda OR minutes of a meeting.

  e Display Documents:
     i An invitation with a menu OR programme (a creative design should be used).
     ii A flow chart OR organisational chart (with or without use of template).
  f Legal Work
     i A lease OR hire purchase agreement OR Will + endorsement.
     ii A contract of employment.
- A bibliography listing the resources you used.

Each document in the portfolio will be checked for mailability. For a document to be considered mailable it must:

- Be free of typographical, grammar and spelling errors.
- Be completely accurate.
- Meet the accepted document processing styles, complying with rules on punctuation, capitalisation and typing of figures.

> **tip**
>
> **CXC states that you 'may make any number of attempts to achieve a mailable specimen.' So you have no excuse not to get the full 25 marks for your portfolio.**
>
> **You should be very comfortable with adjusting margins, indentation and tab breaks (Part 3, Chapters 9 and 12) before you attempt your portfolio.**

The information above was taken from the CXC EDPM syllabus, which goes into much more detail that I can go into here. If you get a chance, you should obtain a copy and look through it for yourself.

2 Practice paper 1

This practice paper is actually longer than the exam will be in order to expose you to a wider range of questions. However the difficulty is in keeping with what you can expect from the actual paper.

Answer all questions.
Time: 1 hour and 45 minutes

1 The image above shows a typical desktop PC.
   a Label items A to E. [5 marks]
   b Which of those items are **i** input devices, **ii** output devices? [4 marks]
   c Which input device is best suited for data entry? [1 mark]
   d Give one output device and one input device that are not listed here. [2 marks]
   e In which component would you find the CPU? [1 mark]

2 Dorothy wants to type a report with a graph in it. Give two types of software she might use. Would you classify this software as systems software or application software? [3 marks]

3 Give three functions of operating systems. [3 marks]

4 List three icons commonly found on the desktop. [3 marks]

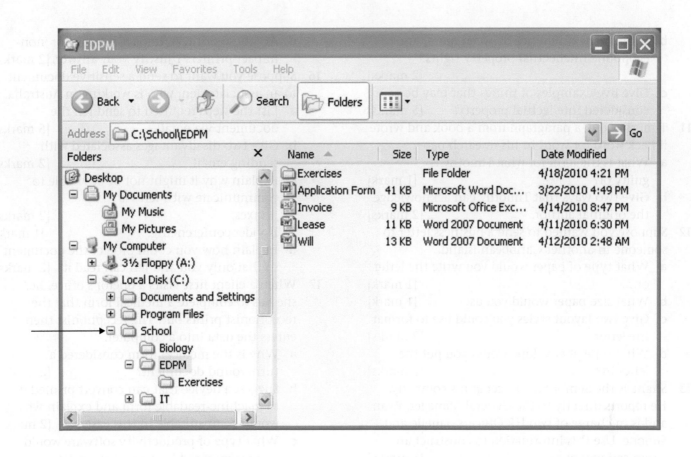

5 Look at the image above and answer the following
   questions:
   a What is the path of the current folder? [1 mark]
   b How many files are in that folder?   [1 mark]
   c Which is the biggest file?   [1 mark]
   d Explain what would happen if you were
      to click the minus (–) sign indicated by
      the arrow.   [2 marks]
   e Explain how you would create a new folder
      inside the Biology folder.   [3 marks]
   f What file extension do programs usually
      have?   [1 mark]
6 Copy and complete the following table.   [7 marks]

Action	Shortcut
Cut	
	Ctrl + I
	Ctrl + V
Move the cursor to the next page	
	Ctrl + Home
Make the selected text bold	
Insert a Page Break	

7 List the steps required to move a paragraph to the
   bottom of a Microsoft Word document. [5 marks]
8 Correct the spelling and grammar errors in the
   following paragraph:

   How are you he asked its definately been a
   long day she replied. "Would you beleive that
   my computer, along with the files on it, were
   stolen?"   [10 marks]

9 Write the manuscript signs for EACH of the
   following:
   a joining two paragraphs   [1 mark]
   b cancelling a deletion   [1 mark]
   c putting text in spaced caps   [1 mark]
   d writing out an abbreviation in full. [1 mark]
10 Cindy explained to Jason that he should not copy
   a DVD and give a copy to his friends because he
   would be infringing on someone elses intellectual
   property rights.
   a What intellectual property right would he be
      violating?   [1 mark]

b Explain the difference between moral and economic intellectual property rights. [2 marks]

c Give five examples of things that may be considered intellectual property. [5 marks]

11 Timothy took a paragraph from a book and wrote it back word for word in his research paper.

a What is the term for what Timothy is guilty of? [1 mark]

b Give two ways that Timothy can acknowledge the original author. [2 marks]

12 Suppose you wanted to send a business letter to someone in another Caribbean island.

a What type of paper would you write the letter on? [1 mark]

b What size paper would you use? [1 mark]

c Give two layout styles you could use to format the letter. [2 marks]

d What type of envelope would you put the letter in? [2 marks]

13 Shane is the Senior HR Officer at his company. He reports directly to the General Manager, Ryan and is in charge of two HR Officers, Janelle and Simone. Use this information to construct an organisational chart. [5 marks]

14 Tamika has been asked to speak to her class about the history of Caribbean music. She decides to take her PC to school so her class can watch and listen to a slideshow that she has prepared.

a What type of productivity software is best suited to this task? [1 mark]

b List two output devices she would need for her slideshow. [2 marks]

c What type of PC should she carry? [1 mark]

d List two other types of PCs. [2 marks]

e A PC is only one type of computer. What are the two other types? [2 marks]

15 Jesse wants to buy two new printers – one for his office and another for his home. He expects that the office printer will be very heavily used but plans to use the home printer to occasionally print photographs and colour documents.

a What type of printer should he buy for
 i work,
 ii home? [2 marks]

b Which of these printers would you expect to print higher quality text? [1 mark]

c Explain why these printers are not line printers and give a term that more accurately describes them. [2 marks]

d Are these printers 'impact printers' or 'non-impact printers'? Justify your answer. [2 marks]

16 Suppose you want to send a sensitive document to an associate, Jen, who is working in Australia.

a List the steps required to send Jen the document via email. [5 marks]

b Give two disadvantages associated with sending email. [2 marks]

c Explain why it might not be advisable to communicate with Jen via
 i faxes, [2 marks]
 ii videoconferencing. [1 mark]

d Explain how you could protect the document so that only you and Jen can read it. [2 marks]

17 When a client first visits a doctor's office, he/she has to complete a medical form that the receptionist prints out. The receptionist then enters the data into a computer.

a Why is the medical form considered a turnaround document? [2 marks]

b Suggest a device that can convert printed data to machine-readable form and explain why it would be unsuitable in this case. [2 marks]

c What type of productivity software would you recommend for storing the patient records? [1 mark]

d Explain why the doctor would want to have both the manual and electronic filing systems. [2 marks]

e The doctor is thinking of moving old records from the filing cabinet and putting them in boxes at the back of the office. What is the term for what he is doing and why is this preferable to discarding the records entirely? [3 marks]

18 Mrs. Samaroo wants to back up her important files on secondary storage media.

a List two types of media she could use. [2 marks]

b Give two suggestions on how the backups should be stored. [2 marks]

c Describe three ways to take care of electronic storage media. [3 marks]

19 Explain how you would protect the files on your hard drive from:

a Accidental deletion. [1 mark]

b Hackers. [2 marks]

c Viruses. [2 marks]

20 How many spaces should you leave after:

a An opening parenthesis. [1 mark]

b A sentence. [1 mark]

c A colon. [1 mark]

3 Practice paper 2

Answer all questions.

Question 1
Time: 30 minutes

[25 Marks]

Type the following letter on A4 paper, following all instructions. Set the left margin to 1.5″ and the others to 1″.

> Address the following letter to the manager of Cheap Cheap Hotels which is located in Montego Bay, Jamaica. It is from Simon Coward who lives at 123 Baker Street, London and was written on February 19th, 2012.

Use indented layout with standard punctuation

Dear Sir,

It is out of great disappointment that I am writing ~~you~~ to you this morning. I and my wife stayed at your hotel during the period February 11th to February 15th. During that time, what should have been an enjoyable honeymoon was an exercise in frustration. From the ~~Wednesday~~ Saturday we got there, until the Wednesday ~~when~~ when we left, it wasn't one thing it was another.

From the beginning, it was clear that this dream vacation was going to be <u>anything</u> but. Although we asked to be picked up at the airport, the person who was supposed to do so either forgot or couldn't be bothered. So we were there waiting for over an hour, until it became clear that no one was coming for

(NP)

us. [We eventually were able to get a taxi but our problems

were far from over ^for that night. When we got ~~at~~ ^to the hotel, and

tried to check in, the receptionist was busy talking on the

telephone and did not so much as look (ital) in our direction. We had

to wait at least 5 minutes (in full) before she finally (U/S) acknowledged our

presence. And even then she was not the least bit accommodating.

She didn't tell us welcome, ask us how we were doing or anything

and made it seem as if she had somewhere else she would rather

be.

After all that had happened, it was no surprise that she

couldn't find our reservation. So we tried to make another one,

only to be informed that the honey moon suite was no longer

available. Eventually we had to settle for a tiny room in which

nothing worked.

When I say nothing, I mean nothing. The television didn't

work, the bed was creaky, there was no hot water and the A.C. (in full)

was broken. Even the lights kept flickering.

The food was nothing to shout about either. When it wasn't too salty, it was cold or took ages to arrive. The waitresses were frequently getting our orders wrong and clearly took the same course in courtesy as the receptionist.

So, imagine our surprise when we went to check out and we handed a bill that contained $50 in PPV movies.

I have several friends who were thinking of coming to stay at your hotel, but I will have to tell them to look elsewhere unless you get your act together. And it is a real pity, since your prices were quite cheap. Unfortunately, this seems like a classic case of getting what you pay for.

Insert signature block

Question 2

[23 Marks]

Time: 20 minutes

Centre the following on A4 paper with 1″ margins. Make sure you follow all instructions.

The CSME is conducting a study on the population density in the Caribbean. Below are 10 Caribbean countries along with their populations and the size measured in sq. miles (in brackets).

Cuba: 11,204,000 (42,803)

Dominican Republic: 10,090,000 (18,704)

Haiti: 10,033,000 (10,714)

Puerto Rico: 3,982,000 (3,515)

Jamaica: 2,719,000 (4,181)

Trinidad and Tobago: 1,339,000 (1,978)

Guadeloupe: 431,170 (628.6)

Martinique: 429,510 (435.5)

Bahamas: 304,837 (5,358)

Barbados: 275,330 (166)

Type the information into a spreadsheet with appropriate column headings in the Comic Sans Ms size 14 font. Centre the heading "Caribbean Population Statistics" across the spreadsheet in an underlined Arial Black size 18 font.

Add a column to calculate the population density (population/size) to 1 decimal place. Also calculate the total population and the average size. Sort the countries in descending order by their densitites.

Question 3

[22 Marks]

Time: 30 minutes

Type the following on Legal-sized paper with 1″ margins. Follow all instructions.

Create a letterhead for the Better Body Gym. Give Better Body Gym an address, telephone number and website of your choosing.

Application for Membership ——— centre and put in Arial size 18

Last name _ _ _ _   First name _ _ _ _ Middle initial _

Address _ _ _ _ _ _ _ _ _ _ _ _ _ _

Home number: _ _ _ _   Cell Number: _ _ _
                                                           lc

bf

Membership Plan   w/s

Choose an option below

☐ One Month: $100

☐ One Year: $800 (save up to 50%)

☐ Two Years: $1400 (Best value! Save up to 70%)

I am paying:

trs.   ☐ By cash

☐ By cheque

☐ By credit card. My credit card number is _ _ _ _

and it expires on _ _ _ _

I have read and agree to all the Better Body terms and conditions

Signature _ _ _ _ _ _   Date _ _ _ _ _ _

Please detach the following form if it is not applicable.

(Insert dotted line here)

I am bringing my spouse/relative/friend _____ with me to become a member of the gym. I want to be entered a chance at winning a free month's membership.

Question 4 [30 Marks]
Time: 40 minutes
Type the following brochure on A4 paper with 1˝ margins. Follow all instructions.

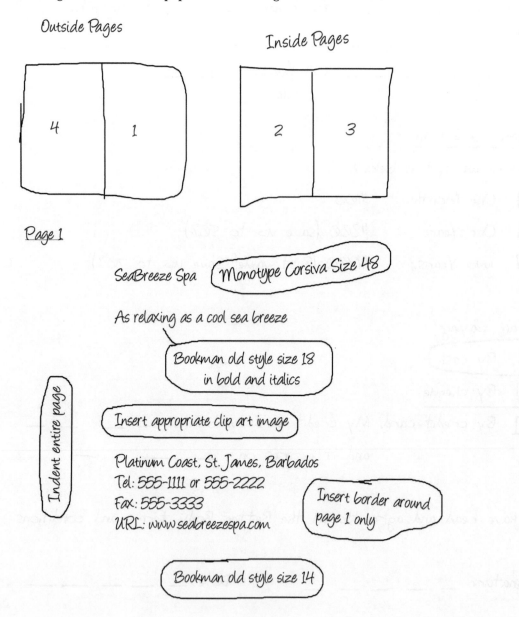

Outside Pages

Inside Pages

| 4 | 1 | | 2 | 3 |

Page 1

SeaBreeze Spa — (Monotype Corsiva Size 48)

As relaxing as a cool sea breeze — (Bookman old style size 18 in bold and italics)

(Insert appropriate clip art image)

Indent entire page

Platinum Coast, St. James, Barbados
Tel: 555-1111 or 555-2222
Fax: 555-3333
URL: www.seabreezespa.com

(Insert border around page 1 only)

(Bookman old style size 14)

Pages 2 and 3

Our Massages *[annotation: Bookman Old Style 18]*

[annotation: Underline all shoulder headings]

Swedish Massage

Sooth your tense muscles and distress with this classical European full-body Massage. Your muscles will be realigned to their natural equilibrium in order to increase circulation and promote healing.

Neck, Back and Shoulder Massage

This traditional upper body massage *[annotation: #]* is designed to help you relax, get better circulation, relieve stress and feel a general sense of well being.

Hot Stone Massage

In this customer favourite, hot stones are used in the massage process and placed on the body's key tension points. The warmth from the stones, combined with the soothing pressure of the massage strokes loosens stiff muscles and releases stress.

Deep Tissue Massage

Have chronic stress or sports related problems? This therapeutic massage is right for you! It:

Focuses on specific problem areas.

Loosens tight muscles and areas of tension *[annotation: use bullets]*

Eases pain   Promotes healing

Our Facials

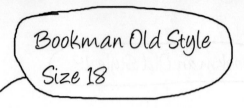
Bookman Old Style Size 18

Normal facial

Cleanse, steam and massage. Simple but extremely effective.

AHA (Alpha Hydroxy Acid)

This facial uses a special cream rich in AHA acids in order to help the skin look smoother and healthier. The AHAs are extracted from fruits and flowers such as bananas, oranges and roses.

Highly recommended for people with skin that is prone to wrinkling easily.

Bio-Lift Facial

This facial uses the familiar bio-mask and targets the dark circles underneath he eyes. *leave 2 line spaces*

Still Can't Choose? Tell us your needs and we'll choose the perfect ~~massage~~ treatment for you.

About Our Massage Therapists

Ini Caps

All our massage therapists are registered massage therapists with a minimum of five years experience

Underline all shoulder headings

Page 4

Monotype Corsiva Size 24

SeaBreeze Spa

Bookman Old Style 18

Service and Prices

size 11, italics

(All prices are in US Dollars)

Underline all ~~paragraph~~ shoulder headings

Massages

Swedish Massage (50 min) – $125

Deep Tissue (80 min) – $175

Neck, Back and Shoulder (50 min) – $125

Hot Stone Massage (60 min) – $115

Use bullets and dotted leaders

Facials

All facials are $100 for ~~50~~ 60 minutes

In-Room Wellness Services

Yoga Session (55 min) – $85

Pilates Session (55 min) – $85

Indent entire page

Glossary

Absolute cell reference
A cell reference that has a $ symbol in front of both the column letter and the row number (e.g. A1). Absolute cell references are used to keep a cell reference from changing when you copy the formula.

Agenda
A list of the topics to be covered at a meeting.

Antivirus software
Software designed to protect your computer from known computer viruses as well as programs that display virus-like behaviour.

Application software
Programs used to perform tasks that are not computer-related.

Archiving
The process by which inactive data is moved to long-term off-line storage.

Attestation clause
The clause at the bottom of a legal document which states that the conditions under which the document was signed.

Backing sheet
A cover page stating the type of legal document as well as the date, parties involved, and solicitors.

Backup
To make a copy of data and store it in another location.

Bandwidth
The maximum amount of data that can be transmitted over a communications channel each second.

Banker envelope
An open-sided envelope with a commercial style flap.

Barcode scanner
An input device which scans patterns of parallel black lines (called barcodes) that are used to identify items.

Baronial envelope
An open-sided envelope with a pointed flap which is commonly used for holding greeting cards.

BCC
Blind Carbon Copy. A copy of an email sent to a particular person without the other recipients' knowledge.

Bibliography
A detailed list of the references that were used while preparing a document.

Bit
The smallest unit of storage. It may be either 0 or 1.

Blocked layout
A layout in which all the elements are aligned to the left of the page.

Bond envelope
A durable, high-quality type of envelope.

Bond paper
Thick, uncoated paper that is very durable and has a high quality.

Boot up
To load the operating system from the hard disk into memory.

Burning
The process by which information is written to an optical storage device such as a CD or DVD.

Byte
A group of 8-bits (the space required to store a single character).

Carbon paper
Thin paper that is coated 'underneath' with a dark, waxy, pigment which is used to create duplicates.

Carpal Tunnel Syndrome
A painful condition which affects the wrists and arms and is common among people who do a lot of typing.

Catalogue envelope
A large open-ended envelope that is perfect for holding magazines, reports and catalogues.

CC
Carbon Copy/Courtesy Copy. A copy of a letter, memo or email message.

CD
Compact Disc. A small, optical disk used to store data or music.

CD-R
Compact Disc – Recordable. A type of CD with a special dye layer that allows data to be 'burned' (recorded) to it. However, once you have finished burning a CD-R, it becomes read-only.

CD-ROM
A type of read-only CD normally used to distribute programs.

CD-RW
Compact Disc – Rewritable. A type of CD that allows data to be recorded and erased several times.

Chairman's agenda
A special copy of a meeting agenda which contains additional information to guide the chairman, as well as space for him to write any notes.

Character
A single digit, letter or symbol e.g. 8, A, @

Checkbox
A special type of box which, when you click it, works like an on/off switch. When it is 'on', a tick appears inside the box.

Circular letter
A letter that will be sent to several people. It normally has a general salutation such as Dear Sir/Madam.

Click
To quickly press and release the left mouse button, while the mouse pointer is over the intended target.

Clipboard
An area in memory where items such as text, images and files are temporarily stored after you Cut or Copy them.

Column break
A special symbol you can insert in a document in order to force the text which follows it into a new column.

Combo box
A text box with a down arrow to the right which you can click to view the list of available options.

Complimentary close
'Yours truly', 'Yours sincerely' or a similar line which closes a letter.

Computer
An electronic device that can accept data and instructions, process them, then store the result or produce output.

Context menu
A menu that appears when you right-click on an item, showing only the options that apply to that particular item.

Copy paper
White paper that is pretty light and does not curl easily, making it suitable for use in copiers.

Copyright
'The set of exclusive rights granted to the author or creator of an original work, including the right to copy, distribute and adapt the work' (Source: Wikipedia).

Counterpart
A copy of the finished legal document.

Cover paper
A stiff, fairly heavy type of paper used for presentation covers, greeting cards and business cards.

CPU
Central Processing Unit. This chip, also called a microprocessor, is the 'brain' of the computer.

CRT
Cathode Ray Tube. This type of monitor uses similar technology to old television sets and as a result is very bulky and heavy.

Cursor
The flashing black line that indicates the current position in a text box or document.

Customised software
Programs that have been modified to meet a client's needs.

Custom-written software
Programs that have been written from scratch to meet a client's requirements.

Data
Raw facts and figures.

Data corruption
When data is lost or damaged.

Database
A structured collection of related data, organized into tables.

DBMS
Database Management System. A piece of software that allows you to efficiently store, retrieve and manipulate data stored in database tables.

Decryption
Decoding an encrypted file in order to obtain the original information.

Desktop
The rectangular background of a graphical user interface on which you will find icons such as the Recycle Bin.

Desktop PC
The largest type of PC, typically consisting of a separate monitor, tower, keyboard and mouse.

Digital camera
A camera that uses an electronic sensor instead of film.

Double-click
To click on an item twice in quick succession, without moving the mouse.

Download
Copy a file from a remote computer on to your local computer via a communications channel.

Drag and drop
To put the mouse over an item, hold down the left mouse button, move the item to a new location, then release the mouse button.

DVD
Digital Video Disk or Digital Versatile Disk. An optical storage device that looks just like a CD and is commonly used to storage movies.

DVD-ROM
A type of read-only DVD normally used to distribute programs.

Electronic filing system
A filing system where documents are stored in computer files and organised hierarchically into folders on electronic media.

Email
Electronic Mail. Mail that is electronically sent and retrieved over a network such as the Internet.

Embedded system
A specialized computer system that is part of another device such as an MP3 player, household appliance or digital camera.

Enclosure notation
The word Enc or Encs. at the end of a letter or memo which indicates that attachments are being sent with it.

Encryption
Encoding a file so that it bears no similarity to the original.

Engrossment
A finished legal document.

Enumeration
A numbered list.

Field
A piece of information about a particular type of entity e.g. an employee's salary or a car's price.

Firewall
Hardware or software that secures a network, protecting it from hackers.

Flash drive
See USB drive.

Flash memory
A form of secondary storage which utilises solid-state electronics.

Flimsy paper
Very thin, low quality paper that is much more opaque than onionskin paper.

Floppy disk
A portable 3.5-inch magnetic disk enclosed in hard plastic.

Font
A style of text such as Times New Roman or Arial.

Footer
Text which appears to the bottom of each page in a section.

Form letter
A personalised letter generated by a mail merge.

Formatting
The process by which a disk is prepared for use. It also erases any information already on the disk.

General-purpose software
Off-the-shelf software designed to perform a wide range of tasks.

Gigabyte (GB)
Roughly 1 billion bytes.

Graphics tablet
An input device that allows users to draw on its pressure sensitive surface using a stylus.

GUI
Graphical User Interface. A user interface containing visual elements such as windows, icons, buttons and menus.

Hacker
Someone who tries to gain unauthorised access to areas on a network.

Hard copy
Printed, human-readable output.

Hard disk
A rigid, large capacity disk that stores data magnetically.

Hardware
The physical components of the computer (the ones you can touch).

Header
Text which appears to the top of each page in a section.

Home position
The position where you place your hands on the keyboard before starting to type.

Homophones
Words that sound the same but are spelt differently.

HTML
HyperText Markup Language. This is the language that web pages are written in.

HTTP
HyperText Transfer Protocol. The protocol that governs how web pages are transmitted.

Human-readable document
A document that is in a form for humans to read.

Icon
A small picture used to represent a file or document.

Impact printer
A printer (e.g. a dot-matrix printer) that prints by striking the paper.

Inbox
A special folder in your email account containing the (non junk mail) messages you have received.

Index paper
Smooth, stiff paper that is fairly inexpensive and not particularly thick.

Information
Data that has been processed so that it is in a useful form.

Inkjet printer
A small printer which prints by squirting tiny droplets of ink on to the paper.

Input device
A device that allows you to enter information into the computer.

Inset
Text such as a quotation, enumeration or table that has been indented from the margins in order to set it apart.

Integrated package
A software package that combines several applications into a suite of programs such as Microsoft Office. Most of these packages combine a word processor, spreadsheet and database program.

Intellectual property
'Creations of the mind – creative works or ideas embodied in a form that can be shared or can enable others to recreate, emulate, or manufacture them' (Source: United States Patent and Trademark Office).

Internet
A worldwide network consisting of millions of smaller networks which provides features such as the Worldwide Web and Email.

ISP
Internet Service Provider. A company that grants subscribers access to various Internet services. For example: LIME or Flow Jamaica.

Joystick
An input device consisting of a vertical lever and some buttons, primarily designed for playing games.

Keyboard
The most common type of input device which contains keys for each letter of the alphabet, the numbers 0–9 as well as common symbols like the full stop and question mark.

Kilobyte (KB)
Roughly 1 thousand bytes.

LAN
Local Area Network. A network that spans a limited geographical area such as a building or campus. The computers are linked using cables and wireless as opposed to telephone lines and satellites.

Landscape orientation
Orienting a sheet of paper so that its top and bottom edges are longer than its left and right ones.

Laptop PC
A small, portable PC which comes with the monitor, keyboard and CPU in a single unit.

Laser pen
A portable laser used for pointing.

Laser printer
The biggest, fastest, most expensive type of printer which prints by using a laser to fuse toner onto the paper.

LCD
Liquid Crystal Display. This type of monitor has replaced CRT monitors since it is much thinner and lighter.

Legend
A key indicating which colour in a chart represents a particular series or slice of a pie.

Light pen
A light-sensitive input device that allows users to draw on CRT monitors.

Line printer
A printer that appears to print an entire line at a time.

Machine-readable document
A document where the data is encoded in a way that can easily be read by computers.

Magnetic tape
A long, thin strip of plastic with magnetic coating used for secondary storage. It comes in the form of a reel or cartridge.

Mail merge
The process by which a series of personalised letters are generated by inserting information from a recipient list at specific points in a main document.

Main document
A special Word document that acts as a template from which personalised letters will be generated.

Main heading
A heading that appears to the top of the entire document.

Main memory
See Primary Storage.

Mainframe
A large powerful computer that can support hundreds of simultaneous users via connected terminals.

Major version number
The number before the dot in a traditional version number. For example in the number 4.1, the major version number is 4.

Manila envelope
An envelope made of strong, relatively thick paper which has a distinctive light brown/beige colour.

Manual filing system
A filing system where the documents are arranged by hand into folders and stored in filing cabinets.

Manuscript
A handwritten or roughly typed document that has not yet been typed up professionally.

Marginal heading
A heading that is positioned to the left of the paragraph, possibly inside the left margin itself.

Megabyte (MB)
Roughly 1 million bytes.

Memo
Short for memorandum. A short letter used for inter-office communication.

Menu bar
A bar underneath the Title bar of a window that contains a list of the available pull-down menus.

Microcomputer
A computer that uses a microprocessor. It is more commonly called a PC.

Microfiche
A rectangular sheet of film used to store images of documents.

Microfilm
A roll of film used to store tiny images of documents.

Microprocessor
A processor on a single integrated chip.

Minicomputer
A multiuser computer that is smaller and less powerful than a mainframe but still much larger than a PC.

Minor version number
The number after the dot in a traditional version number. For example in the number 4.1, the minor version number is 1.

Minutes
A record of what happened during the meeting.

Mixed cell reference
A cell reference with a $ symbol in front of either the column letter (e.g. $E2) or the row number (e.g. E$2) in order to prevent it from changing when the formula is copied.

Modem
A device that allows computer data to be sent over a telephone line. It converts digital data to analog and vice versa.

Monitor
An output device, also known as a computer screen, used to view information.

Motherboard
The main circuit board inside the tower of a computer which contains the CPU, main memory and expansion slots. It contains circuitry connecting peripheral devices to the CPU and main memory.

Mouse
An input device with two or more buttons, used to move a pointer across the screen, select items and click them.

Multimedia projector
An output device that connects to a display port on your PC and uses a lens to project whatever is showing on your screen onto a flat surface such as a wall or a board.

NCR paper
'No Carbon Required' paper. Multipart paper, where the bottom of each intermediary sheet is coated in a special dye and the top is coated with clay that reacts to the dye.

Network
A group of computer devices that are connected in some way, allowing information and resources to be shared.

Non-impact printer
A printer which does not rely on striking the paper in order to print.

Notebook PC
See Laptop PC.

Notification area
An area to the right of the Taskbar containing the clock, volume icon as well as icons that provide notifications for currently running programs.

OCR
Optical Character Reader. This input device detects characters in printed documents.

OMR
Optical Mark Reader. This is a type of input device that detects pen and pencil marks on multiple-choice and survey forms.

Onionskin paper
Translucent (partially see through) paper that is thin and light but relatively strong.

Open end envelope
An envelope which has its flap along the shorter side.

Open side envelope
An envelope which has its flap along its longer side.

Operating system
A special program that manages the hardware resources as well as the other programs on the computer.

Optical storage media
Storage media such as CDs and DVDs that are read using light (or lasers).

Output device
A device that allows you to get information out of the computer.

Page break
A special symbol which you can insert at a particular point in a document in order to force the text which follows it on to a new page.

Page printer
A printer which prints so fast that it appears to print an entire page at one time.

Palmtop PC
A small, handheld PC with a touchscreen which may be operated either with a stylus or by making gestures on the screen with your fingers. Smartphones fall into this category.

Paragraph heading
A heading that is actually part of the paragraph itself so it is left aligned or indented depending on the layout used.

Password
A combination of characters used to prevent unauthorised computer access.

PC
Personal Computer. See microcomputer.

Peripheral
A device that is connected to the computer but is not on the motherboard.

Physical access restriction
Putting measures in place to prevent unauthorised users from gaining physical access to your manual or electronic files.

Piracy
The illegal copying/distribution of products such as music or software.

Pixel
One of the tiny dots that make up an image on the screen or on paper.

Plagiarism
The act of presenting someone's work as your own.

Point of sale terminal
Terminals that process transactions at the 'point of sale' such as checkout counters. They are usually connected to a central computer such as a mainframe.

Portrait orientation
Orienting a sheet of paper so that the sides of the paper are longer than its top and bottom edges. (This is the 'Normal' paper orientation.)

Primary storage
Storage that is directly accessible by the CPU (e.g. RAM and ROM).

Printer
A device that produces output on paper.

Processing
Manipulating data to produce information, for example: by sorting it or performing calculations on it.

Programmer
Someone who writes, tests and maintains computer programs.

RAM
Random Access Memory. This volatile type of primary storage stores the instructions of currently running programs as well as any temporary data that they generate.

Read/write head
A small electromagnet, attached to a mechanical arm in a drive, that reads information from, and stores information on, the disk surface.

Records
Rows of data in a database table. Each record corresponds to a separate entity or transaction.

Recycle Bin
A special folder on your Desktop where deleted files are temporarily stored.

Relative cell reference
A cell reference that does not contain a $ (e.g. D5). Relative cell references change when you copy the formula down or across.

Resolution
The number of pixels per unit area. Higher resolutions allow you to see more fine detail and have higher quality images.

Right-click
To quickly press and release the right mouse button, while the mouse pointer is over the intended target.

ROM
Read-Only Memory. This non-volatile type of primary storage can (usually) only be read and stores the instructions needed to boot up the computer.

Salutation
The greeting that appears just before the body of a letter, for example: Dear Mr. Doe.

Scanner
An input device that scans existing photographs or printed documents and converts them to digital images.

Scan-to-mail
The process by which a document is scanned then sent as an email attachment.

Search engine
A program or website that allows you to find web pages that contain the words you specify.

Secondary storage
Storage that is NOT directly accessible by the CPU. Also called backing storage or auxiliary storage.

Section break
A special symbol you can insert in a document in order to start a new section after the point where it was inserted.

Section heading
A heading corresponding to a particular section in the document.

Series
A set of values plotted on a chart.

Server
A computer on a network dedicated to managing a particular resource and sharing it with remote clients.

Shoulder heading
A heading that is found above the first paragraph of the section.

Side heading
See marginal heading.

Slide master
A special PowerPoint slide which allows you to specify which items appear on every slide.

Soft copy
The digital form of a document.

Software
The programs that run on the hardware of the computer.

Software access restriction
The process of restricting access to programs and computerised data using measures such as passwords and encryption.

Source document
The original document that the data was recorded on.

Specialised software
Software designed to perform tasks specific to a particular field.

Spreadsheet
A giant table containing figures, related labels as well as formulas indicating how values are to be calculated.

Start button
The button to the left of the Taskbar which you click to activate the Start menu.

Start menu
A special menu containing links to the programs on your computer, organised into groups. It also contains commands allowing you to shutdown, log off or restart your computer.

Stencil paper
Tough, white, translucent paper that is covered in wax.

Stet
A symbol used to tell the typist to disregard a correction.

Subheading
A heading found underneath a document's title.

Taskbar
The rectangular bar underneath the Desktop which is used to switch between currently running programs.

Telecommunication
The electronic process that enables communication across large distances.

Telecommuting
The process by which an employee works remotely from the office by utilising telecommunication channels such as a telephone line.

Teleconferencing
The use of computer technology and communication channels to enable people in different locations to talk with each other in real time.

Terabyte (TB)
Roughly 1 trillion bytes.

Terminal
A device, usually a display monitor and a keyboard, that is connected to a mainframe computer.

Thermal printer
A low cost printer which prints by applying heat to heat-sensitive paper.

Title bar
A bar at the very top of a window that displays the title of the window (usually the name of the program and the document currently open).

To the right of the Title bar you can find the Minimise, Maximise and Close buttons.

Toolbar
A bar containing buttons for the most common program tasks. These buttons usually have icons on them.

Transposition error
A type of typo in which letters are typed in the wrong order e.g. 'tihs' instead of 'this'.

Turnaround document
A document that has been output by a computer, then filled out and used as an input document.

Typescript
A typewritten copy of a manuscript.

Upload
Send a file from a local computer to a remote one via a communications channel.

URL
Uniform Resource Locator. The address of a website or web page such as http://www.microsoft.com

USB drive
A tiny portable drive which uses flash memory and can plug directly into your computer's USB port.

Videoconferencing
The use of computer technology and communication channels to enable people in different locations to see and talk with each other in real time.

WAN
Wide Area Network. A network that spans a large geographical area.

Watermark
A faded image or piece of text that appears in the background of a page.

Web browser
A program used for viewing web pages.

Web page
A multimedia document that is written in HTML and can be viewed using a web browser.

Web server
It is a dedicated network computer or program that stores web pages and transmits them as requested.

Webcam
A small camera that you use to send live video over the Internet.

Website
An organised collection of web pages, usually stored on a single web server.

Word processor
A type of program that allows you to create and manipulate textual documents such as letters, reports and manuscripts.

WordArt
A text graphic which is great for making titles stand out.

Workbook
A group of related worksheets.

Worksheet
An individual spreadsheet within a spreadsheet document.

World Wide Web
A global collection of interlinked documents (web pages) that are written in HTML. These documents may contain text, images and video.

Write
To store information on a storage device.

Write-protect tab
A tiny square in the corner of a floppy disk or flash memory which you can slide open to make it read-only.

WWW
See World Wide Web.

Index

Note:

Word refers to Microsoft® Word. Likewise Excel, PowerPoint, Access, refer to Microsoft® Excel, Microsoft® PowerPoint, Microsoft® Access respectively.

@ symbol, typing 77, 77 (fig.), 77 (table)